HORIZON
BEDSIDE
READER

EDITED BY CHARLES L. MEE, JR.

AMERICAN HERITAGE PRESS NEW YORK

CONTENTS

INTRODUCTION

CHARLES L. MEE, JR.

My bedside table is piled high with books and magazines that represent a thousand and one nights of disappointed expectations—bedtime reading that kept me awake, or put me to sleep, or gave me nightmares, or tripped me when I got out of bed in the morning.

There is the half-finished Rex Stout mystery that left me tossing and turning through the night as I fitfully considered how I might myself write a better mystery. There is the James Bond that was so gripping I couldn't get to sleep until I had finished it—at four in the morning. There is the volume of Schopenhauer that a friend told me was lilting and mindless and would put me to sleep like Muzak, but made me hear disquieting strains of Beethoven. And then under the bed are the copies of *Encounter, The New York Times* magazine, *Harper's,* filled with those vexing articles about Mayor Daley and impoverished blacks, ecological horrors and the unrest in our universities—problems that left me with a gnawing guilt when

I wasn't able to keep my eyes open but rather drifted off to sleep in the face of all those troubles.

No, bedtime reading is no simple matter. For when we go to bed—if we go to bed, that is, to sleep—our powers are at their lowest. It is no time to read a new poet, or follow the intricate, soul-searching arguments of Noam Chomsky in the *New York Review of Books,* or pay attention, *really* pay attention, to Nabokov's latest novel. Such things require our full powers, or at least, they require my full powers.

There are some books, to be sure, that serve well at bedtime. Among them are old novels that I have read before, whose styles are reassuring, comforting, and infused with a cadence that resembles a constant pattering of sheep's hoofs. I recommend Jane Austen at bedtime. I keep Miss Austen by my bed, and I enjoy having her there. My wife knows it, and she does not complain.

Then there is Gibbon. You always know how *The Decline and Fall of the Roman Empire* is going to end, so there is no urgency to get to the end of it. You can fall asleep in the middle and pick it up again weeks later without feeling you've let precious time slip by before you *knew.* The style has the roll of the ocean's waves: for that reason I particularly recommend it to city dwellers.

And Boswell's *Life of Samuel Johnson,* of course. It is a book that can be put down—or be permitted to drop out of one's hand—at any moment; for you can begin reading again on any page, near the middle or the end or wherever, some other night. Continuity is irrelevant.

Anthony Burgess keeps Burton's *Anatomy of Melancholy* by his bed, and there is much to recommend it. Burton's mind was so tumultuous, and his great work is so packed with odd bits of knowledge and rumination, that the book is a peerless source of the stuff that dreams are made of.

Well, I have my favorites, as I am sure everyone does, and I am incessantly asking friends for recommendations to supplement my bedside library. But I am omnivorous. And I have always felt the lack of a dependable collection of current magazine nonfiction—one in which I will not encounter troublesome articles that in all good conscience I cannot overlook once I have seen.

Now, *Horizon* happens to be a magazine that contains a good deal of the kind of bedtime reading I enjoy. But *Horizon* has a number of built-in problems. First, it is too large to really curl up with, and its hard covers are too penetrating to rest comfortably on the stomach. Then, too, it is full of imposing articles on art, and essays by such men as Arthur Koestler that tell us how the human brain is put together and why it doesn't function properly, and vast histories about guerrilla warfare that explain what the Pentagon apparently never knew before it went into Vietnam. In short, it is full of articles that demand full attention. So, here, I have removed all the courses save coffee, brandy, and dessert. It is bedtime.

It is not a time, however, for only "light" reading. Gibbon and Burton are not light reading. Nor are some of the literary and historical essays in this book. Only two rules apply implacably to bedtime reading, I find. First, it must be something that one can fall asleep in the middle of—and not care. Thus the articles here are either short enough that one can sprint to the end of them, knowing that victory is in sight before sleep becomes irresistible. Or else they are not so long that one cannot begin at the beginning the following night without feeling that too much of the same ground is being covered again profitlessly. (We have also made sure that the book is not heavy enough to cause serious damage when it falls from the hand.)

Second, although one may fall asleep while reading them, the articles are not soporific. They are good yarns, good wit, or simply good writing. One should never regret, after all, being awake. And these are writers who will repay us at our most attentive, our most alert, our most insomnious.

This anthology is not the "best of *Horizon*" in any sense; it is only the best of a certain kind. And it is, in any event, some of the best bedtime reading I have ever done.

A SEIZURE
OF
LIMERICKS

CONRAD AIKEN

The Limerick, to put it mildly, is an art form of no great repute. The vast majority of limericks are not intended—even assuming that they are fit—to be printed. They are remembered, and passed on by memory from one aficionado to the next, to enliven a dull occasion (or ruin a good one by stopping all other forms of conversation) and eventually to form a part of the folk memory of the race. Periodically attempts are made to collect and (sub rosa) *publish the unpublishable limericks, ranging in time from* Cythera's Hymnal *of 1870 to the awesomely scholarly and complete* The Limerick: 1,700 Examples, with Notes, Variants, and Index, *brought out by Gershon Legman in 1953. Now and then a poet of stature essays the limerick, seeking to do the impossible and make something more of the printable examples than the master, Edward Lear, could make of them. One such daring renovator is Conrad Aiken, eminent winner of many poetry* prizes, who has delivered himself of the limericks on these pages—in an unusual circumstance. They were, he writes, "the immediate result of a coronary which I suffered in Savannah. For some inexplicable reason I at once had a seizure of limericks, beginning the day after the attack, and at the rate, for a while, of two or three a day—my wife took them down. It was, I suppose the psychologists would say, the attempt of the unconscious to keep me amused, and it worked very well."

The limerick's, admitted, a verse form;
A terse form, a curse form, a hearse form;
    As pale and as frail
    As the shell of a snail,
It's a whale of a tail in perverse form.

Said Isolde to Tristan: How curious!
King Mark is becoming quite furious.
    Since we got off that boat
    It's been *all "Liebestod"!*
Is it *possible* Wagner is spurious?

Said a Point being approached by a Locus:
I regard this as sheer hocus-pocus.
    What good will it do me
    If it never gets to me?
Will someone *please* tell it to *focus*?

I don't give a hoot, said a particle,
If I can't have the definite article.
    If *cogito sum*
    Pronounces my doom,
Then down with all systems Descartes-ical!

Said a lovely Greek muse known as Clytie
I look very nice in my nighty,
　　But beyond all compare,
　　I look better when bare,
And when I am bare I am bitey.

Farewell to the old days of Genesis.
We do all these things now by synthesis.
　　And who would not rather
　　Have a test tube for father
Than a *homo in loco parenthesis?*

Lithpt a thad little man from Duluth
I've got a thore tooth and itth loothe.
　　What I needth a Martini
　　With O, jutht a teeny,
Or even not any, vermouth.

A lovely young lass in Sesuit
Was in love with a lad from Cotuit.
　　Said the preacher from Wareham
　　Who proceeded to pair'em
"Sesuit-Cotuit go to it!"

All's quiet along the Potomac.
The Skybolt's asleep with the Bomarc.
　　The Kennedy sings
　　To the last of the kings
And the diplomat fills his *estomac.*

A delectable gal from Augusta
Vowed that nobody ever had bussed her.
　　But an expert from France
　　Took a bilingual chance
And the mixture of tongues quite nonplused her.

Nan, Saw, and Paw, of Setucket,
Between them had only one bucket.
    Nan took it and ran
    And the trouble began:
Sawtucket, Pawtucket, Nantucket.

Great archers, and hitters of bull's-eyes!
You wingers of wren's eyes and gull's eyes,
    Ulysses and Tell,
    And Achilles as well!
Where stalk you now baring your skull's eyes?

There was once a wicked young minister
Whose conduct was, shall we say, sinister.
    By methods nightmarish
    He seduced his whole parish,
Except for one squamous old spinister.

I'm a most highly literate cat
I've had my Litt. D., and all that.
    When in New York, my dear,
    And I read "Litter here,"
Why, I litter at once, and then scat!

There was an old party named Cassidy
Who was famed far and wide for mendacity.
    When asked did he lie,
    He replied: To reply
Would be to impugn his veracity.

Said a curve: I'm becoming hysterical.
It is hell to be merely numerical.
    I bend and I bend,
    But where will I end
In a world that is hopelessly spherical?

WATER
OF
LIFE

FERGUS ALLEN

Tested with a glowing splint under favorable conditions, the breath of a habitual whisky drinker will light with a pop and burn with a blue flame; it will also discolor paint, shrivel foliage, rot delicate fabrics, and asphyxiate a swarm of bees. I mention these facts simply to attract attention and not from a love of the sensational. Whisky marches under a variety of flags or banners, copiously advertised, so that words like "Scotch," "Irish," "Bourbon," and "Rye," which once had distinct and useful meanings of their own, are now little more than signals to alcoholics. Although it can be made in a bath with the aid of a kettle, whisky—which may alternatively be spelled w-h-i-s-k-e-y—is normally produced by means of a pot still or a patent still. The relative merits of the whiskies distilled in one or the other of these pieces of apparatus are the subject of prolonged, repeated, and very tedious argument among those who claim to "know about whisky." The real differences are small, and those which are discussed are largely imaginary. (Ask such a debater to draw diagrams of a pot still and a patent still; his inability to do so may persuade him to change the subject.) This is not to say that all whiskies are equal. Age is of some importance. If whisky is matured in wooden casks for several years, some of the more quickly acting poisons may be leached out, precipitated, or decomposed. This process also serves to impart the characteristic and encouraging color to whiskies which may have emerged from the still quite colorless—and therefore visually indistinguishable from gin, vodka, or water. Should it fail to do so, the manufacturer will not scruple to color the whisky with caramelized sugar.

Setting aside all these trivia, I can now summarize the characteristics of this undeniably important fluid.

Definition: A spirit distilled from malted barley or other grain (*Concise Oxford Dictionary*). Note that it is not described as "good to drink" or even "fit for human consumption." In this, as in other ways, it resembles sulphuric acid.

Etymology: The name "whisky" is derived from the Gaelic *"uisge beatha,"* meaning "water of life," a designation which can hardly be anything but ironic.

Color: More or less yellow, the color associated with bile, jaundice, anxiety, envy, jealousy, cowardice, treachery, and decay.

Taste and Smell: Nauseating; offensive to the mucous membranes.

Other Properties: Inflammable; can be used as fuel for spirit lamps. A good solvent for varnish and shellac. Germicide. Occasionally used for maturing tobacco pipes and cleaning windows.

Effects on Human Body: Taken internally, whisky separates the nerve endings and produces a short-lived exhilaration. This is quickly succeeded by dizziness, partial to total loss of balance, nausea, retching, vomiting, complete loss of muscular control, and coma. On recovering consciousness the normal symptoms are violent headaches, biliousness, liverishness, intense thirst, lassitude, and bad breath. Prolonged dosing

19

over many years gradually mortifies the tissues and the mind, brings madness and premature death.

Methods of Introduction: Many people like to take whisky neat to get the ordeal over as quickly as possible. Others, less sensitive, prefer it diluted. The most common vehicles for dilution are water and soda water, but ginger ale and sweet vermouth are also used from time to time. There are cases on record of whisky having been drunk with such diluents as tonic water (in mistake for soda), port, coffee, milk, honey, and lemon juice. Oddly enough, it is seldom injected directly into the blood stream.

It would, I suppose, be unfair to pass judgment on whisky and its consumers without hearing a defense of some sort. But what defense can there be? What would the articulate whisky drinker hoarsely mutter? Something like this, perhaps:

"Whisky is golden. Whisky is the elixir of happiness, the softener of sorrow, the easer of pain; a tonic, a stimulant, the fountainhead of conviviality and the harbinger of revelry. It tides the sick over crises, fires the wounded with a will to live, transmutes cowardice to bravery. Whisky is sunlight to friendship and moonshine to love, lighting with laughter the seamed face, freeing the tongue tied by fear, evoking the improbable story and hilarious applause. See the men smilingly grouped about their golden glasses; their expanding spheres of benevolence intersect, comrades for the nonce. After the party, homeward bound, the giggling pedestrian assuredly steps, the rosy motorist laughingly swerves. Stretched in bed, the feet perpetually rise, delightful delusion. Memories of jokes cracked renew laughter, sleepy now and slower. Nip from plated flask brings courage to maiden speaker, fortifies traveler plodding through snowdrifts. Revenue to benign government, profit to philanthropic manufacturer, living to open-hearted publican. Whisky, golden panacea, bottled wonder-worker."

SEX AND
THE KING
OF FRANCE

JOSEPH BARRY

By whatever avenue you arrive you are led ineluctably to it. All three avenues of Versailles converge on the Royal Grill of the great palace—the medial Avenue de Paris like a three-hundred-foot-wide shaft of a giant arrow—and they point across the courtyard, not to the Royal Chapel, but to the royal bedchamber.

That the Sun King should install his bedroom at the very center of his palace, then the center of Europe and thus of Western civilization, is piquant enough. More to the point, he had installed it in the little château, the hunting retreat, of his father, Louis XIII. The château—the touching, visible heart of the great palace of Versailles—can be seen clearly by climbing the vast cobbled courtyard of the entrance: a little castle of fairylike beauty with walls of faded brick and white stone, poised above its own tiny courtyard of marble and surrounded on three sides by the monumental wings and façades of Le Vau and Mansart.

That "little castle of cards" was the beginning, for Versailles was born not of Louis XIV but of Louis XIII; not out of love for, but a most un-Bourbon fear of, women.

Louis XIII's mother, Marie de Médicis, felt the first labor pains of Versailles's future begetter at Fontainebleau. Feverishly—he was many times a father, but this was the first legitimate offspring—Henry IV sent for the midwife. He also sent for his cousins, the princes of the blood, to witness the birth. It was a custom and precaution that did not originate with the Bourbons. Questions of legitimacy could instigate civil war. In the case of Henry IV it was a particularly wise precaution. As a rollicking folk song of the period expressed it: he could drink, he could fight, and he could make love.

The royal bed in the queen's oval chamber was covered in crimson velvet; so was the smaller bed next to it, in which she labored, and the chair next to that, in which she gave birth. The midwife sat on a smaller chair before her and received the child. The king beckoned the three princes closer. They bent and looked. The cord was cut, the baby put into its crib. It moved feebly. The midwife called for wine. Her hands were full; the king held the wine bottle to her lips. She filled her mouth, then filled the child's from hers. It stirred more strongly.

"*E maschio?*" the queen asked twice, and rose to her feet to look. Across the room the midwife uncovered the child for the king. "We have a beautiful son!" he cried, thanked God, and let the tears fall. The queen, too, cried and fainted. The king threw open the doors to the antechamber. Two hundred of the court pressed in. The midwife protested. "This child," the king replied, "belongs to everybody."

As the newborn dauphin's governess, he named Madame de Montglat, a tall, thin, and domineering woman, "her character as sharp as her elbows." As the dauphin's personal physician, the king appointed the remarkable Jean Héroard, whose meticulous journal of Louis XIII's life, beginning with the day of his birth in September, 1601, and ending with Héroard's own death some twenty-six years later, fills six folio volumes. It may be the most faithful case history of any king of any time, recording everything from food to evacuations, temper to temperature, conversations to love life, or rather, in Louis's instance, its relative absence.

For the first few days, Héroard notes, the dauphin had difficulty taking his milk, until an encumbering membrane was cut under his tongue. Then he needed two nurses (his father had sucked a legendary eight dry), but he was left the rest of his life with a speech defect. Within weeks he was taken on tour for another public exposure—from Fontaine-bleau to Melun, Villeneuve-Saint-Georges to Paris. Finally, after a stop at the Louvre and the Tuileries, the procession ended at the grim, gray-stone château of Saint-Germain en Laye, eleven miles west of Paris, which had been chosen by Henry IV as the dauphin's residence.

Throughout Louis's infancy affection came from his father, but it was not undivided. The king continued to distribute his energy among his affairs of state, his second wife (he had divorced Marguerite de Valois), his many mistresses (particularly Henriette d'Entragues), and his dozen or so other children. At one time there were nine children by five different mothers living at Saint-Germain; they were familiarly referred to throughout the land as *le troupeau* (the flock). Henry would come to the dauphin's room with the queen and then return shortly afterward with Henriette. Louis, it might be noted, liked neither lady, and with reason. Marie de Médicis may have been many things, but she was not a good mother. The little dauphin also took a pained view of mistresses. When he was seven, the king had taken him for a walk in the gardens of Fontainebleau, pointed to the Comtesse de Moret, and said, "My son, I have given this beautiful lady a child. He will be your brother." The dauphin had blushed and stammered, "He is no brother of mine." And he turned his own "affection" to birds with such a ferocity that he became perhaps the greatest killer of winged game in the history of that royal sport.

As a child Louis was very neat, tidying up Héroard's room, to which he often crept, when he found it in disorder. And, yet a child, he was whipped by the king when he crushed the head of a live sparrow. He was frequently whipped by Madame de Montglat, who would sternly command, "You, sir, bare your arse!" ("Whip him," the king had advised her. "There is nothing better.") Her language was famously coarse and repeatedly shocked Louis.

Before he was one year old, according to Héroard, it was decided that the Spanish infanta would be his wife. At two he was asked if he would be as ribald as his father. No, he said, "coldly." Not yet four, he tried to strike his younger sister. "I am afraid of her," he explained. Why? he was asked. "Because she is a girl." At seven he was teasingly asked if he were in love. "I flee from love," he answered solemnly. "And from the infanta, Monsieur?" asked Héroard. "No," he said; then: "Ha, yes. Yes!" (He knew Héroard was noting his remarks and would sometimes shout after one, "Write that down!")

When he was still only six, the dauphin found himself at the château of Noisy-le-Roi one day and was seized with a sudden desire. "Tétay," he cried to his steward, Ventelet, "prepare the carriage and the birds. I want to go hunting!" That evening he returned with a small hare run to earth by his hounds, and five or six quail and a brace of partridge taken by his hawks. At supper he talked of little else. It was his first hunt in his father's favorite woods, the woods of Versailles.

Louis was past seven when he was switched from the hard but feminine hands of his governess into those of a tutor, put into a ruff, and taught to shoot. He was not yet nine when he had dinner with the king on May 12, 1610. It hadn't happened often; it didn't happen again.

Two days afterward, before a shop with the sign of a crowned heart pierced by an arrow, Henry IV was stabbed to death by François Ravaillac. Hurriedly he was brought back to the Louvre, carried to his bedroom on the second floor, and laid out on the bed. The dauphin, riding elsewhere in Paris, was also hurriedly brought to the Louvre and taken to his father. "The king is dead," he heard from the queen. "Your Majesty must excuse me," he heard the chancellor tell her, "but kings never die in France. *Voilà*," he pointed to the eight-year-old Louis, "the living king!"

And the king cried like a baby.

Later that day Louis was again facing his public—the crowd that filed through the Louvre to stare at its new sovereign. Finally, exhausted, he went to bed, but he could not sleep. He rose, went to his tutor, said pathetically, "I am afraid of dreaming," and lay down beside him until almost midnight, when he was carried back to his own bed. There he slept with his half brother, Henriette's son, fetched by order of the queen.

Never was a king mourned more widely in France than Henry IV. "The village poor," said an eyewitness, "massed on the highways, stunned, haggard, arms crossed, telling people passing of the disastrous news . . . finally disbanding like sheep without a shepherd." Louis's inheritance, in short, was the crushing legacy of a great father. "If only," he sighed to his nurse, "my father the king had lived another twenty years!"

A few days later the new king of France was spanked for obstinately refusing to say his prayers. "At least," he said to his tutor, "don't strike too hard." Afterward he went to see the queen, now regent, who had ordered the whipping. She rose to make him the curtsy due him as king. "I would rather," he said wistfully, "not have so many curtsies and honors, and not be whipped." On September 17, 1610, Louis XIII was again spanked; on September 21, he signed a military alliance with England.

At ten Louis was writing verses and slaughtering game. And from that age on he was taming falcons; ultimately, he reached the height of taming the great eagle. He was to hunt wild duck with falcons, quail with merlins, partridge with goshawks, hares with sakers, and to train teams of birds as if they were commandos. And he was to find his father figure in the form of an ambitious falconer, Charles d'Albert, Duc de Luynes, twenty-three years his senior. Rapidly Luynes rose in power, becoming Louis's favorite, and his bedroom Louis's refuge. Thus Louis flew his birds, painted, danced, and composed, dreamed of—and wrote verses to—Luynes, cooked poached eggs, played the lute, and at the age of fourteen married the Spanish infanta, who was five days older than the king. She was blonde and might have been pretty had it not been for her long Habsburg nose. Indeed, Anne of Austria (her mother was Margaret of Austria) looked remarkably like Louis, which in view of their Habsburg consanguinity was no coincidence.

They were married in Bordeaux on November 25, 1615. After the ceremony they each went to separate chambers in the archbishop's palace and supped. Tired, the little king ate in bed while Messieurs de Guise and de Grammont and other cavaliers, according to Héroard, "regaled" him with coarse stories that were aimed at giving him "confidence." Toward eight o'clock that evening, the queen mother came to his chamber.

"It is not enough, my son," she told him, "to be married. You must go to the queen, your wife, who is awaiting you."

"Madame," said Louis, "I was but waiting your command. If it pleases you, I will go to her with you."

He was handed his bathrobe and small, furred boots, and he went down the passage with the queen mother, his and the little queen's nurses, Messieurs de Souvré (his tutor) and Héroard, the Marquis de Rambouillet (master of the wardrobe), and Monsieur de Beringhen (first *valet de chambre*), who lighted the way with a candle.

"My daughter," said the queen mother to the queen, "I bring you your husband. Receive him well, I pray you."

Anne replied in Spanish that she had no intention other than to obey and please him, and Louis was put into bed beside her. Marie de Médicis whispered something to them in a low voice, then ordered all but the two nurses to leave.

Two hours later Louis called for his bathrobe and furred boots and returned to his bedroom. France was in the midst of civil war. But the rebellious nobility opposed to the marriage would now find it all but irrevocable. As for Louis he was to recall that night with revulsion the rest of his life. It was three years before he could be brought to bed again with Anne; it was another twenty years before he became a father. But before either event could take place, there was Luynes to be removed as an inhibiting factor.

With this in mind, Marie de Médicis and the entire court connived to marry Luynes off to the pretty, charming, highborn, and rich Marie de Rohan. They were successful; the marriage was successful, but subsequent approaches to Louis were not. Pressed by the Spanish ambassador and the papal nuncio to give France an heir, Louis resisted, pleading, "I am too young. It would be bad for my health." Then his half sister, Mademoiselle de Vendôme, daughter of Gabrielle d'Estrées, was married to the Duc d'Elbeuf, and efforts were redoubled.

"Sire," said the papal nuncio to Louis, now seventeen, "I do not believe you would want the shame of your sister having a son before Your Majesty had a dauphin." Embarrassed, Louis allowed that he would not.

By no accident, he was invited to the wedding chamber and encouraged to stay on as a spectator, the bride and groom lending themselves for a royal lesson. "Their act," the Venetian ambassador was to report, "was repeated more than once, to the great applause and particular pleasure of His Majesty. It is thought that this example has excited the king to do the same. It is also said that his half sister encouraged him, saying, 'Sire, you do the same with the queen, and you will be the better for it.'"

The king's pleasure and applause seem to have been greatly exaggerated. Five days later, at eleven at night, Luynes himself had to go to Louis to coax him to the queen's bed. Louis resisted. Luynes insisted. Annoyed, then anguished, Louis was carried weeping in Luynes's arms down the corridor to Anne's chamber. And once again Monsieur de Beringhen lighted the way with a candle. The two adolescents were left

alone together, except for Madame de Bellière, the queen's
first *femme de chambre*. It was presumably she who provided
Héroard with the matter of the day. The king, he noted,
"s'efforce deux fois, comme l'on dit" (did his best twice, it is
said). Louis returned to his bedroom at two and slept unusually long, until nine o'clock.

The public concern for so private an affair reached such a
peak that not only the pope (to whom the nuncio wrote on
April 14, 1618, that the Huguenots were using Louis's chas-
tity for their own purposes) and the king of Spain (father
of Queen Anne) felt legitimately involved but the Duke of
Savoy as well. An enemy of Spain, he was told by *his* man at
court that the farther the king could be kept from the bed of
the queen, the closer he would be to the house of Savoy. In
a dispatch dated February 16, 1618, the Savoyard ambassador
related his own efforts to persuade the Duc de Luynes to
prevent the consummation. "What wouldn't the Spanish do,"
he quoted himself saying to Luynes, "of what would they not
be capable, once *their little queen* had the person of the young
king in her arms every night?"

The day following Louis's noble efforts Anne joyfully sent
her Master of Ceremonies to the papal nuncio and the Spanish envoy to tell them of it, and couriers were booted for the
ride to the capitals of Europe. On January 30, 1619, the
nuncio wrote Pope Paul V: "The king finally decided *con-
jiungersi colla Regina* . . . Since the first night, except for one,
their majesties continue to come together . . . but for the sake
of the king's health, it will be seen to that His Majesty goes
to the queen at properly spaced intervals." An interval of two
weeks was recommended by the court doctors as more likely
to result in a dauphin.

Louis continued to have but one friend—the Duc de Luynes
—and he died in 1621. Moreover, France was again in fratri-
cidal war. At this moment Armand Jean du Plessis de
Richelieu reached the foot of the throne and eventually became the iron-willed ruler of Louis's reign. A kind of equilib-
rium was established. If it was not quite the glamorous time

of Dumas's *Three Musketeers*, in which the dashing Duke of Buckingham publicly pleaded his love to the neglected queen, Anne of Austria, life was gay enough, it seems, for all but the frustrated king. He had lost Luynes. He had Richelieu but no intimate.

He had only Versailles.

Increasingly, Louis escaped to the woods near the little village of Versailles au Val de Galie, a cluster of huts with four or five hundred inhabitants. It had a rude inn or two, a windmill and twelfth-century church on the butte, the half-ruined château of the Gondi, and a little nearby stream, the Galie. It was a rendezvous for hunters, not a place to spend the night. It was a halt for carters and wagoners, their vehicles heavy with beef from Normandy for the markets of Paris.

But there were the sweet woods of the Ile de France, full of game and grace. They were worth the long ride back after dark to Saint-Germain, eight miles distant. But why the ride back?

Modestly Louis planned a small château, no larger than a hunting lodge. Guardedly he budgeted it under *menus plaisirs* —we might call it light entertainment—rather than *bâtiments*, or buildings. Discreetly he had it constructed, pausing during his hunting to watch its progress, as he did on August 2, 1624, when he saw the battery of kitchen utensils installed.

This very first Versailles structure was of brick and stone, in the style we now know as "Louis XIII." It was about eighty feet in all along the façade facing the small park, and only nineteen feet in depth. It was, in the words of Bassompierre, "but a *chetif château* [paltry country house] which any ordinary gentleman wouldn't boast having built." There were three or four rooms for the king and a dozen or so for his suite, but none for the queen, the queen mother, or any of the ladies of the court. They might be invited for a fete, but they had no overnight privileges. This Versailles was a male paradise. But it need not hold us for long, for it was soon to be replaced, after the famous Day of Dupes.

Leagued against Richelieu—to whom Louis relegated full

power, if only to assure himself repose— were the king's only legitimate brother and his wife and mother, the two queens of the "Spanish party," who were not above conspiring with their relatives among the enemy (Anne of Austria's brother was now Philip IV of Spain). And this struggle against the cardinal was to reach its climax at Versailles.

Convalescing from an almost fatal illness, harassed by Marie de Médicis, Louis seemed about to acquiesce in the dismissal of his minister. The critical conversation took place on November 10, 1630, in the queen mother's Luxembourg palace. Unexpectedly, as it was ending, Richelieu appeared. Outraged, Marie de Médicis denounced and insulted him in a flowing mixture of Italian and French. He fell to his knees. He wept: out of office could have meant out of life. He begged pardon. He promised to do whatever Marie demanded. Louis paled and tried to interrupt. Haughtily Marie asked him whether he preferred "a valet to his mother." Louis then ordered Richelieu to rise and leave the room. He himself soon took leave of Marie. It was late, and he had to reach Versailles before it was too dark. In the courtyard Richelieu desolately watched as Louis departed without a look or sign. Inside the palace the cardinal's many enemies celebrated with Marie de Médicis. Richelieu returned to his own palace, the Petit Luxembourg, ordered his silver and his papers packed, and prepared for flight. Then word arrived from the king: Richelieu was to join him immediately at Versailles.

Away from Paris, the court, and his mother, Louis recovered his composure in the late-autumn serenity of Versailles. He went up to his cabinet and waited. Soon the cardinal came to him, fell at his feet, wept, offered his resignation—and allowed himself a refusal. He stayed that night directly below the king. The next morning those who had gone to sleep in victory awoke in defeat. Richelieu had triumphed.

Following that Day of Dupes, when Versailles first entered history, Marie de Médicis was banished, eventually to die in exile in The Netherlands. The Maréchal de Marillac, who had aspired to Richelieu's office, was tortured and put to death; the Duc de Montmorency, a childhood playmate of Louis's, was beheaded. (Refusing to give clemency, Louis remarked, "I should not be king, if I had the sentiments of private persons.") And parcel by parcel, in a series of forty-six separate purchases, the royal domain of Versailles was doubled. Land and rights were bought from Jean-François de Gondi, Archbishop of Paris, and Louis's modest little hunting lodge was completely remodeled.

To begin with, it was enlarged—under the direction of the architect Philibert Le Roy—but not enough to include rooms for the ladies. Femininity was reserved, one might say, for the building itself, for the brightness of its color, the gaiety of its architecture. It was blue, white, and red: roofs of blue-black slate, walls of red brick "chained" by white stone. It was gay with balconies of wrought iron, gilded terminals, tall white pinnacles, chimneys with decorative blue ornaments. The moat, too, was more decorative than defensive, its stone balustrade out of a fairy tale. And at each corner of the château, symmetrically placed, was a free-standing pavilion.

It was this "little castle of cards," as Saint-Simon called it, that the Sun King, not yet born, was to discover in his adolescence and preserve in his maturity as the center of his own great palace, court, and power. But it was here that Louis XIII went to escape his court and the cares of power, the intrigues of courtiers and their plots. Here in Versailles Louis felt secure, free of women, less spied upon. When smallpox threatened Saint-Germain, he sent the queen to Noisy, not to Versailles. "I fear," he explained to Richelieu in one of his almost daily letters, "a great number of women who would spoil everything for me."

Inevitably there were women as "mistresses." The son of the Vert Galant perhaps had no alternative. There was the teen-age blonde, Marie de Hautefort, who terrified him. (He talked to her "only of dogs, birds and hunting," she complained to Madame de Motteville, *femme de chambre* of the queen.) And there was the teen-age brunette, Marie-Louise de La Fayette, who may even have loved him; but when

31

Louis said, "Come live with me at Versailles," she crossed herself and went to live in a convent in Paris. Louis's relief was almost audible, though he wrote a letter to Richelieu telling him of his melancholy (the writing wavers, a tear drops, one still sees the traces).

The pious, inhibited—and possibly tormented—Louis visited Louise, now Sister Angélique, a number of times at the convent of Sainte Marie (part of which still stands near the Place de la Bastille). His visit early in December, 1637, on the way to Saint-Maur from Versailles was to effect an odd reconciliation—with the queen. As Louis and Sister Angélique talked—and talked—in the parlor, a storm rose of such violence that he could neither return to Versailles nor go on to Saint-Maur, where his bed, linen, and service had already preceded him. His apartment at the Louvre, a mile down the Seine, was not prepared for him. Guitaut, captain of the guard, now spoke up with his customary boldness. Since the queen was at the Louvre, he pointed out, the king would find supper and lodging. Louis rejected the idea and said they would wait out the storm. They waited. The storm became even more violent. Again Guitaut proposed the Louvre. Louis replied that the queen supped and went to bed too late for him. Guitaut said she would surely be glad to conform to his wishes. At last Louis agreed to the Louvre, and Guitaut galloped off to advise her of his coming and his desires.

"They supped together. The king spent the night with the queen, and nine months later Anne of Austria had a son, whose unexpected birth brought universal joy to the entire kingdom."

The account is that of Father Griffet, an eighteenth-century historian, and it is told with such a simple directness that it almost disarms one's suspicions. (The fatherhood of Louis XIV is still disputed.) And one could close this account of the birth of Versailles with the birth of its Sun King. Or one could—and perhaps should—close it with his father's last wish and leave out the unbecoming affair with the "beautiful Cinq-Mars." But if the affair is beyond the framework of

Versailles's first château, it is still revelatory of the character of its begetter.

Always preferring that anyone close to the king be as close, politically, to himself, Richelieu had pushed forward the comely son of an old friend, and the young man had predictably caught the eye of the king. "Never," wrote Chavigny to Mazarin, "did the king have a more violent passion for anyone." Arriving at seventeen, Cinq-Mars's rise at court in the next two years was meteoric—from captain of a regiment of guards to "Monsieur le Grand," the Marquis de Cinq-Mars.

As Luynes had been thirty-nine to Louis's sixteen, so Louis was now thirty-nine to Cinq-Mars's nineteen. For Tallemant, who retails tawdry stories of the intimacy between Cinq-Mars and Louis, the relationship was clearly homosexual. On the other hand, this has never been "proved," and Cinq-Mars's own preference for Marion Delorme, a famous courtesan, has been well established, if only by Louis's spies and Louis's jealousy of her. That it was a turbulent and passionate relationship, however, is part of the archives: Richelieu himself drew up peace treaties for their joint signature.

Restlessly Cinq-Mars overreached himself. Turned enemy of Richelieu, he joined the "Spanish plot" against him, alienated Louis—and lost his head. At the hour of his scheduled decapitation the king, according to an apocryphal story, paused during a chess game, looked at his watch, and cynically remarked, "I would like to see the expression on Monsieur le Grand's face now." Poor Louis. "His loves," as Tallemant notes, "were strange loves, and he had nothing of the lover but jealousy." "He took no pleasure, as other men, in *la belle passion*." says Madame de Motteville. "Accustomed to bitterness, his *tendresse* was only that he might feel pain and suffering the more."

To no one's surprise Richelieu's death on December 4, 1642, was swiftly followed by the king's. Long ailing, Louis was not long in dying, being aided enormously by his doctors. In a single year Dr. Bouvard bled him forty-seven times, gave him two hundred and fifteen enemas and two hundred and twelve different drugs. Before dying the king bitterly accused Bouvard of his death.

And before dying Louis also confided his last wish in life to his confessor. If God should give him back his health, he said (he was, after all, only forty-one), he would, "as soon as I see my son able to ride and of majority age [thirteen] ... put him in my place and ... retire to Versailles with four of your priests, there to discuss holy matters, and to think no longer about anything but my soul and my salvation."

One month later, on May 14, 1643, Louis XIII was dead.

THE
BELLY DANCE

MORROE BERGER

For centuries the principal ingredients in the popular Western image of the Middle East have been spirituality and sex. As early as the sixteenth century, European writers were using the second half of this irresistible combination to describe and define a venerable Eastern art form, the belly dance; and the ignorance or laziness of countless popular writers and artists ever since has only reinforced the stereotype. Thus, when the belly dance made a tardy but spectacular debut on the American scene at the World's Columbian Exposition in Chicago in 1893, it was in a carnival atmosphere that made it impossible to take it seriously. Nowadays it is more often called the Oriental dance, a label apparently designed to lend modesty by shifting the point of reference from anatomy to geography. Yet the sexual stereotype remains, and most of the belly dancers one can see in America do little to shake it off. The "Oriental dancers" who suddenly became popular in New York five or six years ago are more in the tradition of American burlesque than of anything else. And it was no doubt this sort of thing that Representative H. R. Gross, Republican of Iowa, had in mind when he sought to defeat the bill to aid the arts by offering an amendment to include the belly dance. As the Congressman jocularly put it, he saw no reason to exclude from federal assistance "the irregular jactitations and/or rhythmic contraction and co-ordinated relaxations of the serrati, obliques, and abdominis recti group of muscles—accompanied by rotatory undulations, tilts, and turns timed with and attuned to the titillating and blended tones of synchronous woodwinds."

As the fame of the belly dance spread to the Western world, it became something of an embarrassment to the cultural and political custodians of the East, who began to consider themselves above their own popular arts. More than a century ago a ruler of Egypt banished all belly dancers from Cairo; the present regime, less extreme in this regard, contents itself with requiring them to cover themselves from neck to ankles. Although the growth of tourism has brought about a revival of belly dancing in Egypt, and Egyptian intellectuals have begun to discuss and analyze its significance, the quality and character of the dance itself are in a state of decline. This is because the government encourages instead the performance of a sort of folkloric dance that only vaguely resembles the belly dance; it offers no help to the real belly dance, perhaps in the hope that it will be confined to the tourist trade and benighted masses.

The most artistic form of the belly dance, which emerged in the nineteenth century and reached a high point in our own times, called for movement across space as well as muscular virtuosity while standing in one place, and was performed by well-trained dancers. This dance, which has already been debased in the West by its assimilation to the strip tease, now is in danger of being "elevated" and modified into folklore by the solemn new regimes of the Middle East.

No one can say exactly how and where the belly dance originated. Nor does it matter. There are enough differing forms of this elemental dance to permit the assumption that it must have developed in several places a very long time ago. The dancers themselves always tell tourists and writers that their costumes, movements, and gestures are deliberately based on the dances of ancient Egypt. They may be right, but they are hardly experts, for, whatever their accomplishments, Egyptology is not one of them. They make these claims for the same reason that they minimize the sexual aspect of the dance: to give themselves what they consider greater respectability, as if their art alone were not enough to recommend them. Yet so great an Orientalist as Edward William Lane professed, in his classic *Manners and Customs of the Modern Egyptians,* to have found similarities between the belly dance he witnessed in Cairo in the 1830's and the ancient dances represented in the tombs of the Pharaohs; he even thought that the dancers themselves might be descended from those of ancient Egypt.

The possible affinity between the belly dance and the Pharaonic dance is not a subject that many Egyptologists have seen fit to explore. There was, however, a Czech scholar who was so incensed by the suggestion of any link between the two that he set his daughter to studying all the illustrations in the tombs. In her book, published in 1935 by the Oriental Institute in Prague, she, like her father, concluded that the modern belly dance came not from their beloved ancient Egyptians but from the Etruscans of Italy. Unfortunately for this thesis, the tomb paintings did reveal gestures and costumes similar to those of the belly dance. Something like the belly dance also reached Spain in early times, as we learn from the first-century Roman poets Juvenal and Martial. The former disapprovingly describes the dancing girls of Cadiz as "sinking down with quivering thighs to the floor," while the latter warns his guests not to expect to be entertained by these dancers who "with endless prurience swing lascivious loins in practiced writhings." The dance has also been attributed to the Gypsies, who, since they are not given to writing articles and books, have no means of refusing all the dubious honors heaped on them.

Whatever its origins, the belly dance in recent centuries has been thought of as Middle Eastern. There is good reason for this identification, because the dance has long been cultivated there. One thousand years ago the great Arab historian al-Mas'ūdī related this story in his account of the world since creation, which he called *Meadows of Gold and Mines of Gems:* In the ninth century, just after the golden age of Baghdad, Caliph Mu'tamid asked a scholar what qualities made a dancer great. The scholar began with a brief statement about the eight kinds of rhythm. Then he described the temperament and physique a great dancer must have, mentioning one quality which indicates that he probably had something like the belly dance in mind. A great dancer, he told the Caliph, must have "loose joints and a great agility in twirling and in swaying her hips."

Despite all this, the cultural authorities of Egypt today are trying to disown the dance. The director of the folklore section of the Ministry of Culture told me that there is no trace of such a dance in ancient or Arab Egypt; it appears in Egypt only under the Turks (whom Arabs blame for most of the things that they dislike in themselves). He has even issued a memorandum on the subject which says that belly dancing "came to us during Turkish and Mamlūk rule and was performed by slaves. It was further degraded when it left the palaces and went into the streets." There is no doubt that the belly dance flourished in Turkey—and among Gypsies, too. Sulukule, the old Gypsy quarter of Istanbul, was famous for its dancers. But nothing can refute the well-attested fact that, however much the official guardians of culture in Cairo may regret it, the belly dance is justly identified with Egypt, and has been since the nineteenth century.

Today, there are three main variations of the belly dance. One is the folk dance of the masses in the villages and cities, in which the sexual element is definite but subdued. Another is the traditional dance of the professional entertainers and the teachers of amatory arts to the ladies of the harem; in this there is not much locomotion but considerable muscular

38

movement, especially of the pelvis. Finally, there is what we might call the cabaret style; it is based on the second variation, but some locomotion and considerable grace have been added to it by dancers with serious training.

It has never been easy to describe any of these forms. A French savant who accompanied Napoleon on his Egyptian adventure in 1798 was so overwhelmed by the muscular dances he saw that he wrote: "It is impossible to describe this sort of dance with exactitude in our language." Fifty years later Gustave Flaubert, whose affair with a famous dancer in Egypt left an indelible mark on his spirit (and perhaps on his body, for a later medical analysis suggests he might have died of the effects of syphilis contracted in her company), attributed the inadequacy to himself rather than to the French language. After he had been favored with a private performance, he lamented in a letter to a friend: "I spare you any description of the dance—it wouldn't come off."

An American traveler of the time was not so reticent. He was George William Curtis, the scion of a respected New England family, a well-known orator, essayist, and earnest social reformer who had beeen at Brook Farm and knew Emerson and the transcendentalists. He visited the same dancer-courtesan with whom Flaubert had spent a night "such as one seldom experiences in a lifetime." She was Kutchuk Hanem, who had been banished from Cairo to Esna, five hundred miles up the Nile, when the ruler of Egypt discovered that she had sold his presents to second-hand dealers in the bazaar. Curtis, then only in his twenties, had the courage to describe her dance in Horace Greeley's New York *Tribune*. "Kutchuk stood motionless . . ." he wrote. "The sharp surges of sound swept around the room, dashing in regular measure against her movelessness, until suddenly the whole surface of her frame quivered in measure with the music. Her hands were raised, clapping the castanets, and she slowly turned upon herself, her right leg the pivot, marvellously convulsing all the muscles of her body. When she had completed the circuit of the spot on which she stood, she advanced slowly, all the muscles jerking in time to the music, and in solid, substantial spasms. It was a curious and wonderful gymnastic. There was no graceful dancing—once only there was the movement of dancing when she advanced, throwing one leg before the other, as Gypsies dance. But the rest was most voluptuous motion . . ."

In one significant respect Curtis was more restrained than Flaubert. Far from abandoning himself to the entertainer, as Flaubert did, he exhibited a self-control that must have pleased his *Tribune* readers. "Farewell, Kutchuk!" he wrote. "Addio, still-eyed dove! Almost thou persuadest me to pleasure. O Wall Street, Wall Street! because you are virtuous, shall there be no more cakes and ale?"

It was only a matter of time until some enterprising man would bring the belly dance to the West. It arrived at the Paris International Exposition of 1889 in the form of an "Algerian Village." A young American promoter of popular entertainment, Sol Bloom, saw it. "I doubt very much," he wrote in his autobiography six decades later, after a varied career that included a quarter-century in the House of Representatives and chairmanship of the powerful Committee on Foreign Affairs, "whether anything resembling it was ever seen in Algeria, but I was not at the time concerned with trifles." With all the judgment of his nineteen years, Bloom paid a thousand dollars for the exclusive right to present the "dancers, acrobats, glass-eaters and scorpion-swallowers" in America.

Where? After finding no enthusiasm to match his own, Bloom heard that an international exposition was planned for Chicago and that a Midway Plaisance was being built to house all the entertainment. Under the direction of the fair's Department of Ethnology, headed by a Harvard professor, things were going slowly. Then Bloom became manager of the concessions and the whole Midway was placed in less academic hands. In his new post he had no trouble bringing his Algerian Village to the World's Columbian Exposition of 1893. "All I had to do," he said, "was approve it myself." Bloom's own favorites in the village were the belly dancers. "It is regrettable . . ." he pointed out in his autobiography, "that more people remember the reputation of the *danse du ventre* than the dance itself. . . . When the public learned that the literal translation was 'belly dance' they delightedly concluded that it must be salacious and immoral. The crowds poured in. I had a gold mine." Money did not, however, exclude art for Bloom. "As a matter of strict fact," he insisted, "the *danse du ventre,* while sensuous and exciting, was a masterpiece of rhythm and beauty; it was choreographic perfection . . ."

Two eminent Americans who took a special interest in the Chicago Fair were among those who had made a trip up the Nile and seen the belly dance in its own setting. Henry Adams was in Egypt on his honeymoon in 1873 but left no published record of his reactions. His wife, however, who was easily shocked, wrote disapprovingly from Karnak to her father. "Last evening," she told him, "we saw some dancing girls at the consul's house, but were not amused or pleased." Twenty years after Karnak, Adams saw the belly dance again, this time at the Chicago Fair. In a letter to his friend John Hay (later Secretary of State), Adams wrote that he found the Midway a "sweet repose," adding: "I reveled in all its fakes and frauds, all its wickedness that seemed not to be understood by our innocent natives, and all its genuineness which was understood still less."

The dance that the nineteenth-century audience saw was the traditional muscular one. Out of it has developed the superior, more recent dance, in which there is greater movement and less exposure of the body. The performer begins with a veil wrapped around her head and shoulders and walks about for a few moments. She soon removes the veil and executes rhythmic movements of various parts of the body, as the music alternates fast and slow in accordance with her preference and arrangement. One early movement is made by the belly alone: it is pulled in and pushed out smoothly. The dancer may next move her breasts sideways as she walks

41

about or stands still. Then she may start rolling her hips upward, sideward, and downward as she moves her belly in the opposite direction; this popular movement is executed while stationary or while making a side step. In the next stage of the performance the dancer strikes a series of dramatic tableaux during which the music is slow and consists of a series of solos by various instruments. She follows with quick, swinging movements that carry her around the floor to lively rhythms, and then takes up her "castanets" (that is, metal clappers called *sagāt* in Arabic and not to be confused with the wooden castanets of the Spanish dancer), and the audience reinforces the rhythm with hand clapping; if the atmosphere is not too modern and forbidding, some men in the audience may rise and dance at their places or even with the dancer. Further conventional and special movements follow in accordance with dancers' talents: shaking of shoulders and breasts and hips, and, a deep back bend; a few turns in place conclude the dance.

Although the dancers now move about much more than they did in the nineteenth century, the belly dance is still essentially one of form rather than locomotion. Most Western dancing involves movement across large spaces, but in the belly dance the main movements are not of the legs but of the arms, hands, torso, and hips. The good belly dancer strives for smooth, circular, elliptical, and undulating motions rather than sharp, angular ones. Hoda Shams Eddin, a leading dancer in Egypt for more than a decade now, says that the effect must be sinuous. "The flute," she told me, moving her hands expressively through the air, "makes the *sound* of the serpent. So I must make his movements." Indeed, like the serpent, the dancer moves slowly, in undulations. Both are in a sense all torso and no legs. Because locomotion is only incidental, good belly dancers train themselves in the graceful movement of as many parts of the body as possible. To achieve proper use of the arms, hands, and head, the best of them have studied ballet with Mlle Sonia Ivanova. Born in Russia and trained in England, she has been Cairo's leading ballet teacher for more than a quarter of a century; she has never felt the contempt or condescension for the belly dance that is now increasingly expressed in the Middle East.

I should like to emphasize three features of the belly dance: it is a series of "stills"; it stresses sexual modesty as well as display; it is sedative as well as stimulating.

Since the belly dancer achieves her main effects by moving various parts of her body while standing still or in a graceful but slow walk, the total impression is one of a succession of still pictures. Like Arab art in general, it depends upon form, the arrangement of parts within a compressed area, as in a mosaic or geometric pattern. For it is not only abandon that the dancer aims for, but also restraint and control. Though the cumulative effect and denouement of the dance are often compared (by inexperienced observers quick to adopt profound metaphors) to the rise and fall of the sexual act itself, I do not think this is any truer of the belly dance than it is of most others. Many kinds of temporal art, of course, build up to an emotional impact and then offer release, just as forms in nature move in waves and cycles.

The belly dance is sexual, to be sure, but it is so in the tension it creates between display and modesty, exposure and concealment. The dancer alternates provocative movements with sedate poses and gestures. At the start she uses the veil to reveal and conceal, without (if she is good) any overtones of the coquettish or coy. She uses her hands and arms gracefully for the same purpose, now hiding her face and now revealing it, for in some sections of Middle Eastern society, where the West has penetrated least, it is still more modest to conceal the face than other parts of the body. This attitude induced Flaubert to write to his mother when he arrived in Alexandria: ". . . if you don't see their faces, you see their entire bosoms. As you change countries, you find that modesty changes its location, like a bored traveler who keeps shifting from one seat in the carriage to another."

By combining modesty with display and by its flowing, undulating movements, the belly dance has a pacifying quality that attenuates its sexual excitement. Upon the Arab, perhaps more than upon the Westerner, the dancer's regular, smooth, and liquid movements often have a semi-hypnotic effect, alternating with a stimulating one that makes him want to dance, too. The sexual side is by no means lost upon him, but, I am convinced from observing many kinds of audiences, it is counteracted by a purely visual pleasure in the motion of the dance and an aural delight in the music. In its own milieu the appeal of the belly dance is one of pure voyeurism.

It is instructive to compare the belly dance with that similarly popular but often depreciated American (and now European) attraction, the strip tease. The differences are profound. Just as the essence of the belly dance is motion within a limited space, so the essence of the strip tease is display during locomotion. The key to both is in the climax: in the strip tease, nudity (or as close to it as the dancer can safely get); in the belly dance, motion. In the Western dance, the music is incidental; in the Oriental dance, it is enjoyed for its own sake and moves the audience to participate by clapping hands, swaying the body, and even by getting up to join in the dancing. In the strip tease, display is so central that attention is riveted upon the dancer's clothing and her manipulation of it; in the belly dance, the eye follows the dancer's body beneath her clothing, for the movements of her head, shoulders, arms, and hands are as important as those of her torso. The one is meant to excite sexual desire, the other to excite but also to pacify. The strip tease is voyeurism, too, but in it the prospect of nudity promises something which is never delivered; the belly dance promises nothing beyond itself, no imagined climax. So the strip tease is Western in its logical emphasis upon the ultimate—nudity—and its coy retreat from climax, while the belly dance is Oriental in its partially sedative quality and in the acquiescence of an audience that demands less from the dancer but gets all that is promised.

Modernization has wrought changes not only in the belly dance itself but in the life of the dancers as well. No longer do they come primarily from families of dancers; the decision to follow the career is now a more deliberate and personal one. Nor do they instruct ladies any more in the arts of seduction and love. The leading cabaret dancers in the Middle East today are Westernized young women who think about managers, contracts, and films. Some move in a world of sports cars, Paris gowns, fancy villas, and real-estate deals. They are, moreover, no longer prostitutes available to anyone with the price of admission. Their private moral character is probably no worse or better than that of young women in America or Europe who want to be paid for their beauty or talent in the entertainment business.

In one respect, however, belly dancing as a career today is similar to what it was a hundred years ago and more: it is still an avenue (narrow and uphill, but open) to fame and material success for girls who would otherwise wind up as the wives of underpaid factory and farm laborers or minor clerks, raising five or six children in poverty, dirt, and ill health. The average laborer in a Middle Eastern city makes about ten dollars a week. Even a cheap dancer who spends her nights in a bar cajoling men to buy drinks makes twice as much, and the good dancers in cabarets make thirty dollars a night; a very successful dancer may draw as much as five hundred dollars a week in a night club, and earn more for special appearances. She doesn't keep it all, of course. Most dancers have agents, who take the usual ten per cent fee, and publicity costs; all have to provide their own costumes, which cost from fifty to five hundred dollars each. What success costs the belly dancer in favors she must return for favors given is another matter. Middle Eastern show business is populated by the same kind of promoters, hangers-on, and phony movie producers as its Western counterpart.

Until a decade or so ago, a girl became a belly dancer by convincing a cabaret owner or director that she had enough talent to join the chorus. She would learn a few rudiments in rehearsals, carefully study the famous dancers in cabarets and films, and work for a break that would enable her to become a soloist. Nowadays the system is not much different, except that the learning period seems to be shorter, and there is a small number of men who give formal instruction in the art. One of the best is Ibrahim Akif, who comes from a family of acrobats and dancers. In a dilapidated building in one of Cairo's big squares just beyond the downtown area known to tourists, he has a shabby, dimly lit studio unannounced by any sign. To it come ambitious girls who think they are attractive and talented enough to convince Akif to give them lessons. Several months of instruction cost about two hundred dollars. This is so high for most of the pupils that they usually pay a small amount as they learn and the rest after they are employed. A typical aspirant I saw was Raga', the twenty-year-old daughter of a retired government clerk. She was small and had a pretty face but was a bit heavy for a modern cabaret dancer. Weary of her menial, low-paying clerical job, she was determined to become a popular dancer at any cost. Though she was afraid to tell her father of her plans, she meant to realize them even if she had to face banishment from home. Her instructor, a young assistant to Akif, was more cynical about her situation. Her father, he said, probably knew about her activity but winked at it in the hope that he might benefit if she succeeded. Raga' was willing enough, yet to me it appeared that her body would never do the things that were demanded of it. She was always good-natured about her excessive weight, her clumsiness, and her inability to imitate her instructor's extraordinary muscular control. Despite Akif's assurances that she would become a star, I felt she could never be more than one of the solo dancers in a cheap cabaret, a status to which she would soon adjust herself however.

One of the streets leading from the square in which Akif has his studio is called Shari'a al Qal'a, Citadel Street. For more than a hundred years it has been the center for Cairo's native professional musicians, and it continues to be the home of famous dancers who perform the traditional dance at native celebrations such as weddings and birthdays. Here is the school of the old muscular dance which Flaubert, Curtis, and

Adams saw and which formed the basis of the more artful modern dance we have been discussing until now. Another such district in Cairo is Bab al Sha'riyah. One street there still bears traces of the past in its name, Shari'a al Tabila, Drum Street. In one of the buildings on this street lives Hurriyah Ahmad, whose life and career are typical of this class of dancers—a class now more than ever hidden from the foreigner.

Hurriyah is about forty years old and lives with her husband, an accordion player and owner of a musical instrument shop, and her three daughters and two sons. Her mother and grandmother were dancers, as are her sisters. Sometimes Hurriyah accepts solo dates for herself, but more often she supplies a troupe of singers and dancers whom she trains and manages herself. For the latter kind of date, she gets thirty to fifty dollars, depending upon the number of entertainers and the client's capacity to pay, out of which she pays each established dancer in her troupe about seven dollars. A dancer also gets tips from members of the audience, who, following an old custom, place coins or bills on her forehead, shoulders, or in her bosom as she approaches them in turn. Hurriyah also teaches singing and dancing to her own daughters; to others who come for free lessons, join her troupe, and are paid a dollar or so when they perform until their training period is over; and to a succession of girls who, under special circumstances, come to live with her as members of the family.

One such girl was Samia, seventeen years old when I saw her in Hurriyah's home last year, who was "adopted" by Hurriyah's husband and took his name, Abu Kahla. Born into a poor peasant family in Tanta, a city about halfway between Cairo and Alexandria, she became interested in dancing when very young. She used to visit an aunt from time to time who lived in a Cairo suburb. One day she told her parents she was going to stay with her aunt, but instead took a job as a servant-girl in Cairo and went often to Citadel Street to try to become a dancer. On her rounds she met Hurriyah's husband and asked him to help her. "She had talent," he told me, "and needed help. If she continued in the same way, she might soon end up in a bad way, as many country girls do. So I had her examined physically to be sure of her purity and then we took her into our home." There Samia was one of the family, and was a companion to Hurriyah's sixteen-year-old daughter, Labiba, also a dancer. The two girls never went out alone. They usually stayed up most of the night even when they did not dance, slept during the day, and spent their spare time practicing, watching television, and going to the movies.

Hurriyah holds Samia in a customary apprenticeship that is a combination of kindness and exploitation. She pays Samia about five dollars for each performance but keeps the money for her. Out of it she buys the girl her costumes and takes a small amount for her board. If Samia marries while she is still in the household, Hurriyah and her husband will act as her parents. In five years or so, if she has not yet married, Samia will probably leave Hurriyah anyway to make her way as a dancer and, of course, to try for stardom in the limited circle of the traditional belly dancers. Meanwhile, she is both protected and used. Yet, from Hurriyah's point of view, it is not always clear who is exploiting whom. She says she has had several such girls living with her who, when they made good elsewhere, have forgotten her.

Hurriyah emphasized that she is not an "artiste," that is, a dancer who works in cabarets, drinks with customers for a percentage of the bill, and gets ahead by pleasing powerful men. She is, she insists, a *fanāna*, which is simply the Arabic word for "artiste" but without the immoral connotation of the French word. The *fanāna* is married, usually to a musician, and professes to live a conventional life. On the surface she usually does, and indeed her home is often a model of pathetic respectability, but many people who claim to know the facts often deride these protestations of virtue.

Dancers like Hurriyah are not encouraged by the Egyptian government. Yet the regime, with all its involvement in economic development and a busy foreign policy, has still found the time to deal with the dance. The government promotes folkloric dancing and ballet, and tries to chasten the kind of belly dancing that is seen by foreign tourists. It has given the recently created state Ballet Institute the very highest priority in an extensive cultural program, and has sent several Egyptian girls to study ballet in the Soviet Union.

The press, which is owned and operated by the government, gives favorable treatment to folklore and ballet and either ignores belly dancing or points up its presumed decline. Last year, for example, an article in a popular illustrated weekly extolled ballet as the finest type of dance, one without provocative shaking, a dance "addressed to the soul." Ballet reached its peak in Russia, the writer generously granted, but it is now returning to Egypt, the land of its origin. As for the folkloric dancing encouraged by the government, it has a certain affinity to the belly dance, and is certainly Egyptian in spirit and origin. Some observers, however, wonder whether the influence of Russian teachers has not made it into something else—interesting and pleasing, but not very Egyptian.

As a further step to discourage the belly dance, the government in 1955 required the dancers to cover themselves from shoulders to ankles, even if with nothing more than the most diaphanous of materials. Not that they were unduly exposed, anyway; cabaret dancers customarily wore much less than any belly dancer who might be appearing on the same program. (But cabaret dancers are "Western" and so do not reflect upon Egypt's cultural reputation.) Because the modern belly dance does not depend much on muscular display, it has not been hampered by the new requirement—although Egyptians associated with belly dancing have been quick to point out the hypocrisy of a policy that requires entertainers to cover their bodies while permitting men and women in shorts and bikinis close contact on crowded beaches.

The belly dance has gone through many changes over the centuries and has often enough in the past been the object of official condemnation and restriction. It has been vulgarized and chastened in turn. Its name has been euphemized. But since its continuing popularity in its various forms has never depended on governmental support, Egyptians feel that it will survive because it arises from something in their spirit that goes deeper than the policy of any political regime.

HOW TO
INSULT
EVERYONE
REGARDLESS OF RACE,
COLOR, CREED,
OR NATIONAL ORIGIN

CHARLES F. BERLITZ

There is a current variation of a military joke that may have had its counterpart in the Roman legions. A visiting Congressman asks a wounded American soldier in a base hospital in Vietnam how many VC he got before he was wounded. The soldier replies that he wasn't exactly fighting the Vietcong when it happened and explains that he had been taught to flush out Vietcong among the peasantry by saying "Ho Chi Minh đù me!" a scurrilous reference to Ho's parents that would enrage and penetrate the disguise of any true Vietcong. One day he tried it on a suspicious-looking peasant on the far side of a road who simply looked up and replied, "President Johnson đù me!" And, he explains, "as we were shaking hands in the middle of the road, we were both hit by a weapons carrier."

The world traveler finds that insults, while displaying a wide variety of imagery, tend to fall into three general classes. The first includes the multiple variants of "idiot," or "fool," and the second accuses the recipient of moral or physical degeneracy on the part of himself or his parents, usually his mother. The third, a simple insulting reference to the other person's nationality, religion, or color, can almost be predicted from the geographical position or national composition of the country or language in question. For example, call a Greek a Turk, or vice versa, and you have already insulted him magnificently. The Chinese can always insult a white man by referring to him as *yang kuei* ("foreign ghost," because of being so pale). However, this sort of slur should not be considered a true insult, since it cannot be used between people of the same nationality.

The traveler to France may easily recognize such standard insults as *imbécile, animal,* and even *crétin.* It is more serious to call someone a *vache* ("cow"), *chameau* ("camel"), *salaud* or *saleté,* these last two having the meaning of "dirt." For the sake of effect, all of these insults can be prefaced with *espèce de* . . . ("kind of" . . .). French possesses also a frequent and unusual use of the "stupid" category of insult wherein the word *con* (the female organ) is used to describe a stupid or unlikable person. This is often lengthened to *connard,* a word that is familiar to anyone who has driven a car in France and that is occasionally accompanied by the holding of the right index finger to the right temple and twisting it.

The supreme insult for a woman in Latin countries is the common term for "prostitute"—*putain* or *pute* in French, *puta* in Spanish and Portuguese, and *putana* in Italian. However, the subtle French have converted the regular word for "girl" or "daughter"—*fille*—into a like meaning. So, when in France, be especially careful how you use the word *fille;* the best plan is always to say "young girl"—*jeune fille*—rather than fille by itself.

Spanish goes one step farther, using *tu madre* ("your mother") so often as an insult that there is a tendency to avoid or disguise the term *madre* in polite conversation. Thus, if you wish to inquire about someone's mother, you may say *su señora madre* (literally, "your lady mother") or *su mamá* ("your mommy"). Of course it is all right to refer to your *own* mother, because everyone knows you would never insult *her*, motherhood still being very much "in" in the Spanish-speaking world. An even more violent insult is a two-syllable word (*chinga*) prefixed on *tu madre*, suggesting an illogical and improbable course of action, an expression so well known among speakers of Spanish that it can be whistled or even sounded out on an automobile horn in the rhythm: long, short, short, long, short.

In Germany the guttural force of the language tends to make the insult seem even nastier. What could sound worse than *verdammter Schweinehund* ("damned pig-dog")? *Schuft* is the equivalent of "jerk," and *Trottel* corresponds to "fool" or "idiot," to be emphasized by banging on your right temple with your fist.

Russian contains an insult for a worthlesss drifter, *b'yezpasportnik* ("one without a passport"), since local passports have been required in Russia by both old and new regimes. A sort of elegant insult in modern Russia is *nyekulturniy* ("uncultured"). The older and more violent insults still exist, however, such as *durak* (the village idiot), *sukin sin* (bitch's son), *huy sobaki* (dog's member), and even *huy morzhevyi* (walrus's member).

When we come to Greece, we find an unusual gesture that has the force of the strongest spoken insult: holding your hand palm outward to the person you are insulting. This is called the *mountza* and usually provokes violence in the insultee, or perhaps a reply in the form of a double *mountza* —both palms, or striking the back of the right palm with the left as if to push the *mountza* even closer to your opponent. By an amazing linguistic coincidence, a recent American car was named the Monza—an interesting example of stacking the cards against a sales potential to Greeks.

In Moslem countries the most effective insults have to do with dogs. Dogs are generally in disrepute throughout the Moslem world because one of their number, about one thousand, three hundred and forty-two years ago, barked at and thereby caused the betrayal of Mohammed when he was hiding in a cave. Turks express this insult by saying *it* ("dog"), and the Arabs by *Ya, ibn kalb!* ("Oh, son of the dog!").

The favorite Chinese insult is *too-tze* ("turtle"), suspected by the Chinese of incestuous proclivities. Further, there is *tieu na ma*, which is similar to the standard Spanish insult about one's mother.

Insults may be interesting to consider and to compare, but not to use. The tourist or traveler should rather consider the Chinese proverb *fan she shih tzu erh ho shuo*—"turn tongue ten times, then speak."

THE
BODY
IN THE
BOG

GEOFFREY BIBBY

The business of the archae-
ologist is the digging up of the past, the reconstruction of
remote history. He does his best to find out what our remote
ancestors did and thought and felt from the material remains
they left in the ground. A distinguished archaeologist has
unflatteringly described himself and his colleagues as sur-
geons probing into the workings of the human brain with
picks, shovels, and builders' trowels. "Fortunately," he adds,
"our patients are already dead."

This comparison must not be taken too literally. When Sir
Mortimer Wheeler describes the archaeologist as investigating people who are dead, he means, I am afraid, that we are
trying to find out about these dead-and-gone people by studying the things they left behind them, their implements and
weapons and coins and pots and pans. The nearest we normally get to the people themselves is their skeletons, and
there is a limit to what can be deduced from dry bones.

I wish to tell an archaeological detective story that is different—a detective story that begins with a body and no artifacts.

My part in the story began on Monday, April 28, 1952, when I arrived at the Prehistoric Museum of Aarhus, in mid-Denmark, to find a dead body on the floor of my office. On an iron sheet stood a large block of peat, and at one end of it the head and right arm of a man protruded, while one leg and foot stuck out from the other end. His skin was dark brown, almost chocolate colored, and his hair was a brownish red.

He had been found on Saturday afternoon by workers cutting peat in a little bog near Grauballe, about twenty miles away. He lay a yard below the surface, but peat had been dug for generations there so that the "surface" had lain much higher, even within living memory. The finders had informed the local doctor of their discovery, not so much because he was a doctor but because he was known to be an antiquary of repute. And he had informed Professor Peter Glob, who was the director of our museum.

This was not Professor Glob's first "bog body"; he knew what to expect and made preparations accordingly. The next day he drove out to the bog, cut a section through the peat exposing the lie of the body, drew and photographed that section, took samples of the peat surrounding the body, and then cut out the whole block in which the body lay and brought it in to the museum in a truck.

That Monday we carefully dug away the peat covering the body, taking samples every two inches. The body lay face down, with one leg drawn up and the arms twisted somewhat behind it. It was completely naked. When we removed the peat from below the body (after turning it over in a plaster cast to preserve its original position), we still found nothing, no trace of clothing, no artifacts—nothing except the naked body.

At this point we turned for help to the professor of forensic medicine at Aarhus University, who carried out a thorough autopsy and presented us with a lengthy and detailed report:

"This most unusually well-preserved body has, as a result of the particular composition of the earth in which it has lain, undergone a process of conservation which appears to resemble most closely a tanning. This has made the skin firm and resistant, and has to a high degree counteracted the various processes of decay which normally commence soon after death. . . . the subject is an adult male, and the condition of the teeth suggests that he was of somewhat advanced age. . . . On the front of the throat was found a large wound stretching from ear to ear. . . . This wound may with certainty be interpreted as an incised lesion, probably caused by several cuts inflicted by a second person. The direction of the wound and its general appearance make it unlikely that it could be self-inflicted or accidentally inflicted after death. . . . The investigation of the hair suggests that the subject was dark-haired. The reddish coloration is presumably accounted for by the body having lain in peat."

So the man from Grauballe had had his throat cut, and we had a murder mystery on our hands.

The investigation went on. The police expert reported: "There is nothing unusual about the fingerprints obtained. I myself possess the same type of pattern on the right thumb and middle finger—without therefore claiming any direct descent from Grauballe Man. Among the present-day Danish population the two patterns occur with a frequency of, respectively, 11.2 and 68.3 per cent."

More important were the results we got from the peat samples and from a portion of the liver region that we had excised and sent to the radioactive-carbon laboratory.

It happens that the botanists of Scandinavia have worked out in great detail the changing composition of the vegetation of the region since the last ice age ended more than ten thousand years ago. They do this by means of the thousands of infinitesimal grains of pollen to be found in any cubic centimeter of peat. The time within this sequence when any particular specimen of peat was formed is shown by the proportion of certain types of pollen grains, particularly of tree pollen. And the pollen analysts could tell us that the peat immediately below Grauballe Man had been formed early in the period the Danes call the Roman Iron Age, a period extending from the beginning of the Christian Era to about A.D. 300.

But they could tell us more. The peat *above* the body was of *earlier* date than that directly below and around the body, and the peat at a little distance to either side of the body was earlier still. The body had clearly been buried in a hole cut in the peat—but not in a hole cut to receive it. The only explanation to fit the facts was that a hole had been cut, probably to obtain peat for fuel, had stood open for some years (long enough for new peat to form in the water at the bottom of the hole), and then Grauballe Man had been thrown into this new peat and the hole had been filled in with peat from the surface layers.

The radio-carbon laboratory—which determines the age of organic substances by measuring the residual carbon-14 in the specimen—could tell us that this had occurred and that Grauballe Man had died in A.D. 310, with a possible error of a hundred years in either direction. This did not surprise us; for, though local newspapers and gossip had made much of a certain "Red Christian," a drunkard farmhand who was said to have disappeared one night some sixty years before, not far from the Grauballe peat bog, we should have been very surprised indeed if the pollen laboratory and the radio-carbon laboratory had *not* given us a date in the region of 100 B.C.– A.D. 300.

For Grauballe Man was far from being an isolated example. Bodies have always been turning up in the peat bogs of Denmark—and not only in Denmark. They are frequently found in northwest Germany and even as far south as Holland. In that area there are records of something like two hundred bog bodies. Since the earlier records are not very detailed, sometimes merely an entry in a parish registry of the "body of a poor man drowned in such and such a bog," the statistics are far from exact. The earliest doubtful record of this nature is from 1450, at Bonstorf in Germany. And the first detailed report is from 1773, when a completely preserved body of a man was found three feet deep in the peat at Ravnholt on the Danish island of Fünen. The body lay on its back with its arms crossed behind it—"as though they had been bound," says the parish clerk. Apart from a sheepskin around the head, it was naked. When the sheepskin was removed, it could be seen that the man had had his throat cut.

In 1797, in southwest Jutland, another well-preserved male body was found, naked save for one oxhide moccasin but covered with two calfskin cloaks. The cause of death is not recorded, and the body was hurriedly buried in a nearby churchyard when it began to dry out and decompose.

And so it went. Every few years a body would be found, would be a nine-day wonder in its immediate locality because of its surprising state of preservation, and would be buried again when it began to smell.

A few of the bodies achieved more than local fame. In 1853, about fifty miles south of Copenhagen a body was found, probably that of a woman, though there was little left besides the skeleton and the long, fair hair. The body was noteworthy because it was accompanied by a bronze brooch and seven glass beads, which even then could be dated to the Iron Age and which we can now date to about A.D. 300.

Eight years earlier a much more complete female body had been found at Haraldskaer, in south Jutland, not far from the burial mounds of Gorm, the last heathen king of Denmark, and his queen, nor from the site of the first Christian church in Denmark, built about A.D. 950 by Gorm's son, Harald Bluetooth. The body lay in the peat with its hands and feet held down by forked sticks, and it achieved some notoriety in Denmark because some learned antiquaries claimed that it was Queen Gunhild of Norway, who, according to legend, had been enticed to Denmark by Harald Bluetooth and drowned by him in a morass. Even at the time of discovery, though, the evidence for this identification was regarded as too slender.

The first photograph of a peat-bog body dates from 1873 and is of a body found near Kiel. It was a man's body with a triangular hole in the forehead. He was naked except for a piece of leather bound around the left shin, but his head was covered with a large square woollen blanket and a sewn skin cape. An attempt was made to preserve him for exhibition by smoking, and several photographs were taken, some extravagantly posed. The first photograph of a body *in situ* was taken in 1892. The body was found not many miles away from the place where Grauballe Man was discovered sixty years later, and very close indeed to another recent find, the Tollund Man.

The list could be continued almost indefinitely. But it is only within recent years that pollen analysis has been developed to a stage where the bodies can be accurately dated. And all the bodies found since have proved to date to the same restricted period of Danish prehistory, the first three centuries of the Christian Era. This fact makes it possible—indeed essential—to regard them as a single "case."

Apart from Grauballe Man, four bodies have been found in the peat bogs of Denmark since World War II, and all have been subjected to the same thorough analysis that we gave Grauballe Man. Three came from the same bog, the large peat area of Borremose in north Jutland. The first was a man, naked like so many of the others but with two cloaks of skin beside him. Around his neck was a rope noose, which may have been the cause of death, although the body was too badly preserved to be certain. There were odd features about the noose; it had been knotted at the neck, and both of the fairly short ends had been bent over and lashed with leather thongs to prevent them from unraveling, surely an unduly elaborate treatment for an ordinary hangman's noose.

The second body was that of a woman, again poorly preserved. The upper part of the body appeared to have been naked, while the lower part was covered with a blanket, a shawl, and other bits of clothing. There was a leather cord around the neck, but the cause of death was apparently a crushing blow on the skull.

The third body was also a woman's, a rather stout lady who lay face downward in the peat with only a blanket wrapped around her middle and held in place by a leather strap. She was no sight for squeamish archaeologists—she had been scalped and her face battered to pieces, though perhaps after death.

It is with quite unjustified relief that one turns from the rather macabre Borremose bodies to the well-known Tollund Man whose portrait has been in the press of the world and who has had the honor of appearing on British television. Tollund Man was discovered in 1950, two years before Grauballe Man and under the same circumstances, by farmers cutting peat. The discovery was reported to the police, and they called in Professor Glob, who described what he saw:

"In the peat cut, nearly seven feet down, lay a human figure in a crouched position, still half-buried. A foot and a shoulder protruded, perfectly preserved but dark-brown in color like the surrounding peat, which had dyed the skin. Carefully we removed more peat, and a bowed head came into view.

"As dusk fell, we saw in the fading light a man take shape before us. He was curled up, with legs drawn under him and arms bent, resting on his side as if asleep. His eyes were peacefully shut; his brows were furrowed, and his mouth showed a slightly irritated quirk as if he were not overpleased by this unexpected disturbance . . ."

Tollund Man was found to be naked except for a leather belt around his waist and a leather cap upon his head, a cap made of eight triangular gussets of leather sewn together. There was one other item. Around his neck was the elaborately braided leather rope with which they had hanged him.

It is clear, I think, that we have a case of mass murder. There are too many points of similarity between the killings for it to be possible to consider each independently of the others. I should point out, though, that their generally fantastic state of preservation is not one of these points of similarity. It is merely our good fortune. The preservation is due to the fact that the peat bogs contain sufficient humic acid and tannic acid to halt the processes of decay and start a tanning process that can preserve the body. (This process, incidentally, we have carried to its logical conclusion with Grauballe Man. Eighteen months in an oak vat in a concentrated solution based on oak shavings has completed the tanning process that nature commenced some eighteen hundred years ago. Grauballe Man, on exhibition at the Prehistoric Museum in Aarhus, needs only a little linseed oil now and then in order to last indefinitely.)

There is one condition for preservation, however, for otherwise the peat bogs would be full of the bodies of every animal that falls into them. The body must be *buried* in the peat, deep enough down to be below the oxygen-containing surface levels. And this—the fact that all these bodies were disposed of in old cuttings in the peat—*is* one of the common factors that cause us to regard all the killings as a single phenomenon.

Another is the fact that all the bodies are naked. Though it is the rule rather than the exception for articles of clothing to be found with the bodies, and sometimes wrapped around the bodies, they are never regularly clothed in the garments. But the most obvious similarity is that all have died violent deaths and that all are found in bogs.

And that leads to the next step in the inquiry: the question of motive. Why are these bodies there at all?

These are not ordinary burials. Archaeologists are very well acquainted with the burials of this period of Danish prehistory. They were elaborate, clearly showing evidence of belief in an afterlife in which the dead would have need of material things. The graves are large and edged with stones. The body lies carefully arranged on its side, together with a whole set of pottery vessels, or in the case of the wealthy, with glass and silver ware imported from the Roman Empire. The vessels must have held provisions for the journey to the afterworld, for there is often a leg of pork or of mutton with the rest of the provisions, and even a knife to carve the joint.

It is clear that whatever it was that resulted in the deaths of the bodies in the bogs also deprived them of regular, ritual burial.

We must dismiss the most obvious explanation—that the bodies were victims of robbery with violence. All are dated to the comparatively short period of three hundred years at the beginning of our era. It may have been a lawless time—though farther south it is the period of the Pax Romana—but certainly it was no more lawless than many other periods: the period before, of the great Celtic and Germanic wanderings; or the period after, when the Roman Empire was breaking up and all the vultures flocked to the kill; or the Viking period; or much of the Middle Ages. We should expect a much greater spread in date if the bodies are to be explained as the victims of robber bands.

We must widen our scope and look not so much at the bodies as at the bogs. What do we find there?

Any Danish archaeologist can answer that question at length. And he can illustrate his answer at the Danish National Museum in Copenhagen, where room after room is full of things found in bogs. More than half of the best treasures of Danish prehistory have been found in bogs, and the archaeologist will tell you that these treasures were offerings to the gods.

Now, archaeologists have often been accused of calling in hypothetical gods and cult practices whenever they find anything they cannot explain by obvious mundane means. A theory of offerings in the peat bogs must not be accepted uncritically. But how else is one to explain why a Stone Age farmer, some four thousand years ago, very carefully laid seven large, new, unused stone axes side by side in a row in a peat bog? How is one to explain why several pairs of the big bronze trumpets known as lurs, the finest known products of the Danish Bronze Age, have been found in the bogs in good working order?

It begins to look as though anything of prehistoric date found in the bogs of Denmark is a priori likely to be an offering to the gods. If we move forward to the actual period of the bog bodies, we find the offerings in the bogs getting more numerous and more varied and richer. In the early 1950's I spent three years a few miles south of our museum, helping to dig out an immense offering of weapons—several thousand iron swords and spearheads and arrowheads and shield bosses —all of them burned, bent, hacked to pieces, and then deposited in a lake in the middle of a peat bog. They had been deposited at various times—it was a regular place of offering —but all during the period A.D. 150–300. Among the weapons lay the skeletons of two horses—and here perhaps we approach quite close in spirit to the bog bodies, for the horses had been beheaded before they were offered, and marks on the bones showed quite clearly where spears had been stuck into the carcasses, before or after death.

We are entering a dark region. Our probings into the minds of our distant ancestors are lifting a corner of a veil that seems to cover an area of deep superstition, a time when the peat bogs were the abodes of gods and spirits, who demanded sacrifice. When we look now at the bodies in the bogs it seems by no means impossible that they, too, were offerings; that the sacrifices to the gods also included human sacrifices.

We must ask ourselves what we know about the gods and goddesses of this period.

At the northern end of that very bog at Borremose in which three of the bodies were found, there was discovered in 1897 a large caldron of solid silver. In itself the Gundestrup caldron is far and away the most intrinsically valuable of all the bog offerings. But it is more than that; it is a picture book of European religion around the beginning of the Christian Era. Its sides are decorated, inside and out, with a series of panels bearing pictures, in relief, of gods and goddesses, of mythical animals, and of ritual scenes. Admittedly the caldron is believed to have been manufactured in southeast Europe and to have been brought to Denmark as booty, but the deities portrayed are like the native Danish gods of the period.

It is particularly noteworthy that each one of these deities, although otherwise naked, bears a torque, or broad necklet, at the throat, which appears to have been a symbol of kingship and of divinity. It has even been suggested—perhaps not entirely fancifully—that the oddly elaborate nooses around the necks of Tollund and Borremose Man in some way set them apart as consecrated to the gods. We know from the sagas, not many hundreds of years later, that in Viking times hanged men were sacred to Odin, the chief god of the Viking pantheon.

One of the interior caldron panels shows clearly that the idea of human sacrifice was not alien to the religion of the time. It is admittedly a different ceremony of sacrifice, with the victim dropped headfirst into, or perhaps slaughtered above, a caldron, perhaps the Gundestrup caldron itself. The cutting of the throats of animal victims and the draining of their blood into a caldron was not unknown even among the civilized Greeks and Romans—and Grauballe Man, like many of the victims in the Danish bogs, had had his throat cut.

Speculation concerning details of ritual, though fascinating, can hardly be justified by the slender evidence at our disposal. But the general picture cannot be questioned: the Danes of the early Christian centuries worshiped torque-bearing gods and goddesses; they were not averse to human sacrifice; and the holy places of the divinities were the peat bogs.

There is one source of information that we have not yet tapped. The historians and geographers of the Roman Empire wrote books, some of which describe the manners and customs of peoples beyond the imperial frontiers. The books must be used with caution; few of the authors had visited the regions they describe, and their accounts may well be as full of misunderstandings and fanciful explanations as anything the modern archaeologist can invent to explain what he finds.

But there is a passage in Tacitus's *Germania*, an account of the peoples beyond the Rhine written in A.D. 98, that bears on our study of the Danish bog bodies. Tacitus names seven tribes to the north of Germany, including the Angles, who are known to have lived in south Jutland before they invaded England in the fifth century together with the Saxons and Jutes. And he says: "these people . . . are distinguished by a common worship of Nerthus, or Mother Earth. They believe that she interests herself in human affairs and rides through their peoples. In an island of Ocean stands a sacred grove, and in the grove stands a car draped with a cloth which none but the priest may touch. The priest can feel the presence of the goddess in this holy of holies, and attends her, in deepest reverence, as her car is drawn by oxen. Then follow days of rejoicing and merrymaking in every place that she honors with her advent and stay. No-one goes to war, no-one takes up arms; every object of iron is locked away; then, and only then, are peace and quiet known and prized, until the goddess is again restored to her temple by the priest, when she has had her fill of the society of men. After that, the car, the cloth and, believe it if you will, the goddess herself are washed clean in a secluded lake. This service is performed by slaves who are immediately afterwards drowned in the lake. Thus mystery begets terror and a pious reluctance to ask what that sight can be which is allowed only to dying eyes."

Here we may be getting close to an answer. Nerthus—Mother Earth—is clearly a goddess of fertility; she may be the "goddess with the torque." And the time of peace and rejoicing when the goddess is driven around the countryside in her draped carriage will be the time of sowing, the vernal equinox. Pagan survivals of this spring festival still exist in many parts of Europe, in mummers' plays and Maypole dancing and Queens of the May. And in the National Museum in Copenhagen may be seen one of the ox-drawn carriages that almost certainly was used to carry the image of the fertility goddess around the fields. It was found—inevitably—in a peat bog, Dejbjerg in east Jutland, in the 1880's. Richly carved and decorated with ornaments of bronze, it is far too fine a wagon to have been used for mundane purposes. Upon it stands a palanquin, a carrying chair with a canopy, within which the image of the goddess must have rested.

A final point brings the evidence full circle to the bodies in the bogs. Microscopic examination of the stomach contents of the men from Borremose, Tollund, and Grauballe shows that their food for several days before death had been vegetarian. It seems to have consisted of some sort of porridge or mash composed of various kinds of corn, or sorrel and heart's-ease (both cultivated during the Iron Age), and of the seeds of such weeds as were accidentally harvested along with the corn. It has been suggested that this was a ritual diet, part of the ceremony needed to make the corn grow. Be that as it may, it is significant that there was no trace of any of the edible plants or fruits of summer in the stomach contents. So whatever our uncertainty about the precise year of death, we can say with confidence that the season of the year was winter or early spring.

Further we cannot go. We have been probing, with our picks and shovels and builders' trowels, not merely into the brains but perhaps also into the souls of men, and we must be content if our diagnosis is imprecise and inconclusive. But it does take us a little way beyond the conventional archaeological picture of the material lives of the simple peasants of barbarian Europe. Behind the material life, interleaved with it and perhaps dominating it, was the world of taboos and magic and superstition, the spirits of the earth and of the heavens, who had to be bribed or placated or bought off. One of the occupational risks of Iron Age Europe, right up to the end of the Viking period scarcely a thousand years ago, was that of being chosen as victim, as the price to be paid for prosperity in the next harvest or victory in the next war. It was only with the coming of Christianity that human sacrifice ceased in Europe; looking on the bodies from the Danish bogs we should do well to realize that there, but for the grace of God, lie we.

THE FATE OF JACOB STALIN

MICHAEL A. BUDEK

I first saw him on the parade square of Oflag Xc at a prisoner-of-war roll call on a cold and cloudy morning late in 1942, a youngish man of middle height with dark, tousled hair and a long and sullen face. He wore a Russian military greatcoat that looked as if he had slept many nights in it, navy-blue breeches, and jack boots far too big for him. We, the Polish officers, were lined up on the right of the square, followed by Belgians, French, Yugoslavs, and finally the French Jews, who were kept apart. Just as our battalion commander, Captain Schulze—a Mecklenburg landowner and reserve officer—began to call the roll, four guards appeared with the dark-haired stranger.

"Your place is there with the staff officers' company, Colonel Antonov," Schulze told him, pointing to the front rank of Polish officers.

"I am no Colonel Antonov," the stranger shouted excitedly in Russian. "I am Lieutenant Yakov Dzhugashvili!"

To the other prisoners that name meant nothing, but we

Poles knew at once that this rather sickly young man was Stalin's eldest son. After the roll call was over, we talked with him. He told us he had been captured in July of 1941 near Liozno, while the Germans were driving through Smolensk toward Moscow. At that time he had been in command of a field artillery battery. He had been wounded and his battery overrun by the Germans, who would have killed him if a Russian soldier had not warned them that the wounded officer was Stalin's son. After the interrogation he was sent to a prisoner-of-war hospital and then, though still in poor health, to our Oflag Xc in Lübeck.

Oflag Xc, commanded by an old, monocled hussar officer, Colonel Freiherr von Wachtmeister, was one of the two special camps that the Germans had built for high-ranking officers and lower-rank officers who came from noted families or who were considered dangerous. Surrounded by a double line of barbed-wire fence thirty feet high, and by a series of turrets with machine guns, it contained about twenty-six hundred prisoners. From the turrets guards watched the whole camp day and night through binoculars and were instructed to shoot anyone who approached the "warning wire."

Within our group were about twenty Belgian generals, including the commander in chief, General Vandenbergh, as well as serving members of parliament and several international financiers. Among the two hundred and fifty or so Poles was the chief of the Polish general staff, General Piskor. Of the several hundred French officers, many bore internationally known names, the most conspicuous among them being René Rothschild and Lieutenant Vigée Lebrun, the son of the French president.

It was natural enough that the son of the Russian dictator should end up at Oflag Xc. But that I, a reserve horse artillery captain, should have been there among all the generals and colonels and counts came about through my chance and brief meeting with Herbert Hoover in 1919, when he was head of the children's relief mission in Europe.

As a young officer in the new Polish Army, speaking five languages, I had been appointed a liaison officer with the Allied Military Mission and afterward assigned to duty with children's relief. When Hoover came to Gorlice shortly before his return to the United States, I happened to be at the railroad station in uniform. Being the only person present with a camera, I took several snapshots of him at the railroad station. He walked over to me, shook hands, and asked me to send him copies of the pictures.

Not until 1926, when I had left the army to become a lawyer, did I remember my promise and send the snapshots. I then visited some of the families who had received the American supplies seven years before, to see what the children now looked like. In one village I found a peasant's hut with the usual small altar in the corner but with a battered empty tin of American condensed milk among the plaster saints. When I asked the peasant why the tin was there, he said it was out of respect for the American mission that had saved the children from starvation. I took a photograph of the altar and sent it to Hoover.

In 1937 Hoover paid a visit to Poland, and to my surprise I received an invitation from the president of the republic to attend an official dinner in Warsaw for the former American president. Hoover gave me a small memento—a theatre ticket on the back of which he had written: "With best wishes, Herbert C. Hoover."

In August, 1939, I was called back to the army to command a territorial cavalry squadron in defense of Gdynia. On September 14 I was wounded, and while in the hospital was taken prisoner. Eventually I was sent to Oflag Xa in Itzehoe, a camp in northwestern Germany containing about six thousand war prisoners.

In Itzehoe I learned that my wife and children were in distress in Cracow. There was not much I could do, but I did know two addresses abroad—one in England and Hoover's in California. Wanting to help my family in any way I could, I sent an official prisoner-of-war card to England and to

California, saying that I had been wounded and that my wife was still at the old address. The cards did not help my family, but a few months later I received a huge parcel of food marked from Mr. Herbert Hoover. The name caused a stir among the Germans, and I was called to the camp commander and asked what my connection was with a former American president. I refused to say, but the Germans must have thought me an important person, for shortly afterward I was sent, along with two or three hundred others, to the special international camp at Lübeck.

After his explosive arrival in our camp, Stalin's son remained a curiosity. We never referred to him as "Dzhugashvili" but as "Stalin's son," and then simply "Stalin." Since Polish-Russian relations had been resumed, he declared it his duty to stay with the Poles and reported to General Piskor, introducing himself and asking advice as to how he should behave.

General Piskor asked Lieutenant Colonel Mazdzenski to take care of Stalin and offered the Russian two of the American Red Cross parcels that every officer in the camp got twice a month. Stalin refused to accept them, saying that he did not want to eat American food under any circumstances.

From the time of his arrival, Stalin was constantly invited to our prisoner parties, which he attended regularly even though he found himself exposed to innumerable questions about high-level world policy, about which he seemed to know little or nothing. We were aware that his relations with his father were not the best and had not been for some time, although we did not then know the cause of their estrangement. In spite of the fact that he knew less than most of us about world politics, he did his best to answer each question and was never impatient at being forced to repeat himself.

Stalin was billeted in the corner room of Barracks 11, next to Captain Robert Blum, the son of the former French premier. The barracks, a wooden building apart from the others and close to the barbed-wire fence, had huge windows through which the German guards could observe both of the prisoners.

At the beginning of his stay in camp, Stalin could move anywhere he liked, though always guarded by a specially assigned watchman. Then, because of a ridiculous incident, he lost his privilege of free movement. The incident occurred when he went to a tea party in Polish Barracks Number 3, guarded by a German who was old and shortsighted and wore thick glasses. During the course of the tea party, one of the Polish officers got up, said good-bye to the others, left the barracks, and started his daily stroll around the camp. After a while he noticed that he was being followed by the near-sighted guard. Realizing that the man could be severely punished for abandoning Stalin, the Polish officer turned to the guard and told him, "You are mistaken, I am not Stalin!"

The stubborn guard insisted that the Pole was Stalin, until a burst of laughter from the other Polish officers convinced him of his mistake. "My God," he said, his face gone white, "I shall be shot!" "Go to barracks three, room ten, and there you will find your Stalin," the Polish officer told him. The guard followed this advice and found his Stalin, still there drinking tea.

The whole incident would perhaps have remained unnoticed by the Germans, but because it was talked of so much in the camp, the commandant learned about it. From that time on, Stalin was restricted in his movements, although he could still receive other officers in his room.

My duty in the camp was to supervise the preparation and distribution of all rations. A second and more private duty was to barter with the German guards. In exchange for American or English cigarettes that the other officers entrusted to me, I acquired letter forms and other documents necessary for anyone trying to escape. During my whole stay in the camp kitchen, I dealt in this kind of smuggling without once being caught. Instant coffee was the most precious camp money; in exchange for it we managed to get parts for three radio receiving-sets, which we were able to keep concealed in spite of searches by the Germans and through which we kept in touch with the world outside. Whatever the language, one of use was able to understand it; altogether we spoke sixty-four languages, including a number of Asiatic and African dialects. One Belgian major spoke twenty-three languages.

Since I spoke only five, I was rather surprised when Stalin, who appeared every day in the kitchen to collect his food ration, asked if I would tutor him. The kitchen was hardly a place for conversation, and I agreed to visit him in his room. Shortly afterward I was ordered to report to General Piskor, who told me: "Because of your previous confidential work as a liaison officer, I have decided at the request of Lieutenant Dzhugashvili to assign you to him as a teacher of foreign languages."

I thought Stalin would like to learn English because it was the most widely spoken language in the camp; but when I suggested this his face darkened, and he replied that he was not interested in English at all. What he wanted to learn was German. I thought perhaps he was planning to escape and wanted to pick up a few useful German words and phrases to help him on his way. But to my astonishment he gave me another reason. After the war, he said, many German war prisoners would be employed in Russia, and since he was an engineer by profession it would be extremely useful for him to know German. I accepted his answer and asked nothing about any escape plans. And we began our German lessons.

Stalin, though he studied hard, had considerable difficulty in both pronunciation and grammar. He showed continued astonishment over the intricacies of construction and wondered why Germans—"such a clever folk"—had such a ponderous vocabulary. During one of our lessons a prisoner in the same barracks was playing the "Song of the Volga Boatmen." I told Stalin that this song had become popular everywhere in the world and that I had often heard it played in South America. He didn't like it much, saying that under the communist regime the music was gay and spontaneous, whereas under the czars they sang only sad and hopeless songs.

Sometimes he would talk to me about his lost motherland, saying that no land in the world was more beautiful than Russia. He spoke once of happy days in the country when he sat on the bank of the Volga at sunset and looked out over the immense fields of ripening wheat. He said he remembered one such evening, sitting with his father and his family, surrounded by friends. While they all fished in the river, Yakov's father told tales of things that had happened long before.

Only once did Stalin ever mention his half sister, Svetlana, and then fleetingly. "Malenkaia," he called her, "the little one." Once he asked me what I was going to do after the war. I told him I wanted to find my children. I said I still had two boys and a girl, but that my wife had been killed in the concentration camp at Auschwitz. He asked me if I had a picture of my family, and I showed it to him. He looked at the snapshot and became thoughtful. I then decided to risk asking him about his personal affairs.

"Have you a family?" He looked at me, hesitated, and said, "Yes, I have a wife and two children." I asked him if he would visit them immediately after his return to Russia. He replied, "Of course I will!" Then I put another question: "Lieutenant, is it true what your Russian soldiers say, that every prisoner will be punished for getting into captivity?" He paused. "Yes," he said, "it is true, but you must bear in mind that in my case I was severely wounded and was unconscious when I was taken prisoner." And after a while he added, "It was not my fault that they saved me. What could I do?" I agreed with him on this point, but I had the feeling that we were both unconvinced. Joseph Stalin's order that Russians who surrendered would be ruthlessly punished regardless of the circumstances was already known to all the Russian prisoners, and many of them were afraid to return home. Young Stalin was fully aware that his fate would not be different from that of his comrades.

Stalin was correct and friendly to his fellow prisoners, but to the German officers he was always rude, replying insultingly even to routine questions. Once, while we were having our German lesson, the door of his room opened and Colonel von Wachtmeister walked in, followed by two junior officers. Stalin jumped to his feet, furious. When the commandant asked him a simple question, instead of replying he threw himself on the bed with his back to the Germans, cursing them and making an obscene gesture. For this he was given ten days' arrest, and our lessons were temporarily discontinued.

Escape attempts were frequent in the camp. I remember an Alsatian, Lieutenant Kruger, who with another French officer somehow got hold of a German uniform and in this disguise walked out of the main gate and into the German barracks. Three months later the news filtered through that the two had reached their unit in North Africa. Another French officer, a quiet, bookish man, managed to cut his way unobtrusively through the barbed wire while the rest of the prisoners were taking their daily walk. It took him an hour to get through the fence and crawl out the other side, but he managed to find his way back to France. Others were not so lucky. One day we had a visit from the Gestapo. Instead of their usual uniform, the Gestapo men were this time in civilian clothes. They ordered us outside, stripped us, and spent the next five hours searching our quarters. After they had finished, we were ordered to return to our barracks. The Gestapo men left the camp in small groups. As they did so, seven of our officers in civilian clothes slipped through the front gate, among them Lieutenant Lebrun. The seven were all captured, executed, and their ashes returned to camp in urns to be displayed as a warning.

Another group of Polish, French, and Belgian officers had planned an escape tunnel. They dug it under Barracks 11, where Stalin and Blum were billeted, since this building was closest to the fence. Because a guard was posted there day and night, the other Germans paid little attention to the premises, and the prisoners were able to hide underneath the flooring and start their tunnel in relative safety. Stalin knew nothing of this escape attempt going on under him, although ironically enough it would eventually cost him his life.

The tunnelers first dug a well five feet deep, and from there began to tunnel outward. Using a stolen electric motor, they built a device for hoisting earth. The work went quickly, and soon they were able to surface in a wheat field ten or fifteen yards beyond the fence. That evening, twenty-two officers disguised in civilian clothes hid under Barracks 11. At ten o'clock, on signal, the first man crawled through the tunnel and into the field, the next following him after an interval of five minutes. Three of the prisoners had already escaped through the field and down the road. The fourth, creeping through the wheat, met a tipsy German corporal on his way back to the quarters. The corporal thought at first that it was some soldier and his girl in the bushes and called out as a joke, but the other, unnerved and unfamiliar with the language, stammered that he was a prisoner-of-war officer. Immediately the sobered corporal covered him with his pistol and fired an alarm shot. Those under Barracks 11 knew then that the game was up and stayed where they were until seven o'clock the next morning, when all prisoners were allowed to move freely in the camp. They managed to sneak back to their quarters and change into uniform before roll call.

Meanwhile, the corporal had taken the escaped officer to the guardhouse, and since no one was there to interrogate him, he was locked up overnight. At roll call it was discovered that three other officers were missing. The recaptured prisoner refused to tell how he had got outside the camp, and a searching party failed to find the exit in the wheat field. Not until the following day did a sergeant, investigating on his own, finally locate it. When he crept into the tunnel, he found that it led under Stalin's barracks.

Wachtmeister was very upset because the diggers had been able to operate so freely, because the prisoner's interrogation had been delayed, and because it had taken so long to discover the tunnel. An investigation committee was coming from Berlin, and he feared a court-martial. Attempting to cover up his negligence, he announced that the tunnel had been dug from the wheat field to Barracks 11 by Lübeck communists for the purpose of rescuing Stalin. To prove it he produced a number of communist leaflets that he asserted had been found in the tunnel, and he asked to have his dangerous prisoner removed to another camp. The Berlin committee accepted the commandant's fable as fact. The next night Stalin was taken away to an unknown destination, which I later learned was Oranienburg. I never saw him again, although I did hear that his father had refused to exchange him for Field Marshal Paulus, the commander of the German army conquered at Stalingrad.

Since the war there have been conflicting stories about what happened to young Stalin after he was taken to Oranien-burg. One of the more colorful recent reports maintains that he escaped from prison, had a son by an Italian woman now living in Piedmont, and fought against the Nazis as a member of an Italian partisan group. When his group was surrounded, he killed himself by holding a hand grenade to his chest.

Another account was given last year by Walter Usslepp, a former SS platoon leader at Oranienburg. According to Usslepp, Stalin was treated with consideration in the hope that he might undertake propaganda against the Soviet Union. In the spring of 1944 he was driven to a Berlin armaments factory, where he was supposed to make a speech to slave laborers and German workers denouncing Russia and com-munism. Instead he shouted in broken German "Stalin big—Hitler *kaputt*!"

This account would accord with the end of the story as I heard it shortly after the war, while I was attached to British 30th Corps at Lüneburg. This version came from several camp inmates and a German noncommissioned officer at Oranien-burg who said that Yakov Dzhugashvili-Stalin was executed on Himmler's direct orders. The SS guards stripped him in his quarters, taped his mouth, dragged him naked into the yard, and shot him.

JOHNSON (?)
ON
JOHNSON

ANTHONY BURGESS

No, not Lyndon, but Samuel, LL.D. (honorary)—lexicographer, biographer, satirist, critic, wit. A series of brief lives of English poets was commissioned from Johnson late in his life, and a number of corrected galley proofs of this were recently discovered in the home of Lord Vestige (a British peer not famous for his literary interests, as fellow members of the London Playboy Club will know). Attached to these proofs was a yellowing manuscript in no known hand—evidently an intended addition to the Lives of the Poets. *Its authorship can only be guessed at. The manuscript came to* HORIZON *via one of its contributors, the English novelist Anthony Burgess, whose longtime admiration for the great lexicographer, coupled with his known linguistic versatility, have aroused suspicion in certain quarters as to the manuscript's authenticity. It is, in any event, reproduced here without emendation.*

The illustrious subject of the ensuing pages will, as is to be presumed on the anticipatory evidence, receive so large a treatment, not less candid than encomiastik, in the projected *Life* of Mr. Boswell, that the present proposed summation must seem alike insufficient and supererogatory. However, it was considered by the book-sellers who were its sponsors, that the *Lives of the Poets* would be deemed wanting by its readers unless the author himself, in respect of both his life and his productions, were accorded the due of inclusion. To determine the scale of such exhibition, whether to honour with the enlargement proper to a Milton or dismiss with the brevity apt for a Cibber, must always set nice problems of judgment when posterity, whose adjudication alone is final, cannot be consulted as an aid; the author, in his joint office of biographer and critick, must accept with frigid resignation that he has said both too little and too much. And yet the sun is not reviled for an excess of effulgence nor the candle for the paucity of its light. Who seeks luminosity will always be thankful to find it.

Samuel Johnson was born in 1709 in the town of Lichfield in the midlands of England. That, when he had long elected to be considered a Londoner, he thought with kindness on his birthplace, may be adduced from the entry in his Dictionary under "Lich," where he interpolates the gratuitous apostrophe *"Salve magna parens."* His father was a book-seller, and it may be conjectured that the propinquity of works of both learning and delight determined the future preoccupations of the son. But, in such circumstances, incli-nation must precede opportunity: he who lives among sheep is not preordained to a gust for mutton. That the bookish inclination was strongly present in the young Johnson cannot, however, be doubted. He read voraciously, though not always with commensurate understanding, from the variety of his father's stock, nor was appetite matched more by the selective faculty than by the power of digestion. That he retained much of what he read, however, seems certain, possessing as he did an inherent capacity for incontinent memorization: what he got by heart he got without effort.

Large-framed and sturdy from his earliest days, he was yet afflicted with certain corporeal infirmities that physick could not alleviate. At the age of three years he was taken to London to be touched by Queen Anne for the king's evil, or scrofula, a belief in the thaumaturgick properties of the royal person being still superstitiously prevalent. Additionally to this ailment, of which the queen's condescension provided neither cure nor palliative, he was afflicted with near sight, of such a morbidity that, when on his way to school, he would crouch down in the street to ascertain whether he was in danger of involuntary precipitation into the gutter. On one occasion, so it is credibly recorded, his nurse was dispatched after him to forestall such an eventuality, but he turned in rage to beat her, being then, as thereafter, both jealous of his independence and physically equipped to defend it. His sole bodily endowment was strength; his father had failed to transmit to him a comeliness that had, without the elder Johnson's immediate knowledge, so inflamed a young woman with love that she had literally languished and died. The son was neither damned nor blessed with a patrimony of such tragick propensities; no female heart was doomed to shipwreck on his shore.

It is proper, though painful, to add other, less palpable, afflictions. Johnson was always subject to a profound hypochondria, or melancholy, so intense as intermittently to deprive him of the ordinary faculties of sensation, or even of visual recognition: he would pass a whole hour unable to read the time on a publick clock. This infirmity could also take a religious manifestation, inducing a conviction that he was eternally damned, but this was doubtless fed by an awareness of genuine culpability: he was given, which is not venial in one of declared philosophick bent, to the practices of Onan. He also suffered from a number of spasmodick impulses, such as unpremeditable and uncontrollable jerks of the limbs and head, which must strike all who did not know him well as, at best, distractive oddities and, at worst, the marks of idiocy. The habit of gulosity, despite his invective in *The Rambler,* was a controllable failing which he did not wish to control, though it may, in charity, be referred back to a morbid predisposition. He was not over-clean and had, on his own admission, no love for fresh linen; in his life of Dr. Swift he seems, with his term "Oriental scrupulosity," to castigate the Dean's predilection for washing as unnatural and eccentrick. Johnson's aversion to the habit may be called a fault of character more than an innate morbidity, though charity again may relate it to an indolence that is one of the sad fruits of hypochondria. But I digress, or anticipate.

Johnson was educated at Lichfield Grammar School and, in 1728, was accepted for Pembroke College, Oxford. When introduced to the latter, he was at first shy and awkward in the presence of the erudite, but he suddenly struck into the conversation by quoting Macrobius, thus giving evidence of a scholarly precocity rare in a freshman. It was generally acknowledged among his preceptors that he was better fitted for the benisons that the university life could bestow, than any they could recollect being committed to their instruction. But aptitude can no more burgeon in conditions of indigence than a rose can flourish in Arabian wastes, and the penury that had overtaken the father rebounded on the son. A poor scholar, he exhibited his poverty in the very nakedness of his toes, though his innate independence rebuffed the gift of shoes from a fellow student, anonymous in his charity. A year after his admission, he was obliged for lack of funds to suspend his courses, and he went down but little advanced up the ladder of a degree.

So often is genius betrayed by circumstance, and aspiration revealed as the bondman of subsistence.

His father died in 1731, and the destitution of his family was his sole, though unpurposed, bequest. Johnson worked as an usher of a school in Market Bosworth but found in the instruction of careless youth little sustenance for the body and none at all for the spirit. It appears that he then secured literary employment of a degraded kind, contributing essays to a Birmingham newspaper. In 1735, he published his first book, though this was no original composition but a translation from the French of Father Jeronimo Lobo's *Voyage to Abyssinia,* a mechanical task that wholly merited its anonymity. Yet no work is wasted, and it is certain that the scenery of *Rasselas* was derived, however partially and inchoately, from his drudging perusal of the worthy priest. In this same *annus mirabilis,* he fell in love and married, the bride being Mrs. Elizabeth Porter, a widow twenty-one years his senior. Fired by the uxorious ambition proper to his new station, he started a school at Edial, near Lichfield, but the enterprise languished for lack of pupils. One of these, however, if a proleptick view be admissible, attained such distinction in his subsequent career as to bring retrospective honour to the establishment. This was David Garrick, the lustrous ornament of the English stage. His zest for the observation of life, as well as his gift for the mimesis of its passions, were, it must be confessed, but meanly employed in this phase of his youth; for he would watch through the keyhole of the marital bedchamber the caresses his master bestowed awkwardly on his bride, and subsequently entertain the small audience of his fellows with impertinent mimicry of those intimacies.

It was with this forward pupil as travelling-companion that Johnson and Mrs. Johnson set out, in 1737, to engage the vaunted opportunities of the metropolis. For a poor scholar with no connexions and small hope of patronage, London had little to offer but, at best, the derisory rewards of Grub Street and, at worst, the sloping path to rags and the debtor's jail. Yet the confidence of the one will always prevail against the experience of the many, else history had long ago come to an end; what men learn from others is that they must teach themselves. Johnson entered the service of Mr. Edward Cave, the printer and founder of *The Gentleman's Magazine,* in whose columns the young aspirant displayed his facile ingenuity in the modes of literature that a periodical then accommodated, contributing essays, odes, occasional poems, Latin verses, biographies, and the reports of parliamentary debates. These last were neither verbatim transcripts nor close paraphrases, but original compositions founded on speeches actually made, in which current issues of policy were treated with an eloquence of which the discutants in the Chamber must, with rare exceptions, be considered hardly susceptible. With genius, it is always easier to create than to copy, and the hues on the canvas of a Reynolds may, with some justice, be accounted superior to their correspondences in nature. Who would not choose to be exalted with the ideal, than merely to be informed by the actual?

In 1738, Johnson published his *London,* a poem written in imitation of the Third Satire of Juvenal, wherein the vice and degeneracy of the New Rome were castigated, as well as the oppression of the poor and the insolence of the rich. The "Thales" who speaks his disgust has, by many, been identified with the unfortunate Richard Savage, who was the companion of Johnson's own penurious drudgery, and it was perhaps no accident that a life of this struggling poet, in whom the expectations of a gentleman were thwarted by an unnatural mother's unremitting persecution, should appear as Johnson's next notable composition. The literary labours continued, but the material rewards were coyly withheld. Yet ambition will, with a kind of perversity, flourish most when least sure of fulfillment. It was in 1747, while still a stranger to fame, that Johnson issued the plan of a work that must, if realized, infallibly procure it. Planting his pennant high, he addressed to the Earl of Chesterfield the proposal of a Dictionary.

This eminent nobleman had represented himself as an arbiter of manners and a friend to literature. To a project that should settle the flux of the English language and determine for a whole age the principles of lexical correctness and stylistic elegance, it might be expected that he would respond with an exemplary ardour. Its proponent he indeed flattered with promises of help, and a retiring scholar, unacquainted with the ways of the *beau monde,* might be forgiven for a credulousness that men sophisticated by disappointment would not so readily conceive. The Tory principles of the lexicographer were disposed to a faith in the rectitude of the aristocracy, and here was aristocracy's most exquisite bloom. And yet the term "patron," which first connoted the condescensions of help, assumed, as the work progressed, ever more pejorative tones. The indifference and even insolence of one who was but a paragon of exterior forms, pusillanimous in substance beneath the mask of speciousness, bred in the nominal protégé the postures of stoicism and the dispositions of bitterness. The appearance of the *Dictionary* in 1755 was celebrated by the tardy laudations of his lordship. But years of neglect could in no wise be exculpated by belated gestures of facile praise, and Johnson very properly repudiated them in a letter compact of stoick dignity and frigid politeness.

While the *Dictionary* proceeded, the man of words did not forget that he was a man of letters, and philology intermittently yielded to his primary avocation. In 1749, he published *The Vanity of Human Wishes,* an imitation of the Tenth Satire of Juvenal, in which Johnson illustrates the futility of ambition, whether in the field of war, learning, or statesmanship. It is a powerful but melancholy dissertation, and the reader does not have far to seek for its causative springs. In the same year, Garrick, having achieved fame ahead of his old mentor, and mindful of the obligation of a former pupil, produced the tragedy *Irene,* which Johnson had written at Edial, in the days of a less equitable relationship. The play was not much liked, being little more than a parcel of moral disputations in the exotick setting of the Mussulman, but it yielded £300, a not inconsiderable sum at that time, and was thus the occasion of mitigating straits that had too long continued. In 1750, Johnson commenced *The Rambler,* a demihebdomadal magazine which he wrote practically without assistance, and in which grave moral essays were variegated with humorous flights hardly less grave. Levity was not easily associable with either his frame or his disposition.

The Rambler ceased publication on the death of Mrs. Johnson, in 1752. Whether the conjugal state was one to which this philosopher was naturally suited, is a question perhaps too delicate for publick consideration, and it is proper to respect Johnson's own reticence on the intimate conduct of matrimonial life. Whatever the moral virtues and intellectual endowments of the lady, these were not matched by corporeal beauty: she was excessively corpulent, and a preternaturally high complexion was exacerbated by the liberal potation of cordials. No record of her dicta lends credence to a compensative mental acuity. And yet her posthumous memory was consistently revered by her relict, who, as her living memory receded, was heard often enough to ejaculate on her putative charms. Whether Johnson's failure to remarry was due to his unwillingness to desecrate a bed of felicity with a new incumbent, or else to satiety with a state whose pleasures are rarely augmented by prolongation, must stay in the decent shades of ignorance, or be left to idle speculation. Johnson once described second marriages as the triumph of hope over experience, and *The Vanity of Human Wishes* admits no exception to the vacuity of hope.

Johnson eventually partook of the heady brew of fame, or rather of the regard of the learned, though this was never to be complemented by the acquisition of wealth. Unlike Pope, he achieved no swelling parterre or Twickenham grotto. His fiftieth year saw the solace of a competence still unattained, and he found it necessary to dash off the tale of *Rasselas* to defray the cost of his mother's obsequies. In 1762, he received a pension of £300 a year from Lord Bute, and this was to suffice for needs that long indigence had schooled to moderation. With the securing of manumission from the tyranny of the pen, the pen ceased to exercise even the sway of a limited rule, and the habits of indolence were quick to supervene. With the founding of the Literary Club, the pleasures of converse soon usurped the place long given to the pains of authorship. Convivial friendship pleased more than solitary study, and the drawing room afforded easier gratifications than the library. Moreover, in 1763, Johnson first grew acquainted with Boswell, the young Scotsman who was to propose the eternization of a biography, and here was as certain a passport to posterital notice as the continued labour of his own hand. He who has written to live, will generally scorn those who live to write, and if immortality be the aim of the literary endeavour, this may sometimes be conferred by easier means than the sweat of application. Johnson doubtless preferred to enter a book in prospect, rather than write a book in fact.

Notwithstanding, he continued to give to the world, though more sparsely than hitherto, and with a ponderous reluctance, such fruits of his genius as the publick hunger demanded. His edition of Shakespeare, which appeared after long delay in 1765, had been subscribed for much earlier, and it might not have come to birth at all had it not been for the Caesarean knife of Mr. Charles Churchill's satire. These present *Lives of the Poets* were, however, commissioned in the time of his independence, though it must be thought that only the united pressure of his friends attained what inclination alone could never have accomplished. A number of fugitive pieces accommodated the requests of his friends or the needs of the times, or else, as with the elegy on the death of Mr. Levett, the obligations of sad affection. Otherwise Johnson basked in the autumn of achievement remembered, or awaited, in the symposial sodality of his admirers, the closing of the crepuscular shades.

The residue of his days may be tentatively computed out of the common expectation, but it were presumptuous to set a term to them, or to anticipate the dispositions of the Almighty. To succeeding editors may be left the task of memorializing his consignment to futurity. [Johnson died in 1784.—Ed.] Those late years that had been irradiated by the hospitable friendship of Mr. Thrale, the brewer, and Mrs. Thrale, the beauty, were at length saddened by the demise of the one and the defection of the other, who must now be denominated Signora Piozzi. That innate melancholy, exacerbated by events, sought alleviation in the composition of meditations and prayers, which, to those granted the grave privilege of access, must impress with the eloquence of their

terror of mortality, and of their deprecation of condign per-
dition. But all men must die, and all men must be judged,
and the evasion of the common lot is accorded not even to
a Johnson. *In die illa, fonte pietatis aspergetur.*

Of his character, it may be said that he hid a sufficiency of
sweetness beneath an exorbitant rugosity, that he could love
without the extravagance of constant asseveration, and that
his prejudices were but the obverse of his convictions. If he
hated Whiggery, it was not out of the spite of personal disappointment, but from a philosophical awareness of its being
intrinsically pernicious, since it was, in the very declaration
of its principles, inimical to the established order and dedicated to its destruction. If he abominated Americans, it was
because they were a sort of aggravated Whigs, in whom re-
pudiation of loyalty excused itself in the canting avowal of a
plausible libertarianism. If he despised the Scots, it was because of their betrayal of ideals of national rectitude, their
apostasy from the true religion, their neglect of agriculture,
and their murder of the English tongue. What many, indeed,
termed prejudice, he would term a just and reasoned hostility, whose complement was an infrangible faith in a monarchy from which he could expect nothing, a social order
that had failed him, and a system of religion that had bred a
fear of damnation.

As a friend, he was just, candid, and forgiving. In the
forms of amical intercourse, it was accepted that he must
lead, and that his voice must prevail; that he must have the
right to censure insolence and overrule unreason, though it
may be admitted that his love of argumentative conquest
would deafen him to the rationality of an opponent: he must
win, by fair stratagem if possible but, in the main, by whatever stratagem seemed expedient. He asked nothing more
than that his *mots* should be applauded, his excesses of ex-
patiation condoned, and his dogmatisms accepted. Such indulgence of the drawing room must be matched by both an
exquisiteness and an amplitude of table hospitality, for,
though he could eat grossly, he was yet sensible of the charms

of culinary delicacy, and fierceness of appetite could yield to the niceness of gustatory discrimination. With wine, he was capable of abstinence but not of temperance, and where the latter could not be encompassed by philosophick self-control, the former could always be induced by fear of the devastation of excess.

His piety was genuine, and his generosity notable. This latter virtue was exercised as much to the animal or, to be strict, feline order, as to the human. His house was never without retainers, and his purse was as liberal as his means could accommodate. Of courage he was granted an heroick endowment, whether it were opposed to the pains of the body, or to the desolation of the spirit. By disposition inclined to pessimism, he yet displayed, when occasion called it forth, a contagious cheerfulness or even a controlled hilarity. Sage in precept, he could be extravagant in jest, as apt for the apophthegm as for the shaft of fancy. Whatever posterity may judge of his works, of his life it may find little to censure. Yet the exterior man is but half of the totality, and the interior must face the severer test of futurity, whose sentences no human lenity can abate. In this regard, his friends can but pray that one human wish shall not be informed by vanity.

It remains to deliver a general opinion of his works. What Johnson wrote in Dr. Goldsmith's obituary, viz. that he touched nothing that he did not adorn, cannot in fairness be predicated of his own compositions. In the fields of the drama and the romance, it must be held that he was deficient, possessing no power to animate his personages or inform their shells with aught but sententiousness. To read *Rasselas* is to be instructed, but rarely to be delighted. We carry from that book a variety of maxims that hold the memory and attain the force of proverbs, but never a sense of human passion. Who does not know by heart such sentences as the following? "Human life is everywhere a state in which much is to be endured, and little to be enjoyed"; "Marriage has many pains, but celibacy has no pleasures"; "Example is always more efficacious than precept"; "Integrity without knowledge is weak and useless, and knowledge without integrity is dangerous and dreadful." Yet who ever formed a distinct impression of Imlac or of the Abyssinian prince himself, and who ever cared for the outcome of their acts or the unwinding of their destinies?

In the moral essay, however, he must be considered supreme, whether in the prose of *The Rambler*:

There are minds so impatient of inferiority that gratitude is a species of revenge, and they return benefits, not because recompense is a pleasure, but because obligation is a pain;

or in the verse of *London*:

This mournful truth is ev'rywhere confess'd:
Slow rises worth by poverty depress'd.

And, even in the fugitive pamphlet, as "Taxation No Tyranny," on the unrest in the American colonies, true sense informs the most ephemeral apophthegm:

How is it that we hear the loudest yelps for liberty among the drivers of negroes?

As a poet, he rarely produces harsh numbers, but there are times when, looking for melody, we find only correctness and, seeking the enlightenment of fancy, discover only the strictures of precept. And, it must be admitted, he is not above the redundancies of *The Vanity of Human Wishes*:

Let observation with extensive view,
Survey mankind, from China to Peru;

where he would seem to demand of observation that, with extensive observation, it observe mankind extensively. Such tautology he condemned in others, but missed in himself. But a tendency to swollen ventosies may be attributed less to want of ear or of care, than to habits of Latinate balance that prevailed above the demands of sense. Yet the *chiasmus* frequently triumphs:

And, bid him go to Hell, to Hell he goes.
                    —*additions to Goldsmith's "Traveller"*

and:

Hides from himself his state, and shuns to know,
That life protracted is protracted woe.
                              —*The Vanity of Human Wishes*

What has been argued against this poet's claim to excellence is that, pursuing the general, he too often betrays the particular, so that he appears to impose on the diffused experience of mankind the contracted vicissitudes of his own life; as in the following:

There mark what ills the scholar's life assail,
Toil, envy, want, the patron, and the jail.   *ibid.*

where "patron" must not be supposed to be a legitimate term of disparagement in all vocabularies, but bears a private bitterness of very particular signification.

Poetry is less harmed by such disclosures than is the impersonal art of the lexicographer, which should inform without prejudice and enlighten without reserve. In his Dictionary, Johnson too frequently admits the gratuitousness of implicit or explicit animosities, as in the definition of "excise": "A hateful tax levied upon commodities"; or of "oats": "A grain, which in England is generally given to horses, but in Scotland supports the people"; or of "patron," which, as may be anticipated, bears a load of wholly personal acerbity: "Commonly a wretch who supports with insolence, and is paid with flattery"; or of "Whig," in which elucidation is forbidden by contumely: "The name of a faction."

Of his vocabulary, it has been objected that it prefers the exotick Latin to the indigenous Saxon, much to the harm of clarity; as may be exemplified in his definition of "network"; "Anything reticulated or decussated at equal distances, with interstices between the intersections." Even in his private conversation, he seemed to evince a prejudice against the plain, and a correspondent predilection for the ornate, so that he would sometimes emend the one to the other in a single utterance; as when he observed of Buckingham's *Rehearsal* that "it had not wit enough to keep it sweet," and then corrected himself to: "I mean it possesses insufficient vitality to preserve it from putrefaction." Such a predisposition to the locutions of learning cannot always escape absurdity, and it is capable of translating a pithy proverb into a pretentious aphorism, so that "Birds of a feather flock together" must become "Ornithological bipeds of identical plumage invariably congregate in the closest proximity." The truth is, that there is a time for the Latin, as there is a time for the Saxon, and to confuse the two argues no niceness of discrimination: where we doubt the judge in one capacity, we infallibly doubt him in others.

Yet Johnson could contrive, on occasion, a style as easy as Addison's, as trenchant as Swift's, as dignified as Gibbon's; witness his letter to the Earl of Chesterfield, in which we introduce his word of most particular opprobrium for the last time:

Is not a Patron, my Lord, one who looks with unconcern on a man struggling for life in the water, and, when he has reached ground, encumbers him with help? The notice which you have been pleased to take of my labours, had it been early, had been kind; but it has been delayed till I am indifferent, and cannot enjoy it; till I am solitary, and cannot impart it; till I am known, and do not want it.

Of his obiter dicta it would be premature to speak, until those meticulously recorded by his friends have been exhibited to the publick. Let it suffice to say, that his power of conversation was unmatched in this age, and his gift of the apt riposte, the epigrammatical summation, the pleasantry homely but never indecent, and the rebuke just but never obnoxious, was as diligently cultivated by art, as it had been lavishly imparted by nature. It may happen, that he who sought immortality by what he did, may more readily attain it by what he was; that the words he spoke, may instruct more than those he has written; and the example of his character may elevate, where the precepts of his work may fail to instruct. Happy the man who may reach posterity by two roads, of which, if one be blocked, the other will be open.

THE TALE
OF THE
PURLOINED
SAINT

CURTIS CATE

Yes, saintforsaken was the word for it. A girdle of angry cliff faces, a murmur of mountain waters, a shiver of naked poplars by the arched Roman bridge, and there suddenly it was, half-hidden by the rocky ledge guarding the entrance to the secluded valley: the little town of Conques, a cluster of gabled roofs and timbered walls watched over on the left by a tiny helmeted castle and in the center by the rainwashed bulk of its basilica, as squat and stoop-shouldered as a medieval man-at-arms. A pale winter sun cast a faint clambering shadow across the tufts of brownish grass as I trudged up the *chemin de Charlemagne,* trying not to slide back down its mossy flagstones. I doubt that the great Frankish emperor ever got near this remote mountain glen, but it was up this steep and slippery slope that for centuries the pilgrims struggled with their mules, though few of them can have been so foolhardy as to undertake the trek in midwinter.

Farther up, by the basilica, I found the Auberge de Sainte-

Foy resolutely shut, its ornate ironwork sign deceptively promising hearthside warmth and Yuletide cheer. But a few steps down—for half the streets of Conques are steps—was a weather-beaten hostelry dimly advertising itself as the "Hôtel Boudou." I sat down inside on a bench at one of its bare wooden tables and found myself being waited on by a smiling crone, her head wrapped in a shawl and her feet in woolen slippers, who padded up and down the steps between kitchen and dining room with the sure-footedness of a mountain goat. This presumably was la mère Boudou, whom the Grimm brothers would no doubt have identified as Mother Goose's stepsister.

As I sat there watching my breath rise in the heatless chamber, I was reminded of Chaucer's pilgrims, who would have recognized that poor struggling sun skirting the leafless ridge across the way as their own palefaced Kentish orb.

The colde frosty seson of Decembre. . . .
The bittre frostes, with the sleet and reyn,
Destroyed hath the grene in every yerd.
Janus sit by the fyr, with double berd,
And drinketh of his bugle-horn the wyn.

To be sure, the two bereted yokels who had followed me into la mère Boudou's Merovingian establishment were not exactly double-bearded, and they had left their bugle horns behind; but the determination with which they dipped their mustaches into their wineglasses was unmistakably Chaucerian. No, nothing much had changed hereabouts since the Middle Ages, and Chaucer would have found an admirable subject in the story of Conques, a rollicking medieval tale of pilfering monks and purloined bones.

The first known inhabitant of these wild parts was a pious recluse named Dadon, who sought refuge here in the latter part of the eighth century. The poor fellow had seen his house sacked and his mother hideously mutilated by the Moors—a spectacle that had confirmed him in the belief that this earth is a vale of tears. He accordingly removed himself to this deserted valley "unknown to man, long repelled by its wild aspect, and the abode of beasts," to quote from an ancient script. The chronicler for once was not exaggerating. This is still a fair description of the Aveyron—or the Rouergue, as it was known in the Middle Ages—which is one of the poorest regions of the Auvergne, in southwestern France. Here the rolling hills and broad green pastures that elsewhere provide some of the choicest beef and butter in France have been compressed into wrinkled valleys. At Conques the ground is so steep that the little town's vegetable patches have been built into escarpments. Terraced vineyards still dot the slopes, though it is now cheaper to buy wine produced in more favored climes. Pork is still the *pièce de résistance* in most humble houses, and only yesterday the chestnuts harvested every autumn from the surrounding woods were used for feeding humans as well as hogs. Which explains why many of Dadon's modern descendants have concluded that there are less painful ways of keeping the wolf from the door than hoeing a few feet of unproductive soil; they have chosen to emigrate, with the curious result that four out of every five barmen and café owners in Paris today come from this backwoods region.

But in the devout Dadon's day the remoteness of the valley was its saving grace. Word of the good hermit's exemplary devotion eventually got back to the ears of Louis the Pious (later rechristened "the Debonair"), whom Charlemagne, his father, had appointed Duke of Aquitaine. Louis had the holy man brought to him, and after engaging him in lengthy theological discourse he encouraged him to set up a Benedictine abbey in the hitherto uninhabited glen. It was Louis, so posterity claimed, who gave the wild spot the name of Conques (in Latin *concha*), supposedly because it had the shape of a shell (which it doesn't).

Founded in 790, the abbey proceeded to prosper—enough at any rate to persuade Louis the Debonair's son, Pepin of Aquitaine, to extend its jurisdiction over the Benedictine monastery of Figeac. This was asking for trouble, which was perhaps what Pepin was after. Though only twenty-five miles distant as the crow flies, Figeac belonged to another world—a Latin world of Roman laws and flat tiled roofs which to this day offer a striking contrast to the steep Gothic eaves and the fan-shaped grey-brown slates which shelter the sons of the Auvergne. The idea of having to take orders from their hillbilly cousins to the east was too much for the Figeacians, and the result was a long and bitter feud, which the abbots of Figeac sought to settle in their favor by forging a fake charter to prove that they were and had always been an independent monastery. The row was still smouldering merrily in 1096, when the Council of Nîmes put an end to the mischief by giving the Figeacians their freedom.

Poor the *Auvergnats* may be, but they more than make up for it in guile, as was to be proved once and for all by the crafty monks of Conques. France at this time was in a highly unsettled state, as the pillaging Vikings stormed their way up the Garonne in 850 to sack Toulouse. Encouraged by the Vikings' success, the Moors staged a brief comeback, recrossing the Pyrenees and plundering in their turn. To complete the confusion a wild Mongol host smashed across northern Italy and Provence. Fifty years after his death Charlemagne's empire was a shambles, the barons who should have been defending it being more interested in feuding with each other.

The ultimate beneficiary of this chaos turned out to be the Church, which could at least pose as a disinterested body anxious to limit the damage. But the Church at this time was anything but a unified force. This was an age of *sauve qui peut*, in which each parish had to struggle as best it could to survive. The popes in distant Rome could issue bulls and distribute anathemas, but they did little to meet local needs, which were of a more urgent character. Feudal Europe responded by producing a plethora of saints to fill the void. Jesus Christ, like his vicar in Rome, was no longer enough. Each locality had to have its patron divinity, its own guardian, its *genius loci*—as he would have been known in pagan times—who was simply the religious equivalent of its secular lord.

The French language, amusingly enough, has retained the word *"invention"* to designate the discovery of the sacred relics that each parish had to have in order to claim a saint's protection. Probably the first Frenchman to pull off a major "invention" of this kind was a monk from Fleury called Aigulfe, who journeyed down to Monte Cassino in the year 655 and brought back the bones of Saint Benedict and his sister, Saint Scholastique.

Tours was lucky enough to boast a genuine fifth-century saint—the generous Saint Martin, who had split his cloak with a beggar and who was honored by the construction of a Romanesque basilica that rose to be the finest church of its day. In Paris the devotees of Saint Denis, its first bishop, had "invented" a wood fragment from the Cross and ever several of the nails used to pierce our Saviour's palms and feet. In Autun a local saint called Saint Nazaire was identified with "Lazare" (Lazarus) and was reported to have reached France with his sister, Mary Magdalene. She herself was said to be buried in the vicinity of Aix-en-Provence. This was still too far away for an enterprising Burgundian monk called Badilon, who journeyed down to Aix-en-Provence and brought back the sacred bones to Vézelay. Nîmes could boast the remains of Saint Gilles—notwithstanding a rival claim advanced by the Hungarians, who were too far away and too barbarous to matter. Poitiers had Saint Hilary, and even Angely—a one-horse hamlet if ever there was one—claimed to shelter the venerable head of John the Baptist.

One can imagine the mounting frustration of the friars of Conques as they heard about all these wondrous "inventions" in the bitter realization that their own godforsaken glen had been unhaunted prior to the good Dadon's time by anything more glamourous than the occasional footprint of a wolf or the creepy hoot of an owl. The holy fathers set about solving the problem in their own resourceful fashion. To be sure, their first experiment in the genre was not a conspicuous success. In 855 two monks, Hildebert and Audald, journeyed from Conques to Valencia fired with a zeal to lay hands on the remains of Saint Vincent of Zaragoza. Probably they reckoned that by penetrating this deeply into Moorish territory they could have the theft written off as a piece of infidel sacrilege. They actually got hold of the bones, but on their way back they were ambushed at Zaragoza, the good saint's home town, and forced to relinquish the booty.

Some fifteen more years passed while the monks of Conques gnashed their teeth in helpless wrath. Then, in 870 or thereabouts, another commando force was dispatched to recuperate the bones of another Saint Vincent, buried in the village of Pompéjac, near Agen. The expedition succeeded brilliantly, and the relics were brought safely back to Conques; but to the dismay of the friars the transplanted saint failed to attract the slightest attention.

It was during this raid, however, that the monks first heard of Saint Foy and of the extraordinary miracles that her relics had begun to accomplish in Agen. Located on the banks of the Garonne about eighty miles upstream from Bordeaux, Agen—or Aginum, as it was called by the Romans—had been one of the most important centers of Roman Gaul. Foy, or Fides (to give her her Latin name), was born around A.D. 290, the daughter of a local patrician who paid homage to the city's Roman gods—Jupiter and Diana; she and her sister were brought up in the Christian faith by their governess. At a very tender age she began to display a deplorable solicitude for the wants of the needy, even going so far as to steal bread from the family kitchen, which she distributed to the poor. Caught red-handed one day by her suspicious father, who wanted to know what it was she was carrying bundled up in a fold of her dress, she had answered: "Flowers!" And lo and behold—for so it is written in the *Liber Miraculorum Sanctae Fidis* (which dates from the eleventh century)—she opened her dress and a cluster of beautiful red flowers flashed forth where the loaf had been.

Fides was just twelve years old when the emperor Diocletian, in the year 303, ordered a ruthless purge of all Christians in the empire. The man sent to Aquitaine to take care of the job was Dacian, the governor of northern Spain, a man for whom orders were orders. In the *Liber Miraculorum Sanctae Fidis* he is depicted as a dark, bloodthirsty horror, but the anonymous author of the *Canczon de Santa Fe* (probably a monk of the eleventh century) portrays him, less harshly, as a kind of subtle scoundrel whose slumbers are troubled, like Pontius Pilate's, by a nagging sense of shame. Here Fides is draped in all the attributes of a heroine in a *chanson de geste*:

Lo corps es belz, e paucs l'estaz;
Lo senz es gencer, qe dinz jaz.
Los oils a gentz, e blanca faz . . .
(Beautiful is her body and small of size,
But fairer still the sense within her.
Lovely are her eyes and white her face . . .)

The bard launches into a rapturous description of all the rich things of this world she has fallen heir to but has had the stout Christian courage to disdain:

Great were her lands and castles strong
And furs from wild beasts she had and buttons
And on her fingers precious rings,
And plates well made of gold and silver.
All these she fears are evil snares
Wrought for her by the black Devil;
With them she feeds the lepers and the poor.
Poor she made herself, like a beggar,
And remained with God, this being better.

Such is the radiant creature who is brought before Dacian, the instrument of the abominable Diocletian. The rogue begins by promising her the sun and the moon if she will but renounce Christ and agree to sacrifice to Diana, the city's pagan goddess. He promises her a belt made of gold and *"de vera purpral vestiment"*—a raiment of real crimson. A hundred damsels will wait on her, a thousand cavaliers escort her if only . . . But no, the stouthearted virgin refuses, even going

98

so far as to revile the official gods, who she says are fed a daily diet of toads and perfumed by the hand of the devil in the incense of burning wool. On hearing this outrage *lo mendiz pudolenz* (the stinking wretch—which is to say, Dacian) rolls his eyes and gnashes his teeth. An iron grid is brought forth and a bonfire of walnut trunks is built beneath it. Like Saint Lawrence, Fides is to be roasted alive. At the prospect of this frightful immolation, the people weep and the entire city goes into mourning. But as the flames rise, an angel, white as a dove, comes down from Heaven and, blowing on the fire, puts out the blaze. The angel then places a golden crown on Fides's head and covers her nude body with a gold-spangled robe—though none of this is seen by the Roman governor.

Furious at seeing the blaze dwindle to a heap of tepid ashes, Dacian orders her beheaded. The job is done by the Basques, who drag Fides from the grid and unsheath their swords. One of them, raising his flashing blade, severs her head at a stroke—as Herod did with John the Baptist, adds the poet.

Such was the virgin saint and martyr. Tradition has it that following her glorious death Fides's body, together with that of her sister, was dragged away by the pagans and left to rot beyond the city walls. But the surviving Christians secretly took possession of the truncated bodies, wiping the holy blood off onto pieces of precious cloth—tattered fragments of which later turned up in Saint Foy's reliquary along with locks of hair, bits of jewelry, tiny silk and leather pouches containing cinders, and even bits of blood-stained amianthus. These remains were duly elevated a century later by Saint Dulcidius, Bishop of Agen, who had a tiny brick chapel built to house Fides's marble tomb. Next the sanctuary became a shrine, and later a Benedictine abbey, which is what it was in the second half of the ninth century when the friars of Conques raided the tomb of Saint Vincent de Pompéjac.

Saint Vincent having failed them, the friars of Conques now hatched a scheme for annexing the remains of Saint Foy of Agen. They realized that this was an infinitely more delicate operation and that there was no point in trying a crude frontal assault. As luck would have it there was at hand just the man for the job. His name was Ariviscus, and he was a priest of exemplary piety who in the administration of a neighboring church had displayed "remarkable prudence and a consummate skill in the commerce of life"—which can only mean that he was crafty, taciturn, and tenacious, and thus an *Auvergnat* to the tips of his prayer-joined fingers.

Exchanging his monastic habit for the cloak and staff of a pilgrim, Ariviscus hied himself to Agen with a lay companion and took his time reconnoitering the enemy camp. There was only one word for his performance—masterly. So assiduous was his devotion, so manifest his piety, so simon-pure his comportment, so elevated and yet amiable his conversation, that it never occurred to the good monks of Agen that they were admitting a wolf to the fold. They welcomed the newcomer as one of their own and even allowed him to become a guardian of the monastery's prized possessions.

Tradition says that the prudent Ariviscus took ten years to mature his diabolical plan. But even if he only took half that time, his tenacity is awe-inspiring. Having duly taken stock of the habits of his companions, Ariviscus concluded that the most propitious moment for a coup was January 6, the night of the Epiphany. The wintry night would be conveniently long, but even more important, the occasion would be celebrated with an unusually copious dinner, in the course of which even the most vigilant spirits were apt to be numbed by food and drink. And so it happened on this particular Epiphany, in the year 877 (or thereabouts). Excusing himself on the pretext that the abbey's holy relics required a particular watchfulness on this festive night—a gesture of self-sacrifice that won him the enthusiastic acclaim of his colleagues—Ariviscus quietly repaired to the chapel. Unable to lift the marble slab covering the saint's remains, Ariviscus calmly took a crowbar and a hammer and smashed open a hole at the foot of the tomb. He then dragged out Saint Foy's bones, slipped them into a large potato sack, and stole out of the abbey while his fellow monks continued to carouse.

What must have been their dismay the next morning on entering the chapel to find—oh, horror of horrors—the tomb of their revered saint desecrated! The sudden absence of the devout Ariviscus made it clear who the miscreant had been, but the flabbergasted monks lost a number of precious hours vainly wringing their hands and wondering what to do. Saint Foy was not only their saint but also a patron of Agen, and loud and bitter were the recriminations when the dreadful tidings swept through town.

A few horsemen were hastily assembled and sent after the blackguard. They succeeded only in getting lost. A new expedition was forthwith prepared, and this time the riders actually caught up with the villain at the village of Lalbenque, near Cahors. Ariviscus and his companion were resting under a large tree when the horsemen trotted up and asked if by any chance they had seen an absconding monk pass that way. They described the abdominable scoundrel in full, dark detail, and the trembling Ariviscus had barely enough courage to answer no, neither he nor his companion had seen the rogue. His disguise—probably a wig and certainly a hat to conceal his tonsured pate—luckily fooled his pursuers. The medieval chronicle ascribes his narrow escape to "divine protection."

The horsemen then rode on to Conques, where they were greeted with expressions of bland surprise. What? The bones of Saint Foy had been stolen from Agen by a monk called Ariviscus? Heavens, what was the world coming to? No, they hadn't seen him and hadn't the slightest idea what had become of him. Years had passed since he had vanished from these parts. Fatigued and dispirited, the horsemen turned about and rode sadly back to Agen. Here again one can detect the masterly touch of the shrewd *Auvergnat* friar. Instead of making straight for Conques, Ariviscus had decided to take his time and return by a deliberately circuitous route.

Loud was the rejoicing when the two tired travelers finally

heaved into Conques with their treasure. It was the four-teenth of January, eight days after the coup had been pulled off. For centuries thereafter this date was celebrated as the beginning of the golden age of Conques.

For from that moment the fortunes of this backwoods val-ley changed. The first to benefit from Saint Foy's magic touch was a former steward named Guibert, who had had his eyes torn out during a violent altercation with his master, a local landlord called Géraud. Forced to choose another form of livelihood, Guibert had ended up a *badin,* which is to say, a wandering storyteller and entertainer. On the eve of her first day, now celebrated on October 6, Saint Foy appeared to him and promised that if he made the pilgrimage to Conques and lit two candles—one for the altar of the Saviour, the other for her tomb—he would recover his sight. In his home village of Espeyrac, situated on the uplands east of Conques, his description of his vision was greeted as the hallucinatory raving of a madman. But Guibert finally managed to pry a few coins out of a neighbor to buy the candles. He lit them as instructed and prostrated himself in front of the saint's relics. By and by he saw, as though in a daze, two shining globules the size of olives descend from on high and fix them-selves in his eye sockets, and when he awoke the next morn-ing, he was startled to *see* the church full of candles lit for the celebration of matins.

News of this miracle spread over the countryside, attract-ing a host of pilgrims from near and far. The abbot, who knew a good thing when he saw one, gave Guibert a job as a wax salesman, and soon not only Saint Foy but the fortunate Guibert himself was being showered with presents by persons hoping to be healed by the saint. Fame went to Guibert's head, and finally, to put a curb on his boasting, Saint Foy was forced to reimpose his blindness. After a few months of darkness he was readmitted to the light, only to be deprived of it again when he reverted to his braggart ways. No one was quite sure whether he was blessed or mad, but nothing could dim the prestige of this *"illuminé,"* as he was called, and of the saint who had given him back his sight.

The significance of the tale is unmistakable. Behind it one can detect that struggle between the rational and the irrational that rent the Church throughout the Middle Ages. But the moral is not simply that the inner light of faith is more precious than the outer, and that a blind man can regain his sight if he concentrates on God and walks in the way of the Lord. The story alludes to the elevation that may be granted to a *badin* who will place his talents as an entertainer at the disposal of God. The *badin* was first cousin to the jongleur, who was part acrobat, part juggler, part mime, part bard, part storyteller, and as often as not a lute player as well, and who haunted not only the courts but the porches of the churches. In a largely illiterate age the minstrels were as influential as the monks in educating the common herd, regaling their audiences with the heroic exploits of King Arthur and Lancelot and Roland and the rest. They entertained pilgrims all over France and over vast areas of Europe, and just as they helped kindle the fervor of those who were undertaking the pilgrimage to Santiago de Compostela in Spain, so it was they who more than any others were to spread the fame of Saint Foy across the length and breadth of Christendom.

Giving sight to the blind became one of the special virtues of the saint, and her cult in the eleventh, twelfth, and thirteenth centuries can only be compared with that of Our Lady of Lourdes in our own time. The waters of the Auvergne have long been noted for their health-giving properties, and the cult of Saint Foy at Conques was encouraged by the purity of the mountain spring that continues to bubble forth not far from the basilica's southern tower.

To house the saint's skull a special gold statue was wrought and embossed with a fabulous quantity of precious stones and antique cameos. These came from pious "donations," which the gentle saint was particularly resourceful in extracting. The abbot of Beaulieu was so hounded by a series of visions that he finally agreed to part with two beautiful gold doves, which went to embellish her throne. Arsinde, the barren wife of Guillaume Taillefer, Count of Toulouse, who finally consented to part with two precious bracelets, was rewarded with two sons in exchange. When Countess Richarde, the wife of Raymond III, Count of Rouergue, refused to give up a gold brooch, Saint Foy punished her by causing her horse to rear and the brooch to get caught on a branch. A few days later it was brought to the abbey by a pious woman of the neighborhood who had found it.

Saint Foy's ingenuity in circumventing the wiles of avarice soon won her the title of *sancta joculatrix*—the prankish saint. For a while she swept all before her, and from Rouergue her fame spread over a good part of the Auvergne. Soon Conques was besieged with requests to have the miraculous statue brought over to bless this or that community. Such outings were almost invariably attended by miracles, each miracle necessitating the celebration of a special mass to the repeated flourish of trumpets and the ceaseless pealing of bells. On one of her more memorable excursions—to the town of Molompise, which lies in the heart of the Auvergne—the miracles, falling almost as thickly as snowflakes, kept the hard-pressed monks of Conques from having time to eat anything for more than twenty-four hours.

For such occasions the statue, preceded by a jewel-studded cross, would usually be placed on a richly caparisoned horse, though she was also carried at times on a tapestried litter. Torches and candles accompanied her, joyously clashing cymbals heralded her triumphant approach as well as the deep-throated sound of oliphants—horns hollowed out of elephants' tusks. No instrument was more prized in the Middle Ages, at any rate by knights and crusaders. It was on an oliphant that Roland blew the final heroic blast, heard for thirty leagues around, that informed Charlemagne that his rear-guard was in trouble.

Conques was a stopping point on one of the four major pilgrimage routes to Santiago de Compostela, and the same martial fervor that made this for a while the greatest pilgrimage in Europe can be detected in another facet of Saint Foy's miracle-working powers. She was responsible for miraculously freeing an extraordinary number of prisoners, who then brought their locks and their chains to Conques as a token of their homage. In all probability many of these "miraculous" escapes were organized by resourceful prelates. The fathers of the Church, who were no fools, recognized what was demonstrated once again during the last war— that former criminals and jailbirds make excellent commandos and singularly resourceful soldiers, whom the Church needed for the pilgrimage to Santiago and to fight the Moors in Spain. The banner they fought under was the banner of Saint James—Sant Iago—transmuted from a humble Galilean pedestrian into a sword-wielding horseman, the blood brother of el Cid Campeador.

They also fought under another banner—that of Santa Fe, to give her her Spanish and Provençal name. For as her fame grew, so did the requests for her remains. A church was founded in her honor in Alsace; a priory was dedicated to her in Bavaria, and another sprang up in Liège; several churches were built for her in Italy; and even London acquired a chapel established in her honor. But it was in Spain, where half a dozen churches were dedicated to her, that her fame was greatest. It was she whose aid Raymond III, Count of Rouergue, invoked in liberating Barcelona from the Saracens in the year 987. It was again she who aided Don Pedro Sanchez, the king of Aragon, in chasing the Moors from his kingdom. The memory of these exploits was still very much alive centuries later when the conquistadors crossed the Atlantic, and the Spanish mission fathers once again invoked her help in combating a new kind of infidel—one with a red skin and war paint—as they did at Santa Fe, in what came to be known as New Mexico.

At its height—in the eleventh and twelfth centuries—Conques' abbey numbered close to nine hundred monks, or almost twice the total population of present-day Conques. They were spread for leagues around, tilling the fields and sowing wheat on the uplands above the valley or milling flour down at the old mill (which still exists) a mile or two upstream on the Dordou river. Artisans were imported by the muleload and were kept busy for decades fashioning gold and silver and other precious metals into fabulous new reliquaries. Two new basilicas had to be built as each grew too small to contain the host of pilgrims who came to pay homage to the priceless gold statue of the saint. The hundreds of chains and locks brought to her by escaped prisoners were melted down and reworked into a series of beautiful forged-iron gates and grills, which now surround the pillars of the apse. In the Middle Ages they were used to protect the gold statue and the other treasures of Conques, which were kept on more or less permanent display; the church at night was a sea of candles as scores of pilgrims spent night-long wakes guarding the precious treasure from lurking thieves.

And then, almost as suddenly as it had flared, the cult burned itself out. By 1424 there were only twenty-nine monks left. A century later a pontifical decree turned the abbey into a secular church. In the 1590's the basilica narrowly missed destruction when the Protestants marched up and set fire to the roof; but fortunately they spared the treasure. The revolutionaries who marched up the valley two centuries later were bent on demolishing the treasures, but the resourceful spirit of Ariviscus was still very much alive among these backward yokels, who got advance warning of what was brewing down below. They hastily removed the treasures from the church and buried them, then smashed a couple of locks, bent a few iron bars, and left open one of the grillwork gates. When the rabble marched up the hill, they were greeted by some glum-faced locals who stared at them woodenly before breaking the terrible news: they had been beaten to the spot by a bunch of godless bandits who had broken into the sanctuary and decamped with the loot!

For years there was not a house or a cabbage patch in Conques that did not have some priceless piece of jewelry buried away beneath it, yet such was the continuing faith in their guardian patroness and saint that not one of these religious heirlooms disappeared. One by one they crept back into the basilica as the memory of Robespierre's Terror faded into the past. Today they are housed in a specially constructed wing of the cloister behind panels of protective glass. They constitute the finest collection of Carolingian art in France; and as one descends into the darkened crypt where they repose, one has the impression of having suddenly stumbled into some magic cavern ablaze with the marvels of Aladdin's lamp.

For major feast days the statue is still solemnly brought out, placed on a simple litter, and paraded up the village's one and only tarred street. The procession winds past the timbered façade of the Auberge de Sainte-Foy and on up to a kind of square, shaded by a fine old chestnut. The bells peal, but there are no oliphants any more to fill the echoing valley with the sound of Roland's horn. Gone, too, are the lutes and the split-reed pipes with which the jongleurs of the Middle Ages used to amuse the pilgrims gathered on the cobbles in front of the basilica.

History has passed Conques by, and in a sense it is a blessing. For though a couple of souvenir stores have sprouted, Conques has been spared the dozens of trinket shops which now mar Mont-Saint-Michel and Rocamadour, to say nothing of Lourdes, with its endless cobwebs of booths run by the Sullivans, the Mulligans, the Donovans, and the O'Gradys, O'Haras, O'Reillys, and O'Tooles—and that's only a starter—who have brought the cheer of good Saint Patrick to the land of Bernadette. "We are lucky if we get 50,000 visitors a year," remarked Father Calmels, the rosy-cheeked friar of the Prémontré order who today stands watch over the religious trophies of Conques.

Did I detect a note of regret in his voice? I am not sure. But when I asked him what he thought of Ariviscus and his legendary theft, he shrugged his round shoulders beneath his white robe, and his brown eyes dissolved into a skeptical smile. "Well, you can believe it if you like," he said. "But the monks of Agen had good reason to have Saint Foy's sacred relics brought up here—to save them from the Normans." He nodded philosophically, then added: "And why should they have stolen from each other? After all, the monks of Agen were Benedictines, like those of Conques."

But so, I couldn't help thinking, were their cousins of Figeac.

A NIGHT
AT THE
OBSERVATORY

HENRY S. F. COOPER, JR.

A year ago last summer, I was invited out to Mount Palomar, the big observatory in southern California, to spend a night on the two-hundred-inch telescope. A member of the observatory's staff wrote me exuberantly, "The scientists here feel that the last couple of years have been the most exciting in astronomy since Galileo." He was referring to observations of the quasars, most of which had been made at Mount Palomar. Quasars are thought to be tremendously distant objects that may be almost as old as the universe itself; as yet, not a great deal is known about them. "Dr. Jesse L. Greenstein, Executive Officer of the Department of Astronomy at Cal Tech, will be going down to Palomar soon, and he says he will be glad to have you go along," my correspondent continued. "He says to warn you not to expect any great discoveries." That was an acceptable condition. As a final admonition, he added that the telescope is extremely delicate, and before I went out I had to promise to do my best not to break it. This, I thought, would be an easy promise to keep, since the telescope is as big as a small freighter.

On my way to Palomar, I stopped in Pasadena at the California Institute of Technology, which runs the observatory. A smog that made one's eyes smart hung over the city. I found that Dr. Greenstein was already at Palomar, a hundred and thirty-five miles to the south and fifty-six hundred feet up in the clearer, cooler air. I headed south, too. The road wound through ranches and forest up and up a mountain. Soon I saw across a valley, perched on the edge of a plateau, the glistening aluminum dome of the observatory. The huge slit for the telescope to peer through was shut like a closed eyelid.

On top of the plateau, which was dotted with nine sturdy yellow cottages, I headed toward the Monastery, where I expected to find Dr. Greenstein. The Monastery is the dormitory where the astronomers stay when they are using the two-hundred-inch telescope or the smaller forty-eight-inch Schmidt telescope. The Monastery is a solid building fitted out with black leather blinds for daytime sleeping. It was six o'clock in the evening. Dr. Greenstein, who had been up all the night before, was in the dining room having a solitary supper; a stocky, graying man in his mid-fifties who sported a tiny, pencil-thin moustache, he was the only astronomer on the mountain. Dr. Greenstein complained about not being able to sleep. "The first night I'm down here, I can't sleep at all," he said. "It isn't until the fifth day that I get a full night's, or rather morning's, sleep, and then it's time to go back to Pasadena." I asked him how often he had to go through this sleepless state, and he answered that in his case it was about thirty-five nights a year.

"I get up here whenever I can," he went on, planting an elbow next to a half-empty coffee cup. "Time on the telescope is so valuable that you snatch at it whenever you can get it. Just *having* the two-hundred-inch telescope puts Cal Tech in a tough spot. It's a national asset, so we can't do anything trivial. Any reasonably good astronomer would have to try hard in order *not* to make an interesting discovery with it. In practice it is used mainly by the members of the Department of Astronomy, and even with just sixteen of us, we are forever feuding to get time on the telescope. Cloudy time can be a real disaster."

I said I hoped Dr. Greenstein wouldn't be clouded out tonight, and he replied that he didn't think he would be. Since he had some preparations to make for the evening's work, I accompanied him along a path from the Monastery through a dry, prickly field toward the dome. It was partially hidden over the brow of a hill; for all anyone could tell, a big silver balloon had crash-landed there.

I asked Dr. Greenstein whether he had been involved with quasars lately. He shrugged. "I feel that my work, which is mostly the composition of stars within our galaxy, is more important; and current interpretations of quasars may be obsolete by next week." Although Dr. Greenstein is best known for his studies of the evolution of stars and galaxies, and of the elements within the stars, he is a top quasar man, too, and he has made observations to learn what their composition might be.

Quasars were first noticed in 1960 by radio astronomers as invisible sources of radio waves. One of these sources, 3C-48, was identified with what appeared to be a tiny, sixteenth-magnitude star. Three years later Dr. Maarten Schmidt, at Palomar, managed to concentrate on film enough of the feeble light from a quasar to get a spectrum. It appeared that quasars were not tiny stars within our own galaxy, as had been thought, but instead probably were intense and incredibly distant sources of light and radio waves. Quasar 3C-48 appears to be almost four billion light-years away, and subsequently other quasars have been measured out to almost nine billion light-years away; this is four-fifths of the way back to the "big bang" with which the universe supposedly began.

By studying the quasars, it may be possible to learn whether the universe will expand indefinitely; or whether it will stop some day; or whether it will fall back in upon itself for another big bang—and if so, when these events will take place.

But a great deal more information is needed about the quasars, including the answer to why they shine so much more brightly than even the brightest galaxies. This is a problem that Dr. Greenstein is working on.

"As it happens, I don't like working with quasars," Dr. Greenstein continued as we trudged along. "They're tricky little things. I don't even like the word 'quasar.' it was invented by a Chinese astronomer in New York who doesn't speak English well. Chinese is like Hebrew, which has no vowels. He saw the letters QSRS, which stand for quasi-stellar radio source, on a chart, and called them 'quasars.' We shouldn't have a vocabulary for what we don't know, and when we do know what the quasars are, we will have a better word for them. Quasar sounds as if it's short for quasi-star, and that's the one thing we know a quasar isn't." Dr. Greenstein observed that the sky, darkening fast now, was beautifully clear. The moon, about half full, was rising in the east, clear crystal against the dark blue background, which, Dr. Greenstein said, augured well for seeing tonight. The setting sun glinted red on the dome. Dr. Greenstein glanced at the cirrus clouds in the west, which were reddening as the sun sank. "Sunsets are nice," he said, "but you haven't seen anything until you see a sunrise at Palomar."

The dome, which is nine stories tall and as much as that in diameter, rises from a round, yellow, cement drum. Dr. Greenstein, fitted a key in a latch, and soon we were blinking our eyes inside a cavernous, pitch-black room three stories below the telescope. Dr. Greenstein said he had some work to do in his darkroom and suggested I go to the third floor and take a look at the telescope.

The inside of the dome was stuffy, dim, mysterious, and silent except for the echo of some approaching footsteps. The telescope loomed in the center of the room, shadowy and intricate, its works mostly exposed, like a fine timepiece under a glass bell. The telescope, Dr. Greenstein had told me, works something like a clock. Its tube has to keep time exactly with the movement of the stars so that a star's light can stay riveted to a photographic plate for several hours at a stretch. The telescope, with its reflecting mirror two hundred inches in diameter, serves as a sort of bucket to catch as much light as possible from a star and concentrate it on film: it could pick up the light of a ten-watt bulb a million miles away. The purpose of the telescope is not to magnify, for no matter how great the magnification, no star would ever show up as more than a point of light.

The footsteps I had heard belonged to the night assistant for the telescope, Gary Tuton, a lean young man with short, wavy hair. Tuton is the technician who runs the telescope for the astronomers. He walked over to a control console and pressed a button. The telescope sprang into life. The big mirror, which weighs almost fifteen tons, rests at the bottom of the telescope tube, an open steel cylinder some sixty feet long. The tube swivels north and south inside a huge frame called the yoke, and the yoke swivels from east to west on two enormous bearings, so that the tube, with the mirror at its bottom, can aim at any point in the sky.

Now the yoke spun to the east and the tube swiveled to the north, only, since both these motions happened simultaneously, the movement was one smooth undulation. The tube can be locked on a star, just as the pencil in a compass can be locked at any given radius. Then the star can be tracked along its path simply by turning the yoke, which is fixed on the North Star as if it were the dot at the center of a circle. The movement of the yoke has to be very delicate. Tuton explained that the huge bearings at either end of the yoke are floated on thin films of oil so that the telescope, which weighs five hundred tons, can be turned by hand. The oil pumps under the enormous bearings whined. The observatory sounded like a very active railroad yard.

Slowly and ponderously the two-hundred-and-twenty-five-ton doors that covered the slit in the dome pulled aside, revealing a widening band of dark blue sky. It was like being inside the eye of an awakening animal. "Sometimes, in winter, when the dome is covered with snow, I have to go up top and sweep the snow off the slit," Tuton said. "One night last winter it got so cold that the gears on the doors that cover the slit in the dome froze. No matter what I did, one shutter would shut and the other wouldn't, and there was a snowstorm coming. But by and large the weather is pretty good up here. Last year we used the telescope on three hundred and ten nights."

A door banged and Dr. Greenstein appeared, struggling under a load of lenses and photographic film. Since it was still too early to begin taking pictures, Dr. Greenstein said that he was going up into the prime-focus cage at the top of the telescope tube and invited me to come along. "I want to take a look at a group of stars, a globular cluster called Messier 13," he said. "There's a peculiar star in it that I want to get a spectrum of later on. It's in with such a mass of other stars that I want to make sure I get my bearings straight."

Dr. Greenstein explained that the prime focus was the simplest and most direct way of looking through the telescope. There are several different ways, and none of them is the conventional one, used with binoculars or refractor telescopes, of holding the telescope up to your eyes. Instead of focusing light through a lens, the big mirror bounces the light back up the tube and concentrates it at a point fifty-five feet above. The exact spot is called the prime focus. The astronomer sits in the prime-focus cage, which is like a balloonist's basket high inside the telescope tube, and from this vantage point he can photograph the image directly.

"I like it in the prime-focus cage," Dr. Greenstein concluded. "You feel closer to the stars." Then he frisked himself and me, removing any hard objects, such as coins and pens, that might fall on the mirror and damage it. It had taken eleven years to polish the mirror into exactly the right configuration; a scratch could mean years more polishing. We climbed to a balcony, boarded the dome elevator, and began a long, hair-raising ascent as the elevator rose upward and outward, following the overhanging contour of the dome. Through the slit we could see the ground several stories below, and several thousand feet below that, the lights of the valley floor. The dome elevator is a peculiar, unenclosed contraption like a long spoon; we stood at the outer end of it where the bowl would be. After a bumpy ride, the elevator deposits the astronomer, like a dollop of medicine, inside the mouth of the telescope. At this point, the astronomer is about seventy feet above the floor of the dome, with very little to hang on to.

"People have gotten killed on telescopes," Dr. Greenstein said with what I thought was poor timing as we lurched unevenly up and out. "Sometimes astronomers get squashed by a telescope slewing about, but that doesn't happen very often."

I gripped the railing of the elevator, fixed my eyes firmly on the top of the dome, and asked Dr. Greenstein to tell me more about the peculiar star in Messier 13. "Globular clusters, like Messier 13, are sort of suburbs of our galaxy which contain some of the oldest stars, and for this reason they might have a bearing on the quasars, which are supposed to be primordial objects, too," he said. "However, the star I want to look at now is blue, a color usually associated with younger stars, so in this case it must represent a peculiar stage of evolution. Although this star—Barnard 29—is blue, it has a peculiar energy distribution. Its spectrum is too much in the red, and one possibility I want to check tonight is whether it couldn't in fact be a close pair, a double star, one blue and one red."

Soon we were directly on top of the telescope tube, and Dr. Greenstein flung open a flimsy gate at the end of the elevator platform. The prime-focus cage—a bucket perhaps five feet in diameter and five feet deep—was about eighteen inches below us. Dr. Greenstein explained that the elevator couldn't go all the way to the cage because of the danger of collision with the telescope: we would have to travel across the remaining gap ourselves. So saying, he flung himself into the void and disappeared into the mouth of the telescope.

Inside the bucket was a chair and an empty well that looked straight down at the mirror; the astronomer fits his instruments into the well. When Tuton was sure that we were safely installed, and that nothing could drop on the mirror, he opened the diaphragm that covered it. Slowly, like a water lily, the petals of the diaphragm lifted, revealing what looked like a pond of rippling, shimmering water beneath. The stars, which wouldn't stay still, were streaking like meteors; the mirror, it seemed, was popping a few millionths of an inch with the change of temperature. Tuton slewed the telescope off in search of Messier 13 and Barnard 29. As one side of the bucket dipped suddenly down, the chair, which was on rails, moved around and down with gravity, so that the astronomer was always upright; the sensation was like riding very slowly in a Ferris wheel. Stars shot through the big mirror as we sailed along. The telescope came to a smooth halt, moving just fast enough to keep the stars still in spite of the rotation of the earth. Dr. Greenstein peered into the pool of light for a moment. Then he maneuvered a tiny lens that looked like a magnifying glass—it was tied to the well with a string—until he found the exact spot where the image was clearest. This was the prime focus.

"We're right on the beam," Dr. Greenstein said, handing the lens to me. As I looked down, I felt my glasses begin to slide down my nose; I grabbed them just before they dropped down the well toward the mirror. The lens resolved the chaotic splotches of dancing light, and I saw an enormous rash of stars, each one a point of hard, brilliant light. I couldn't make out Barnard 29. Dr. Greenstein was able to converse with Tuton over an intercom, and he asked him to stop the telescope's tracking drive. No sooner had the telescope stopped moving than Messier 13 and Barnard 29 slipped out of the field of vision. Other stars whizzed across the mirror, following Messier 13 into seeming oblivion; a given star crossed the mirror in about ten seconds, before vanishing. That, Dr. Greenstein said, showed how fast the earth, with the telescope, was turning. Tuton's voice crackled through the microphone, asking how I felt. I replied that I was getting a little dizzy. Tuton started up the tracking device; the telescope passed all the stars that had been whipping by, and soon we were safely back with Messier 13.

"Did Dr. Greenstein tell you about the time I was stuck up there?" Tuton asked; and his voice crackled on, "I was in the prime-focus cage when the power for the telescope shorted out. It was a cold winter night. I had to climb down, which was the hairiest thing I ever did. What made me do it was not the cold so much as what the men who came in the morning would say. I'd never have lived it down."

At last Tuton wafted the telescope toward the elevator platform for us to board. I fixed my eye on the top of the dome again. Dr. Greenstein glanced at his watch and said that he wished the elevator would hurry, because it was already dark enough to start using the spectrograph. He shouted down to Tuton to start setting up the telescope for the coudé focus. The coudé focus is in a room outside the telescope altogether, and the light from a star is deflected to it by a mirror—called the coudé flat—which bounces the starlight in a thin beam down through a hole in the southern foundation of the telescope and into the coudé room one floor below, where the spectrographs are kept. The film to record the spectrum of a star is in this room, which serves something of the purpose of an old Brownie box camera. As we reached the ground, an electronic engine whirred and the coudé flat, weighing a ton and a half, lifted slowly into position just below the prime-focus cage. It glittered like a jewel inside a watch.

Dr. Greenstein fetched the films he had brought with him and disappeared down the steps into the coudé room, a tiny chamber that descends steeply in line with the yoke, pointing at the North Star. It was already after eight o'clock. Barnard 29 was nestled among so many stars that the final zeroing in had to be done by dead reckoning. "There's a sort of triangle of stars," said Dr. Greenstein, who had returned to the control room at the top of the steps. "See it? There ought to be a double star on the upper left. Got it?" He sounded like a man finding his way with a road map. Tuton said he had it. "Do you know what the most difficult object to find is?" Tuton asked as

117

he turned a knob for fine adjustment; I said I didn't. "It's the moon. The moon is so close, and it's moving so fast, that it's like trying to aim a rifle at a moving target close by, instead of at the trees standing behind it."

All of a sudden, Barnard 29 disappeared from view. It was as if the telescope had gone dead. Tuton raced out into the dome and peered up at the sky through the slit; a long, wispy cloud was obstructing the view. "Looks like it's going to be a cloud-dodging night," he said. Quickly Tuton and Greenstein flipped the telescope to another star, called HD 165195, which was in a cloudless part of the sky.

I asked Dr. Greenstein whether we would see any quasars that night. "The moon is up, so we can't work on anything as dim as quasars," he said. "That's probably just as well. There isn't much you can tell by looking at a quasar anyway. Instead, I will be doing long exposures on some of the oldest stars in the galaxy. The procedure is much the same as with quasars; and in fact part of what we'll be doing is related to quasars. There is a theory that has to be explored that the quasars are a remnant of the first formation of galaxies. According to this theory, during the contraction of the gases that formed the galaxies, some super-massive objects formed within them. These objects may have become extremely dense and pulled themselves together so rapidly that they exploded. Perhaps that is what the quasars are. I don't know. I'm fairly neutral on the subject. There is evidence in our own galaxy of a superexplosion far greater than the explosion of a supernova, but less, I think, than a quasar explosion. In any event, if the quasars represent monumental explosions within galaxies during the half-billion years or so that the galaxies and the stars were condensing out of primeval gas clouds, then you would expect that the oldest stars, the first to condense from the gases, would be heavily contaminated by the elements in the quasars. They would have been loaded with the products of quasar evolution."

Dr. Greenstein turned out the lights in the control room and pressed a button to start the exposure. The control room was lit only by the soft-green glow of the dials on the control panel, like the cockpit of an airplane at night. "So I will be looking at some of the oldest stars in our galaxy, like this one, to see whether they have the same elements and in roughly the same proportions, as the quasars. We don't know yet the exact composition of the quasars, but we may be able to do something with oxygen or iron. If they have the same elements, it might indicate quasars were the raw material in forming stars. But if there are other elements aside from those found in quasars, it might prove that the quasars are not important in star evolution, for the oldest stars don't seem to have manufactured many new elements after their formation, such as metals. But if I find a trace of metal in HD 165195, I have to decide whether it might have been cooked within the star after all, or whether the metal was part of the original gases of which the star was composed. The chances are we won't know much more after tonight. I'll need this type of information on hundreds of stars before I can begin to get anywhere."

The time was eight-thirty. I found myself standing in the path of the slender stream of light from HD 165195, and Dr. Greenstein asked me to step out of the way, which wasn't easy, since the control room was cramped and narrow. A ticking sound filled the room. Dr. Greenstein said that the ticking came from the photoelectric scaler, which counts the number of photons coming from a star, like a light meter. Each tick meant twenty thousand photons of light. A dial kept count of the ticks, and Dr. Greenstein said that, for this exposure, he wanted about thirty-three hundred.

He invited me to look through the eyepiece of the spectrograph. A spectrograph, an apparatus in the control room that intercepted the light coming from HD 165195, refracts and spreads out the light from a star into its component wave lights, giving a spectrum something like the light from a prism. The lines in a spectrum show the elements in a star. They also show how fast an object is receding from the earth by how much the lines are shifted to the red end of the spec-

119

trum. This is called the red shift, and it was in this way that Schmidt first decided the quasars were tremendously distant objects. Through the eyepiece, the star appeared as a fuzzy, bright-green spark; the star's light had been shattered by passing through a slit and some gratings inside the spectrograph. Dr. Greenstein said the light had left the star ten thousand years ago. Tuton darted across to the telescope's control panel and slowed down the telescope's tracking drive by a tiny fraction. "We want to make the star trail along the slit in the spectrograph," he said. "This is what we have to do with faint objects. It's like painting one brush stroke over another, until you get the proper intensity on the plate."

With everything squared away, Tuton settled down by the eyepiece, stretched, yawned, and tuned in a radio to a rock-'n'-roll station in San Bernardino. He kept an ear cocked to make sure the ticking didn't stop, and every once in a while he checked the eyepiece to make sure the star was still there. I asked Dr. Greenstein why he and the other astronomers couldn't stay in Pasadena, and phone down to Tuton whenever they wanted a plate taken of a star. "There are too many things that can go wrong," Dr. Greenstein said. "I wouldn't know whether a plate was any good or not unless I was here." Tuton concurred with him. "I've never been trained in astronomy," he said. "I can run the telescope all right, and find a star, but when it comes to astronomy, I just haven't the foggiest idea what's going on. The astronomer never says what he's doing. Half the time he doesn't know what he's done until he's gotten back to Pasadena. I didn't know anything about quasars until I read about them in the papers." Then Tuton pulled out a magazine, which he squinted at by the light of the dials.

Dr. Greenstein suggested that we go out on the catwalk. Except for a gentle breeze, the plateau was absolutely still. I could see the smaller dome of the Schmidt telescope about half a mile to the east. Dr. Greenstein pointed out a spot between the two domes where an Air Force bomber had crashed four years earlier, killing the crew and two horses that belonged to the superintendent of the observatory but miraculously doing no damage to the telescope. Away to the northwest, the smog over Los Angeles glowed—possibly in something of the way the outer gases of the quasars shine, powered by some mysterious force inside. There was a light mist on the mountain, and the half-moon glowed overhead. "Only spectrograph work can be done in full moonlight, and even that is terribly difficult," Dr. Greenstein said. "You have to be very careful that the moonlight doesn't contaminate your plate. I thought I'd made a great spectrographic discovery once, only to find that it was the light of the moon, and not of the star. There is a gadget called a moon eliminator. I wish we could get rid of the moon for good!"

Dr. Greenstein glanced at his watch. It was eleven o'clock. "The night's young yet," he said energetically. He went inside, bustled into the control room, checked the dial that counted the ticks, and shut down the spectrograph. Tuton slewed the telescope to another star, BD 39° 4926, which Dr. Greenstein explained was also very old and might shed light on whether quasars had to do with galaxy formation. Then, since the exposure would last for three hours, Dr. Greenstein went downstairs to his darkroom to develop the plate on HD 165195.

Amid a sloshing of water and the acrid odor of hypo Dr. Greenstein said, "I don't really believe that the older stars are residues of quasars. I don't believe the quasars are a part of galaxies, and therefore I don't happen to believe that they have anything to do with star evolution. There is evidence of giant explosions in galaxies now, but whether these caused quasars or not, we don't know. But what we know of quasars really isn't conducive to the formation of stars. I don't believe quasars come from explosions, though other astronomers do. Speculation is like the stock market. I feel that the quasars instead may be in some kind of balance condition, like a star, and that they are isolated objects, and that they are formed of matter between galaxies. Other people feel they are little things which have been blown out of galaxies. Another group believes that the quasars are extremely dense objects and that their red shifts are caused by gravity, rather than by speed or distance. I don't know. The best we can do is to test the different theories, which is what I'm trying to do now."

Just after midnight, Dr. Greenstein came up from the dark-room. He checked the star, which was ticking away nicely on the slit, and sat on a table. "That's all the developing I do tonight," he said. "It's too risky when you're tired." He had evidently lost his second wind. I asked him if he had been able to tell anything about HD 165195, and he said he hadn't. "It's too late at night for discoveries," he said with a yawn. "There's nothing like making a great discovery that you might absent-mindedly wipe off the plate with a wet finger. I make it a rule never to make great discoveries after midnight."

Dr. Greenstein yawned again. I followed him over to a couple of reclining chairs by the control console under the north bearing. Just visible in the starlight, he lay back with his arms folded behind his head as a pillow and his eyes shut. The moon, for the time being, was obscured, so it was unusually dark inside the dome. As I became more accustomed to the darkness—it was much darker than in the control room, which contained a number of luminous dials—I could make out more and more of the telescope. Dr. Greenstein opened his eyes. "I could look at it forever," he said. "No matter how long you look at it, it always looks different. It looks different now, when you can barely see it in the dim starlight, from what it did a few minutes ago in the light of the half-moon. It's different from whatever side you look at it. Right now, it just sits there and broods. It is a remarkable subordination of brute force for delicate ends. All this mechanism is for is to move one piece of glass; and all the glass is for is to carry one thin layer of aluminum that reflects star-light. I wish it were quieter! We must get rid of those oil pumps."

At last Dr. Greenstein's voice drifted off. He was fast asleep. After a time he sat bolt upright and looked at his watch. It

122

was two fifteen. Above him, the telescope was almost completely on its side, as if it, too, had been asleep. Over the last three hours, its tracking of BD 39°4926 had caused it to assume this position. The ticking ceased abruptly when Dr. Greenstein checked the meter and ended the exposure. After rummaging around in the inky coudé room to change plates, Dr. Greenstein came back to the control room and decided to return to Barnard 29. "We need about three hours, though with this much moon, I doubt if we'll get it," he said briskly as he zeroed in the telescope. As he was talking, the ticking became more and more sporadic, slowing down; finally it stopped altogether. Tuton, who had had no nap, and who looked a little scruffy, went out under the dome and squinted up through the slit. Barnard 29 was obscured by clouds again. "What do we do now?" Tuton asked Greenstein. Tuton said that what he would like to do now would be go home and go to bed.

"We're getting only about ten minutes' exposure time to the hour, but as long as I can get even that much, I can't shut down," Dr. Greenstein said, and added unhappily, "the telescope's time is more valuable than my own." It costs one thousand dollars a night to operate the telescope. Suddenly a great rift appeared in the clouds, and the moon emerged. It was greeted with a terrific burst of ticks. Dr. Greenstein shouted to Tuton to shut off the spectrograph. "We're better off wasting exposure time and not getting contamination," Dr. Greenstein grumbled, exhaling a cloud of cigar smoke that glowed derisively in the moonlight. It was a little after two forty-five, and I had the impression that Dr. Greenstein was about to call it a night.

At three fifteen the sky cleared and Tuton started the exposure once more. Since he was stiff and tired, Dr. Greenstein suggested another spin around the catwalk. There was low-lying mist on the plateau, and not far away a jay woke up raucously. The air was chill and damp. The east was as dark as ever, but Dr. Greenstein said he could see the zodiacal light, which heralds the dawn. "We won't be able to keep the exposure going much longer," he went on. "The sun is already beginning to heat up the atmosphere to the east, which makes it bubble a bit." Groggily, I looked for bubbles in the east, but saw none. A flush of pink appeared and spread rapidly; the stars to the east blinked out, though the ones to the west were, for the time being, as hard and brilliant as they had been for most of the night. Shadows grew where none had been before, and we could begin to see colors—the green of the pines, the pink clay of the road. Dr. Greenstein went back inside and called down to Tuton to turn off the exposure before it was contaminated.

The inside of the dome was suffused with pink; the dome's interior, too, was of brilliant aluminum, and caught the dawn through the slit. The telescope was visible again, like a dinosaur emerging from a misty bog. "This is *my* time on the telescope," Tuton said, "the time after dawn, but before all the stars are washed out. It's useless for spectrography or photography, so I just aim the telescope at what I want to look at. I think Saturn is in a good position for viewing."

He consulted an astronomy book and quickly swung the telescope to a new position. He snapped the eyepiece into place, focusing it. He stepped aside, and I took a look. There was Saturn, as big as a football and, with its rings forming an oval around it, somewhat the same shape. Through the two-hundred-inch telescope, Saturn was so brilliant that it hurt the eyes. Dr. Greenstein squinted through the eyepiece, grunting. "I never particularly liked the solar system," he said, relinquishing the telescope. I looked again; Saturn was less brilliant than before, and it was fading fast in the sunlight. Soon it vanished altogether, like the Cheshire cat, leaving nothing behind but a patch of pale-blue sky.

WILL SOMEONE PLEASE HICCUP MY PAT?

WILLIAM SPOONER DONALD

O ne afternoon nearly a hundred years ago the October wind gusted merrily down Oxford's High Street. Hatless and helpless, a white-haired clergyman with pink cherubic features uttered his plaintive cry for aid. As an athletic youngster chased the spinning topper, other bystanders smiled delightedly—they had just heard at first hand the latest "Spoonerism."

My revered relative William Archibald Spooner was born in 1844, the son of a Staffordshire county court judge. As a young man, he was handicapped by a poor physique, a stammer, and weak eyesight; at first, his only possible claim to future fame lay in the fact that he was an albino, with very pale blue eyes and white hair tinged slightly yellow.

But nature compensated the weakling by blessing him with a brilliant intellect. By 1868 he had been appointed a lecturer at New College, Oxford. Just then he would have been a caricaturist's dream with his freakish looks, nervous manner, and peculiar mental kink that caused him—in his own words

—to "make occasional felicities in verbal diction."

Victorian Oxford was a little world of its own where life drifted gently by; a world where splendid intellectuals lived in their ivory towers of Latin, Euclid, and Philosophy; a world where it was always a sunny summer afternoon in a countryside, where Spooner admitted he loved to "pedal gently round on a well-boiled icicle."

As the years passed, Spooner grew, probably without himself being aware of the fact, into a "character." A hard worker himself, he detested idleness and is on record as having rent some lazybones with the gem, "You have hissed all my mystery lessons, and completely tasted two whole worms."

With his kindly outlook on life, it was almost natural for him to take holy orders; he was ordained a deacon in 1872 and a priest in 1875. His unique idiosyncrasy never caused any serious trouble and merely made him more popular. On one occasion, in New College chapel in 1879, he announced smilingly that the next hymn would be "Number One seven five—Kinkering Kongs their Titles Take." Other congregations were treated to such jewels as ". . . Our Lord, we know, is a shoving Leopard . . ." and ". . . All of us have in our hearts a half-warmed fish to lead a better life. . . ."

Spooner often preached in the little village churches around Oxford and once delivered an eloquent address on the subject of Aristotle. No doubt the sermon contained some surprising information for his rustic congregation. For after Spooner had left the pulpit, an idea seemed to occur to him, and he hopped back up the steps again.

"Excuse me, dear brethren," he announced brightly, "I just want to say that in my sermon whenever I mentioned Aristotle, I should have said Saint Paul."

By 1885 the word "Spoonerism" was in colloquial use in Oxford circles, and a few years later, in general use all over England. If the dividing line between truth and myth is often only a hairsbreadth, does it really matter? One story that has been told concerns an optician's shop in London. Spooner is reputed to have entered and asked to see a "signifying glass."

The optician registered polite bewilderment.

"Just an ordinary signifying glass," repeated Spooner, perhaps surprised at the man's obtuseness.

"I'm afraid we haven't one in stock, but I'll make inquiries right away, sir," said the shopkeeper, playing for time.

"Oh, don't bother, it doesn't magnify, it doesn't magnify," said Spooner airily, and walked out.

Fortunately for Spooner, he made the right choice when he met his wife-to-be. He was thirty-four years old when he married Frances Goodwin in 1878. The marriage was a happy one, and they had one son and four daughters. Mrs. Spooner was a tall, good-looking girl, and on one occasion the family went on a short holiday in Switzerland. The "genial Dean," as he was then called, took a keen interest in geology, and in no time at all he had mastered much information and many technical definitions on the subject of glaciers.

One day at lunchtime the younger folk were worried because their parents had not returned from a long walk. When Spooner finally appeared with his wife, his explanation was: "We strolled up a long valley, and when we turned a corner we found ourselves completely surrounded by erotic blacks."

He was, of course, referring to "erratic blocks," or large boulders left around after the passage of a glacier.

In 1903 Spooner was appointed Warden of New College, the highest possible post for a Fellow. One day walking across the quadrangle, he met a certain Mr. Casson, who had just been elected a Fellow of New College.

"Do come to dinner tonight," said Spooner, "we are welcoming our new Fellow, Mr. Casson."

"But, my dear Warden, I *am* Casson," was the surprised reply.

"Never mind, never mind, come along all the same," said Spooner tactfully.

On another occasion in later years when his eyesight was really very bad, Spooner found himself seated next to a most elegant lady at dinner. In a casual moment the latter put her lily-white hand onto the polished table, and Spooner, in an even more casual manner, pronged her hand with his fork, remarking genially, "My bread, I think."

In 1924 Spooner retired as Warden. He had established an astonishing record of continuous residence at New College for sixty-two years—first as undergraduate, then as Fellow, then Dean, and finally as Warden. His death in 1930, at the age of eighty-six, was a blushing crow to collectors of those odd linguistic transpositions known by then throughout the English-speaking world as Spoonerisms.

A DAY
WITH JUDE
THE OBSCURE

LORD ELTON

The volume of traffic in Oxford's High Street on a July afternoon in 1923 was naturally nothing like what it would be today, and it could move a lot faster. Which meant that from the steps in front of the college we might hope to spot a car slowing down before it drew up at the college gates. "You'll find that they will be punctual," said my companion confidently.

I did not feel so certain myself, for people are by no means always punctual in dreams, and I had not yet altogether shaken off the impression that we were involved in a stimulating but faintly embarrassing dream. For we were waiting to receive Mr. and Mrs. Thomas Hardy, and for me, at the moment at any rate, Thomas Hardy, who was then eighty-three and was generally supposed to have withdrawn permanently into Wessex, was not so much the doyen of English literature and the author of the novels—and particularly in the present context, of *Jude the Obscure*—as well as of the poems which it had recently become fashionable to regard as even more important than the novels: rather, he was a revenant from another age, a prodigious Victorian whom as a schoolboy I had supposed to have died at least a generation before. Indeed, we might have been about to welcome Charles Dickens.

My college, of which I was then junior Fellow, had elected Hardy to an honorary Fellowship in the previous autumn. This in itself had been a highly unusual proceeding, since colleges rarely elect an honorary Fellow who has not been a member of the college or even of the university. It had been my present companion on the college steps, an elderly Fellow of the Royal Society, who had unexpectedly proposed Hardy's name, and after duly stressing his illustrious achievements, he had even contrived to plead a tenuous connection with the college. Its ecclesiastical patronage, he recalled, included no less than eleven benefices in Hampshire, and although admittedly Hampshire was not Dorset, it presumably lay within, if only just within, the boundaries of Hardy's Wessex. However, the Governing Body was more influenced, I think, by memories—some of them no doubt somewhat nebulous— of Jude's thwarted dream of admission to "Christminster," and the notion that we should be conferring a kind of belated consolation prize on his creator. After all, it was already more than a quarter of a century since *Jude the Obscure* was published, and not many of the present Fellows were likely to have read the book lately, while some of their predecessors had probably swelled the outcry that greeted its first appearance, echoing over the common-room port the anguished exclamation of the New York *Herald's* critic: "I am shocked, appalled by this story . . . Aside from its immorality there is a coarseness which is beyond belief." My own recollection of the book was not strong on details, although I remember vividly Jude's desperate expedients in "Christminster," but I was aware that some years ago Hardy had categorically disposed of the myth that it was autobiographical.

Punctually almost to the second, the Hardys' car drew up,

and a smallish, frail old gentleman in tweeds was clambering out of it. Alert, birdlike, and unassuming, he might have been an exceptionally intelligent retired farmer, but certainly not a literary giant, and still less a thwarted student; and it was with such polite small talk as might have been exchanged with a retired farmer that we occupied the crossing of the front quadrangle to the Provost's lodgings. The Provost of that time was a year older than Hardy—it was before the day of compulsory age limits—and was never seen abroad, his duties having devolved on the pro-Provost, who was to preside over a formal lunch that day. Thanks, however, to a rectangular white beard of the chest-protector type which had become fashionable during the Crimean War, the Provost looked, and presumably felt, vastly less contemporary than Hardy, and his manner suggested that he regarded his guest as a mere stripling. For some years past he had himself emerged only once or twice a year on exceptionally warm summer days, to be driven slowly about for an hour, heavily muffled in a coachman's cape, in a hired horse-drawn victoria, and perhaps he could not regard one who had just traveled in a motorcar from Dorset, and picnicked en route, as a coeval. And certainly as we left the Hardys with the Provost and his elderly niece, Hardy himself sitting upright and attentive on the edge of his chair and the Provost embarking on a genial monologue on the weather, I remember thinking, "Such is the English reverence for status as distinct from achievement, and such the academic indifference to mere literary genius, that the Provost is positively patronizing Hardy." But in retrospect I suspect that I was doing him an injustice. The Provost, I fancy, was putting Jude Fawley, a very junior Fellow with a distinctly dubious background, at his ease.

Next morning the Hardys were ritually conducted around the principal sights of the college by a small posse of four Fellows, headed by the pro-Provost. No one could have been better qualified than the pro-Provost to provide factual information, for he possessed a photographic memory and had once continued his lectures on the Peloponnesian Wars, quite unembarrassed and with every quotation and textual reference word-perfect, after the contents of his rooms, including his lecture notes, had been destroyed by fire. But this morning, I couldn't help feeling, he was almost too informative. We would pause before the Grinling Gibbons carvings in the Library or Garrick's copy of the First Folio or the contemporary portrait of one of our more distinguished Old Members, King Henry V, and Hardy would gaze reflectively at it and seem about to speak, when a fresh spate of information would break over his head. One recalled the observation of a rustic character in *Under the Greenwood Tree:* "He can hold his tongue. That man's dumbness is wonderful to listen to," but Hardy's, it was to be feared, had been to some extent involuntary.

However, when the tour was completed there was half an hour or so to spare before lunch, and Hardy asked me to go with him and Mrs. Hardy into High Street, where he was anxious to see the famous curve from the most revealing viewpoint. (Had not the carter assured young Jude that "there's a street in the place—the main street—that ha'n't another like it in the world"?) As usual, bicycles as well as cars were pouring down toward Magdalen Bridge, and Hardy remarked that about 1900 he had done a lot of cycling and believed that he could do it still if it were not for the motor traffic, of which, he confessed, he would be somewhat apprehensive. Once, he said, when bicycling from Bath to Bristol, he had skidded and fallen on the muddy road; and then going into a second-hand furniture shop, he had seen a first edition of Hobbes's *Leviathan* lying in a basin, and when he asked the price, the woman in the shop had eyed his muddy clothes and replied, "Would sixpence hurt 'ee?" He displayed little fear, however, of the cars now swirling past us; too little indeed, it seemed to me, when we crossed the street for a better view of All Souls. Hardy's eye traveled appreciatively along the majestic arc from Queen's to Brasenose. Was he recalling how often the youthful Jude had climbed the hill to gaze at the distant city, seen as a faint halo of light in the night sky, and called it "the heavenly Jerusalem" and "a castle, manned by scholarship and religion"? Evidently not, for he remarked thoughtfully that it was by way of Oxford that Shakespeare had traveled on his first journey from Stratford to London, and that he had put up at Carfax; by which road would he have entered the city? "Just fancy *him* being here!" he murmured. We had some minutes in hand before lunch, and Hardy's thoughts were evidently still running on literature rather than learning. Would it be possible to see the Shelley Memorial? he inquired. Shelley, like Jude, it occurred to me, must have got a good deal less out of Oxford than he had hoped for. I could not remember having seen the memorial myself, but I knew that it was conveniently close at hand, somewhere in University College, and without disclosing my ignorance to the Hardys, I led them through the college gate and made unobtrusive inquiries in the porter's lodge. Hardy did not seem to be very favorably impressed by the memorial when we had reached it, and perhaps the effigy of a naked man spread out on a slab does suggest a failed cross-Channel swimmer rather more than either the undergraduate who was suspended for atheism or the author of the *Ode to the West Wind*.

I remember little of the lunch, at which all the Fellows with their wives were present, but it was doubtless sumptuous, for our college chef was celebrated throughout the university, and beyond it. Afterward, a formal group of Fellows was photographed, with Hardy looking more diminutive and fragile than ever in the billowing recesses of the gown of the Doctorate of Literature. When the company had dispersed, the Hardys invited me to accompany them in a hired car which was to take them sight-seeing where they pleased. I was only too well aware that in respect to dates and architecture my local knowledge might prove sadly unreliable on an intensive tour of the university in company with one who, like the young Hardy, had been trained as an architect or, like the young Jude, must have eagerly accumulated heterogeneous information as to the colleges. I was somewhat relieved therefore, as well as somewhat surprised, when once again his inclination proved to be toward literature rather than the university. We would drive to Boars Hill, a mile or two to the south, he proposed, to call on the Masefields. John Masefield was not then poet laureate, of course, but his *Widow in the Bye Street* and *The Everlasting Mercy* had excited the young shortly before the war, and in 1923 almost any undergraduate with literary leanings could quote "Quinquiremes of Nineveh from distant Ophir . . ." Mrs. Hardy remarked that Masefield had always sent her husband his books, with the solitary exception of *Right Royal,* which, they concluded, he had felt to be not up to standard. Of the younger poets, Hardy said, he liked Siegfried Sassoon best. This suited me, and I asked what he thought of another of my favorites, James Elroy Flecker, but he seemed hardly to know of him. However, they had been seeing a good deal of Colonel Lawrence, of Arabia, recently transmogrified into Private Shaw. Lawrence was stationed near Dorchester and used to ride over to Max Gate; and Hardy described how once Lady Crewe and some peer or other were in the house when Lawrence arrived, and he had refused to come in while they were there and had drawn himself up stiffly to attention against the wall of the porch as they passed him when departing.

So far as I know, the Masefields had had no warning of our advent, but they were at home, and I admired their almost instantaneous control of the incredulity with which they must have heard their maid announce Mr. and Mrs. Thomas Hardy. Very soon we were seated, and Masefield was showing Hardy some of the more macabre vignettes among the tailpieces in an eighteenth-century edition of Bewick's *British Birds.* Indeed, the Hardys' arrival seemed to have turned his thoughts to the darker hinterlands of rural life, and he went on to tell of the ghost of Sidney Ball, a Socialist Fellow of St. John's College, seen thirty times since his death in the house across the road. Hardy listened alertly but without comment; as if to draw him into the conversation, Masefield inquired of their drive to Oxford. Hardy said that they had paused at Fawley (the Hampshire village which, as "Marygreen," was Jude's birthplace and had provided him with a surname), but he mentioned the book with a deprecatory air, and twice referred to Jude as "that fictitious personage."

I had begun to wonder whether, in his insistence on the fictitiousness of Jude, Hardy was defending himself only against a current misconception of the book. When we were being driven back toward Oxford, Mrs. Hardy said something about the advantages of cousinship being that one could make what one pleased of it, and I remarked that Sue Bridehead, Jude's *femme fatale,* was his cousin. Hardy, who was holding a red rose which Masefield had presented to him as we left, replied mysteriously, "I ought to have made them second cousins."

As we approached St. Aldate's the clock was striking the hour in Christ Church, the "Cardinal College" from which Jude had counted the hundred and one strokes at nine o'clock on his first night in Oxford, but Hardy made no reference to that doomed assault on the university: he only remarked that a pre-Reformation bell in their village church was cracked and that, despite their vicar, he hated the idea of its being recast; "Just think of all the people it has called!" He had told the vicar, he added, that he would, at least and at last, be a member of his flock when he was dead; on which Mrs. Hardy, who was his second wife and many years younger, commented hastily that he probably would not, since Mr. Cowley was not likely to stay with them much longer. Hardy now asked that we should visit the Martyrs' Memorial, and I am afraid that I asked him to repeat himself, thinking that I must have misheard him. For amidst so much that was ancient and academic, the choice of that unimpressive neo-Gothic structure seemed inexplicable. "Erected by public subscription" in 1841 as a counterblast to the high Anglicanism of Newman, Pusey, and Keble then spreading through the common rooms of the university, the memorial commemorates the three

Protestant bishops burned at the stake three hundred years earlier in the reign of Queen Mary. I could not believe that Hardy was deeply interested either theologically in the controversies of the Tractarian era, or architecturally in an uninspired pastiche. However, we were duly driven to the south end of St. Giles, and after pensively surveying Sir Giles Gilbert Scott's crocketed pinnacles, Hardy observed that somewhere nearby a small cross in the pavement marked where the stake had actually stood. At this an obscure memory awoke naggingly in my brain, but before I could formulate it, we were on our way to New College, where Hardy had asked to be taken into the cloisters. Was this to be the first of our objectives which could be fairly ranked as academic? Probably not, I thought, for although the cloisters were undoubtedly part of the fourteenth-century college, they were also perhaps the most peaceful, secluded, and, with their ranks of memorial tablets, melancholy enclaves within the university, a fit spot for somber meditation. We did not, however, reach them, for evensong was about to commence in the college chapel, and instead of penetrating farther, we sat for a quarter of an hour in the antechapel listening to the soaring trebles of the boy choristers, Hardy unstirring and apparently entranced.

After this we returned to the Provost's lodgings, where the Provost's niece greeted us brightly with "Well, have you been to all the right colleges?" Fortunately she did not pause for a reply.

I went straight home to leaf through my *Jude*. Yes, Jude's first meeting with Sue, while his hopes were still high, had been beside the memorial, "at the cross in the pavement which marked the spot of the Martyrdoms," and it was past the memorial that he staggered with Arabella in his hour of despair. Something surely in that fictitious personage, although not his exclusion from the university, still mattered much to his creator.

The Hardys were driven back to Wessex next morning. He never slept away from home again.

THE WORLD'S MOST EXCLUSIVE CLUB

PHYLLIS FELDKAMP

Most men in the position of François Schneider, an influential power in French business and industry who figures in Georges Simenon's novel *The Bells of Bicêtre*, would feel that they had won all of life's first prizes.

At sixty-five Schneider is in perfect health. Every morning before he leaves his handsome *hôtel particulier* on the best street in Paris, he is given a treatment in his private exercise room by his yoga professor. Then he is shaved and combed and manicured by his personal barber. When he arrives at the Bourse, he increases his already formidable fortune through stock manipulations; his voice carries heavy weight on several consequential boards of directors; he cuts a mean figure in French racing circles; he is welcomed in the salons of the most clever and beautiful women in Paris.

Yet in spite of his eminent position Schneider is not satisfied. There is only one group that really interests him, and so far it has failed to admit him. Like dozens of others in

France who are exceptionally successful, he wants the crowning status symbol: he wants to belong to the Jockey Club of Paris.

Ever since it was founded in 1834, membership in the Jockey Club has been the ultimate stamp of French social approval. A choice museum piece that outsiders rarely see, the Jockey is the last stand of the remnants of the French aristocracy. Behind a deliberately anonymous façade at number 2 rue Rabelais, near the Rond-Point des Champs-Elysées, the members—descendants of *"les lions"* and *"les demi-dieux du Jockey"* who fascinated Balzac and Proust—relish their privacy and are united in tireless vigil against any intrusion on what they regard as their hereditary rights, even if most people think these were dispensed with a long time ago.

Parisians like to pin the label of "the world's most exclusive club" on the Jockey, although an Englishman might argue for the Royal Yacht Squadron at Cowes. Even if the club does not hold this distinction, it is unique in another respect. There is surely no other place in the world where General Charles de Gaulle can be disposed of in conversation as "the son of old Talhouet's tutor."

Although noble birth is not necessarily a requirement for eligibility, 85 per cent of those who make up the list of twelve hundred members have titles. At least three princes of the blood, two dozen *ducs,* and an array of lesser nobles compose a group whose names sound like a roll call from a French history book—if the book stops at the end of the nineteenth century.

Fame, intellectual brilliance, or distinguished public service are not of stunning significance at the Jockey Club. The Duc de Lévis Mirepoix and Jacques de Lacretelle, both of the Académie Française, do not belong to the club because of their writing talents, but in spite of them. The Duc de Doudeauville, who was the club's president for forty years until he died in 1963 at the age of ninety-three, summed up the prevailing attitude when someone broached the name of the celebrated novelist and Academician Paul Bourget, and began cataloguing his achievements with a view to proposing him.

"Fortunately," said the Duc, "we are still those few in France for whom these matters are, thank God, of no importance whatsoever."

Provided they meet certain conditions, men such as Simenon's fictional François Schneider, who have simply concentrated on making money more or less honorably, stand a better chance. If Schneider belongs to a family of the *haute bourgeoisie,* if his fortune has been ripening for three generations, and if his relations have been kindly disposed toward the idea of marrying off daughters to insolvent sons of the aristocracy, he may even be on firmer ground than a candidate whose pedigree should make him a shoo-in but whose great-great grandfather backed the wrong duke a hundred years before. Many of the Jockey's members have long memories.

The tangible rewards of admission are slight: an unobtrusive letter J after one's name in the *Bottin Mondain,* the French social register; access to the Jockey Club tribunes at the race courses of Longchamp, Chantilly, and Deauville; and, at the club, a passable lunch or dinner for a modest fifteen francs.

Still, the warning of a sophisticated Parisian, "It's useless to knock at the door of the Jockey Club. . . . There hasn't been a new name in the yearbook in fifty years," will not restrain the François Schneiders from continuing to try. Ambitious Frenchmen who have reached the top of the material and social heap figure that the gamble is worth taking; and although they know that the entire membership votes on new entrants under a system whereby one *"Non"* cancels out six *"Ouis,"* they cheerfully risk being blackballed as many as two or three times over. If they fail often enough, they are in good company, and there is even a certain distinction to be gained. The record for blackballs at the Jockey Club is held by Charles Haas, Marcel Proust's model for Swann, who was put down four times before finally being elected.

Men's clubs started in France during the reign of Charles **X** on the wave of Anglomania that swept in with the *Restauration*. Every fashionable young Frenchman wanted to be a fop à la Buckingham or Beau Brummell. It was very bon ton to wear yellow gloves, lean over balconies smoking cigars, and practice looking detached and bored. *Les dandys* ate plum cake and spiced gingerbread and spoke French with a strong British accent. "Goddam," went a popular song, *"Moi, j'aime les Anglais!"*

The moving spirit behind the formation of the Jockey Club and the man chiefly responsible for the introduction of thoroughbred racing into France was an Englishman, Lord Henry Seymour, a leading eccentric of the day. No one in France had ever cared much about sports, much less horse racing, although today some Frenchmen will argue that it began with a contest organized by Charlemagne and won by the legendary Bayard. However that may be, Godolphin Arabian, one of the three founding stallions of thoroughbred racing, was sold for next to nothing by Louis XV and was later discovered pulling a dray cart in Paris, whence he was shipped off to England to breed champions that were later eagerly imported into France. Seymour, a small man, was a sports fanatic whose house in Paris was fitted out with a gymnasium and a massage room, and was packed every day with languid dandies who came to watch him and his muscle-conscious cronies box, fence, and work out with punching bags.

Les dandys much preferred looking at exercise to actually taking it. They thought the size of Seymour's biceps, which was said to equal the span of a young girl's waist, *"un monstrueux développement."* They were appalled that a man of high birth and great fortune would go in for weight lifting and would join a crowd of thugs and rowdies to hang over the rails and shout at dog fights.

But Seymour loved racing, and in 1833 he founded, with the help of a number of like-minded and wealthy associates, the *Société d'Encouragement* for the improvement of horse breeding in France. Among his colleagues were the Russian Count Anatole Demidoff, who owned a bathtub carved from a single piece of malachite; Marshal Ney's son, the Prince de la Moskowa; and a Portuguese nobleman, De Gama Machado, who kept two hundred parakeets at home and never went out without one of them on his shoulder. (Seymour himself is supposed to have been the illegitimate son of the Marchioness of Hertford and the Adonis-like Comte Casimir de Montrond, Talleyrand's right-hand man. His money came from his mother's family, for the Marquess of Hertford, on whom Thackeray modeled the insufferable Lord Steyne in *Vanity Fair*, left Seymour out of his will.) Under the sponsorship of the Duc de Nemours and the Duc d'Orléans, the heir presumptive to the French throne, the aristocratic sportsmen set up the framework for thoroughbred racing in France, following the Newmarket regulations which prevailed in England.

Not every man in Paris was as taken with horses as they were. Few dandies cared to risk their skins as gentlemen jockeys; why expose oneself to useless dangers? To attract more supporters, Lord Seymour and his group organized the Jockey Club the next year, with Seymour as its president. Members were required to sign up in the *Société d'Encouragement*. Since the events of 1789, the word "club" had had nasty Revolutionary political connotations, and clubs were, in fact, prohibited by law. The Jockey was officially known as the *"Cercle de la Société d'Encouragement"* until early in the twentieth century.

Among the stated aims of the founders of the Jockey Club was "to make a chain to bind the classes together," but which particular classes was not specified. At least the club got *les dandys* out of Seymour's house for part of the day. As soon as there were two hundred members, they rented quarters conveniently near their favorite restaurant, the Café de Paris, and the ballet dancers' foyer at the Opéra, and had a wonderful time spending money on decorating the premises. They voted to admit the novelist Eugène Sue, who later became a Socialist deputy and was dropped for nonpayment of dues, but they turned down the poet Alfred de Musset.

Seymour, when not busy strengthening his little finger so that it could sustain a hundred-pound weight, was engrossed in his stables at Neuilly and his breeding farm at Glatigny. After the *Prix du Jockey Club* was established in 1836—it is the French Derby, run the second Sunday in June at Chantilly—his horses won the race for three years straight.

The horsy types at the Jockey were quickly outnumbered by the non-horsy types, who belonged to two categories: the gastronomes and the whist players. The gastronomes thought that funds for the encouragement of the breed might better be given over to the encouragement of better dining. Their preoccupation with sedentary, sybaritic meals and all-night high-stake gambling sessions infuriated Seymour. He flew into a temper when the board proposed revising the rules to use some racing funds for the club itself, and after less than two years in office he resigned as president.

He was a rotten loser. When, in 1840, one of his horses failed for the first time to win the *Prix du Jockey Club,* he claimed a foul; and when the charges were dismissed, he sold all his horses and pulled out of racing completely.

Since Seymour's time the club has maintained its ties with the *Société d'Encouragement,* which administers three tracks in France and the training grounds at Chantilly. Roughly half of the thirty-two to thirty-eight member chairs of the *Société* are by statute occupied by owners who are Jockey Club men and who serve on the racing commissions. But most present-day members of the club lack the passion for racing— and the money to keep large stables and breed race horses. Hunting, card playing, and the complex rules of social life concern them more. To the early men of the Jockey, whose idea of interesting gambling was a bet of something like ten thousand dollars on a single throw of the dice, the bridge games of today would seem tame. The members still appreciate the period charm of such exploits as that of Charles Laffitte and the Comte de Chateauvillard, who charged up the stairs on horseback in 1849 and trotted into the billiard room to play a round *a cheval,* but no one has shown any inclination to try anything similar for many years.

The prosperous era of Napoleon III fostered such extravagant gestures, which were epitomized in the Jockey Club set by the Duc de Gramont-Caderousse, who tossed his money around with plenty of panache. His crowning achievement was an Easter present for his mistress: a gigantic artificial egg, which cracked open to reveal a victoria with two horses, a coachman, and a footman. At this time the *beau idéal* of the Continental upper crust was Albert, Prince of Wales, later King Edward VII. He had only to turn up his trouser cuffs or leave the last button of his ample waistcoat undone to create a fashion among the *élégants* of Paris.

On Bertie's annual sprees across the Channel he joined his fellow members of the Jockey Club in paying surprise backstage visits at the theater and the Opéra. "With wavy whiskers and curly hair, square monocles set in the eye, towering stovepipe hats on their heads, the fast young men of the day drifted along the passages to knock at the little iron door which gave access to the wings of the stage." The members of the *corps de ballet* were the biggest snobs in Paris. They graded their suitors according to their clubs. The Jockey came first, and after that, the *Cercle de la rue Royale,* the *Cercle Agricole,* and the *Cercle de l' Union;* the dancers snubbed everyone else.

As an imposing symbol of the good life, Edward VII formed a one-man link between the Second Empire and the golden *Belle Epoque,* which stretched across the 1890's well into the new century. On his official trip to Paris in May, 1903, when laying the groundwork for the *Entente Cordiale* (which was to make allies of those two ancient enemies, France and England), Bertie lunched with Jockey Club intimates as a matter of course and attended the races at Longchamp. His favorite companions included two members who were source material for Proust—Charles Haas and General de Galliffet.

An exotic club member at the turn of the century who was welcomed by all of the elect—with the exception of Edward VII—was that decadent bloom, Comte Robert de Montesquiou, another Proust original. He served as the model for the depraved Baron de Charlus and worked hard at the game of aestheticism. Montesquiou also posed for J.-K. Huysmans's hero, Des Esseintes, in *Against the Grain*. "His Arrogance," as Montesquiou was called by a society belle, belonged to one of the finest old families in France and was descended from Charles de Baatz, on whom Dumas based the character of d'Artagnan in *The Three Musketeers*. His wit was vicious, his manner supercilious, his hair marcelled. Anatole France avoided Montesquiou at parties. "I can't bear that man who is always telling me about his ancestors," he complained.

Kings counted in those days. In 1905 the Jockey Club had among its members the reigning monarchs of five countries: England, Belgium, Holland, Denmark, and Serbia. Keeping up with Edward VII and his peers cost money, and the price of racing stables and social éclat was paid more and more often by great fortunes from across the Atlantic. Such American figures as August Belmont and assorted Wideners, Vanderbilts, and Biddles became familiar on the French turf.

American wives of Jockey Club men helped to strengthen the perverse affection for the United States that has always been shown by the aristocracy in France, despite differences in outlook on the form a proper government ought to take. In the Jockey Club today there are about twenty American members, among them former Secretary of the Treasury Douglas Dillon, U.S. Ambassador to Great Britain David K. E. Bruce, and Mr. Julian Allen of the Morgan bank in Paris. Parisians who are not in the know blink when they occasionally read in the newspapers that a dinner has been given at the Jockey Club for, of all people, "The Sons of the Revolution." These are, of course, sons of the *American* Revolution.

No Nazi goose-stepped into the Jockey during World War II, even if some of the nobility did feel that Vichy was the country's legal, albeit temporary, government. A great many members of fighting age earned the *Croix de guerre* and several, notably Emmanuel d'Harcourt and Comte Robert de Vogüé, were star performers in the Resistance.

After the Liberation the club flung its doors open to American officers. Some confusion ensued. One officer, who was looking for a strip-tease cabaret also called "Le Jockey Club," but in Montparnasse, sat down to dinner and asked the maître d'hôtel when the floor show began.

The club's building, like any other of the Baron Haussmann era, is undistinguished. There are no initials on the door mat. The only equestrian motifs within are the club's collection of racing paintings, the horsehead gold buttons on the footmen's blue livery, and the big brass scale for weighing the gentlemen jockeys at the foot of the staircase in the entrance hall. When footmen present a letter on a tray, they take the precaution of first putting the mail in a fresh envelope—a practice they have followed ever since a member recognized his wife's handwriting on a note being delivered to the man sitting in the next chair.

Whenever they meet, members always shake hands, even if it means putting down a magazine or a hand of cards first. The story of the two Jockey Club members who recognized each other at opposite ends of the bathing area at Deauville and swam the length of the beach to shake hands is probably untrue, as no one who is anybody would dream of going into the water at Deauville.

It is considered beyond the pale to ask anybody in the club his name. The beautiful manners of *la vieille France*, which have practically vanished from the rest of the national landscape, remain in an ideal state of preservation at number 2 rue Rabelais; and any non-U speech immediately chills the atmosphere. Woe to the chance visitor who acknowledges an introduction with the telltale bourgeois *"Enchanté."* "To be received at the Jockey Club," says the Marquis de Rochechouart, a member of the committee who sometimes speaks for the inner circle, "is to be considered 'just like us.'"

The club has been portrayed as "the only place where one

can still be treated as a gentleman and can authenticate one's title; where admission is the equivalent of the honors of the court." Small wonder that eyebrows shot up in the *haut monde* a few years ago when an anonymous genealogist using the pseudonym of "Charondas" printed a little green book, *Un Juge d'armes au Jockey Club,* which was a well-documented tabulation of the number of dubious, and even fake, titles to be found on the membership list. Two weeks after it was published there was not a copy left for sale.

The *Association d'Entr'aide de la Noblesse Française,* to which many of the *ducs et pairs de l'ancien régime* at the Jockey belong, bases legitimacy of title on the direct and masculine line only. Many proud *ducs* were unpleasantly surprised to find themselves in the company of self-made *comtes* and *vicomtes,* ennobled only by hyphenation with their grandmothers' names. The news came at a particularly awkward time, since Prince Philip had just joined the club. (The Duke of Windsor is also a member, as was his late brother, George VI. The Comte de Paris—pretender to the French throne, a descendant of Louis-Philippe and head of the house of Orléans—does not belong to the club but his distant cousin, the Duc de Nemours, does.)

As a result of exposures in the little green book, more than one carefully arranged betrothal crumbled. *Soi-disant* barons downed brandies at the bar like condemned men. A spurious marquis had a nervous breakdown. Self-appointed aristocrats, confronted with the evidence, were invited to tear up their visiting cards and have new ones engraved with their legitimate names.

"We do not simply admit a man," one of the clubmen has said, in describing the special air of the rue Rabelais, "He is accepted into a family." If he is a Broglie, a Ganay, a Gramont, a d'Harcourt, a Vogüé, or a La Rochefoucauld, there will be from five to sixteen members of his own family already in the Jockey. As soon as sons have finished their schooling with the *Frères Oratoriens* at Pontoise or at the *Lycée Janson de Sailly* in Paris, and have got their degrees from "*Sciences-*

Po" (now *l'Institut d'Etudes Politiques*) or spent a few years at the Harvard School of Business, they are introduced into the *Cercle*—"before they are old enough to get into any trouble," says a French aristocrat.

This familiar family climate leaves some men lukewarm. "The principal advantage," grumbled one of them recently, "is that it is the only spot on the face of the earth where you can be sure that your neighbor holds his fork the same way you do."

When they are voted in behind the red screens on the landing of the big staircase, young men of the Jockey Club join a group of courtiers who are without a court. Until the day when they are buried with their illustrious ancestors in the private cemetery of Petit-Picpus, a few yards from the common pit into which the decapitated bodies of some thirteen hundred noble victims of the Terror were thrown during the Revolution, men of the Jockey are assured of at least one refuge in this world from all that is ordinary, all that is vulgar. That is more than most men can look forward to, or perhaps want to.

FOUR SCORE
AND
SEVEN HOURS
AGO . . .

ROBERT S. GALLAGHER

Bringing forth a new nation, despite certain evidence to the contrary, involves a lot more than hiring a cartographer, denouncing the "imperialist, neo-colonial policies" of the United States, and then accepting generous offers of aid and assistance from Washington. Naturally, it helps to have a capital, preferably one with a good view, and enough cash to defend it during the independence ceremonies, at which a strange flag will be raised to the stirring cadences of an unfamiliar anthem. But this is hardly as simple as it might seem. To be sure, the departing colonial masters can be expected to provide a freshly painted government house, and a week's pay for the constabulary may be obtained by raising the fees for exit visas. Anyone, alas, can design a flag—and often has. A national anthem, however, is a different matter, one that demands careful consideration, the utmost in tact, and a touch of creative larceny.

Why have an anthem at all? It is a question most frequently asked by those who have not tried to start a country of their own or who have attempted to memorize all one hundred and fifty-eight Homeric verses of the Greek anthem. The answer is protocol. Without the accustomed rituals of diplomacy, foreign ministers would arrive and depart unheralded and unsung; in fact, they might choose not to arrive at all. International intercourse would be severely curtailed: treaties would remain unnegotiated and unrenegotiated and unsigned; trade would be hampered, alliances unforged, and wars undeclared; foreign aid would not be appropriated, and Keynesian economists would mutter darkly about the growing National Surplus.

But if an anthem is a necessity, as it appears to be, how does one go about composing one? The experience of the long-established nations, whose anthems evolved through tradition and habit, is of little use to the emergent nation. For instance, the Italians are perpetually donning "The helmet of Scipio" and wondering "Where is Victory?" The Poles seemingly never tire of urging: "On! On! Dabruski!" (the general who led their legions at the end of the eighteenth century), and the Portuguese gustily reminisce about their "heroes of the sea." The Dutch, somewhat incongruously, still vocalize the pledge by their valiant prince, William of Nassau, of "a life's loyalty" to the king of Spain. Even mountainous Andorra, with a smaller population than Ravenna, Ohio, remembers that:

The great Charlemagne, my Father,
From the Saracens liberated me . . .
I was born a Princess,
A Maiden neutral between two nations;
I am the only remaining daughter
Of the Carolingian empire.

Though a measure of braggadocio is good for the national psyche, there are limits beyond which chauvinistic pride becomes pretension. For example, the postholocaust archaeologist confronted an eon hence with the parched fragment

Our valor and our writings are the envy of the ages. . . .

149

The Gems of the East are her land and sea.
Throughout the world her good deeds flow from pole to
    pole,
And her name is her glory since time began

might, without more evidence, have difficulty assessing
Lebanon's actual role in the current galaxy of nations.

Actually, the best solution to the lyrics problem, if the
new African states are valid examples, seems to be a sprightly,
innocuous blend of optimism and necessity. Very often the
African anthems spell out a particular trinity of national
need: in the Congo it is "unity, work, progress"; in the bor-
dering Central African Republic it is "work, order, and
dignity"; in Mali, the chant is for "one people, one goal, one
faith"; the natives of Rwanda seek "peace, truth, comprehen-
sion"; and the Malawians sing to "put down each and every
enemy/Hunger, disease, envy."

The question of who will write the anthem is immensely
simplified by electing a poet as president. Senegal did in
1960, and Léopold Sédar Senghor rose to the occasion:

Sound, all of you, your Koras,
Beat the drums,
The red Lion has roared,
The Tamer of the bush with one leap has rushed forward
Scattering the gloom.

But this solution has its obvious limitations; so do official
commissions, although it is worth noting that it was not a
committee that produced the ear-jarring opening couplet
of the second verse of "God Save the Queen":

O Lord our God arise,
Scatter her enemies . . .

From a political standpoint, there are certain advantages to
be gained from conducting a nationwide anthem contest; if
nothing else, the competition has the effect of informing the
population that it now belongs to such-and-such country.
The winning entry, of course, should receive an appropriate

state award, say political amnesty. An act of the legislature is all that is necessary to make the song official, but if a general consensus is more desirable, then there is always the example of Kenya, whose anthem was adopted by the public acclamation of its school children.

One caution: as a rule, it is best to avoid politics, ideologies, and especially personalities. The Soviet Union, faced with the pragmatic exigencies of turning back Germany's "barbaric hordes" in 1943, scrapped the "Internationale" in favor of a more patriotic ballad extolling Lenin and Stalin. All was harmonious until 1956, when Khrushchev announced that his predecessor wasn't worth singing about. The Russians, past masters at the loose-leaf approach to history (the *Great Soviet Encyclopedia* once issued its readers razor blades to help them replace a selection on the NKVD's Beria with one on the Bering Strait), simply deleted the vanquished Generalissimo with a pen stroke. But the Bulgarians, lacking the revisionist experience of their Soviet comrades and confronted with

> *How great is the sun of our Lenin and Stalin,*
> *Whose unequaled splendor throws light on our way!*
> *The hearts which Dimitrov [d. 1949] has fired are flaming*
> *In struggle and work with so dazzling a ray!*

finally capitulated in 1962 and held a new anthem contest.

Finding an appropriate musical score is no problem, so long as it is vaguely familiar and within the octave range of half the population and two-thirds plus one of the legislature. Most hymnals are a veritable trove for the unimaginative composer (a practice that originated with the English, who launched the anthem fad in the eighteenth century). If a hymn doesn't seem apropos—and mention of a Supreme Being is now passé—the leitmotifs of native folk songs interspersed with swatches of the "Marche Consulaire" will suffice. For thirteen nations, such as Spain, Afghanistan, Saudi Arabia, and Mauritania, the music is enough; even Kuwait, which could afford a regiment of Alan Jay Lerners, prefers to do without words. But such caution runs counter to that daring impulse pounding in the breasts of all those who, having almost ruptured their vocal cords singing the "Star-Spangled Banner," secretly long to launch a new nation on a Gregorian chant.

THE
GAME OF
GO

J. A. MAXTONE GRAHAM

About four thousand years ago a warlike Chinese emperor called Yau (or, according to dissenting authorities, another warlike Chinese emperor called Shun) invented the game of Go. Doubtless trying out crafty military tactics with pieces of stone arranged on a plank of wood, he soon developed his idea into a formalized game that in the ensuing centuries has kept billions of Orientals happy and quiet for hours, sometimes days, on end.

Chess, also of Oriental origin, is normally regarded as the classic war game: indeed, it is not hard to see the military comparisons—with the pawns, those cheap scouts and disposable cannon fodder, driven on from behind by a ponderous king surrounded by his variously versatile court. That, at least, is the way wars used to be waged.

Today, kings and queens in real life are thinning out; cavalry, despite their knightlike ability to leap over obstacles, are not to be found in the best armies; the humble infantryman, slogging forward one square at a time, is an anachronism. War today is not chess; war, as fought in Vietnam for example, is Go.

Go is essentially a game of surrounding, of isolating, of capturing an area and imprisoning all the enemy therein; a game of threat and counterthreat, of infiltration, of communications cutting, of the swift and unexpected parachute drop. If chess is a battle, Go is an entire war, with pockets of action going on at several different points of the board simultaneously. You think you are doing fine around Quang Ngai, and suddenly you observe your opponent developing a beastly plot against your territory near Danang.

In Go, encirclement is all, and its strategy seems to govern the subconscious thinking of Oriental militarists. In September, 1965, Marshall Lin Piao wrote a fifty-thousand-word article on the subject of global war, pointing out that Chinese support of revolution in underdeveloped countries was just a step toward the eventual encirclement of America and western Europe. At the same time he commented on Mao's theory that rural revolutionary base-areas must be established so that cities can be surrounded from the countryside. Any Go player who has watched his secure little group of men gradually threatened by encroaching guerillas will know just how this feels.

Go is now played more in Japan than in China. The equipment for the game, which is played by 10 per cent of the hundred million Japanese, is as simple as can be: one flat board, squared by nineteen lines each way; one hundred and eighty white counters; one hundred and eighty-one black counters. (The total, they say, equals the number of days in the year. Actually . . . Oh well, never mind.) The pieces are shaped like small, fat buttons. You go on placing them on the board until neither of the two players can make another valid move. You place the men on the intersections of the lines, not in the squares, as with chess and checkers. You make no *moves*: play consists only of placing men on the board, encircling an area, and removing enemy prisoners.

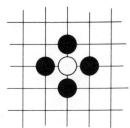

The basic prisoner-taking situation works as shown at left.

This results in the capture of the white piece, which is removed from the board. The vacant area has been conquered by Black. Often a great number of prisoners are taken in one operation:

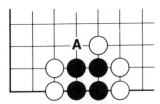

By placing one soldier at point A, White can capture all the enclosed black men. (The edge of the board is more or less the equivalent of the sea.) A group can keep "alive" if there are two breathing spaces, or *eyes*, open in the ranks. White cannot play in either spot without being captured. If Black is unwise enough to play in one, White can play in the other and claim capture of the whole

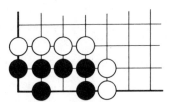

lot. So Black leaves the position as shown, and the battle stops in that part of the country—with White having a decided advantage.

Go is to Japan as baseball is to America or cricket to England. There are massive collections of Go proverbs ("There are times when even a fight over nothing means something.") There are Go professionals, Go magazines, Go championships. When a big game is being waged between two leading players, the moves in the contest are televised, and on boards in cafés and at street corners each new move is reproduced, its subtleties and future implications to be marveled over—and argued about—by passers-by.

Writers on Go can earn a more-than-respectable living once they have mastered the particular journalese of their profession: "Now the clouds are gathering in to inundate the valley"; "Black's three moves comprise an ideal, masculine pattern." The technical instructions seem complicated at first, even though there's always a helpful diagram: "Black 2 and 4 comprise a frequently employed *tsuke-hiki* pattern. Should White resort to a *katetsugi* move by occupying 5, Black is advised to occupy the *san-san* point in the corner position. Black 6, moreover, is an extremely exquisite move, inasmuch as it helps defend Black's corner position from a possible *uchikomi* by White."

For many centuries excellence in Go tactics has been a ready recommendation for promotion in the Japanese business world and in the armed forces. Indeed, in the seventeenth century they started a National Academy of Go from which generals and admirals had to graduate to prove their mastery of war strategy. The game is still avidly played, as an extracurricular activity, in Oriental war colleges today.

You can learn the three essential rules in five minutes—and then spend a lifetime working your way up toward proficiency. Go players are graded, as in judo, by *dans*, ninth *dan* being the highest. Top player of all is given the title of Hon-inbo, from the unbeatable player of that name who lived three hundred years ago.*

No Occidental player has ever got anywhere near stardom. When in 1966 a middle-grade (fifth-*dan*) Japanese professional visited America, he played nine simultaneous games against New York's best players, and gave them all a handicap. He lost only twice. To become a first-class player, it is best to start within a few years of learning to walk, and then to play, with a suitable handicap, against as good a player as you can find. Until the start of the last war, Go was hardly played outside Japan, Korea, and China; but curiously enough, in recent years, while the Japanese have been taking up bridge and golf with nearly as much skill as energy, the British and Americans have been plunging into Go. Takashi-

* Hon-inbo-Sansa, the first great champion, left a number of *waka* (thirty-one-syllable) poems for Go players to ponder, including this scrutable precept: "Ridiculous indeed is he who forgets to consider *his* shortcomings while he points out those of others."

maya, a Japanese department store in New York, sells half a dozen six-dollar sets a day. Every large city has its Go circle: the American Go Association, founded about 1933, numbers twenty clubs and six hundred players, and there are at least a hundred thousand unaffiliated players. One American woman, a computer programmer, took the trouble to learn Japanese so that she could read technical Go books in the original. So far, Bell Laboratories and IBM are the only large corporations that have Go teams. Go is not part of the curriculum at West Point or the Harvard Business School—not yet. But various pundits, admittedly Go buffs themselves, have forecast that the game will oust chess to become the leading intellectual game for men who have IQ's between 110 and 190.

As a keen and (so many friends say) ruthless competitor in any indoor contest from ticktacktoe to Scrabble, I became eager to find out what there was about Go that could appeal to so many people for forty centuries. I wrote to the secretary of the Nippon Club in London to ask if anyone could help me, and a few days later I played my first game of Go with Mr. Takizawa, the London representative of a Tokyo import-export firm.

Mr. Takizawa is in his thirties, but since he took the game up only a couple of years ago, he belongs to no *dan* at all. He volunteered to give up some of his working hours to play with me. I met him at his office in Finsbury Square at one o'clock on a Saturday. After lunch we went to the Nippon Club, which commands a fine situation on the Thames Embankment. Upstairs, Mr. Takizawa ordered tea and got out the board, while I pondered a huge notice on the wall that was all in Japanese characters except for the solitary word "adjust" somewhere about the second paragraph.

The board was not one of the best, just a plain slab of ex-otic-looking wood a couple of inches thick and about twenty inches square. It couldn't have cost more than five or six dollars. Mr. Takizawa lowered his nose to the wood. "Is not *kaya*," he said. "No smell." *Kaya*, I learned later, is the Japanese name for the fetid yew, which gives off a noxious odor pleasing to Go players. The best sort of *kaya* board, six inches thick and mounted on short, ritualistically carved legs, can cost as much as nine hundred dollars, including the black counters carved from heavy gray slate, and the whites from shells of specially bred clams. The same game, when played in Korea, is called Pa-tok, and the hollow board, which incorporates an arrangement of hidden strings, gives off a musical sound each time a stone is played. It must be very distracting.

"I give you nine stones," said Mr. Takizawa. "Thank you," I said, bowing slightly. (Nine stones at the start of the game constitute the biggest handicap the game allows.) I started to arrange nine black stones to encircle a useful chunk of territory. "No, please," advised Mr. Takizawa. "You must put them there, and there, and . . . ," he said, pointing to nine darkened spots at the intersections of certain of the lines. "Here is where you put handicap stones." In four thousand years of play these points have been found to be the most effective, and I obeyed, arranging my nine stones in a square.

"I commence," said Mr. Takizawa, taking a white stone and slapping it firmly down about halfway between two of my handicaps. I placed a black—fairly craftily I thought—next to his stone, with the subtle idea of eventually pinning him down at the edge of the board. It wasn't a good move, apparently, and he counseled me to start another operation in the opposite corner of the board, away up near Hanoi or somewhere. By joining up my scattered forces I could quickly encircle and control quite a large area of country, but Mr. Takizawa made a quick parachute drop just where I'd planned to create a solid, invincible stronghold. "Aha! Now I cut your communications," he said. In an effort to surround and remove him, I placed a stone to the landward side of his last play. He smiled politely, exposing a complete set of gold teeth. "That move is very meaningless. You should go here now. See, if you stay there, then I do this, and you do that, and I do this, and those black stones are in *great peril*."

Gradually I got the hang of the guerilla tactics involved,

and my very meaningless plays became less frequent. We reached some kind of deadlock in one corner, with Mr. Takizawa clearly in a commanding position but just unable to bring about my total surrender because of my two *eyes*. In another corner, thanks largely to my immense handicap, I had complete mastery, and even captured five of his white stones in one brief and bloody skirmish. In yet another area Mr. Takizawa took one of my stones by surrounding it with four of his. After a few moments' study I saw that by putting down one of mine, I could take the last white he had placed. I did so.

"No," said Mr. Takizawa, pained at my ignorance. "That is *ko*."

"*Ko?*"

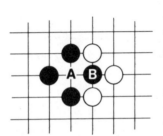

He explained to me about the *ko* situation, which necessitates about the only artificial rule in the game. Here is the simplest *ko* position, and the one that we were in. Obviously the game could go on forever in this way: White plays at A and takes Black, Black plays at B and takes White, White plays at A, etc. So there has to be a rule that the second player, faced with a *ko* position, make one play elsewhere, and of course this gives his opponent time, if he wishes, to seal up the hole.

"If you do not do something good soon, you will lose all those thirteen stones," said Mr. Takizawa sadly. I did something soon, but something bad, and within a couple of moves he was picking up a fistful of my army and dumping them unceremoniously on the table. In another section of the fighting, at a loss to embarrass my opponent by stealth, I shut my eyes and dropped a black stone at random. For ten minutes there was no sound from Mr. Takizawa except a heavy and worried breathing.

"That is *very* good play, *very* meaningful," he hissed. I

blushed. It had been immediately obvious to him, although not to me, that his situation in one entire quarter of the board was completely hopeless; he did not risk any more troops by playing there again. All the same, it *was* obvious to me that Mr. Takizawa was gaining ascendancy wherever we had clashes—a square or two here, a stone or two there—although he was making little of the central portion that was more or less enclosed by my nine handicap stones.

"There, we cannot play more," he said, after I had concentrated for two hours. (Top players in important matches sometimes battle on for twelve or more hours.) "Now we score." Heavy at heart, as I visualized my ignominious defeat, I helped him fill in the *dame* positions, empty spaces not vital to either side, and then we each took the prisoners we had captured and used them to fill in the holes in the territory held by that color.

Then, with a calculating series of maneuvers that my simple Occidental brain could not follow, Mr. Takizawa moved everything around rather quickly and transformed the areas controlled by each of us into trim rectangles. I wondered, bitterly, how much he would beat me by.

"Very good," said Mr. Takizawa graciously. "You have win. Eighty-nine to forty-five."

I must say, I felt rather surprised, rather as President Johnson would have if Ho Chi Minh had sent him a message that it had been a great game—but that a seven-stone handicap would be quite enough next time.

HIGH-SEAS SOCIETY

TIMOTHY S. GREEN

Whenever that prince of art dealers, Lord Duveen of Milbank, boarded an Atlantic liner on his yearly pilgrimage to and from Europe (in keeping with his irrefutable observation that Europe had plenty of art and America plenty of money), his first task invariably was to scan the passenger list. Having picked out a wealthy passenger who might well be persuaded to invest at least a part of his fortune in works of art, Duveen would go in search of a friendly deck steward, hand him a one-hundred-dollar bill, and ask him to be so kind as to place his deck chair next to that of his potential client. Then, as the two men, snugly wrapped around in steamer rugs, sipped their morning bouillon in mid-ocean, Duveen would casually strike up a conversation, and it was never long before he turned it to his favorite topic—art. In more than fifty years of Atlantic travel, right up to his death in 1939, Duveen became, understandably, a popular man with deck stewards. But his investment in them was handsomely rewarded. On one occasion an obliging steward placed the art dealer's deck chair next to that of Alexander Smith Cochran, the millionaire carpetmaker from Yonkers. The acquaintance thus begun resulted in Cochran's buying more than five million dollars worth of art objects from him over the years.

It was a rare voyage when Duveen could not find some distinguished patron—or potential patron—of art among the galaxy of tycoons, politicians, writers, and actresses who crowded the luxurious first-class accommodations of the Atlantic liners before World War II. Indeed he found that the unique atmosphere aboard the liners helped to soften his clients' resistance to the extraordinarily high prices he invariably charged. The fifty years of Duveen's voyaging coincided, happily for him, with the high-water mark of Atlantic sea travel, when the watchword was "the best of everything" —whether the champagne and caviar, the marble baths in the staterooms, or the Persian carpets in the lounges. Coupled with this opulence were snobbery and social pressures quite as potent as any on dry land.

The Atlantic ferry—or "ocean railway," as Samuel Cunard, whose *Britannia* pioneered a scheduled Atlantic passenger service in 1840, liked to call it—developed in time a mystique and tradition all its own. The splendor of the ships became a matter not just of commercial pride but of national prestige among the British, the Americans, the Germans, the French, the Italians, and the Dutch. Governments were frequently persuaded to subsidize luxury liners far beyond their economic value. As a result no other shipping route in the world has ever spawned such extravagances or such follies. Where else have ships had Byzantine chapels and Pompeian swimming pools, dining rooms styled like the palace of Versailles, lounges decorated in mock Inigo Jones, and Turkish baths like eastern harems?

The rivalry between these colossi was so intense that one Frenchman, writing at the time of the maiden voyage of the *Normandie* in 1935, speculated: "What palace, what Triumphal Way, what memorial have we built to perpetuate our civilization, as the cathedrals perpetuate that of the Middle Ages, the castles of the Loire that of the Renaissance, and Versailles that of the age of Louis XIV?" His answer was, of course, the *Normandie*.

The special snobbery that blossomed aboard the ships often made it easier for captains to pilot their way around the drifting icebergs off the Grand Bank than to chart a course through the social shoals of choosing guests for the six or eight places at the captain's table. One captain recalled in his memoirs that his sole bedside reading during his first three years in command was the British and American *Who's Who*, so that he could whittle out from the passenger list the right half-dozen to join his table.

The beginnings of the liners, of course, were much more humble. The *Britannia*, the wooden paddle-steamer that sailed from Liverpool for Boston with sixty-three passengers on July 4, 1840, inaugurating Samuel Cunard's "ocean railway," was a mere two hundred and seven feet long. She would have fitted snugly on the foredeck of either of the *Queens*. The real achievement of the voyage, which took fourteen days, was the comforting knowledge that because the *Britannia* and her three sister ships in Cunard's infant fleet were steam-driven, they would arrive at their destination close to schedule. This was true luxury after the days of occasional sailing packets when an Atlantic voyage might take anywhere from thirty to one hundred days, with passengers supplying their own food.

Charles Dickens, who made a crossing on the *Britannia* in the winter of 1842, was hardly impressed by the opulence of the accommodations. The stateroom of " 'Charles Dickens, Esquire, and Lady,' " he recalled in his *American Notes*, was an "utterly impracticable, thoroughly hopeless, and profoundly preposterous box." As for his bunk: "nothing smaller for sleeping in was ever made except coffins."

Once Dickens had recovered from the worst throes of seasickness, he managed to sample the minimal charms of the saloon of an Atlantic passenger ship of the 1840's. "At one, a bell rings, and the stewardess comes down with a steaming dish of baked potatoes, and another of roasted apples; and plates of pig's face, cold ham, salt beef; or perhaps a smoking mess of rare hot collops. We fall-to upon these dainties; eat as much as we can (we have great appetites now); and are as long as possible about it. If the fire will burn (it *will* sometimes) we are pretty cheerful. If it won't, we all remark to each other that it's very cold, rub our hands, cover ourselves with coats and cloaks, and lie down again to doze, talk, and read . . . until dinner-time."

Sailing the stormy Atlantic was still high adventure, and William Makepeace Thackeray, on his voyage across the Atlantic on the *Canada* in 1852, was almost overcome with admiration for captain and crew. He says in *Round-about Papers*: "We trust our lives to these seamen, and how nobly they fulfill their trust! . . . Whilst we sleep, their untiring watchfulness keeps guard over us." Mark Twain declared that those "practical, hard-headed, unromantic Cunard people would not take Noah himself as first mate till they had worked him up through all the lower grades and tried him ten years . . ."

The immediate success of the Cunard fleet did not go long unchallenged. In 1849 the New York shipowner E. K. Collins announced he was building a steamer fleet "to sweep the Cunarders off the Atlantic." The United States government was persuaded to forget its traditional hostility to subsidies and grant the Collins Line nearly twenty thousand dollars per voyage for mail carrying. The ships were to be faster and more luxurious than the Cunarders, with steam heat in the staterooms and electric bells for summoning the stewards.

The Collins challenge ended, however, in tragedy. In 1854 the line's *Arctic* sank after a collision in fog with a French ship; more than three hundred lives were lost. Less than two years later the Collins's *Pacific* sailed out of Liverpool with one hundred and fifty-nine passengers and crew and was never seen again. Not surprisingly, the United States government now began to fight shy of maintaining the mail subsidy, and in 1858 the Collins Line collapsed.

But the spirit of transatlantic competition continued to thrive. The commercial and national rivalries that were to blossom into such extravagance at the end of the century had already been born. The Germans had entered the fray with the Hamburg-American Line in 1848 and the North German Lloyd Line in 1857; the Compagnie Générale Transatlantique (French Line) started operations in 1861; the Holland-America Line began as a private Dutch company in 1872. In Britain itself the White Star Line, the Inman Line, and the Guion Line were all attempting to woo passengers away from Cunard ships.

When Dickens traveled on the *Britannia,* there had been a cow on deck in a padded stall to supply fresh milk for the voyage. By the early 1870's the breakfast menu alone offered beefsteaks, mutton chops, pork chops, veal cutlets, smoked salmon, broiled chickens, eggs, and mushrooms. The wine and spirits bar was open from 6 A.M. to 11 P.M., selling first-quality claret at six shillings per quart and brandy at three shillings a pint. There were still some regulations, however, that would have been entirely alien to the next generation of transatlantic passengers. Lights were put out in the saloons at 11:30 and had to be out in staterooms by midnight. Little notices reminded passengers: "As the labor of the servants must be very great, and the space required for a larger number absolutely prevents an increase, the passengers are requested to spare them as much as possible between the Meal Hours, and particularly preceding dinner."

But comforts were slowly creeping in. Private bathrooms were first introduced in the *Abyssinnia* and the *Algeria* in 1870, while the *Gallia,* launched in 1879, gave the first hint of the opulence of later years. Her saloon was decorated "in Japanese style, the walls being in panels of jasper red lacquer, with delicate Japanese designs in gold and soft colors portraying birds and flowers." There was even a fountain spouting in the center of the smoking room. Pianos were now installed in the saloons, and concerts took place. The *Aurania*

News recorded in 1888 that on one voyage "Lord Henry Grosvenor took the chair at the concert. Lady Henry Grosvenor sang 'The Brook,' a duet called 'Oh, wert thou in the cauld blast,' and 'Home Sweet Home.'" It was a perfect replica of a genteel musical soiree at an English country house.

The real heyday of Atlantic travel came, however, only after considerable engineering and other technical advances. Even in the 1870's and 1880's the real triumph of Atlantic travel was still the sheer feat of getting across the ocean safely on time. Only with the advent of steel ships, of twin and then quadruple screws driven by turbines, of electric lights and refrigeration, could real luxury be offered.

Lillie Langtry, the actress, found how trying an Atlantic voyage could still be when she first crossed from Liverpool to New York on the *Arizona*. "There were rats on the *Arizona*, long-coated and tame," she wrote in her autobiography, *The Days I Knew*. "Poor Mrs. Labouchère [her traveling companion], who was a victim to *mal de mer*, remained in bed nearly the whole of the voyage, and one morning, on opening her eyes, she was horrified to find a fat, genial rodent sitting on her chest. Alas, I knew that fellow! He used to sit and listen while I read to the invalid, and, with unwelcome familiarity, would indicate his need of water by rattling the chain in the washbasin."

John Burgess, the historian who crossed from Boston to Liverpool in 1871, wrote: "There were no napkins at the table, and when our passengers made a sort of protest to the company in regard to what we considered our hardships, on our arrival at Liverpool . . . old Mr. McIver [one of the early Cunard partners] replied that going to sea was a hardship, that the Cunard Company did not undertake to make anything else of it . . ." Vastly different sentiments were expressed in a Cunard "logbook" that was handed to each passenger in 1902. "From the moment of booking a berth the passenger's welfare is studied with the solicitude and aptitude born of long experience in conveying passengers between the Old

World and the New. He is gently encouraged to do all that will add to his comfort and convenience but guarded against falling into the many little errors to which the untraveled are prone, with a nicety which is quite an art." As for the ships— they were now what Cunard liked to call "a silent sermon in good taste."

In the space of thirty years a revolution had taken place in Atlantic travel. In 1876 the White Star Line's *Britannic*, holder of the Blue Riband for the fastest crossing, was a mere five thousand tons. The *Mauretania*, launched in 1907, displaced thirty-two thousand tons, while the giant *Bismarck*, launched at Hamburg in 1912, was more than fifty-six thousand tons. The liner, in the sense that we understand it today, had arrived. There was now space enough not only to carry ample crew to minister the travelers' every whim but to install gymnasiums, swimming pools, public rooms, and luxurious private suites. The first of the new generation were Cunard's *Lucania* and *Campania,* which the company labeled "the aristocrats of the Atlantic."

Actresses, opera singers, authors like Oscar Wilde, now found pleasure in crossing the Atlantic in comfort on their way to theatres or lecture tours in the United States. In 1893 alone, Cunard carried 18,500 first-class passengers across the Atlantic—far more than any of its rivals.

"Lily Langtry was installed in Twenty-third Street, New York," wrote F. Lawrence Babcock in his book *Spanning the Atlantic;* "Sarah Bernhardt, Yvette Guilbert, Eleanora Duse, Emmy Destinn, Ellen Terry, and dozens of other beautiful and talented women had crossed the ocean to find the metropolitan portions of American youth ready to fall at their feet. Hardly a Cunarder arrived but there was a throng of 'stage-door Johnnies' of the best quality waiting at the pier to greet some celebrity."

The traffic was not one way. Now that the Atlantic crossing was no longer an ordeal, it became fashionable for young American men to be seen sipping a glass of wine in Montmartre cellars or for daughters of rich New Yorkers to be allowed a year in Paris to round out their education. This was the age of tourism on a grand scale.

For the less well off, enterprising American travel agents advertised European cycling tours at one hundred dollars for the round trip. "Try steerage," one advertisement suggested. "As Hazlitt said of the 'Fairy Queen,' it won't bite you." Indeed steerage class was at last beginning to enjoy some of the benefits already accorded to the upper decks. The majority of the millions of emigrants who crossed the Atlantic in the last half of the nineteenth century had traveled in steerage. They were crammed into the bowels of the ship, bedded down on straw mattresses that were thrown overboard before it arrived at New York. They were fed from iron buckets. Some steamship companies even carried cattle in the steerage accommodations on the return voyage from New York to Europe.

Now, as the first-class passengers tucked into their champagne and caviar, steerage passengers were at least getting three meals a day served properly by stewards and even had a piano in their lounge. They no longer had to bring their own towels, and after 1900 the very term "steerage" was often replaced by "tourist" class.

Meanwhile, up on the first-class decks the splendors of the Edwardian era ashore were being emulated at sea. Orchestras, which became a regular feature of the liners after 1905, played the melodies of Lionel Monkton or the operettas of Gilbert and Sullivan far into the night. The steamer trunks were now crammed with white tie and tails for the men and a constant change of gowns for the ladies. "Remember . . . the one essential garment for a man aboard ship is a dinner-jacket," wrote Basil Woon in *The Frantic Atlantic,* a guide to Atlantic social etiquette. "He can (and frequently many of us do) dispense with all else, but the dinner-jacket is as necessary to an ocean traveler as a tailcoat is to a waiter. Without it you may not, except on the first and last nights out, come down to dinner. Without it you will have to sneak out of the smoking-room at eight P.M.

"Without it you will have no dances and no Great Moments with the young thing in crêpe-marocain on the lee of the starboard ventilator."

The pursuit of excellence aboard fomented national rivalries to build larger, faster, and more de luxe ships; and safety, as the *Titanic* was to demonstrate so tragically, was sometimes sacrificed for high living afloat. Together with the *Titanic*, the White Star Line's *Olympic* and the German trio *Imperator, Vaterland,* and *Bismarck* were all giants of more than forty thousand tons. All were decorated in a potpourri of styles.

The final glory was Cunard's *Aquitania*, which made her maiden voyage on the eve of World War I. The main drawing room was based on Robert Adam's plans for Lansdowne House in Berkeley Square, London. It had a high dome with lunettes in the center and a perfect Adam fireplace. There were large bay windows (not a porthole in sight). Over the chimney piece of carved statuary-marble was a copy of a painting by Giovanni Cipriani. The walls were decorated with classical fluted pilasters supporting an Adam frieze of scroll foliage surmounted by a cornice, and were hung with copies of paintings by Copley and Reynolds of the Duchess of Devonshire, the Marchioness of Hertford, and the daughters of George III.

The first-class dining room, complete with minstrel gallery, was supposed to convey to the passengers the sense that they were eating in the palace of the Sun King at Versailles. Over a marble buffet was a view of the park of the Grand Trianon; in the center of the ceiling was a massive oval painting, *The Triumph of Flora*, described as "after Jean Jacques Lagrenée" (a minor, late-eighteenth-century French painter). In the midst of the clouds floating across the sunlit sky the Goddess of Flowers welcomed other divinities who had come to pay her court.

The *Aquitania* boasted eight luxury suites named after famous painters—Holbein, Velázquez, Vandyke, Rembrandt, Reynolds, Gainsborough, Romney, and Raeburn. Copies of their paintings adorned the walls of each suite. This exotic decoration was responsible for inspiring perhaps the most notable of Lord Duveen's mid-Atlantic art coups. The astutely positioned deck chair was only a part of the art dealer's seagoing campaign to wear down his clients' resistance to his high prices. He made sure, too, that his suite was strategically placed near that of a potential client.

Thus on one memorable *Aquitania* voyage Duveen was installed next door to the California railroad magnate H. E. Huntington and his wife Arabella, who had booked the Gainsborough Suite. Huntington was a regular client of Duveen's, and naturally the art dealer was invited to dinner in the Gainsborough suite. Pride of the place in the private dining room went to a reproduction of *The Blue Boy*. During dinner, conversation turned to the picture. In his biography of Duveen, S. N. Behrman faithfully reports the exchange:

" 'Joe,' said H. E., with the confidence of one who knows that he can get the answer to anything, 'who's the boy in the blue suit?'

"Duveen said, 'That is a reproduction of the famous "Blue Boy." It is Gainsborough's finest and most famous painting.'

" 'Where's the original?' Huntington went on, with even more confidence. Duveen did not let his inquirer down. 'It belongs to the Duke of Westminster and hangs in his collection at Grosvenor House, in London.'

" 'How much is it?' asked H. E.

"Duveen was discouraging. 'It can probably not be had at any price,' he said."

Huntington, however, was not a man to be thwarted so easily. He pressed Duveen for a price, and finally the dealer said it might be six hundred thousand dollars—which was far more than the millionaire had ever paid for a painting.

"I might see my way clear to pay that much," Huntington said.

The Huntingtons disembarked at Cherbourg, but Duveen went on to Southampton. When the boat train deposited him in London, he hastened to call on the Duke of Westminster at Grosvenor House. He found the duke, whom he knew to be rather in need of some ready cash, quite happy to sell *The Blue Boy* and anything else in his collection that Duveen fancied. Duveen settled for *The Blue Boy*, together with Reynolds's *Sarah Siddons as the Tragic Muse* and Gainsborough's *The Cottage Door*. He paid about six hundred thousand dollars for all three, then hurried off to Paris to deliver *The Blue Boy* to the Huntingtons, whom he charged six hundred and twenty thousand dollars for the one picture. They were delighted at the coup; their sole complaint was that the original *Blue Boy* was not as blue as the reproduction in their *Aquitania* suite. But Duveen assured them that was no problem; he would have the painting cleaned and thus restored to the fresh blue that had first entranced them in their suite in mid-Atlantic.

Many other Duveen clients—Andrew Carnegie, Henry Clay Frick, and J. Pierpont Morgan—were regular Atlantic voyagers. They were treated with reverence by the shipping lines. Morgan was even shown the plans for the *Titanic* before she was built so that he could choose where he would like his suite to be. Whenever Morgan was returning to New York, his private yacht *Corsair* put out from the harbor with pennants flying to greet the incoming liner. Morgan would stand at the rail and wave his handkerchief enthusiastically as the ship came into berth. Then, the moment the lines were made fast to the dock, the *Corsair* would come alongside, and Morgan would step aboard her and steam off direct to his home. Once, when his wife was arriving alone on the *Oceanic*, Morgan took the *Corsair* out of the harbor to meet her and had his crew skillfully bring the yacht alongside the liner at sea. He grabbed for a perpendicular steel ladder running down the ship's side and began the long climb of sixty feet up to the deck with a cigar between his teeth and a straw hat on his head. He was then sixty-two years old and hardly a fit man. But, as passengers on the *Oceanic* placed bets on whether or not he would make it, he clambered over the rail, his face dripping with perspiration, and hurried off toward his wife's suite.

Not surprisingly, the close confines of these liners heightened all the social snobbery of dry land. Before the voyage
the captain and the purser spent as much time scrutinizing
the list of perhaps one hundred and fifty passengers whom
the head office had pointed out as being particularly important as they did debating fuel supplies or studying advance
weather reports. It was not simply a question of a person's
social, political, or business importance—the captain had to
be the perfect diplomat in not, quite unwittingly, selecting
violent adversaries to sit side by side at his table for five days.

The guest list for cocktail parties caused equal agonies of
mind; some people clearly rated an invitation from the captain, others were equal only to the purser. One liner captain
recalled tentatively suggesting a particular couple at his early
morning social strategy session with his purser. "Oh no, sir,"
replied the purser, appalled, "*they* are not for *you*. Leave
them to me."

The passengers, in turn, waited anxiously for the printed
white cards inviting them to this table or that party. A lavish
1920's promotion booklet, in the form of an ecstatic diary of
an *Aquitania* voyage, notes: "Tuesday—Tonight I had the
honor of being invited to the captain's room for cocktails
before dinner. I enjoyed the little party tremendously. The
captain of such a famous ship must always be a great sea-
man but I was not prepared for so much wit and charm—
and knowledge to boot—and I do not wonder that his invitation is the most coveted honor on board ship."

The old lady who, on being invited to sit at the captain's
table, snapped back to the purser, "young man, I haven't
paid all this money to eat with the crew" was indeed a rarity.
And half of the pleasure of an Atlantic voyage was the intimate shoulder-rubbing with the great.

Over the years passengers developed special devotions to
captains, to officers, to particular tables or cabins or even
stewards. The true art of being an Atlantic purser was to
know exactly which cabin this judge or that colonel liked;
the art of the restaurant manager was not just to conjure up

food but to know every whim of a whole generation of Atlantic travelers. For example, Henry Ford, Jr., met his first wife in the Verandah Grill aboard the *Queen Mary;* for many years afterward the same table at which he had first been introduced to her was always reserved for him on subsequent voyages. Even in the lounge or smoking room the stewards stayed on for decades, and on the first night a regular passenger would be greeted automatically with "Good evening, sir, your usual table is waiting."

They were, of course, well rewarded. Tips on the Atlantic have always been nearly three times as high as on the other main sea routes of the world. Captains and pursers often received handsome boxes of Havana Havanas from grateful passengers. One American lady even went so far as to bequeath almost her entire fortune to the officers and crew of the *Lucania,* with a special fifty thousand dollars set aside for her commander, Captain McKay.

The First World War did nothing to dim the enthusiasms or the prejudices of the Atlantic traveler. Indeed the 1920's ushered in the final fling of the giant liner. The competition to begin with was a little one-sided, for the three German liners *Imperator, Vaterland,* and *Bismarck* had all been taken over as part of Germany's reparation payments. They now became the *Berengaria* of the Cunard fleet, the *Leviathan* of United States Lines, and the *Majestic* of the White Star Line.

The social whirl continued undisturbed—although the *Berengaria* had a stock exchange aboard so that anxious investors could keep an eye on Wall Street and the City in London in between Turkish baths and before-lunch drinks in a smoking room that looked like a baronial mansion. One English baronet was so entranced with the ship that he used to fly around the world to pick up the *Berengaria* in New York or another port when she was cruising, solely to challenge her chef to culinary contests.

"Everybody on the *Berengaria,* even the dogs, were 'socially prominent,' " wrote one Cunard captain. "There was Gertrude Lawrence's dog, which she liked to exercise on deck each morning in defiance of regulations, and the melancholy incident when I caught her doing so and escorted her in grim silence back to the kennels. She sobbed all the way, bitterly and magnificently . . . [the *Berengaria*] was principally a gleaming and bejewelled ferry boat for the rich and titled: for the Sultan of Johore, Lord Duveen, the Earl of Warwick and many Cortlandts, Vanderbilts and Swopes." There was so much wealth aboard that a junior purser would regularly walk through the smoking room announcing "Ladies and gentlemen, we have reason to believe there are cardsharpers on board" just so no one could claim they had not been warned.

The liners were a happy hunting ground for a small army of swindlers and cardsharps who sometimes cleaned up with a five-thousand-dollar profit in one evening. Charles T. Spedding, *Aquitania* purser in the early twenties, wrote in his memoirs, "there was practically not a voyage but at least one gang was on board." Although one cardsharp threatened to shoot a purser when he was unmasked, most of them behaved outwardly with as much decorum as their fellow passengers. Indeed one, whom Spedding called "a perfect gentleman," made a fortune from traveling on Cunard and White Star Line ships and finally retired to write a book on the iniquity of gambling. By the end of his career he was so well known aboard the ships that he could no longer cheat, but he enjoyed such a colorful reputation that many passengers asked to play with him just to be able to impress their friends ashore with tales of gambling at sea.

Not all mid-Atlantic gambling ended so peacefully. One young German was swindled into thinking he was playing for a shilling a hundred instead of a shilling a point, then had to settle his debts out of his firm's money. He committed suicide a few weeks later.

Confidence tricksters worked a multitude of schemes. The simplest and most profitable was for a "lady" to strike up a conversation with her victim in the bar before dinner. After a couple of drinks she would suggest they adjourn to her stateroom, confiding that her "husband" was off having cock-tails with the captain. Then, at the crucial moment, the "husband" would burst in. The compromised passenger almost invariably reached for his checkbook; many parted with a thousand dollars to avoid a scandal.

Passengers' wealth was also tapped, perfectly legally of course, for seamen's charities at the daily tote on the ship's run and at concerts. It became a tradition for actors, actresses, or opera singers crossing the Atlantic to give their services at these concerts. Nellie Melba sang arias, P. G. Wodehouse read Jeeves stories, and an entire revue starring Gertrude Lawrence and Beatrice Lillie was staged in mid-ocean when the show was transferring from London to New York. The collections after the concerts occasionally raised as much as ten thousand dollars.

Charlie Chaplin, returning to Europe in the early 1920's for the first time since he had become an international star, reveled in the peace and elegance of first class on the White Star Line's *Olympic*. In *My Autobiography* he remembers: "At last I was alone in my cabin, which was stocked with flowers and baskets of fruit from my friends. It had been ten years since I had left England, and on this very ship, with the Karno Company; then we had traveled second class. I remember the steward taking us on a hurried tour through the first class, to give us a glimpse of how the other half lived. He had talked of the luxury of the private suites and their prohibitive price, and now I was occupying one of them. . . . A few hours out and the atmosphere was already English. Each night Eddie Knoblock and I would dine in the Ritz restaurant instead of the main dining-room. The Ritz was à la carte, with champagne, caviar, duck *à la presse*, grouse and pheasant, wines, sauces, and crepes suzette. With time on my hands I enjoyed the nonsense of dressing each evening in black tie. Such luxury and indulgence brought home to me the delights of money."

Even princes found that in the heady atmosphere of an Atlantic liner they could relax more easily than ashore. The

Duke of Windsor, when he was Prince of Wales, once hired the *Berengaria*'s orchestra to stay aboard the ship late at night after she was docked at Southampton so that he could conduct his own private concert. Before a tiny audience of startled ship's officers, the prince took the stand, Lord Louis Mountbatten took over the drums, and they whipped through a serenade of popular music that went on into the night. The prince explained afterward to the officers that this was the one place he could think of where he could escape the stiff formalities that inhibited him ashore.

Prohibition in the United States gave an added stimulant to the hilarity of Atlantic crossings. The moment the ship left her berth on the New York waterfront, a thirsty crowd of passengers gathered outside the bars, waiting for them to open the moment the magic three-mile limit was crossed. Then they drank as if they expected the ship to run dry at any second. On the return voyage there was even greater determination to knock back that final extra drink before the Ambrose lightship hove into view and the bar shutters snapped shut.

By the late 1920's national rivalries on the Atlantic were reasserting themselves as the North German Lloyd's *Bremen* won the Blue Riband that the Cunard liner *Mauretania* had held since 1907. The Italians with the *Rex*, the Germans with the *Europa,* and the French with the *Normandie* were all fighting for the prestige of having the newest and fastest ship on the run to New York. Cunard responded with the *Queen Mary* and later the *Queen Elizabeth* (which was completed only on the eve of war and did not make her proper maiden voyage until 1946).

Yet by the time most of these ships were in service, the grand era of the Atlantic ferry was almost over. The onset of the Depression had halved in one year the number of passengers crossing the Atlantic. Only for a few years immediately after World War II—when there were too many passengers chasing too few berths in the handful of remaining luxury liners—did the Atlantic trade return to anything like its former glory. But it was a short-lived finale. Already the character of the ocean liner business was changing. Shipping companies had to admit—and it took some of them a long time to do it—that they could not compete with air transport. The arrival of long-haul jets finally drove home the point to any shipowners who still dreamed nostalgically of the old days. On the liners that remain today there is a spirit of democracy that would have caused a mid-ocean crisis a generation ago. Instead of issuing that treasured handful of invitations to the captain's cocktail party, most captains now give a cocktail party for *all* their passengers, including those in tourist class. Cunard's new *Queen Elizabeth II* is essentially a one-class ship.

While the recent sales of the *Queen Mary* and the *Queen Elizabeth* have marked the final eclipse of Samuel Cunard's ocean railroad, many connoisseurs of the art of Atlantic travel saw the true end to the great era in 1950 when the thirty-six-year-old *Aquitania* steamed off on her final voyage to the breaker's yard. The *Aquitania* even more than the *Queen Mary* was a symbol of a unique period of ocean travel. "She was," as the British newspaper proprietor Lord Northcliffe once wrote, "a country house at sea with just the right number of people in it and plenty of room for them all."

THE
MAN WHO
CLEANED UP
SHAKESPEARE

E. M. HALLIDAY

One of my poignant memories of high school is the day when in third-year English we began to read *Othello*. Our teacher, who may as well be called Miss Jones, had ordered a neat, single-volume edition of the play because, as she explained, it was so much nicer to have each of Shakespeare's works all by itself. The books arrived in the middle of a May morning, and it was decided that we would plunge right in. Miss Jones undertook to read the first act aloud to us, and we listened with considerable attention as she declaimed the lines the Bard had invented for the introduction of Iago and Roderigo.

Everything went smoothly until the part where the two conspirators are outside Brabantio's Venetian home, ready to reveal to the senator his daughter's elopement with Othello. Miss Jones had really caught the spirit of the scene by this time and was delivering Iago's speech with a venom I never would have thought her capable of:

Zounds, sir, you're robb'd; for shame, put on your gown;

Your heart is burst, you have lost half your soul;
Even now, now, very now, an old black ram
Is tupping your white ewe.

A dead silence fell upon the room. Outside, on a nearby branch, a bird chirped; through the wall I could faintly hear Miss Kenyon, in history class, going on about the Reformation. A slow flush had crept up Miss Jones's neck and was diffusing across her cheeks.

"Miss Jones," said a plaintive voice from the back of the room, "What does that mean? About the ram?"

It was, as they say, a good question. Miss Jones, who by this time had turned back to stare raptly at the title page, answered by announcing amid some confusion that a mistake had been made—this was *not* the edition of *Othello* she had ordered. And so the neat little volumes were collected again; and I, for one, gave up my copy reluctantly.

I thought of this episode recently when I encountered the famous edition of Shakespeare smugly put forth in 1818 by Dr. Thomas Bowdler, F.R.S., S.A.; *The Family Shakespeare*, he called it: "In which nothing is added to the original text; but those words and expressions are omitted which cannot with propriety be read aloud in a family." I flipped through Volume VIII until I came to *Othello,* and sure enough, the old black ram was gone. It was clear to me that Dr. Bowdler and Miss Jones would have seen, if the expression may be pardoned, ewe to ewe.

A skimming perusal of the rest of the play provided several obvious samples of the sort of thing Bowdler thought too raw for the family circle. Totally absent were such touches of lyrical eroticism as, "Make love's quick pants in Desdemona's arms"; "They met so near with their lips, that their breaths embraced together"; and "He hath not yet made wanton the night with her, and she is sport for Jove." Dr. Bowdler could hardly pretend to his readers that sexual love had nothing to do with the plot of *Othello;* but he was going to make sure it was not presented as sport, spectator or otherwise.

It turns out, moreover, that "nothing is added to the original text" cannot be taken literally. Bowdler does add many words in the form of substitutions, and although these seldom amount to more than two or three at a time, the alteration they produce in Shakespeare's effect is often jarring. In that same opening scene of *Othello*, for instance, Iago lines out another famous metaphor to dazzle Brabantio, Dr. Bowdler, and Miss Jones: "I am one, sir, that comes to tell you your daughter and the Moor are now making the beast with two backs." Since this is in answer to Brabantio's question, "What profane wretch art thou?" Bowdler did not feel that he could dispense with it entirely; so he changed it to: "I am one, sir, that comes to tell you your daughter and the Moor are now together." This, of course, is not at all what Iago has come to tell, and such an impotent conclusion seems somewhat inadequate to explain Brabantio's fury at his midnight informer. After all, the family reader might conclude, perhaps Othello and Desdemona are just off in a gondola somewhere, holding hands.

The man who was first responsible for the systematic purification of Shakespeare—whose name, indeed, has become a synonym for genteel expurgations—came by his pious occupation all too legitimately. The atmosphere of the English family into which he was born, near Bath, on July 11, 1754, was inescapably moral. His mother had dabbled for years in religious poetry and essays, and she raised two daughters, Henrietta and Jane, to do likewise. Both of them, while failing to achieve matrimony, became popular authors of works on the Pleasures of Religion, the Advantages of Affliction, et cetera; and their elder brother, John, was also a best seller with his *Reform or Ruin* (1797), a pamphlet strenuously exposing the moral corruption of British society. Thomas Bowdler satisfied his father's wish by studying medicine at Edinburgh, but he had no taste for the profession and promptly gave it up upon receiving his inheritance in 1785. His concern, like that of his siblings, was more with the human soul than with its house of clay.

Settling down in London, Bowdler moved happily among the most polite and cultivated people of the 1780's. A frequent visitor at the bluestocking literary salons of Elizabeth Montagu and Hannah More, he seems, on the whole, to have preferred the company of ladies. This was good preparation for his task of pruning Shakespeare, and since his edition is dedicated to the memory of Mrs. Montagu, it may be assumed that what he changed or cut was what might have offended the ears of that paradigm of gentility.

It cannot be said that Bowdler came immaturely to the magnum opus that was to immortalize his name: he was sixty-four in 1818, when the first run of *The Family Shakespeare* came off the press. He had traveled widely in Europe, and in England had become well known for an active part in various social reclamation groups like the Proclamation Society—forerunner of the Society for the Suppression of Vice. The time was ripe for his project. The age of romanticism was well begun, and the swooning heroines of early nineteenth-century fiction were sentimentally in perfect phase with the audience Bowdler hoped to reach. Just over the horizon of history gleamed the Victorian era.

Although Bowdler is scarcely humble in his preface to *The Family Shakespeare*, he maintains a surface modesty. It is the peculiar advantage of literature, he points out, that unlike painting or sculpture, it can be modified without danger of permanent injury: the original work remains unimpaired and always available, even if the emendations "should immediately be consigned to oblivion." The risk of error therefore need not disturb the courageous reformer; nor should Shakespeare's acknowledged eminence over all other poets cause him to tremble. Even Homer nods; and even Shakespeare has his defects—principally a regrettable tendency to use lewd words and expressions. Bowdler's explanation of this fault falls back on stock eighteenth-century Shakespeare criticism: the Bard of Avon was an untutored genius, a child of Nature who warbled his native wood-notes with "unbridled fancy," insufficiently aware of the proper rules of art. On top of that, Shakespeare no doubt deliberately sauced up his creations "to gratify the bad taste of the age in which he lived." But, says Bowdler, "neither the vicious taste of the age, nor the most brilliant effusions of wit, can afford an excuse for profaneness or obscenity; and if these could be obliterated, the transcendent genius of the poet would undoubtedly shine with more unclouded lustre."

That they could be obliterated, and by himself, Bowdler felt highly confident. Like most censors he was perfectly convinced that his own taste was somehow in tune with the music of the spheres: where he found offense, surely all persons of sound moral judgment would also find offense. Behind his complacency lay the assumption of a Deity who had chosen to infuse into the Best People a practically infallible sense of what was right, what wrong. Just as litmus paper detects acid by turning red, a blush on a sensitive cheek would certainly indicate those passages where Shakespeare had gone awry. With his built-in detector as a guide, Bowdler was ready for action; when he finished, he doubted not of his success: "I hope I may venture to assure the parents and guardians of youth, that they may read the FAMILY SHAKESPEARE aloud in the mixed society of young persons of both sexes *sans peur et sans reproche.*" The Bayard of Avon had fulfilled his quest.

Looking back on the changes Bowdler made nearly a century and a half ago, the modern reader is likely to be impressed as much by what he left in as by what he took out. Fluctuations of taste are precarious. Words which today have acquired an unsavory aura failed to strike him as obnoxious: thus he allows Othello to call Desdemona a "whore," yet avoids the word "bawd" as if it were contagious. A society which, like ours today, considers it indecent for a mother to be seen nursing her baby in public would be unlikely to regard Bowdler's substitution of "teat" for "dug" (in *Romeo and Juliet*) as an improvement. Again, "His friend's with child by him," in *Measure for Measure*, sounds little different to the twentieth-century ear than Shakespeare's original "He hath got his friend with child"; evidently it was the word "got" that Bowdler could not stomach. And when, in the same play, he changes Claudio's "The stealth of our most mutual entertainment" to "The stealth of our most mutual intercourse," the switch seems to be in the direction of clinical specification rather than propriety.

Despite shifts in semantics and taste, however, these examples offer clues to Bowdler's sensibility. Two things he will not tolerate: the suggestion that sexual relations can be fun, and the suggestion that human beings belong to the animal kingdom. Out goes any patently joking reference to sex, like the marvelous foolery between Pompey and Elbow in *Measure for Measure;* out goes the Nurse's delighted account, in *Romeo and Juliet,* of her late husband's prediction that Juliet would "fall backward" when she had "more wit." Bowdler habitually changes "body" to "person"; he refuses to let Isabella, in *Measure for Measure,* call her brother a "beast"; and in Hamlet's celebrated catalogue of the characteristics of old men the one that gets dropped is "most weak hams." Pigs were pigs, but men, young or old, could not be allowed to have hams.

Like any alert censor, Bowdler took no chances with suspicious passages, even if he was not quite sure what they meant. It is doubtful that he fully understood (since editors still argue about their precise meaning) "groping for trouts in a peculiar river" (*Measure for Measure*) or "change the cod's head for the salmon's tail" (*Othello*), but he threw them out: they smelled, shall we say, fishy. Sometimes he slips in a way that one is tempted to describe as Freudian: for instance when he knocks out Hamlet's teasing question to Ophelia, "Lady, shall I lie in your lap?" and replaces it with the stage direction, "Laying [sic] down at Ophelia's feet." And sometimes connotations quite unsuspected when he made his careful emendations have cropped up in the intervening years to rob them of their dignity, as when he changes Iago's "twixt my sheets / He has done my office" to "in my bed / He has done me wrong." Shades of Frankie

183

and Johnny! This is also a nice illustration of how ordinary words can pick up a connotative load through idiomatic use —a problem Bowdler was uncomfortably aware of. "No words," he observed, "can be more harmless than the short words 'to do'; yet in the mouths of Pandarus and Cressida the words are unfit to be repeated." On that point, I might add, times have not changed too much: I remember my father's forbidding my sister to sing aloud the apparently innocent words of a popular ditty called "Let's Do It."

Bowdler's detergent labors met with great applause. His first edition sold out quickly, and by 1824 three more had appeared. There were a few cavilers, but they did not intimidate the editor; they were critics, he felt sure, "who do not appear to have made any inquiry into the merits or demerits of the performance, but condemn every attempt at removing indecency from Shakespeare." He nevertheless was at pains, in the preface to his fourth edition (1825), to defend his purpose and method at some length. One objection that had stung him was that Shakespeare could not be expurgated without injuring the dramatic structure of the plays, and this he set about to refute as smartly as he could.

"It is indeed a difficulty," Bowdler admits, "and a very great one, under which I labor, that it is not possible for me to state the words which I have omitted; but I think that I may adduce one instance, which, without offending the eye or the ear of modesty, will sufficiently . . . prove that a whole scene may be omitted, not only without injury, but with manifest advantage to the drama." The scene he is talking about, it develops, is the one in *Henry V*, Act III, where the French princess, Katherine, makes a lighthearted effort to learn a little English from her maid, Alice. It seems, as viewers of Sir Laurence Olivier's screen version will concede, a delicious interlude amidst the alarums, flourishes, and orations of a Shakespeare history; but its true and sole purpose, Bowdler assures us, is a dark one. It is no less than to introduce, "through the medium of imperfect pronunciation, the two most indecent words in the French language." The whole scene, therefore, can be chopped out not only to the advantage of morality but of dramatic structure.

It appears never to have occurred to Bowdler that hundreds of his readers would scurry to an untinkered version of *Henry V* to see what in the world those two French words might be. It is a fair guess that for a decade or so he gave that particular scene a secret vogue it had never previously enjoyed. For the ease of the present reader, let me remind him that the two words are Katharine's crude attempts to pronounce "foot" and "gown"—which may suggest little even to some who have spent years studying French. Yet Bowdler assumed that these words would be nastily meaningful to English ladies of Jane Austen's generation: at their mention, he says, "the princess is shocked, as every virtuous woman would be, if she were either here or elsewhere, to see them written, or hear them repeated."

Is it true that Bowdler's excisions and euphemisms seriously damage Shakespeare's plays? I think they do, and not merely from the point of view of dramaturgy or diction, but even more with respect to his matchless vitality. For my taste, Bowdler was deceived in supposing that he could remove whole scenes without violating dramatic structure, and that a change like watering down Hamlet's "Remorseless, treacherous, lecherous, kindless villain!" to "Remorseless, treacherous, unnatural villain!" was not an affront to poetry. He was much more deceived in depreciating Shakespeare's whole and steady vision of life in all its fullness. The role of sex in human affairs was not, for Shakespeare, something superficial and meretricious, to be exploited in his plays as a lure for prurient minds. It was of the essence. Like any other essential theme, it had its humorous highlights as well as its tragic depths, and with the marvelous completeness which no other playwright has ever equaled, he displayed them all. "Purify" *Othello, Lear, Hamlet,* and a dozen others of their sexual overtones and specific passages, and they lose half their meaning.

It must be admitted, indeed, that Bowdler himself seemed

to become aware of this to some extent as he worked at his job of snipping and clipping. He confesses in his preface to the fourth edition that he is not entirely satisfied with *Othello, Measure for Measure,* and the two parts of *Henry IV:* they had proved too recalcitrant to his shears. From the latter he utterly banished Doll Tearsheet without a qualm; but he shows that he understood at least dimly that the Falstaff who remained when he was done with him was only a feeble shadow of the lusty rogue whose capon-stuffed belly presided at the sessions of the Boar's Head Tavern. It is a pity that Bowdler was unable to assimilate, instead of expurgating, Lucio's sage observation in *Measure for Measure:* "A little more lenity to lechery would do no harm . . . it is impossible to extirp it quite, friar, till eating and drinking be put down." As for *Othello,* it would seem that Bowdler found Shakespeare's searching portrayal of sexual jealousy rather overwhelming: he added a postscript to the play in which he suggested a slight change of plot that would make the alleged adultery of Cassio and Desdemona more believable. Thus we find the purse-lipped editor collaborating with Shakespeare in the dramatic representation of sexual intrigue.

When all is said and done, it may well be that history has been a bit unfair to Bowdler's memory. The verb which has grown out of his name is seldom used except contemptuously, and it is a cliché of reference books to describe him as a foolish bigot who made (as the *Dictionary of National Biography* puts it) "sad havoc" of Shakespeare's text. It was, to be sure, a pallid version that he offered the nineteenth century, drained of much of its living sap. Yet there is no doubt that he carried the great poet's work to an audience which otherwise would have been almost totally deprived of it. Algernon Charles Swinburne, certainly no prude, put it bluntly enough at the close of the century: "More nauseous or foolish cant was never chattered than that which would deride the memory or depreciate the merits of Bowdler. No man ever did better service to Shakespeare than the man who made it possible to put him into the hands of intelligent and imaginative children."

Today, when almost all moral censorship has been laughed out of our manners (and out of our courts and the Post Office as well), one would assume that bowdlerization was a thing of the past. Yet not so, when it comes to our precious young and Shakespeare. Miss Jones, apparently immortal, remains on Bowdler's side, and most school boards across the land stand squarely behind her. The Shakespeare texts chosen for official high school use in America today follow Bowdler's excisions pretty closely; they are, as a textbook editor put it recently when pressed, "lightly expurgated."

This leaves the imaginative child of our time still wondering what Hamlet *really* said to Ophelia, or just why the Nurse in *Romeo and Juliet* has the reputation of being so bawdy. If he wants to find out, of course, he has only to walk to the nearest drugstore, where he can purchase, for little more than the cost of a sundae, a copy of Shakespeare alive with all its pristine impurity. Just possibly, too, he may notice a copy of *The Tropic of Cancer* on the stand, and be off into orbits that neither Dr. Bowdler nor Miss Jones ever dreamed of.

RASPUTIN
RECONSIDERED

E. M. HALLIDAY

Accord to Sir Bernard Pares, the eminent British historian who spent World War I as an observer with the Russian army, it was taken for granted by the soldiers at the front that the Empress Alexandra was the mistress of Grigori Rasputin, the Siberian wanderer and "man of God." Pares, who knew the empress and her Victorian background, disdained the notion; yet he was embarrassed, both as a gentleman and as a historian, by certain documents —for example, this letter from Alexandra to Rasputin:

"My beloved unforgettable teacher, redeemer and mentor! How tiresome it is without you! My soul is quiet and I relax only when you, my teacher, are sitting beside me. I kiss your hands and lean my head on your blessed shoulders. Oh how light, how light do I feel then! I only wish one thing: to fall asleep, forever, on your shoulders and in your arms. What happiness to feel your presence near me. Where are you? Where have you gone? . . . Come quickly, I am waiting for you and I am tormenting myself for you. . . . I love you forever."

One has to remember firmly, when reading that, that the empress was literally a Victorian. A German princess, she was put under Queen Victoria's tutelage at the age of six, and in that chin-up *ambiance* she grew to be a very model of a reserved and proper young Englishwoman. She was shy, and nobody was much taken with her in St. Petersburg when she visited there in 1889. Nobody, that is, except twenty-one-year-old Nicholas, heir to the Russian throne. He fell completely and irrevocably in love with her.

The marriage that resulted, after a suitably long and difficult courtship ("Alix," who was enormously religious, was most reluctant to abandon Protestantism for the Eastern Orthodox faith), was as comfy-middle-class and free from internal stress as can be imagined. One's first impression in reading what Alexandra wrote to Nicholas right from the start—and went on writing over some twenty-two years, for her wifely ardor never flagged—is that of having injudiciously untied the ribbons on a packet of letters penned by somebody's grandmother in her youth. It is difficult not to wish, sometimes, that Alexandra had written in Russian instead of English; some dignity might have been gained in the translation. But she was never at ease in Russian, and this is what we get:

"Sleep well my Sunshine, my precious one & thousand tender kisses fr. yr. own old Wify. . . ."

"Sweet Many mine, beloved One, huzy my very own Treasure, good-bye. . . ."

"Yes, me loves oo, my little Boy Blue. . . ."

That's not fair, obviously—pulling out a few lines of love talk from her long, detailed, frequent letters (she wrote every day whenever they were apart). Still, such lines do suggest something about the scope and timbre of Alexandra's mind. It was tremendously active, but its horizons were close. She had an ample lack of general knowledge—Queen Victoria's tutors had done a remarkably bad job, it seems; she had very little imagination and very little capacity for empathy beyond the circle of her family and a few friends. She felt briefly for the mangled soldiers whom she attended as a half-trained nurse in a hospital near the palace, but was unable to contemplate the meaning of multiplying what she saw by hundreds of thousands. The war itself she tended to regard as a personal affront; she thought Wilhelm (the kaiser) ought to be ashamed of himself.

As for politics, Alexandra was perfectly sure of one cardinal point: God had indeed anointed her husband as the absolute ruler of all the Russias, and any challenge to his authority should be ruthlessly cut down. From first to last, and with increasing frequency, her communications to him are studded with admonitions to "show that you are the master," "remember who you are," "be more autocratic." " . . . they shall be *made to bow down* before you and listen [to] your orders," she insists; " 'Russia loves to feel the whip'—it's their nature. . . . How I wish I could pour my will into your veins." She makes little distinction between liberal politicians and outright revolutionaries; they are all of "the left" and ought to be destroyed—it's they or Russia, she feels.

The man to whom her hundreds of epistles were sent was a small, trim-looking, affable person, almost invariably courteous and calm—at least outwardly. His inward demeanor may be more accurately reflected by his remarking to his mother that he often thought he was going to be sick just before a public appearance.

It was the importunities of royal responsibility that upset him: for this he had no stomach. Nicholas became czar unexpectedly early, when his tall, domineering father, Alexander III, died quite suddenly in 1894. The young man was not ready to step into those iron-heeled boots—but then, he never would have been ready. By temperament he was barely interested in problems of government, and he chose what only appeared to be the easiest course: "I shall maintain the principle of autocracy just as firmly and unflinchingly as it was preserved by my unforgettable dead father."

It was not in him to do so. Trotsky, whose contempt for

Nicholas was naturally Gargantuan, quotes with satisfaction Rasputin's pithy characterization: "He lacks insides." That is too harsh. The emperor had his inner life, but it was not adjusted to his larger obligations. He was genuinely and immensely fond of his family, the four pretty girls the empress bore him before producing, finally, a male heir; he was even fonder of the boy. To Alexandra herself he was unshakably devoted, in a more quiet way as the years went by, perhaps, but without deviation. He loved the out-of-doors—walking, running, climbing, shooting, rowing, bathing; the family vacations, spent in the sunny Crimea or cruising the fjords of Finland on the royal yacht, were his happiest times. In the evenings he thoughtfully played dominoes, or read light, romantic English novels recommended by the empress. Of his official duties, the only ones he really enjoyed were those involving the army and navy. He loved his many fancy uniforms; he loved military bands; he loved parades and reviews —fine horses prancing, lances flashing in the sun, a thousand visored heads (Dre-ess *right!*) turning smartly as one, to receive his Imperial Majesty's pleased and benevolent appraisal.

And Nicholas did try to follow in his father's autocratic footsteps. To be a successful autocrat in a gigantic nation that is teeming with the revolutionary impulses of a backward society awakening to new knowledge and a new technology, however, requires stark concentration. The mailed fist must come crashing down at the right moment and in the right place; both rewards and punishments must be dealt, not capriciously, but with a view to consequences. Alexander III was good at this; he was also good at picking talented men to execute his will. Count Sergei Witte, who more than any other man jacked Russia out of the nineteenth century and into the twentieth, was Alexander's best executor, and Nicholas relied on Witte after his unforgettable father's death.

But not enough. Witte was opposed to the disastrous conflict with Japan in 1904–05, but Nicholas allowed himself to be talked into launching what was anticipated as "a small, successful war" on the ground that it would unite the nation and cool off revolutionary hot spots. When it all went badly, Witte was dispatched to New Hampshire where, working smoothly with Theodore Roosevelt, he pulled the Russian chestnuts out of the fire in a surprisingly good peace settlement. But when Witte convinced his doubtful master that the revolutionary pressure, intensified instead of reduced by the war, must be met by real political concessions, Nicholas granted a mildly representative government—the Duma—only with the greatest reluctance: "this terrible decision," he called it, writing to his mother in October, 1905. (He did his best to renege as fast as possible, dissolving the First Duma after only two months, the Second after three.) Witte, meanwhile, fell abruptly out of favor.

Eleven years of his reign had now passed by, and the smiling and ever-courteous Nicholas had achieved the reputation among the revolutionaries of being worse than Alexander. But his ruthlessness was born of indifference and inattention rather than deliberate despotism. Even more than his spouse, he was deficient in empathy. His impressions of his subjects' sufferings were always terribly vague, very hard to keep in mind for more than a moment.

When hundreds of peasants were trampled to death in a crowd gathered to celebrate his coronation in 1896, Nicholas looked the other way and proceeded to a glamourous ball. He was in the middle of a set of tennis when, in 1905, the news was brought to him that a whole Russian fleet had been destroyed by the Japanese at Tsushima; he remarked, "What a terrible disaster" and went on to finish the set. And after the infamous "Bloody Sunday" of 1905, when hundreds of petitioning peasants and workers were killed or wounded by over-eager police as they peacefully approached the Winter Palace, Nicholas allowed a delegation of workers to visit him and hear his reaction: he scolded them severely about their faltering loyalty to their czar. "What a fine fellow!" he noted on a report complaining about a provincial official who had been executing suspected seditionists without trial.

Was he, then, incapable of deep feeling? Not at all. "The

whole day after it happened I never stopped crying," he wrote his mother in 1902 when "dear old Iman," his favorite dog, died.

Into the midst of this looking-glass Camelot abruptly walked Grigori Rasputin. It was the autumn of 1905. Not only had the royal couple been badly shaken by the failure of the Japanese war and the establishment of the Duma, but they were in a state of anxiety about Alexis, the czarevitch. The little boy, Russia's heir apparent, had inherited through his mother that curse of European royalty, hemophilia. The empress prayed for a saving miracle—and lo, Rasputin appeared!

Nobody knew much about him, and indeed his background is still obscure. Legends festoon such a character like seaweed around a sunken ship. By the time he was lured to his death in the basement of a St. Petersburg palace in 1916, he had aroused such intensities of hatred and loyalty that the facts of his early life already had slipped beneath the surface of reality; they shimmer murkily there, distorted by the refracted light of partisan views. Was he, truly, at sixteen already known in his part of Siberia as an insatiable lecher whom the peasant girls somehow could not resist? Did he, at the same time, show gifts of second sight and prophecy that cast a glow of religious mysticism around his head? Did he disappear from home for long intervals, wandering about Russia and even to the Holy Land as a starets, a pilgrim of God, who was still a drunkard and an indefatigable satyr? Was he a member of the secret group known as the *Khlysts*, outlawed fanatics who held frenzied rites in torchlit forest glades that ended with wild, naked dancing and abandoned sexual orgies?

All these suppositions were part of the Rasputin legend long before he died, and there probably is a kernel of truth in most of them. It is known on better evidence that he was born, about 1870, in the village of Pokrovskoe, in a fertile and prosperous part of Siberia, the son of a relatively well-to-do peasant. He was christened Grigori Efimovich, and it has been claimed that "Rasputin," which means "dissolute," was a nickname given him later for sufficient reasons; but it has also been claimed that it was an alternate name for his village, which stood at a crossroads. In a slightly different form, "Rasputin" means just that. He grew up as a farm boy and in his teens was a carter. Soon after that his wanderings began, as well as his reputation as a mystic, and from there on it is more and more difficult to sift fact from legend until he moves into the limelight of St. Petersburg after 1905.

What we know for sure is that Rasputin possessed one of those charismatic personalities that mysteriously exude an aura of singularity. He stood out in any crowd—not for his size (he was of ordinary height and build, not huge or hulking as he has often been described) but for that radiating singularity. In attempts to explain it physically, most people who knew him attributed it to his eyes. They were large eyes, but the pupils were small and bright and had a "piercing" quality; many felt that there was something distinctly hypnotic about them.

Then there was his manner. He was rough and uncouth, yet there was about him none of the deferential humility of the typical Russian peasant only half-escaped from serfdom, whose costume he persisted in wearing no matter what high echelon of St. Petersburg society he touched. There was instead a disconcerting self-assurance, as if he knew some unique secret and was on easy terms with unseen, supernal forces.

The empress was sure he came from God. He was introduced to her and Nicholas by a grand duchess who had seen him perform impressive acts of faith healing. Rasputin was curiously at ease with the royal couple from the start, greeting them like old country cousins; in no time, it seemed, he was addressing them as "Papa" and "Mama" and kissing them casually whenever they met.

"The Czar needed a peasant," wrote one of Nicholas's head courtiers; and the czarina needed one too, for she cherished a romantic notion that, despite her unpopularity with the upper classes, the millions of obscure Russian *muzhiks* were lovingly loyal to her and to the czar. Even Rasputin's air of supernatural sponsorship did not strike Alexandra as contradictory to the idea that he was typical of the people, since she devoutly believed that in their untutored faith the simple peasants of Russia were more directly in touch with God than the priests of the Church.

Rasputin soon showed what he could do for young Alexis. The boy fell under the spell of those hypnotic eyes, and whether or not he liked the faith healer from Siberia—it is a matter of dispute—he must have believed him when the starets stroked his brow and said that the fever would subside, that the headache would go away, or that the bleeding would stop. For that is what happened, much to the consternation of the royal physicians.

The effect of all this on the empress, whose religious fervor often crystallized into superstition, can readily be imagined. It was the miracle she had been praying for, incontestable proof that "our Friend" (as she and Nicholas called Rasputin) had been "sent to us by God." No matter that the starets, pleasantly surprised at the shower of good things that began to descend on him now that he was a favorite of the royal family, set up an elaborate establishment in St. Petersburg from which rumors of high living and low pursuits soon began to filter back to the palace. It was all just jealous calumny, Alexandra believed, the kind of thing true saints had often had to endure; Jesus Himself, she sometimes reminded the emperor, was woefully maligned. The analogy appealed to her, and in her letters she almost invariably upper-cased the H in personal pronouns referring to Rasputin.

It is true, of course, that palace favorites always stir up much jealousy and spite, and the spectacle of the bearded peasant living in epicurean luxury and enjoying first claim on the attention of the czar and czarina was more than most upper-class Russians could stand. Above all, it was Rasputin's free and easy sex life that galled them. There probably was as much sexual license in St. Petersburg between 1900 and 1916 as anywhere in the world (the lascivious tradition established by Catherine the Great had never died), but peasants were not supposed to act like that, especially peasants who claimed to be more than usually religious. Rasputin never disavowed the Church, and he prudently attended mass often enough to spike any charge of overt heresy; but to the extent that he was credited with having special lines to heaven, the hierarchy inevitably felt by-passed as well as insulted. Openly lewd behavior from such an individual was simply intolerable. As for the sturdy industrialists and country squires who made up the larger part of the Duma, the thought of Rasputin bedding down a ballerina one night and kissing the empress the next was enough to raise their blood pressure to dangerous heights.

So was born the legend of Rasputin as a sexual ogre. It was avidly promoted by his many enemies during the last decade of his life, and since then it has produced a garbage slide of lurid books and articles. M. V. Rodzianko, the last president of the Duma—an enormous man with a deep voice, an impressive belly, and a talent for indignation—enjoyed referring to (but never exhibited) "a whole mass of letters from mothers whose daughters had been dishonored by Rasputin." A fanatical monk named Illiodor, who at first was one of Rasputin's disciples, then a competitor of sorts, and finally his bitterest enemy, wrote a book called *The Holy Devil*—an alluring title that has since been used repeatedly—telling many spicy details of "our Friend's" behavior with the opposite sex that allegedly were based upon Illiodor's observations and the word of Rasputin himself. Rasputin was not modest, and such stories, especially when recounted by a man who hated him, might have been thought of doubtful historicity; yet Sir Bernard Pares did not hesitate to use them in drawing his character sketch of the imperial favorite. It must be admitted that some of Illiodor's revelations are irresistible; for example, when Rasputin's wife (for he did have a wife, and three children) was quizzed on her reaction to her husband's sexual exploits, she replied, with something resembling family pride, "He has enough for all."

Pares, however, who apologizes for having to introduce

such unsavory matters into a serious work of history, prefers to document Rasputin's debauchery from police reports. Plainclothesmen were stationed outside the prophet's apartment at all times to keep notes on who went in and out; when Rasputin himself went out, he was followed. On the basis of this evidence it is possible to reach a reasonably objective conclusion about his venereal habits. And the interesting point is that when the circumstances are considered, those habits seem to have been nothing very extraordinary. There was, to be sure, a fairly steady procession of actresses, dancers, and upper-class ladies who for one reason or another were careless of their reputations; and it does indeed appear that Rasputin was extremely direct in his approach to sex. He was not inclined to waste much time in dalliance.

What was admittedly extraordinary was his situation. A strong and healthy peasant, with strong and healthy appetites, he was so influential at the royal household that in St. Petersburg he could actually do what most men achieve only in erotic dreams. He could enjoy a different woman every day, whether she came to him out of piqued curiosity, as a trembling offering in return for a political favor to her husband, or as a religious devotee whose Christian ecstasies had somehow gotten mixed up with her orgasms.

For he was attractive to women; there can be no doubt of that. He was nothing if not masculine, and the mesmeric quality of his eyes evidently was an effective complement— or, when necessary, an effective palliative—to the blunt probing of his peasant hands and the wet kisses that he distributed among his female acquaintances like invitations. As for the charge so assiduously pushed by his male detractors—namely, that he was physically "filthy" and had a strong body odor— it does not seem to comport well with the acknowledged fact that a favorite place for his "orgies" was the public baths.

Once the idea that he was sexually grotesque has been set aside, it is quite possible, as a matter of fact, to see Rasputin in a favorable light: he was really, in modern terms, a good guy. He was undeniably crude, but there is little evidence that he was cruel. On the contrary, as Pares is quite willing to admit, Rasputin was strongly bent toward a kind of Robin Hood generosity. Often he took large sums of money from the wealthy—bribes for favors—and handed them out to poor people without even troubling to count: he was not personally avaricious. He drank—but seldom anything stronger than wine and always, if possible, in company; he loved singing and dancing, and was perpetually ready for a party. Russian folk songs and gypsy music were two of his passions.

On more important questions, Rasputin comes off surprisingly well. He foresaw what World War I would mean for Russia and tried desperately to make Nicholas see it, too, sending him telegrams and notes conveying his vision of the impending calamity. It was a very lonely and unpopular view to take at the start of the war, for Russia was caught up in the frenzied, romantic patriotism of 1914 as much as any of the participants. Pares dutifully records a fact that he was sure would strike his readers as anomalous: Rasputin was a close friend of that shrewdest of Russian statesmen, Count Witte, who was also firmly opposed to Russia's involvement in World War I. ". . . but there is nothing surprising in all this," Pares concludes, giving the devil his due; "Rasputin's views were very long-sighted and they coincided with Witte's."

There was another subject on which Rasputin took an unpopular stand, particularly for a Russian peasant. He was sure that all races and religions were equal in the sight of God, and he spoke out boldly against anti-Semitism whenever he thought it might do some good. Over a long period of time this had some effect on Nicholas and Alexandra, in whom the prejudice was deeply ingrained.

No, the image of Rasputin as "the evil monk" simply does not hold up on the basis of the record. Yet now comes the paradox. It can reasonably be argued that without the influence of this *bon vivant* who so ardently preferred Eros to Death, the Russian Revolution of 1917, with all its agonies, might never have occurred.

To make such an argument, it is necessary, of course, to

entertain the idea that individual personalities do matter in history. It is a non-Marxist idea, although Trotsky, confronted with the fascinating triumvirate here considered—Nicholas, Alexandra, and Rasputin—concedes that "the great, moving forces of history, which are super-personal in character" do, after all, "operate through people," and he proceeds to a penetrating character sketch of the czar and the czarina.

It was Nicholas who set the stage for a denouement in which Rasputin's influence would be the catalytic force. In the summer of 1915, with Russia reeling under the blows of the Kaiser's armies and the responsibilities of wartime government painfully stretching his limited attention span, he decided to leave the helm to Alexandra while he went off to the front to personally lead his soldiers in defense of Mother Russia. It was a farce that fooled almost nobody but Nicholas himself; he had no practical experience as a military commander and only the haziest concepts of military strategy and tactics. It was his quaint notion that nothing could boost the morale of Russian army units more than the living sight of their emperor, and when he was not playing dominoes, walking in the woods, or reading, he spent much of his time visiting troops—always, of course, at a safe distance to the rear of the actual fighting.

Back in St. Petersburg and Tsarskoe Selo, the seat of the imperial palace, Alexandra and Rasputin were, as the saying goes, having a ball. Both of them had encouraged Nicholas to go to the front, overpowering the eloquent protests of his ministers, and the shape of things to come was suggested by a fond exchange of notes between Alexandra and her spouse shortly after the event.

"Do not fear for what remains behind [she wrote]. . . . Lovy, I am here, don't laugh at silly old wify, but she has 'trousers' on unseen . . . It is all much deeper than appears to the eye . . . you showing your mastery, proving yourself the Autocrat without wh. Russia cannot exist. . . . God is with you and our Friend for you—all is well. . . . Sleep well my Sunshine, Russia's Saviour. . . ."

"You do great service to me and to our country," Nicholas replied not long after. "I am so happy to think that you have found at last a worthy occupation!"

What followed was a governmental debacle. Rasputin by this time was under intense fire from both left and right in the Duma; the only way he could protect his privileged position was to get rid of ministers who were opposed to him and install those who had good reason to be friendly—either because they had bribed him, or because he "had" something on them from his unusual sources of information. It was not a procurement system likely to bring good men to office, and in any case Rasputin's crystal ball fogged badly when it came to picking ministers, however innocuous his intentions. It must be remembered that he was almost entirely uneducated; for all his native insight, he knew next to nothing about the monstrous problems of economics and administration that the war's devastation had brought to Russia. As for Alexandra, she blindly accepted every recommendation that her man of God made to her, passing the word along to Nicholas (who still made the actual appointments) in letters that, as the months went by, escalated from hints to wheedling and from wheedling to hysterical insistence.

The chaotic results, unfolding over a period of a year and a half, would take much space merely to chronicle, but they were epitomized by three of the Ministers of the Interior (in charge of the secret police) who held office during that time. A. N. Hvostov, a prize plum of Alexandra's, turned out to have sinister underworld connections and ended by plotting— unsuccessfully—to kill Rasputin. He was followed by a disaster named B. V. Stürmer, a double-dealing reactionary who was despised by nearly everyone who knew him; and his place was finally taken by A. D. Protopopov, who was so egregiously fumbling that many thought he was on the edge of insanity. Most of the lesser ministers were no better, and Russia plunged toward the abyss of revolution faster and faster as the discontented segment of the public expanded to include many thousands of the upper classes in addition to the workers and the peasants.

Was the revolution, then, Rasputin's fault? Essentially, it was brought about by the overwhelming impact of World War I on Russia: the slaughter of its young men by the millions; the disruption of its economy caused by the national war effort. But it is conceivable that the country might have muddled through to the end of the war and been counted among the victorious Allies—if the czar had remained in charge of his government and allowed himself to be persuaded toward basic social reforms in the direction of constitutional government. The rest of the country was ready. During the first year of the war there was in office one of the most competent cabinets Russia had ever had—a council well aware of the awesome needs of the country in the struggle against Germany and not unwilling to co-operate with the Duma and the spontaneously organized citizens' groups like Zemgor (in effect the Red Cross) and the war industries committees in meeting those needs. The czar was a malleable fellow, especially when he was bored, and he was enormously bored by the war.

No, the revolution was not Rasputin's fault. But when Nicholas presided over a meeting of his Council of Ministers on September 2, 1915, and listened to their urgent pleas that he reconsider his decision to go a-soldiering, it was noticed that he held a religious icon clenched tightly in his hand. It was undoubtedly the same image of Saint Nicholas that Alexandra referred to in a letter shortly thereafter; it had been blessed by Rasputin before the meeting. When everyone had finished speaking, the czar stood up and said simply, "I have heard what you have to say, but I adhere to my decision." A day later he left for the front.

Rasputin was murdered, in a fashion and for reasons never satisfactorily explained, in Prince Felix Yusupov's palace in St. Petersburg on the night of December 29, 1916. The assassins' melodramatic tale of their supposedly patriotic deed has been told too often to bear full repetition: how Yusupov lured Rasputin to a strange basement apartment that had been lavishly furnished for the occasion, plied him with heavily poisoned wine and cake—without effect—and then shot the starets with the revolver of his friend and fellow assassin the Grand Duke Dmitri Pavlovich; how Rasputin later "came to life" and struggled fiendishly with Yusupov, broke through a "locked" door into a courtyard, and finally was shot again by a third conspirator, Purishkevich; how the body was then bundled up and dropped from a bridge through the ice of the Neva River, where the police found it shortly "with water in the lungs."

To say that this is a dubious story is to put it kindly. But then, the chief assassins were rather dubious characters. Prince Yusupov, the twenty-nine-year-old ringleader, was by his own description a spoiled playboy whose "scandalous" diversion for several years had been to dress up as "an elegant woman" and visit St. Petersburg night spots where he drew attention from gallant army officers unaware of his disguise. The Grand Duke Dmitri was one of Yusupov's closest friends. During the war he had exhibited his patriotic zeal by hanging around the czar's military headquarters doing nothing in particular, or by going on long leaves to St. Petersburg to join Yusupov in a variety of nocturnal revels. The third principal member of the murder ring, V. M. Purishkevich, was a far-right member of the Duma known for his passionate hatred of all liberals, radicals, and Jews; he was one of the organizers of a group of reactionaries known as "the Black Hundreds," who worked with the secret police in promoting anti-Jewish riots. Purishkevich was noted for his wit, which on occasion took odd turns: he once appeared at the Duma wearing a red carnation in the fly of his trousers.

However, in the present context the point quite simply is that Rasputin was done away with. Though miserably botched, the crime was in a sense a perfect one: the murderers were never prosecuted because one of them was a member of the royal family. The mismatched troika that had been running—and ruining—Russia was suddenly minus its leader, and no lightning came from heaven to avenge him.

It must have occurred to millions that perhaps it would not be so difficult to get rid of the other two, after all.

When it was nearly over for the Romanovs—when the bread riots of March, 1917, had exploded into irrepressible revolution—two harried members of the Duma, themselves utterly astonished at what had happened, traveled to Pskov to receive the czar's written abdication. The document spoke of the need "to facilitate for our people a close union and consolidation of all national forces for the speedy attainment of victory" and respectfully mentioned the establishment of "legislative institutions" by "the representatives of the people." Shulgin, one of the two emissaries, burst out: "Oh, Your Majesty, if you had done all this earlier . . ." The ex-czar looked at him "in a curiously simple way." "Do you think it might have been avoided?" he asked.

History cannot be lured back to cancel even half a line. Still, half a century later, Nicholas's poignant question invites an answer.

THOREAU:
THE CAMPER
IN THE
BACK YARD

WALTER HARDING

It was in the early spring of 1845 that Henry David Thoreau went out to the shores of Walden Pond, a little glacial lake half a mile long and a third of a mile wide, two miles south of the village of Concord, Massachusetts, and began cutting down the tall, arrowy pines with which to build the cabin that was to make him famous around the world. He had long been thinking of such a move. As early as 1837 he had written in his *Journal*, "I seek a garret"; and in 1841, "I want to go soon and live away by the pond, where I shall hear only the wind whispering among the reeds." He wanted to get down to work on a book about the voyage he and his brother John had taken on the Concord and Merrimack rivers in 1839. And unless he could "get away from it all," it seemed as though that book would never be written.

There was plenty of precedent for Thoreau's taking to the woods. It was, after all, the period of the great migration west. Men, women, and children by the hundreds and thousands were pulling up stakes and moving to new territory to start life afresh. But Thoreau realized that he needed to change something more vital than his mere geographical location: he needed to change his way of life. He was going to stay in Concord and simplify his life there. Remembering what he had said so boastfully at his college graduation, he determined to reverse the Biblical instruction—to work one day a week and rest six, though rest would be only a euphemism. Those six days of each week he would devote to writing and the observation of nature.

Thoreau had already made several abortive attempts to simplify his life. In 1841 he had tried unsuccessfully to purchase the lonely Hollowell Farm on the outskirts of Concord. Shortly thereafter he had tried—again unsuccessfully—to obtain permission to build a cabin on Flint's Pond in nearby Lincoln. Then, in 1845, when he was twenty-seven, his opportunity came, and he did not let it go by. The preceding fall Ralph Waldo Emerson had purchased some land on the shores of Walden Pond. Ostensibly he bought it to save its trees from the woodcutter's axe, for it was a spot he loved and already one landowner there had permitted many trees to be felled along the shore of the pond. But Emerson had also long thought of building himself a rural study along these shores if the opportunity arose. And he thought, too, of giving the land to his sister-in-law, Lucy Jackson Brown, or to Bronson Alcott so they could build houses for their families. As it happened, neither house was ever started at the pond.

Then on March 5, 1845, Ellery Channing wrote Thoreau from New York City suggesting that he go out to Walden Pond, there build himself a hut, and begin the grand process of devouring himself alive. Thoreau quickly obtained permission from Emerson, went out to the pond late in March, and began to chop down the pines. Just how long he intended to live at the pond he had not decided, but it would be at least until he finished the book. "I went to the woods," he said, "because I wished to live deliberately, to front only the essential facts of life, and see if I could not learn what it had to teach, and not, when I came to die, discover that I had not lived. I did not wish to live what was not life, living is so dear; nor did I wish to practice resignation unless it was quite necessary. I wanted to live deep and suck out all the marrow of life, to live so sturdily and Spartan-like as to put to rout all that was not life, to cut a broad swath and shave close, to drive life into a corner, and reduce it to its lowest terms, and, if it proved to be mean, why then to get the whole and genuine meanness of it and publish its meanness to the world; or if it were sublime, to know it by experience, and be able to give a true account of it in my next excursion."

Thoreau began his work at the pond with a borrowed axe. It probably belonged to Bronson Alcott, although after its fame spread it was claimed by both Emerson and Channing. But from whomever he obtained it, he returned it later, he boasted, sharper than when he had borrowed it. He hewed the main timbers, he said, "six inches square, most of the studs on two sides only, and the rafters and floor timbers on one side, leaving the rest of the bark on, so that they were just as straight and much stronger than sawed ones." By mid-April he had every plank mortised and tenoned and the house framed, ready for raising. Meanwhile, for $4.25, he purchased an old shanty from James Collins, an Irish laborer on the Fitchburg Railroad. In a few hours he dismantled the shack, spread out the boards in the sun to bleach them and warp them back into shape, and drew the nails. Those nails, however, disappeared into the capacious pockets of one neighbor Seeley, who helped himself when Thoreau's back was turned.

It took Thoreau only two hours to dig a cellar hole six feet square and seven deep in the soft sandy soil, two hundred feet up a gentle slope from the shore of a cove on the north side of the pond, and in the shade of some small pines at the edge of a brier field. It was not a lonely spot. The well-traveled Concord-Lincoln road was within sight across the field; the Fitchburg Railroad steamed regularly along the opposite shore of the pond; Concord village was less than two miles away; and the house where Thoreau's parents lived was even closer along the railroad right of way.

In early May, adopting the old country custom, Thoreau invited some of his neighbors to help set up the frame of the house and raise the roof—both tasks that took more than one pair of hands. His assistants were a distinguished crew; they included Emerson, Bronson Alcott, Ellery Channing, George William Curtis (who later became editor of *Harper's Weekly*) and his brother Burrill, and Thoreau's favorite Concord farmer, Edmund Hosmer, and Hosmer's sons John, Edmund, and Andrew.

Thoreau was in no haste to move in. Once the frame was up, he did the remaining carpentry slowly, living in the meantime with his parents and walking back and forth to the pond each day, carrying his lunch wrapped in a paper. When warmer weather came, he cleared the brier field and planted two and a half acres, with beans and potatoes for money crops, and with corn, peas, and turnips for his own use.

On July 4, 1845—Independence Day, appropriately enough —he borrowed a hayrack to cart his few articles of furniture out to the cabin and moved in. As yet he had no chimney nor fireplace, and the walls, still unplastered, had wide chinks that let in the cool air at night. Later, when he had completed the cabin, he described it as "a tight shingled and plastered house, ten feet wide by fifteen long, and eight-feet posts, with a garret and a closet, a large window on each side, two trap doors, one door at the end, and a brick fireplace opposite." Out back was a woodshed. Close by—Thoreau was too much the Victorian to say exactly where—was a privy. The pond was his bathtub and refrigerator. And the spring under nearby Brister's Hill provided his drinking water when the pond was too warm.

The cabin cost Thoreau exactly $28.12½; his only extravagance was $3.90 for nails. Despite his boasted dexterity, he was apparently a bad shot with a hammer, and when the site of the Walden cabin was excavated a few years ago, the cellar hole was found filled with hundreds of bent nails.

Ellery Channing, who visited the cabin often, has aptly

described it as a wooden inkstand on the shores of Walden Pond. "Just large enough for one . . . a durable garment, an overcoat, he had contrived and left by Walden, convenient for shelter, sleep, or meditation."

The inside of the cabin was as simple as the outside. Thoreau's total furniture, much of it homemade, consisted of a "bed, a table, a desk, three chairs, a looking glass three inches in diameter, a pair of tongs and andirons, a kettle, a skillet, and a frying pan, a dipper, a washbowl, two knives and forks, three plates, one cup, one spoon, a jug for oil, a jug for molasses, and a japanned lamp." For a time he kept three pieces of limestone on the desk, but threw them out when he found they required daily dusting. When a friend offered a mat for the floor, he declined it, saying he did not want to spare the room for it nor the time to shake it out.

In the fall of 1845 he built a fireplace and chimney in his cabin. Using a thousand secondhand bricks, and stones and sand from the pond shore in his mortar, he worked slowly at his task, laying a few rounds of bricks a day. It was November before the task was completed. Meanwhile he took in a boarder for two weeks—his friend Ellery Channing. They found the tiny cabin so crowded that Channing spent the nights sleeping on the floor underneath Thoreau's low-slung cot.

With the coming of cold weather, Thoreau set about making the cabin more snug. He lathed the interior and then, gathering clean white sand from the opposite shore of the pond, he plastered all the walls. The previous winter he had burned a few clamshells to prove to himself that he could manufacture his own lime, but having satisfied himself that he could, he now bought two casks of lime for $1.20 each. From November 12 until December 6, while he was applying the plaster and letting it dry, he lived at home with his parents. It is a wonder that, having left it to dry in a cold building, he did not find it frozen and disintegrated on his return.

Thoreau ate simply and plainly while he lived at the pond. One of the Hosmers, who spent a Sunday in September of

1845 with him, said his "hospitality and manner of entertainment were unique, and peculiar to the time and place. The cooking apparatus was primitive and consisted of a hole made in the earth and inlaid with stones, upon which the fire was made, after the manner at the seashore when they have a clambake." Their meal included roasted horned pout, corn, beans, bread, salt, and so on. Hosmer gave the menu in English, and Thoreau rendered it in French, Latin, and Greek. "The beans had been previously cooked. The meal for our bread was mixed with lake water only . . . spread upon the surface of a thin stone . . . and baked. . . . When the bread had been sufficiently baked, the stone was removed, then the fish placed over the hot stones and roasted—some in wet paper and some without—and when seasoned with salt, were delicious."

When the fireplace was completed, Thoreau moved his cooking indoors. In his second year at the pond he gave up the fireplace and installed a small stove. It was not as poetic as the fireplace, and he felt that he had lost a companion. But he did not own a forest to burn, he said, and the stove was much more efficient.

At the end of his first eight months at the pond he found that he had spent a total of only $8.74 for food—an average of twenty-seven cents a week. Clothing for the same period cost him only $8.40¾ and lamp oil two dollars. From an economic standpoint the experiment at Walden was a success.

There were those who complained that he balanced his budget by sponging on his friends and relatives. Some Concordians claimed that "he would have starved, if it had not been that his sisters and mother cooked up pies and doughnuts and sent them to him in a basket." It is true that his mother and sisters made a special trip out to the pond every Saturday, carrying with them each time some delicacy of cookery which was gladly accepted. And it is true that he raided the family cookie jar on his frequent visits home. But any other behavior on his part would have hurt his mother's feelings: she prided herself on her culinary accomplishments and dearly loved to treat her son.

The Emersons, too, frequently invited him to dinner, as did the Alcotts and the Hosmers. They had all done so before he went to Walden Pond and continued the custom after he left. Rumor had it that every time Mrs. Emerson rang her dinner bell, Thoreau came bounding through the woods and over the fences to be first in line at the Emerson dinner table. The fact that a mile and a half was an exceptional distance to hear a dinner bell was ignored by the gossips. In *Walden* Thoreau wrote, "If I dined out occasionally, as I had always done, and I trust shall have opportunities to again, it was frequently to the detriment of my domestic arrangements."

Thoreau found plenty to do at the pond. He learned to love having a broad margin to his life. On summer mornings he would sometimes sit in his sunny doorway from sunrise until noon, rapt in reverie, while the birds sang around him or flitted noiselessly through his house. He grew on such occasions, he thought, like corn in the night, and said his hours of idleness were not time subtracted from his life, but so much over and above his usual allowance. Other mornings he devoted to housework, setting all the furniture out on the grass, dashing water on the floor and scrubbing it with a broom and white sand from the pond shore, and returning the furniture to its place before the villagers had had their breakfast.

But most mornings he devoted to his garden. His bean rows added up to more than seven miles in length and required constant weeding. What is worse, the woodchucks nibbled the bean sprouts faster than he could pull the weeds. "My enemies," he said, "are worms, cool days, and most of all woodchucks. They have nibbled for me a quarter of an acre clean. I plant in faith, and they reap."

Thoreau was at a loss for a time what to do about it—the woodchucks, he felt, had prior claims as residents, but if they remained, there would be no garden. He finally consulted a veteran trapper for advice. "Mr. W., is there any way to get woodchucks without trapping them with—" "Yes; shoot 'em,

210

you damn fool," was the reply. But Thoreau ignored that sage advice, and matters got worse instead of better. Finally, in desperation, he procured a trap and captured the grandfather of all woodchucks. After detaining it for several hours, he delivered it a severe lecture and released it, hoping never to see it again. But it was a vain hope. Within a few days it was back at its old stand, nibbling at the beans as heartily as ever. He set the trap again, and this time when he caught the villain, he carried it a couple of miles away, gave it a severe admonition with a stick, and let it depart in peace. He never saw the woodchuck again, but what the farmers in *that* area thought is not recorded.

On a later occasion when another woodchuck trifled with his garden, Thoreau was more bloodthirsty. Abandoning his not-too-strongly-held vegetarian principles, he trapped it, killed it, and ate it as a culinary experiment, reporting the meat surprisingly good.

Despite the woodchucks, the worms, the cool weather, and the weeds, Thoreau's garden was a success. His expenses for tools, plowing, seeds, and cultivator totaled only $14.72½. The garden yielded twelve bushels of beans, eighteen bushels of potatoes, and some peas (the sweet corn and turnips failed to mature). Keeping enough for his own needs, he sold beans, potatoes, grass, and stalks for a total of $23.44. Thus he had his food for a year and a profit of $8.71½. Comparatively speaking, he thought, few Concord farmers did as well.

The second summer at Walden, Thoreau decided he had had enough of agriculture, and so he planted only a third of an acre of garden—just enough for his own use. "I learned from my two years' experience," he explained, "that if one would live simply and eat only the crop which he raised, and raise no more than he ate, and not exchange it for an insufficient quantity of more luxurious and expensive things, he would need to cultivate only a few rods . . ."

In the colder seasons he found other methods of earning a living. For a dollar a day he did fence building, painting, gardening, and carpentering. Once he built a fireplace for a man who would not accept his protests that he was not a professional mason. On another occasion he built a woodshed "of no mean size" for six dollars and cleared half that sum by close calculation and swift work. Going home from one task he suffered a misfortune. As he was about to clamber into a hayrack, he inadvertently frightened the horse with his ubiquitous umbrella. Feet flew, the bucket on Thoreau's arm was smashed, and Thoreau himself was stretched out on his back on the ground. The sudden bending of his body backward strained his stomach muscles, and for a time he had to give up hard manual labor. He also tried his hand at surveying, making use of borrowed instruments and those left over from his schoolteaching days. He found the work both satisfying and remunerative; it enabled him simultaneously to earn a living and to spend most of his time out-of-doors in the fields and woods he loved. The only flaw was that his surveying was all too often a preliminary to woodcutting on the part of his employers, and thus he was playing his part in the destruction of the Concord woods. That fact was to disturb his conscience for some time.

From all these various sources Thoreau found he was easily able to support himself at the pond by working, at the most, six weeks a year. "In short," he wrote his friend Horace Greeley, "I am convinced, both by faith and experience, that to maintain one's self on this earth is not a hardship but a pastime, if we will live simply and wisely. . . . It is not necessary that a man should earn his living by the sweat of his brow, unless he sweats easier than I do."

A good part of his new-found free time he was able to devote to writing. The first work he completed at the pond was an extended essay on Thomas Carlyle. As early as 1842 he had begun making notes on Carlyle's works, but it was probably not until he got to the pond that he gathered the notes together and wrote the essay, which he tried out as a lecture before the Concord Lyceum on February 4, 1846. Although it was apparently a success, it was not what his townsmen expected or wanted to hear. They wanted to know why he, a college graduate, had given up conventional life and gone to live in a cabin in the woods. And so it was that Thoreau started writing the series of lectures that eventually grew into his masterpiece, *Walden, or Life in the Woods.* "Some," he said, "have asked what I got to eat; if I did not feel lonesome; if I was not afraid; and the like. Others have been curious to learn what portion of my income I devoted to charitable purposes; and some, who have large families, how many poor children I maintained." And those were among the questions he attempted to answer in his lectures and in his book.

It was a year later, February 10, 1847, before he delivered the first of these Walden lectures to his townsmen. That evening he read a paper entitled "A History of Myself"—a portion of which was eventually to become the "Economy" chapter of *Walden*—and it was received so well that, quite out of keeping with the regular practice of the Lyceum, he was asked to repeat it a week later for those who had missed it. Prudence Ward, who boarded at the Thoreau house, reported that "Henry repeated his lecture to a very full audience. . . . It was an uncommonly excellent lecture—tho' of course few would adopt his notions—I mean as they are shown forth in his life. Yet it was a very useful lecture, and much needed."

The favorable reactions to this and following lectures persuaded Thoreau that it would be worthwhile to write a book-length account of his life at the pond. So earnestly did he set to work that by September, 1847, he had completed the first draft. (It was seven years and eight complete revisions later, however, before the book was finally published.)

Meanwhile, Thoreau had not forgotten that one of his purposes in coming to Walden was to write another book, the account of his voyage on the Concord and Merrimack. Work on this, too, had progressed so rapidly that just a year from the time he moved to the pond the first draft was completed. Emerson immediately urged him to submit it to a publisher, but Thoreau insisted on taking further time to polish the manuscript. He spent a good many hours at the cabin reading various drafts aloud to such friends as Alcott and Emerson to get the benefit of their criticism. It was 1849 before the book was published. But the bulk of both it and *Walden* was written during his two years at the pond.

Thoreau still had time for strolling through the woods and fields of Concord or boating on its ponds and rivers. Evenings he often rowed out on the pond and played his flute or fished. He was, in his own words, "self-appointed inspector of snowstorms and rainstorms . . . surveyor, if not of highways, then of forest paths and all across-lot routes." He "looked after the wild stock of the town" and "had an eye to the unfrequented nooks and corners of the farm." In the fall he often went graping to the river meadows or hunting for nuts in the chestnut groves of Lincoln. In the first winter he dragged home old logs and stumps to burn in his fireplace.

He became fascinated with the phenomena of the pond. In the spring of 1846, before the ice broke up, he surveyed carefully the size and depth of the pond. He cut holes in the ice and charted his findings with a cod line and pound-and-a-half stone, a compass, and a chain. Native Concordians had sworn that the pond had no bottom, but he quickly put an end to their stories and proved that Walden had a reasonably tight bottom at a not unreasonable, though an unusual, depth. When, a century later, a trained limnologist checked the pond with the latest complex instruments, he was astounded to learn how accurate Thoreau's findings had been.

In February of 1847 Frederic Tudor, the "king" of the New England ice industry, took over the pond for a time. He and his former partner, Nathaniel Jarvis Wyeth, had quarreled. For years they had garnered huge profits by cutting ice near Boston and shipping it to warmer climates ranging from New Orleans to Calcutta. Now Wyeth gained control of the ice-cutting rights on most of the ponds they had been using. Rather than give in, Tudor moved farther from his base and purchased the rights to Walden Pond from Emerson and the Fitchburg Railroad. Shortly afterward a hundred Irish laborers and their Yankee supervisors began coming daily from Cambridge on the railroad. They often harvested as much as a thousand tons a day, stacking it up in a pile thirty-five feet high, banking it with hay, and covering it with boards. Thoreau was delighted. Here was one commercial venture that could do no harm to his pond or his woods, and the ice cutters, he thought, were a merry race, full of jest and sport. When he talked with them, they good-naturedly invited him to help saw the ice and, when the men fell into the water— which they did frequently—he invited them to use his cabin for a warming hut.

Inspired by their activities, he began a study of the temperature of Walden and the various nearby ponds, rivers, and springs. It was the first of the many statistical studies that were to become so much a part of his life. Like many of his contemporaries, he found himself developing a mania for charts of temperatures, heights, depths, weights, and dates. It disturbed him, but he was never able to free himself from the habit. (As for the ice, Tudor's men returned briefly in July and removed a small part of it, but Tudor had won his war and the pile was soon abandoned, not to melt away completely until September of the following year.)

The icemen were by no means Thoreau's only visitors. Hardly a day went by that he did not visit the village or was not visited at the pond. Shortly after Thoreau arrived, five of the workmen on the nearby Fitchburg Railroad dropped in to see what he was doing. When he told them of his plans, one replied: "Sir, I like your notions. I think I shall live so myself. Only I should like a wilder country, where there is more game. I have been among the Indians near Appalachicola. I have lived with them. I like your kind of life. Good day. I wish you success and happiness."

Before the second day was over, his sister Sophia arrived for a visit. She had so worried about him that she had not slept the previous night and now used the excuse of bringing out some food to reassure herself that he had survived what she thought of as the rigors of the wilds. But she soon got over her worries, and he made a point of stopping off regularly at his parents' house to reassure them all.

One of his most frequent visitors was Alek Therien, the French-Canadian wood chopper later immortalized in *Walden*. Therien, almost exactly Thoreau's age, had come down from Canada when he was in his teens. Although their backgrounds were very different, they found much in common. Thoreau admired Therien's overflowing happy nature and the thorough way he went about his work with his axe. Therien delighted in stealing up to Thoreau's cabin from the rear, firing off a stout charge in his gun, and laughing at Thoreau's surprise. Although Therien had had little formal education, he was keen and alert. The two often talked of books. Quite naturally their discussion turned to one of Thoreau's favorite authors—Homer. And when Therien told Thoreau that he thought Homer a great writer, "though what his writing was about he did not know," Thoreau took down his *Iliad* and translated portions for him. Therien was so delighted that he later quietly borrowed Pope's translation from the cabin and forgot to return it. Thoreau was to wonder in *Walden* where it had gone.

Emerson was, of course, a frequent visitor at the cabin, and showed his pleasure in Thoreau's experiment by making out a new will naming him heir to the land on which the cabin was built. When there was a threat of further woodcutting at the pond, Emerson purchased an additional forty-one acres on the Lincoln side of the pond and Thoreau was asked to witness the signing of the deed. Meanwhile Emerson frequently asked Thoreau to come in to the village to help him. When he found he was to be out of town for a few days, he asked Thoreau to supervise the building of a house for Mrs. Lucy Jackson Brown near his own. When he purchased two acres adjacent to his house, he asked Thoreau to survey it and gave him a dollar for his trouble. When he wanted the yard beautified, Thoreau dug up seventy-three pines, hemlocks, and junipers in the Walden woods and transplanted them to an area surrounding Emerson's house. It was then that Emerson said, "It is worthwhile to pay Henry surveyor's wages for doing other things. He is so thoughtful and he does so much more than is bargained for. When he does anything, I am sure the thing is done."

But not all was work between them. On pleasant summer days Thoreau would often join the Emerson family on a picnic or a blueberrying party. Emerson would drive a carryall with his mother and Mrs. Brown; Thoreau would follow in a hayrack loaded with the Emerson children and their friends, the mothers, and the Emerson servants. While Emerson and the ladies sat in the shade, Thoreau would lead the children from one berry bush to another.

Nathaniel Hawthorne, too, as long as he remained in Concord, frequently came out to the pond for a visit. With his almost painful shyness, he sometimes found Thoreau's cabin a welcome relief from the stream of visitors at home. Bronson Alcott was another frequent visitor. He purchased a farm on Lexington Road and set about restoring it. Thoreau helped him transplant evergreens and vines from the Walden woods and climbed a tree to assure him that the site he planned for a new summerhouse would have a good view. Thoreau often attended Alcott's "Conversations" in town. And Alcott, in his turn, spent nearly every Sunday evening for several months in the winter of 1846–47 visiting with Thoreau at his cabin.

Louisa May Alcott was a child at the time of Thoreau's residence at Walden, but he made an indelible impression on her and years later she recalled that he "used to come smiling up to his neighbors, to announce that the bluebirds had arrived, with as much interest in the fact as other men take in messages by the Atlantic cable. On certain days, he made long pilgrimages to find 'the sweet rhodora in the wood,' welcoming the lonely flower like a long-absent friend. He gravely informed us once, that frogs were much more confiding in the spring, than later in the season; for then, it only took an hour to get well acquainted with one of the speckled swimmers, who liked to be tickled with a blade of grass, and would feed from his hand in the most sociable manner."

The Alcotts often took their friends out to the pond to see Thoreau. Frederick L. H. Willis, who is said to be the original of Laurie in Louisa May Alcott's *Little Women,* visited Thoreau in July of 1847, and recalled:

He gave us a gracious welcome, asking us within. For a time he talked with Mr. Alcott in a voice and with a manner in which, boy as I was, I detected a something akin with Emerson. He was a tall and rugged-looking man, straight as a pine tree. His nose was strong, dominating his face, and his eyes as keen as an eagle's. He seemed to speak with them, to take in all about him in one vigorous glance. . . .

He was talking to Mr. Alcott of the wild flowers in Walden woods when, suddenly stopping, he said: "Keep very still and I will show you my family." Stepping quickly outside the cabin door, he gave a low curious whistle; immediately a woodchuck came running toward him from a nearby burrow. With varying note, yet still low and strange, a pair of gray squirrels were summoned and approached him fearlessly. With still another note several birds, including two crows, flew toward him, one of the crows nestling upon his shoulder. I remember it was the crow resting close to his head that made the most vivid impression upon me, knowing how fearful of man this bird is. He fed them all from his hand, taking food from his pocket, and petted them gently before our delighted gaze; and then dismissed them by different whistling, always strange and low and short, each little wild thing departing instantly at hearing its special signal.

Then he took us five children upon the Pond in his boat, ceasing his oars after a little distance from the shore and playing the flute he had brought with him, its music echoing over the still and beautifully clear water. He suddenly laid the flute down and told us stories of the Indians that "long ago" had lived about Walden and Concord; delighting us with simple, clear explanations of the wonders of Walden woods. Again he interrupted himself suddenly, speaking of the various kinds of lilies growing about Walden and calling the wood lilies stately wild things. . . . Upon our return to the shore he helped us gather . . . flowers and laden with many sweet blossoms, we wended our way homeward, rejoicingly . . .

Thoreau's way with wildlife continually astonished his visitors. Mrs. Edwin Bigelow once said of him: "Henry would tell all to sit absolutely quiet and close together—then he would go forward cautiously, sprinkle crumbs before them and then retreating, seat himself a little before the others and begin a sort of rolling or humming sound and so would draw squirrels to come and eat at last out of his hands."

The favorite of all Thoreau's wild pets was a mouse, which he said had a nest under his house and came while he ate lunch to pick the crumbs at his feet. It had never seen the race of man before, and therefore became familiar so much the sooner. It ran over his shoes and up the inside of his pant leg, clinging to his flesh with its sharp claws. When he held out a piece of cheese, it came and nibbled between his fingers, and then cleaned its face and paws like a fly. Like the Pied Piper, Thoreau could summon the mouse out of hiding with his flute and display it to his friends. One of the few decorations he permitted in his cabin was a drawing, made on the closet door, of himself and his pet mouse.

For the sake of science Thoreau was willing, occasionally, to sacrifice a specimen or two. Louis Agassiz, who had arrived in Boston from across the Atlantic in the fall of 1846, was anxious to catalogue the flora and fauna of America. James Elliot Cabot enlisted Thoreau's aid, and in the spring of 1847, Thoreau shipped some specimens in to Agassiz's laboratory. Among them, Agassiz found a number of new species including bream, smelt, and shiners. Thoreau also offered to put the hunters and trappers of Concord to work collecting snapping turtles if Agassiz would pay seventy-five cents to a dollar apiece for them. But that offer was not accepted.

Occasionally whole groups of Thoreau's friends came out together to the pond and swarmed into his little cabin. It became quite the fashion to hold picnics on his doorstep, and when it rained, as many as twenty-five or thirty people took refuge inside the tiny cabin. On August 1, 1846, the Woman's Anti-Slavery Society of the town came to the cabin for the annual commemoration of the freeing of the West Indian slaves, and Emerson, W. H. Channing, and Reverend Caleb Stetson spoke to the assembled group.

The only guests that Thoreau did not welcome were the curious—and there were plenty of them—who used any excuse to see the inside of the cabin. When they asked for a glass of water, Thoreau, knowing their real intent, would point to the pond and offer to lend them his dipper. Once two young ladies thus borrowed his dipper and failed to return it, and he fumed in his *Journal:* "I had a right to suppose they came to steal. They were a disgrace to their sex and to humanity. . . . They will never know peace till they have returned the dipper. In all worlds this is decreed."

But despite the visitors, despite all the trips to Concord village and to his parents' home, despite his surveying and fence building and carpentry, and despite the hours devoted to writing, it must not be forgotten that the experiment at Walden was primarily a period of solitude and of communion with nature for Thoreau. It was a period of observing the loons and geese on the pond, the foxes and hawks in the woods, the woodchucks and meadow larks in the fields, the stars and the clouds overhead, the ants and the grasses underfoot, the flowers and trees all around. And his contemplation was one akin to religious devotion. Frank Sanborn once told Thoreau that when he first moved to Concord in 1855, he was told there were three religious societies in town—the Unitarian, the Orthodox, and the Walden Pond Society. The latter consisted of those who spent their Sunday mornings out walking around Walden Pond enjoying the beauties of nature. Thoreau was unquestionably the high priest of that sect and spent a good part of each day in his devotions.

Although he was never to change the basic pattern of the life he adopted at Walden Pond, by 1847 Thoreau began to feel that he had exhausted the particular benefits of his life there. He had fulfilled his original purpose in coming to the pond—not only had he completed the manuscript of *A Week on the Concord and Merrimack Rivers,* but he had written the first draft of *Walden.* It was time to turn to other fields, he thought, before he got into a rut.

In May, learning of Thoreau's restlessness, Emerson wrote to his brother-in-law, Dr. Charles T. Jackson, urging that Thoreau be included as an assistant on a government geological survey to be made in Michigan. Thoreau would have been admirably suited for the position and wanted very much to go along, but the appointments proved to be political plums over which Jackson had no control and the opportunity was lost.

Then in the late summer of 1847 Emerson himself decided to go abroad for the winter for a lecture tour arranged by his English friends. Mrs. Emerson was in poor health, and the children were too young to travel. Emerson was worried about leaving them alone, but she quickly proposed a solution, suggesting that Thoreau be invited to join them for the winter. His presence would not inconvenience them in the least, for he required no ceremony, and it would assure her husband that his family had the protection and assistance he felt they needed. Emerson quickly agreed to her suggestion, and Thoreau readily accepted their joint invitation.

And so it was that Thoreau left the pond, on September 6, 1847, exactly two years, two months, and two days after he had moved in. He explained in the pages of *Walden*, "I left the woods for as good a reason as I went there. Perhaps it seemed to me that I had several more lives to live, and could not spare any more time for that one." But in the confidence of his *Journal* he later confessed, "Why I left the woods I do not think I can tell. I have often wished myself back. I do not know any better how I ever came to go there. Perhaps it is none of my business, even if it is yours. Perhaps I wanted a change. There was a little stagnation, it may be. . . . Perhaps if I lived there much longer, I might live there forever. One would think twice before he accepted heaven on such terms."

GREEKS
AND
ROMANS
AT THEIR EASE

GILBERT HIGHET

Rich people have always had leisure, and most of them have always used it for the same occupations: killing animals and birds, collecting beautiful women and other works of art, building large houses and filling them with useless but decorative equipment, eating and drinking, and working out systems of social differentiation almost as elaborate as the intestines of a computer. Ordinary people have always had festivals: a time to relax after getting in the harvest, a dance and a few drinks after making the new wine, a big blast to kick out the old year and welcome in the new—all usually tied up with religion, so that a holy day is a holiday.

As far as I know, the Jews were the first people to introduce, not simply seasonal festivals, but regular periods of leisure for everybody, rich and poor alike. Once every seven days, on the Sabbath, "thou shalt not do any work, thou, nor thy son, nor thy daughter," and the commandment goes on through the servants and the livestock and even visitors from outside. This is real leisure: a blessed day of rest. Later the rule was extended, and the Jews were commanded not only to do no work on the Sabbath, but to enjoy it: wear their best clothes, eat three meals, and rejoice. It is a great gift, the Sabbath.

However, it was the classical Greeks who took the idea of general free-floating leisure and improved it by thinking of something to do that was quite different from work. They invented the gymnasium. The word and the idea "athlete" are both Greek. Nowadays we are apt to think of the Greeks as brilliant thinkers and agile conversationalists, but many of them were handsome bodies with much spirit and grace and not a great deal of brain. Everyone who goes to Delphi and sees the bronze charioteer is charmed by the skill of the sculptor and disappointed by the expressionless face of the young man whose victory he commemorated. But this is correct. The Greeks founded the Olympic games in 776 B.C., long before a single philosopher opened his mouth.

"Health is best," begins one of their drinking songs, which does not even mention intelligence. Healthiest and stupidest of all were the Spartans. They did no work at all, ever. They hunted in the rugged mountains and exercised and drilled for the next war and sat around talking laconically, while the Helots whom they had conquered worked on the farms.

The gymnasium was a Greek solution to the problem of leisure. But it became something more than a training school for young athletes and an exercise area for the middle-aged. A Greek who did not have to work all day on his farm or sell goods in a shop gravitated to the gymnasium. The Greeks loved talking, and some Greeks were highly intelligent; so, as they sat in the gymnasium, resting between bouts of physical training or watching the youngsters leap and wrestle, they exchanged ideas. In time the gymnasium became a club, in which serious matters were discussed. It came to embody that fine balance between body and mind that was the best product of Greece. Socrates would often sit in a sunny corner questioning the young men in order to make their minds as supple as their muscles. Greek education kept growing more elaborate. A library was added to the gymnasium, teachers of literature joined the staff, classes were systematized, and what had at one time been a place in which men of leisure could run and jump and take sunbaths grew into a school.

School is a Greek word, *scholé*. If a Greek was really poor, he had to help his father on the farm, grubbing up roots and watching the goats. If he had a little extra cash, he went to the place of leisure.

The Romans were originally not much for leisure. They were too busy conquering the world. This was not primarily an imperialistic plan. It was the expression of their driving restlessness and their built-in love of challenge and difficulty and effort. Work, fight, serve, work, save, plan, work. Old Cato objected bitterly to the time people spent standing around yakking in the Forum: he wanted it paved with sharp-edged shells. Like other Romans he despised the Greeks for wasting hours every day oiling their bodies and wrestling, and oiling their tongues and arguing. Why didn't they get together and build a few decent roads and bridges and aqueducts? They are still there, the great Roman highways, and they symbolize the republican Romans' belief that wasting time and avoiding hard work was a sin.

Rome started out poor and had to work. Rome became rich—so rich that for many of its people work was a waste of time. As the conquest of the world was completed, the small subsistence farmers had their land swallowed up by big landholders; the long-term soldiers were discharged with nothing to do; floating populations from all over the empire drifted into the big cities with no real trade or skill to guarantee them a steady livelihood. Under the republic the city-dwelling Romans worked hard. Under the emperors they worked less and less. Not only Rome but the other big centers. Alexandria and Antioch and many more, were full of surplus people who had to be fed and amused. The government was forced to provide free food and amusement for this mass leisure.

Juvenal called the solution "bread and circuses."

Food was a problem of agriculture, transport, and economics, and it would take a large book to describe how the Roman officials tried to solve it. (Food tickets, extra handouts of oil and wine and sometimes cash, but no guaranteed income.) Once the Romans had adopted the idea of leisure, they arranged it with efficient vulgarity through three large-scale institutions. These institutions satisfied basic human impulses: physical exercise and comfort, competition, and hunting.

Much leisure was spent in the huge public baths: exercising, being massaged, showering, playing handball, swimming, and sun-bathing—and also gambling, chatting, strolling, looking at the exhibitions of paintings and statues, and occasionally listening to poets reciting their own works. The Roman baths were projections of the Greek gymnasiums into a more affluent era: they were superclubs. Admission was a few cents only. Did it matter if you slept in a six-story walk-up if you could spend most of the day in an establishment that would have made a Hilton hotel look like a slum?

The Romans also loved to watch men kill animals and one another. The same impulse that makes Arab sheiks in air-conditioned Cadillacs run down gazelles and butcher them with machine guns made the Romans enjoy seeing men grapple with wild beasts in the arena. The modern descendant of the Roman beast hunt is the Spanish bullfight, in which there can be no satisfaction without a killing. *Arena* is the Latin word for sand; and the sand, like the eyes of the spectators, will soak up blood of beast or man without discrimination.

One of the great spectacles was a hunt. Strange imported animals were driven into the circus (sometimes prepared as a jungle with exotic trees and bushes), and trained hunters tried to capture or kill them. A single man would face a lion. A woman alone would tackle a wild boar. The emperor Commodus personally killed five hippopotamuses and two elephants in two days; one of his stunts was beheading ostriches from the imperial box with a broad-bladed arrow. (The disgusting trick of tying up criminals and setting animals to devour them was a late invention, based on Gresham's law that bad shows drive out good.)

Gladiators—the word means "swordsmen," and a gladiolus is a little sword—were originally war prisoners sacrificed at the funeral of the general who captured them. They fought one another to the death—a more honorable fate than being passively butchered—and their blood fed his spirit. This was the one practice, among the many cruelties and vulgarities of the Romans, that other nations despised most bitterly. But the Romans were rich and powerful, and subject peoples wished to please them, and so the habit spread. Even in the theatre of Dionysus at Athens, where men had once staged noble tragedies to honor the god, trained fighters killed each other, so that the blood splashed the front seats and the distinguished spectators who sat in them. After the emperor Trajan conquered what is now Rumania, he brought back many millions of dollars' worth of gold and booty. He gave Rome public shows that lasted for 117 days of honorific leisure. Nearly five thousand pairs of gladiators were pitted against each other, while the crowds roared.

Horse races were seldom run as they are now, with single horses ridden by jockeys. Each entry was a group of four horses yoked to a light chariot and driven by a skilled charioteer. This was the only spectator sport in antiquity organized by teams. Each team had special horses, stables, drivers, supporters, and colors: red, white, green, blue. The sillier Roman emperors would wear the colors of their favorite team and even sleep in the stables with the drivers. After Christian Rome was founded in Constantinople, the horse races continued there amid wild enthusiasm. Disputes between fan clubs grew into large-scale disorders. During the WIN WIN WIN riots in A.D. 532 the powerful emperor Justinian was besieged in his palace, the cathedral of the Holy Wisdom was burned down, and for five days the mob ruled the city.

Magnificent public baths, savage animals killed by hunters for show; the Colosseum filled with water so that sea battles could be staged to amuse the public; expert swordsmen fighting duels, and in the lunch interval criminals sent in with swords but without armor, to kill each other off as quickly and bloodily as possible; chariot races; and always the yelling mobs. These were the occupations of mass leisure in the Roman Empire.

Where did Roman culture come from, then? It came from the gymnasium and not from the arena. The Greeks founded Western civilization and taught the Romans how to use it. In mind, the greatest Romans were half-Greek. They exercised their bodies, but they developed their minds in leisure. They had nothing but loathing, or at most patient contempt, for the races and the beast hunts and the blood on the sand. The Greeks created an almost complete civilization of the spirit. The Romans have left us a tradition of law and politics, some splendid public architecture, and several hundred fine books written by men in quiet rooms from which they could scarcely hear the voice of the many-headed beast in the circus roaring WIN WIN WIN! Leisure, for the mass, is a narcotic or an intoxicant. For the thoughtful man leisure is the Sabbath in which he can have a conversation with his soul.

YOUR
FRIENDLY
FIDVCIARY

OLIVER JENSEN

There isn't much to hang onto
these days. Take banks. It seems only yesterday, in a sense,
that the greatest banker of all, J. P. Morgan, left us for the
Last Directors' Meeting. Indeed, no one has had the heart to
break the news to the Soviet cartoonists, so that the old image
—silk hat, wing collar, diamond stickpin, and bags of gold—
lives on in many places.

Everyone knew, so very recently, how to tell a bank. It
looked like a Roman temple, at least from the front. There
were columns, polished brass, and at the fancier fiduciaries,
female statuary robed loosely in the style of A.D. 300. All the
ladies in this kind of nineteenth-century Greco-Roman art
form have the same face. They served colleges as Muses, law
courts as Justice, and in banks, I always supposed, they represented Fiscal Stability, or Compound Interest, or maybe
The Resumption of Specie Payments. But this was only the
beginning of the imperial note, which was rendered absolutely unmistakable by the lettering on the pediment, cut

into stone in big Latin capitals with scrupulous attention to the rule that the Romans wrote V when they meant U. The fact that they didn't have a W or J, or use K much either, was quietly ignored to avoid making things difficult in places like Vashington, D.C., and Iacsonville, Fla. New York, or Iorc, however, abounded with MANVFACTVRERS TRVST branches, and lord knows how many GVARANTY's; the latter is a lot easier to pronounce if you are a small boy trying to get things right: *Guh-varanty*. It sounded imposing, like *Suh-vub* Treasury, or Bank of the Vee-nited States; but in mouthing the latter, doubt began to enter even the most literal mind. A good thing, perhaps, since that imposing-sounding depository turned out, during the Depression, to be as bare as Old Mother Hvbbard's Cvpboard.

Old-time banks went in heavily for marble, high ceilings, and a deep cathedral hush. Customers spoke in low tones in order not to disturb the money, and the religious air was heightened by the guard who stood like a verger at the door of the steel vault. Behind all those bolts and wheels and dials lay the holy of holies, full of the bigger bills, the senior securities, and the choicest mortgages. Off to one side, in an atmosphere of plush and mahogany, sat The Officials, and one could detect the higher ranks by the white piping on the vests. You saw them again on Sunday morning, forsaking Caesar's collections for the moment and passing the plate, in spats. Formality was the keynote.

Well, you know what's happened. Now everything is glass, abstract art, and bonhomie. Come in and make friends at the Chase Manhattan. Drop in at our comfy Mortgage & Loan Department. Meet the fellows. See our fashion show, our ice ballet. Let us introduce you to the money.

It all started, I suspect, just the way the deep-dyed conservatives always expected, with Government Interference. One minute the New Deal was guaranteeing deposits, and the next thing anyone knew, there was a mural painter at work in the lobby. Then the Government took away the right of private banks to issue their own paper money, and the senior vice-presidents who used to sign the bills had nothing to do any more. They began to buy art, like David Rockefeller of the Chase, and this, of course, got them to meeting modern architects, and that was the end of the Roman temples. With the glass walls it has become possible to see any banker in New York, indeed, impossible not to see him. The lower echelons of officials are ranged right alongside the wall in such a way that any passerby can read the papers on their desks, and it is difficult to maintain the old air of secrecy, let alone hitch up one's socks or take a little unobserved nap. The money itself has no privacy at all.

Given all this sudden and violent change in tradition, it was obvious that bankers would get to know one another and start merging. The process has gone so far that it is almost as hard to recognize the banks by their names as it is by their buildings. If American bankers, like English ones, used their own names—Messrs. Coutts, Barclay's, Williams Deacon's, and the like—merging would offer no problems of nomenclature, but here it has been necessary to make up all sorts of unlikely combinations. The best example is the union of the Chemical Bank & Trust Company with the Corn Exchange Bank, producing "Chemical Corn." The old image, in both cases, was dignified—thoughtful professors, metallurgists, and inventors dropping into the Chemical Bank to make a deposit, perhaps even to suggest some new advance in alchemy, which the bank, one imagines, followed up with special zeal. Up at the Corn Exchange, on the other hand, fantasy pictures sturdy farmers pulling up the horses and dropping in to salt away the proceeds of the fall crop and conceivably exchange a few bushels of the Favored Commodity for, say, the bank's calendar and a winter's supply of deposit slips. But the new image! Chemical Corn! As if every child did not know this cheap confection, sold ten kernels for the penny and not a very convincing imitation at that.

The heartiness of modern banking is overwhelming, if advertising means anything. You never know whether you are going in to make a small withdrawal or to take part in a wienie roast. Every night on television the First National City Bank of New York reminds one and all that at their far-flung institutions, "You come first!" It is an interesting, Orwellian idea—everyone first, but some, perhaps, more first than others?—although it suggests certain problems of implementation on days when there are long lines at the tellers' windows. There lurks in this slogan, somehow, an implied, mysterious comparison. What comes first at other banks, eh? Does it mean to plant the suspicion that the money-changers in other temples are a mite less friendly, a little less full of the first-name, shirt-sleeve spirit? Who comes second, by the way, at First National City?

But it is petty to question the jargon of modern institutional *Gemütlichkeit,* which has been designed for imprecision ever since the first "better" was used without its "than." The bank is just trying to tell you that it's big and friendly, like a dog, and wants to nuzzle up. And any day now the Christmas Club will hold a taffy-pull, and maybe get up a blazer.

The best way to visualize the change that has taken place, apparently overnight, is to try to re-create J. P. Morgan in the new image. He is sitting behind a little modernistic table —it seems a little dainty for a desk, but that's what it is— and the substantial bottom is perched (is there a trace of unease in the furrowed countenance?) on a fragile contraption of wire and laminated bamboo shoots, designed for him by a clever Japanese. He has on a tweed jacket, suede shoes, and button-down shirt, and he leaps up to greet you, the new depositor. "We're all plain folks here," he booms. "Make yourself comfortable while I get you some coffee and a plastic piggy bank for the kiddies."

Then the face that launched a thousand mergers turns toward you. Beneath the bushy brows and steely eyes there suddenly spreads the smile of Your Friendly Naborhood Banker. "By the way," Morgan says, "just call me Jack."

THE DUKE
OF WELLINGTON'S
SEARCH
FOR A PALACE

ELIZABETH LONGFORD

At the end of the war that began in 1914 Britain promised its returning soldiers "homes for heroes." Not all of them were forthcoming. A hundred years earlier, in 1814, when the Napoleonic Wars seemed to have ended, Britain had made a similar promise to its hero Arthur Wellesley, Duke of Wellington. That time fulfillment appeared easy. The money was there—indeed, it had leapt from an original grant by Parliament of £100,000 (£10,000 of it for the "Mansion and Park or Pleasure Grounds") in 1812, after "the glorious Battle of Salamanca," to £400,000 (£100,000 for the mansion, etc.) two years later, when Wellington became a duke. Parliament voted this sum to "support the Dignity and the Dukedom" and to create "a lasting Memorial" of the nation's "Gratitude and Munificence."

The architects were there, too, eager to compete for such a plum—John Soane, who had built the new Bank of England; Robert Smirke, future designer of the British Museum; and Benjamin Dean Wyatt, member of Britain's most illustrious family of architects, born with a golden trowel in his mouth. Magnificent estates abounded also, conveniently encumbered with debt. Yet eight years and a procession of at least twenty-five possible palaces passed by before Wellington's mind was irrevocably made up.

On July 15, 1814, Wyatt, who had formerly been Wellington's clerk in India and now combined the roles of architect, surveyor, and estate agent, sent in his first report on country properties available. (Wellington was on his way to Paris, where he would take up his new post as British ambassador in August.) Standlynch in Wiltshire, wrote Wyatt, was unsuitable for one of "high rank and fortune." Its grounds were ordinary, it had not a single really fine apartment, and there was no space for sideboards in the dining room. Above all, Lord Radnor's neighboring estate of Longford Castle would always dwarf Standlynch.

During the rest of that year three more "possibles" were produced by Wyatt. Great Tew in Oxfordshire, however, he considered neither sufficiently handsome in itself nor far enough away from Blenheim Palace, which Parliament had bestowed on an earlier military hero, John Churchill, first duke of Marlborough (building had begun only six months after *his* victory). To found a ducal home only ten miles from the Churchills, Wyatt asserted, would be infinitely worse than adjoining the earls of Radnor. In Kent, Somerhill was very beautiful but too much enclosed. On the other hand, Sir George Bowyer, at Radley, was prepared to sell on conditions so advantageous to Wellington as to be "extraordinary." Provided St. John's College at nearby Oxford would add to Radley its estate of Bagley Wood, and provided the course of the turnpike road from Oxford to Abingdon was changed (the town clerk of Oxford was "quite willing"), Radley could become a place of suitable magnificence. Alas, by December Sir George Bowyer's "extraordinary offers" had dwindled away.

As 1814 passed into 1815 there was still nothing but disappointment. Lord Fitzwilliam's Harrowden was not even his principal estate, and it was just out of reach of all the great packs. (Hunting was the Duke's favorite sport.) Busbridge, belonging to Lord Egremont, was too small; while a property in Herefordshire called Hampton Court was ruled out because of its deep woods and flooded rivers. "The Duke of Wellington," wrote Lord Essex confidentially to Wyatt, "might as well attempt to hunt Foxes in London as Herefordshire." The only surviving hope seemed to be Mr. Clarke Jervoise's large estate in Hampshire. Its views of Spithead and the Isle of Wight were "*very imposing*," and the hunting was excellent.

The public, of course, were as anxious as ever to present the liberator of Portugal, Spain, and the south of France with a proper palace. But their hero was still pinned down abroad, at the Congress of Vienna, and his most recent victory, Toulouse, had occurred nearly a year ago. On February 21, 1815, Wyatt wrote that he had decided to besiege Mr. Clarke Jervoise, despite the fact that the London to Portsmouth turnpike road cut through his estate for three miles.

Less than two weeks later, Napoleon had escaped from Elba and was making for the palace of the Tuileries. How would this cataclysm affect the search for Wellington's palace?

Writing on May 22, four weeks before Waterloo, Wyatt was not sanguine. The allied armies were collecting on the plains of Flanders, and perhaps Wyatt feared lest his patron, now their commander in chief, should soon have no more need for terrestrial mansions, whether or not in proximity to the great packs. Gloomily he informed Wellington in Brussels about the latest offer. Houghton in Norfolk had got rid of its foxes, and he doubted whether the local gentry would like to have them reintroduced. Nor did Houghton possess quite the degree of grandeur that the public required for their national monument; besides, it was remote, and its surroundings flat, sandy, and uninteresting.

The Duke of Wellington's prospects seemed no less flat.

Suddenly all was changed. Wyatt's next letter was dated June 27, 1815. The wonder of Waterloo was nine days old; and flat, sandy Houghton was out of the running. After all, it had been founded by Sir Robert Walpole (Britain's first prime minister), and it would always be associated with Walpole rather than with "the British 'Waterloo' of the Duke of Wellington." The Marquess of Bute's estate at Luton was nearer the mark: its timber was positively *"majestic."* "Upon the whole," summed up Wyatt, "after having despaired that any suitable place could be found . . . the features of Luton have excited a cheerfulness in my mind, which it had ceased to feel on this subject."

Wyatt's cheerfulness was premature, for something far grander had to be found now. After Waterloo Parliament stepped up its munificence by an additional £200,000, to mark "this signal and splendid Achievement," thus making £300,000 available for the mansion alone. Not unnaturally, the Duke's trustees (the Speaker, Prime Minister, Chancellor of the Exchequer, and two of Wellington's brothers— William Wellesley-Pole and the Rev. Gerald Wellesley) decided to invite two architects, Soane and Smirke, to submit designs along with Wyatt.

Wyatt fumed: was anyone's taste "so generally ridiculed as Mr. Soane's"? He did not underrate Mr. Smirke, but he, Wyatt, was as good as Smirke and better known to the Duke. As for the trustees' question to all three—could they build a suitable mansion for £150,000?—all three agreed. They could not. The Duke's palace, explained Wyatt, must be something better than "a Confectioner's Device"—referring to the fantastic superstructure of Blenheim. Smirke's minimum turned out to be £250,000, while Soane and Wyatt each hit upon the sum of £210,000. Wellington demanded an explanation of this coincidence. Hastily Wyatt assured him on his honor that Soane had originally estimated £500,000, but hearing of his rival's smaller sum, had brought his own down to the same.

By October Wyatt was working at top speed to beat Smirke's "visionary splendor" with the "practicable splendor" of his own design. His walls and staircases were to be faced with marbles from Italy. Why not, interposed the Duke, the marbles that he had seen in the palace at Madrid, when he entered it in triumph after the battle of Vitoria? Wyatt was enchanted with his Grace's suggestion.

The list of luxuries for the paper palace multiplied: barrel and groin vaults and piers for the basement; porticoes, steps, and walls in the best quality of brickwork, with Bath stone six inches thick; proper architectural furnishings, including columns, pilasters, capitals, bases, entablatures, parapets, blockings, balustrades, chimney pots, imposts, pedestals, spring courses, and window "cills." The entrance steps and landings were to be of Portland stone. The workmen to perform these wonders comprised bricklayers, masons, carpenters, slaters, plumbers, plasterers, smiths, glaziers, house painters, and gilders (the last to be allotted a sum of £4,000 for gilding alone). One suite was to be set aside as state rooms only, and later on Wyatt sent his patron some measurements of other famous state rooms. King James's room at Hatfield, for instance, was 58 feet long, 27 feet wide, and 20 feet 6 inches high. Wellington's palace must not fall short of Lord Salisbury's by so much as an inch.

Wyatt's total estimate, presented in December, 1815, amounted to £215,850 15s. 3d., an agreeably idiosyncratic figure unlikely to be repeated by Mr. Soane. The Duke, however, was not quite satisfied. It seemed to him that Wyatt had neglected the servants' hall—at any rate, there was nothing to light it. A more accurate plan of the kitchen court speedily arrived, together with further references to the splendors abovestairs. The circular colonnade would resemble the colonnade in front of St. Peter's in Rome! For in Wyatt's dazzled eyes the conqueror of Napoleon had soared far beyond Marlborough's fame and now vied with the Supreme Pontiff himself.

But where was the land on which to build all this? The Duke's luck had not yet turned. Lord Gage had a fine estate in "the Garden of England," near the river Wye; but he would apparently sell only to the Crown. Luton Hoo faded away, despite the fervent wish of Lady Salisbury and Sir Henry Wellesley, the Duke's youngest brother, to have him there. The Duke of Buccleuch might sell his property at Beaulieu in the New Forest; but no, a year later it appeared that the Buccleuchs had never dreamed of selling.

If Sir Harry Fetherstonhaugh were willing to part with his estate on the South Downs, Uppark, his price would probably be around the exorbitant figure of £300,000. In any case Wyatt could give the Duke but a tepid report on the amenities of Uppark. Though some of the views were "very handsome" and the park "good," the sea in the distance was "not distinguishable as water" except in *very* clear weather. Turning to the house, Wyatt had to confess that its exterior was "egregiously ugly," for its roof was too high and its windows too tall and narrow, while the front was built—of all things—of "old red brick." If bought for the Duke, it would have to be razed.

"I'll tell you why I don't buy Up Park," wrote Wellington to his friend Mrs. Arbuthnot in October, 1816. "He asks a Jew's paie for it; that is to say £400,000 . . . This is more than I can afford to pay for beauty in grounds." It was also believed that the man who had found Benjamin Wyatt's hall too dark for his servants found Sir Harry's drive too steep for his horses. Thus, one of the loveliest houses in England, where Miss Hart, Lord Nelson's future Emma, once danced for Sir Harry on a table, remains to this day with the Fetherstonhaughs.

There had been other blows to the Duke's hopes. In January, 1816, poor Wyatt announced that he had shown his designs to four of the trustees, who had gazed at them in stony silence, not even commenting upon the great hall and staircase. Afterward they had actually criticized the dome over the staircase for being ugly—yet it had been copied exactly from the dome of the Pantheon!

Becoming desperate, Wyatt plunged into a long-drawn duel, on Wellington's behalf, with an eccentric baronet who might have come straight out of the pages of a Disraeli novel, for the possession of his bankrupt estate, Exton, in Rutland-shire. At the end of this bizarre encounter the vanquisher of Napoleon found himself comically beaten by Sir Gerard Noel, Bart.

An advertisement for the auction of Sir Gerard's life interest in Exton convinced Wyatt that here was the ideal estate: a rental of £20,000 per annum, fine hunting country, and best of all, a burned-down house, so that there would be no necessity to pull it down before rebuilding in the image of the Pantheon. Further inquiries proved satisfactory. Sir Gerard and his eldest son were at loggerheads, and both were up to their eyes in debt. It was therefore more than likely that his Grace would be able to buy the life interest from the father and the "fee simple"—title in perpetuity—from the son.

Wyatt advised the Duke to offer £600,000 of the purchase money at once and the rest (£300,000) later. Part of the total, of course, would come out of the Duke's private money. The offer was duly made, and on August 22, 1816, a reply reached Wyatt, written from Green's Coffee House, Lincoln's Inn, London, in Sir Gerard's extraordinarily large, uncontrolled hand. He thanked the Duke for his "obliging communication" and would answer Yes or No as soon as the "confusion" of his affairs permitted. On August 27 Wyatt received a somewhat unusual No.

The Duke's wish to possess Exton, Sir Gerard began civilly enough, was a compliment to the noble race of Noel, which had come to England with the Norman Conqueror and had been "uninterruptedly possessed of dignity and wealth" until this hour of Sir Gerard's "pecuniary misfortune." The "mysterious advertisement" inserted in the newspapers without his knowledge, and against which he would probably appeal in the court of chancery, justified the Duke's "polite and generous offer." But, he continued with rising indignation, he must at once say No, owing to "the growing & shameful Publicity of your proposition. . . . I find that there are sordid notions afloat concerning my Conduct."

Wyatt replied two days later with one of his immensely long, neat compilations, concluding with an assurance that no one would impute to Sir Gerard a "sordid motive" if he decided "to contribute to the objects of the Nation at large, with respect to that illustrious Individual, who has done more for the Glory of his Country, and for the general Happiness of Mankind than any other Human Being ever did for any Country or Countries, in any age of the world." To this fountain of patriotic persuasion Sir Gerard responded by angrily publishing his own letter of August 27 in the newspapers.

A howl of rage burst from Wyatt. Sir Gerard was "*absolutely* a Madman" if he thought such "pigheaded opposition" would stop the sale. But he still hoped to win over the father, as he had already won the son, by relieving them both of their respective embarrassments. At this point, one of the Duke's trustees, William Wellesley-Pole, wrote to Wellington in alarm. "My dear Arthur," he began, Wyatt's "itch for writing" must be curbed, and he must be prevented from "working among all the lawyers, and attorneys, and auctioneers of the Noel family," as well as among its warring branches and their creditors. He, William, had tried to impress on Wyatt how unpleasant it would be for the Duke to get involved in their hot disputes. It was William's opinion that if Sir Gerard did find himself forced to sell his life interest, the Duke would eventually have a chance of buying it; but this would happen best by "not meddling."

While these sage reflections were steadying the Duke's camp, Sir Gerard was preparing to bring off a devastating coup. True to his threat, he appealed to the Lord Chancellor and secured an injunction against the sale of his life interest on condition that he could raise £96,000 to pay his creditors.

Flabbergasted at first, Wyatt recovered his balance when he considered the feud between Sir Gerard and his son. No son, surely, would help to raise money for a father who had just described that son's overtures to Wellington as "fit for the Palace of Beelzebub"? By the middle of October Wyatt was awaiting with moderate confidence the "crisis" that would soon decide Exton's fate. "I am in daily expectation of some strange violence or other," he wrote to Wellington, "on the part of Sir Gerard . . . he is not unlikely to attack Your Grace, his Son, and me, as a set of Conspirators . . . Your Grace's character, however, is far above any assault from him." Only one small cloud specked the fair skies—"Old Coutts," of the famous banking firm, was willing to accept a mortgage for a sum owed them by Sir Gerard; this being, according to Wyatt, "a latitude which he need not give." Wyatt may have been justifiably aggrieved, for less than a month before, the Duke had lodged with that same old Coutts a deposit of £5,000 for the purchase of a town mansion, Apsley House.

Disconcerting news arrived on October 14. The Chancellor's court had now decided that if Sir Gerard could insure his life for £50,000 by the 24th instant, the injunction against the sale of Exton would remain in force until November. "I have no hesitation in saying that his Grace must pass through my Head into Exton," declared Sir Gerard, and in his next letter he proposed to sally forth on horseback with two of his "loyal" younger sons, like a medieval champion, and accuse the Commander in Chief of the Allied Armies of Occupation in France of behaving in a manner "inconsistent with his overtures as a Man of Honor." He would like to "be certain," however, that his Grace *did* intend to purchase, before he took "the trouble of the Journey."

Two days earlier Wyatt had made a sensational discovery. The snake in the grass was not Sir Gerard, after all, but a Mr. William Leake, his principal assignee. For his own ends this monster was determined to prevent the sale of Exton. "I shall keep my eyes upon him," growled Wyatt; "and shall, I think, be able to defeat his Project." In fact, a fortnight later Wyatt announced triumphantly that "Sir Gerard has struck his Colors," while in confirmation the gallant baronet explained that he had fought his ship "till she was sinking"—in other words, till his son William had backed out of the plan to present Wellington in France with something really "strong." Sir Gerard would now "surrender to the Duke of Wellington upon the best terms his generosity will offer."

The next week the cup slipped from the Duke's lip. Or rather, as Wyatt had to admit, Mr. Leake dashed it down. For the "cunning attorney" at the last moment persuaded Coutts's to "patch up" Sir Gerard's finances, provided that he himself was appointed sole agent. To such "roguery" alone did his Grace owe the loss of a "most eligible Property." Turning at last from this mournful post-mortem, Wyatt announced that there was an estate in Gloucestershire called Miserden that might do.

Miserden did not do. "I feel no great inclination to purchase it," wrote the Duke to Wyatt on February 25, 1817, from France. "First, I am convinced that *I* should never live in any County in which I could not hunt; Secondly *I am not* desirous of placing myself so exactly within a morning's ride of Cheltenham"—whence a stream of visitors to that fashionable spa could descend on Miserden for luncheon. By spring the flooring of Apsley House was being strengthened to receive the colossal statue of Napoleon by Canova, and still Napoleon's conqueror was without his palace.

At long last, on July 8, Wyatt struck lucky. It appeared that a place was really for sale in Hampshire. The second Lord Rivers had stated "seriously" to a neighbor that he wished to sell Stratfield Saye. This time Wyatt begged Wellington to write himself, so that if Lord Rivers's friends tried to dissuade him from selling, he would be "more committed" by his personal exchanges with the Duke. Wyatt's preliminary visit to Stratfield Saye rekindled all his enthusiasm: the happy state of the tenantry, fine carriage drives through splendid plantations, a magnificent park and prospects over distant country, all made it "by far the handsomest estate" hitherto offered. Moreover, the borough of Reading was "very open to the wishes of any popular Person possessing the Property." (This could provide a future parliamentary seat for the Duke's schoolboy son, Lord Douro.) "The present house," however, "is a very bad one, and stands on by no means the best situation." It would have to be pulled down and resited.

It was November, 1817, before Wellington could get over from France to give Stratfield Saye his approval. But negotiations continued. In February the search almost came to an abrupt end for the second time. An attempt had already been made in Paris to set fire to the house in which Wellington was giving a ball. Now, in 1818, a shot was fired at him on his way home. Wyatt trusted that in the future every precaution would be adopted "to guard a life, upon which the Tranquillity of Europe depends"—not to mention the purchase of Stratfield Saye.

In point of fact Wellington's trustees seemed to be hedging on the purchase. They considered its price a dear one. Nevertheless, Stratfield Saye became his, for £263,000, and in June, 1819, he was noting that his French beds were 7 feet 1 inch long and asking Wyatt whether they would fit into the alcoves in rooms 9, 12, and 13. He moved in that autumn or late summer. To Mrs. Arbuthnot he was writing delightedly in 1820. "Do you know that white violets grow wild at Stratfield Saye?" His eight-year search was over—or so it seemed. It is surprising, to say the least, to find the Duke of Wellington just two years later inspecting that notorious Gothic extravagance, Fonthill Abbey, as a prospective buyer, surrounded by a horde of admiring tourists who had been admitted by its eccentric owner, William Beckford, previous to its forthcoming sale. Yet there is no doubt of it. A bundle of letters at Stratfield Saye, dated September, 1822, to January, 1823, bears the uncompromising title, "Proposed Purchase of Fonthill, Wiltshire."

The mystery is not insoluble. Stratfield Saye, as it stood, was no palace. And in view of its high price, stand it very likely must. The further cost of demolition and rebuilding might well prove prohibitive. Wyatt's personal tastes, which were catholic enough to appreciate both strict classical styles and the pure romance of "Gothic revival," stopped short of the seventeenth-century charm of Stratfield Saye. Built about 1630 by Sir William Pitt, its stucco exterior had been added in 1750 by the first Lord Rivers, Pitt's great-grandson, thus concealing the original red bricks. A row of dormer windows broke the long, steep line of the roof on the east side, giving it a pleasantly French air, and this was emphasized on the west, opposite the front door, by a gay vista of pink-washed stables with rococo curves. But the Duke's young friend Lord Francis Leveson-Gower had written off Stratfield Saye in 1818 as "a miserable imitation of a French Château," standing in a swamp, and he secretly regretted that the neighboring Bramshill, high up and Jacobean, had not been bought instead.

When Fonthill came on the market, Wyatt remembered that his own famous father, James Wyatt, had designed it for Beckford in 1795. Though the writer William Hazlitt had denounced Fonthill as "a Cathedral turned into a toy-shop," Benjamin Wyatt felt "extreme regret that this Place should not have been for sale before Your Grace had purchased any other." The Duke was persuaded to view it, and he described himself as "never more gratified and even surprised" than by Fonthill, with its "wild woods," and furniture and pictures "the most beautiful I have ever seen." In October Wyatt obtained for the Duke an option on the estate for £279,125 and was soon making reports on its accommodation, particularly its stables and servants' quarters, followed by plans for new buildings.

One question remained. What was to happen to Stratfield Saye if the Duke bought Fonthill? Wyatt grandly suggested that he should keep both, pulling down the mansion at Stratfield Saye and drawing a big rent from its profitable farms. The Duke's retort that Wyatt must think him mad makes it pretty clear why Fonthill was bought in 1823 by John Farquhar, a contractor for green-powder tea in Bengal, rather than by the Duke of Wellington. The Duke's trustees kept a tight hold on his money and a cold eye on Wyatt's enthusiasms. Of course, as Wyatt insisted, the Duke could always buy Fonthill and resell Stratfield at a profit. The necessary improvements to Fonthill would cost only £93,500 as against a price of £216,000 for a new Stratfield Saye.

A new Stratfield Saye? Those most familiar with the legend of the Iron Duke may wonder whether his heart was altogether in the search for a *palace*. Wyatt obviously hoped that it was. He had been permitted to work on further elaborate drawings for at least three years after he had produced the original designs of 1815, including the dimensions of rooms "to be sent to the Savonnerie factory in Paris for the carpets." Parliament certainly expected something "fitting," that is, splendid: for even the Act as amended in 1813 meticulously enumerated the necessary appendages to a suitable "Mansion" —"Out Offices and Out Buildings . . . Walls and Fences . . . Avenues, Walks, and Rides, Borders and Divisions . . . Trees, Roots, Shrubs, and Plants."

Wellington himself was not the man to ignore what was considered suitable or fitting. A gentleman of rank was expected to present a well-groomed appearance against a handsome background of shining brass and leather in his coach houses, glittering plate on his sideboards, and sparkling gems on his wife. In his person Wellington was immaculate, his horses and carriages were his pride, and he made up for his wife's dislike of jewelry by loading his daughters-in-law with diamonds. At the same time, like many great soldiers, he treasured certain simplicities. His eating and drinking were abstemious. His thought and language were plain. Everything about him was open, honest, direct.

Is it possible, then, to imagine this man, of all people, associating himself with Fonthill—that farrago of the sublime and the ridiculous? Or to believe that the Iron Duke, who slept at Walmer Castle on a soldier's traveling bed, should have longed to raise his eyes to tassels and swags and gilded cupolas? It is tempting to conclude that the Duke never really wanted a palace. That the palace was a dream of his countrymen, his friends, his architect. That his native austerity saw in all private palaces—to borrow a phrase from Sir Gerard— a touch of "the Palace of Beelzebub." He wanted foxes and friends, a fine library, fine trees. Not a pocket borough for Douro. Not a dome but a home.

This view carries us into mythology. Popular imagination has seized upon the hero's camp bed at Walmer, forgetting that at Apsley House he slept in a splendid French affair of mahogany and bronze. Admittedly there were no state apartments at Stratfield Saye, but at Apsley House his new Waterloo gallery was a declaration of sheer magnificence. The hero could take grandeur in his stride. He might well have lived in a palace. The fact remains that he never did. Precisely why we do not know.

Certain events in his life may have had something to do with it. His ailing wife, Kitty, lived until 1831—passionately fond of the old Stratfield Saye, pathetically unfitted to manage a Wyatt palace. As she lay dead inside Apsley House, its windows were broken by the mob. In Hampshire, as elsewhere in rural Britain, there was to be rick burning by the landless poor. With all the social and economic unrest of those dangerous years Wellington may have felt that this was not the moment to start a long-postponed project, both costly and ostentatious. The expense of Apsley House itself certainly made him think twice about a new Stratfield Saye; not to mention the expense of owning a large agricultural estate—which did not prove to be the source of revenue he had imagined. Then in 1834 Mrs. Arbuthnot died. We may guess that one of the most persuasive voices that had earlier spoken up for a palace was thus silenced.

Four years later the die was cast. Wellington was almost seventy and had lived nearly twenty years in the old house. Though there is no written proof that Wyatt's palace was ever formally canceled, the year 1838 marks the final reprieve of Stratfield Saye—signaled by a massive program of expenditure to make it, in its proud owner's opinion, one of the most comfortable houses in England.

And so all ended happily, except perhaps for Wyatt and Fonthill. Wyatt never built his Blenheim. After erecting the Duke of York's column in London under Wellington's chairmanship, he quarreled and eventually broke with his most celebrated patron over the theft from Apsley House, during renovations by his workmen, of three pairs of new shoes, one black coat and waistcoat, both new, three colored waistcoats, and a new pair of gaiters—all belonging to the Duke's groom. But that is another story. As for Fonthill, Farquhar sold its whole fantastic contents within a week of purchase; two years later its soaring octagon tower collapsed; it was twice swept by fire, and today hardly one stone still stands upon another.

Stratfield Saye, on the contrary, stands today much as it stood when the Great Duke first set eyes on it in 1817, with the lovely river Loddon flowing through rushes and water crowfoot between its rising deer park and sloping green lawns. True, much valuable buhl furniture arrived from Paris in 1818, to be followed by marble columns from Italy (some of which, however, remained in their packing cases for a hundred and thirty years), a continual stream of books and pictures to take their places beside Stratfield Saye's original rococo chimney pieces and Chippendale mirrors, and the construction of two new outer wings for the west front.

But the "capabilities" of Stratfield Saye on which the Duke really concentrated were of a different order: windows with double glazing copied from Russia; nine water closets attached to bedrooms for his guests; patent Arnott stoves to warm his new conservatory; and a powerful central-heating system with indestructible iron pipes, to remind visitors, both then and now, that the Great Duke always put service before show.

ENGLAND, THE MELTING POT

DAVID LOWE

The first English saint was Alban of Verulamiun, who was martyred for his faith at the end of the third century. He was a Roman soldier. When the English next felt the need for a national martyr they were lucky in having at hand Thomas à Becket, a Frenchman. Becket, of course, was Archbishop of Canterbury, that prime see of the English church founded in the sixth century by Augustine, an Italian, and whose cathedral, which the English claim as one of their great national monuments, was mostly the work of William of Sens, another Frenchman.

But the English have shown themselves to be as truly catholic in their government as in their church. In that battle upon which all English history appears to swing, Hastings of 1066, the English were led by Harold, whose mother and father were both Danish. As everyone knows, Harold was beaten by William the Conqueror—who was a Norman. But then there never has been an English royal house.

When, in the twelfth century, the English grew tired of the

Normans, they turned to the Plantagenets, who got their extraordinary name from a shrub favored by Geoffrey, count of the French province of Anjou. Geoffrey's son, Henry II, the first of the line to sit on the throne of England, spoke French and laid the foundation of the judicial and administrative system which made English government the model for the world. It was at this time that the legends concerning one of the supreme English literary heroes, King Arthur, were gathered together. It should surprise no one that Arthur was a pure Celt. As a matter of fact, the earliest English literary hero, Beowulf, was a Swede celebrated in a German epic poem which never mentions England.

Having gone to Denmark, Normandy, and Anjou for their royal house, in the fifteenth century the ever-inventive English went to Wales. There they found the Tudors, whose line was descended from the steward of Llewlyn, prince of North Wales. The first Tudor king, the Welshman Henry VII, had the good sense to keep the system of royal councilors which eventually developed into that very English institution, the House of Commons. His son, Henry VIII, was one of the fattest men ever to sit on the English throne. We know because of his portrait by the most popular English painter of the period, Hans Holbein, who was German.

In 1605 the main line of the Tudors died out, and in typical fashion, the English went to Scotland, where they found James I—he was already James VI of Scotland, thus putting the canny Scots five up on the English. The second Stuart, for that was the name of the new royal house, was Charles I, who is remembered because he lost his head and is the only person canonized by the Church of England. Before he lost his head and gained his halo, Charles sported a lovely Vandyck. We know because of his portrait by the most popular English painter of the period, Sir Anthony Van Dyck, who was Flemish.

Under Olive Cromwell's Commonwealth (1649–1660) England had the only thing approaching an English monarch in its history, though Cromwell's great-grandfather was one

Morgan Williams, and that's about as Welsh a name as you can pronounce. Neither the Irish nor the Scots were happy with an Englishman heading an English government, and they fought long and hard against Cromwell. In time the English themselves grew unhappy with self-government—the Commonwealth is still looked upon as the dreariest period in English history, and the English have had the good sense never to put an Englishman on their throne again. As soon as Cromwell was cold in his temporary grave in Westminster Abbey, the English gave the crown to the son of Charles I and his French queen, Henrietta Maria. Charles II had not a drop of English in his purple blood and, as one might expect, he was one of the most popular monarchs in English history.

But after three generations in England the English thought that the Stuarts were behaving too much like natives, and so they drove James II from the throne and offered it to his daughter, Mary, who had been sensible enough to live abroad and to pick for her husband William of Orange, a Dutchman. Thus, with splendid perversity, the Glorious Revolution of 1688 celebrates the seating of foreigners on the throne of England. Due to a lack of direct heirs and other shenanigans, the English royal house eventually became *Deutsch* rather than Dutch. It was under the second of these German kings from Hanover—they were unimaginative and always named their sons George—that a most English event took place, being not English at all. The most popular piece of English classical music, written by a composer from Lower Saxony under the patronage of an English king who spoke only German, was given a foreign première. The music was *The Messiah* by George Frederick Handel, which was first heard in Dublin in April of 1742. The king was George II.

The eighteenth century was not only an era of accomplishment for English music, but for English letters and thought as well. Oliver Goldsmith, born in Ireland, wrote his plays and novels in English; Jonathan Swift, born in Dublin, wrote his satires in English; Edmund Burke, also born in Dublin, made his great Parliamentary speeches in English; David

Hume, born in Edinburgh, Scotland, explained his philosophy in English; Adam Smith, born in Kirkcaldy, Scotland, wrote his *Wealth of Nations* in English. The favorite historical painter of George III—the German King who lost the American colonies for England—was the president of England's Royal Academy, Benjamin West. West was born in Springfield, Pennsylvania.

Nineteenth-century England was dominated by Queen Victoria, Prince Albert, Benjamin Disraeli, and Oscar Wilde. If there was a drop of English blood in any of them, they never spoke of it. When the red of England covered the map of the world rather than the ledger of the Chancellor of the Exchequer, the country had a sovereign who was more German than Kaiser Wilhelm (his mother was English); a prince consort who was the son of the Duke of Saxe-Coburg-Gotha, and a prime minister whose father was a Jewish immigrant from Venice. When good English Victorians wanted a change from the brilliant plays of Oscar Fingall O'Flahertie Wilde, who was, among other things, Irish, they could mope over the poetry of Dante Gabriel Rossetti and Christina Rossetti, the children of an Italian refugee, or have their love of the medieval whipped up by the novels of the Scot, Sir Walter Scott, or have their blood chilled by the tales of the Brontës, whose father, Patrick Brunty, was from Ireland. If they sought something more demanding in the way of history and philosophy, they could always find it in the books of another Scot, Thomas Carlyle. Under these circumstances it is not surprising that when their Parliament buildings burned in 1834, one of the architects the English hired to express their national aspirations in the new edifice was August Charles Pugin, who was French.

During the late nineteenth century, English letters achieved a new glory with the American Henry James, O.M., the Scot Robert Louis Stevenson, the Irishman George Bernard Shaw, and a novelist born of a Polish family named Korzeniowski, Joseph Conrad.

In 1917, after three years of war with the Germans, King

George V, finally announced that the royal house would henceforth be known, not as Saxe-Coburg-Gotha, but as Windsor. This attempt at Anglicization did not alarm the sensible English, who knew very well that no English blood had tainted the royal family since it had come over from Hanover in the eighteenth century. And so England remained a monarchy while native royal families were being thrown out of their palaces all over Europe. It is true that later on one English king, George VI, did marry a lady from the British Isles, the present Queen Mother Elizabeth. But at the time he did not expect to become king and, as it fortunately turned out, she was a Scot.

In the First World War the English found their prime minister, David Lloyd-George, in Wales; in the Second, they turned to Winston Churchill, whose mother, Jennie Jerome (part Iroquois Indian), was from Brooklyn.

During the first half of the present century the most influential Englishwoman was Lady Astor, the former Nancy Langhorne of Virginia, who in 1919 became the first female to sit in the House of Commons. The most influential English poet of the period was T. S. Eliot, O.M., of St. Louis, Missouri. Perhaps it was not mere chance that brought the Bishop of Coventry to Sir Jacob Epstein when he wanted a sculptor who could sum up the triumph of good over evil for the cathedral he was building to replace the one blitzed by the Nazis. Like Sir Winston's mother, Sir Jacob was from Brooklyn. And it is certainly no surprise that half of those English musical phenomena of today, The Beatles, Paul McCartney and John Lennon, are Irish. For further reading see the Encyclopedia Britannica, published in Chicago, Illinois.

POKER
AND THE
AMERICAN
CHARACTER

JOHN LUKACS

The origins of poker are very obscure: encyclopedias and dictionaries give either vague or contradictory information about its origins. Yet it seems more or less certain that something like poker was played in French Louisiana and that it spread to the United States around 1800 and to England afterward. Because of the imitation of English habits, games, and clothes characteristic of much of Europe's aristocracy and upper bourgeoisie in the nineteenth century, poker made its way across the Continent; indeed, it was (and still is) one of the few American things that most Europeans erroneously attribute to England. From scattered bits of information, including literature and memoirs and personal reminiscences of older people, I can say that poker was mildly fashionable among the Orleanist aristocracy of France in the 1860's; it was played in Turin around 1865; it arrived in Vienna in the 1870's, in Hungary in the 1880's, in Russia around 1900. By about 1920 poker, with other formerly aristocratic habits and pastimes, filtered down to the level of the bourgeoisie, which is where I became acquainted with it in 1938, at the age of fifteen, in my native Hungary.

The uniqueness of poker consists in its being a game of chance where the element of chance itself is subordinated to psychological factors and where it is not so much fate as human beings who decide. In this respect poker is the game closest to the Western conception of life, where life and thought are recognized as intimately combined, where free will prevails over philosophies of fate or of chance, where men are considered free moral agents, and where—at least in the short run—the important thing is not what happens but what people think happens.

To some extent, of course, this element is present in a number of sophisticated games of chance in which bluffing, or the character of the player, may become decisive on crucial occasions. But in the playing of poker this factor is not occasional but constant, not secondary but primary. Like certain other games of chance, poker is played not primarily with cards but with money; unlike other games, the money staked in poker represents not only our idea of the value of our cards, but our idea of what the other players' idea of the value of our cards might be.

All other unique characteristics of poker flow from this condition. Thus, in the second place, cards count in poker, but they count less than in any other game. There are good players and bad players in every game: there are, contrary to the supercilious belief of mathematicians, even such things as good and bad roulette players. But even in such an intelligent game as bridge a bad player is almost sure of ending up in the black if, by chance, he has a succession of very good hands all evening. Conversely, the good poker player—like the good artist or the fine *viveur*—may make much out of little on the one hand and, on the other, limit his losses by strict self-discipline.

In the third place, poker—again unlike other games—becomes gradually more interesting the more one plays with the same group of people (provided, of course, they are agreeable partners). Since the important thing is not the cards but the betting, not the value of the player's hand but the player's psychology, as one gets to know the habits, the quirks, the tendencies, the strengths, and the weaknesses of the other players—which, more than often, are reflections of character strengths and weaknesses—the play becomes increasingly interesting. Whereas in bridge there is a certain social charm in getting acquainted with previously unknown partners at a resort hotel, a poker game between four or five characters unknown to each other must, by necessity, be stiff, angular, and unduly cautious—except for the professional cardsharp, of course.

The reason for this is that in poker you play not against chance or fate but against people, human beings; and what is important about them is not so much how they play their cards but how they bet their money. There is, thus, in the game of poker—perhaps alone among games of chance—a unique element of reality. This reality—which is the fourth characteristic of the game—derives from the condition that you must play within your means. Money is the basis of poker: whereas bridge can be played for fun without money, poker becomes utterly senseless if played without it. Note that I said *money*, not *chips*—chips only when they represent money and money only because it represents the daring or the cowardice of other people. Poker, to repeat, can be played only with people and, unlike chess or even bridge, never against an IBM machine.* On the other end of the scale, poker again becomes senseless if the people who play it have too much money—to give a concrete example, if people of, say, $30,000-a-year incomes sit down to play with chips

---

*A relatively simple mathematical computation will show some of the following probabilities out of the 2,598,960 possible hands of classic draw poker played with the standard fifty-two-card deck:
Flush: 5,108 (or once in 509 hands), Straight: 10,200 (or once in 256 hands), Three of a kind: 54,912 (or once in 48 hands), Two Pairs: 123,552 (or once in 21 hands), One Pair: 1,098,240 (or once in 2½ hands), Other hands: 1,302,540 (or once in 2 hands).
I reproduce these figures from John McDonald's *Strategy in Poker, Business, and War*, a book to which I shall return. Yet every poker player will, I think, feel that at closer scrutiny there is something strange about them. It just does not happen that, on the average, one has to wait 48 hands for three of a kind, or 256 hands for a straight. And, besides, what are 2½ hands?

representing nothing higher than pennies. This, of course, is true of other games, too—but only to some extent. Clearly the very rich person, whether at the gin-rummy table or at the horse races, has a certain advantage over others: he can take chances which other players cannot, but he can also lose more—and that rich people gamble more successfully than poor ones is yet to be demonstrated. This is not so in poker, where a group of people with moderate incomes cannot afford to play regularly with a happy-go-lucky millionaire, whose attitude toward money will be different; and this is what counts in the end.

For, in the end, poker is also a game of a thousand unwritten rules. It is a game for gentlemen, and for gentlemen alone; and by this I do not mean that it requires social class but only those unwritten and often hardly conscious social standards and codes of behavior that constitute the subsoil of certain historical cultures. I cannot imagine Syrians or Burmese, including aristocrats or philosophers, playing poker in the way it was played in English or American clubs around 1880. This is not what sociologists call a value judgment: it is a historical condition. It has little to do with the rules of the game. Except for the dealing practices of the cardsharp, it is difficult to cheat in poker, but this is not the point. The point is that there are a thousand different ways in which poker can be played *legally* but *not quite correctly*, where its rules are strictly observed but its human relationships are not. People play poker in the way they want to play it; it is a game based to a large extent on free will, a game that flows from the necessity that we recognize a certain relationship between image and reality and that, for the sake of the game, this relationship be kept reasonably proportionate—an eminently Western game.

Poker, as played in Hungary during the years when I first learned the game, reflected something of the Hungarian national character. It was classic draw poker but with one important variation: the lower cards were excluded from the deck. Thus, for example, in a game of four (the minimum for a poker table) the lowest cards were sevens; when five persons played, the sixes were left in the deck; when seven were playing (the reasonable maximum), the fives were added. This kind of playing with a thirty-six- or forty-card deck did make the game quicker and perhaps more exciting: there were more good hands, and the hierarchy of hands was slightly changed. This lent the game a certain jaded but very Hungarian grandiloquence and *brio*. On the other hand, there was a slight but appreciable class difference between the several varieties of the game: certain people played with a gin-rummy deck, including the two Jolly Jokers which were naturally wild. "To play poker with a joker," I once heard my mother superciliously observe, "is a lower-class game."

All of my family were Anglophiles: indeed, my mother Anglomaniacally so. I remember the profound expression of shock on her face when two German visitors, business acquaintances of my stepfather, assured her in 1943 that many Germans, especially in Hamburg, played poker too; her incredulity was only partly assuaged by the subsequent assurance that those were anti-Nazis. It was around that time, during what had become the ritual practice of listening to London short-wave broadcasts over a large Telefunken radio, that we heard a human-interest background report about General Eisenhower: among other things, we were informed that he liked to play poker for relaxation. This piece of precious intelligence about the new Supreme Allied Commander filled us with great joy and hope. A poker-playing American general, we agreed, would be a general with nonchalance and dash and that loose-limbed, easygoing, natural elegance of action characteristic of Americans: this was the image that rose before us immediately; he would give short shrift to the methodical Germans.

This was before the invasion of Sicily. Our hopes were to be disappointed; the Italian front, the one closest to Hungary, bogged down in a largely senseless campaign. It took Eisenhower nearly a year to get from Naples to Rome, then another year from Normandy to Berlin. By that time the Russians, not the Anglo-Americans, had conquered Hungary, a bloody and prostrate country mostly in ruins, where no more poker was to be played for a long, long time. Not until eight or nine years later, during the Presidential campaign of 1952, did I learn that while Truman was a poker-playing President (and a President, too, with a great deal of historical sense), Eisenhower was not a poker player but a bridge addict.

I had many illusions about the United States when I landed in Portland, Maine, on a converted troopship in October, 1946. These illusions included poker. I was coming, I told myself, to the fatherland of poker, to the classic country of poker, where everybody plays poker, where I would have unlimited opportunities to amuse myself during the long American weekends. I understood that the American public was saturated with knowledge of the game and even "absorbed its language," as John McDonald put it; "every American, poker player or not, knows what it is to have an ace in the hole (or up the sleeve) or to be in the chips, to bluff or call a bluff, stand pat, four-flush, put his cards on the table, have a showdown, or otherwise get into a situation where the chips are down; and finally to meet the end of life itself by cashing in the chips."

I have now lived in the United States for twenty-four years; and I have played less poker here than during an average month in Hungary. Some of this undoubtedly has been the consequence of the strenuous quality of American life: I have certainly had less time (and, strangely enough, also less money) for poker playing than in Hungary. The main reason, however, is that the overwhelming majority of my friends now play a game that is still called poker, but its relationship to poker is about as distant as that of General Lee's horse, Traveller, to the President's bubble-top limousine—no, to his electric golf-cart. In twenty-four years I have been able to organize a classic, or draw, poker game but once. At best, I have been able to compromise, on a one-sixth or one-seventh basis, meaning that when we play dealer's choice, I choose five-card draw on my turn.

I must now explain, in brief, the differences between classic (or draw) poker on the one hand, and *all* other variations of poker on the other. In *every* other variation of poker—from the mildest (one card wild) to the wildest (seven-card stud, high-low)—the human factor is weakened and the factor of chance is correspondingly increased; seven-card stud resembles a gambling game with poker nomenclature but not very different from flipping seven pennies and betting on them in turn. In these games the unique character of poker is damaged, and perhaps ultimately destroyed. I need not enumerate here the many variations of the game—"baseball" or "spit-in-the-ocean," for example—that are widely and extravagantly played in America today. My point is that these "improvements" fatally affect the character of the game, so that it would be perhaps proper and just not to call them poker at all.

The most important of these fundamental changes is the considerable reduction of the unique poker opportunity of bluffing. Thereby the four essential characteristics of poker, mentioned earlier, no longer exist. It becomes a gambling game, with a few conventional variations remaining; it is a contest not between human personalities who represent themselves through money and cards, but between cards held fortuitously by certain individuals.

What has happened?

It is very difficult to know anything definite about the historical development of the game. It is, however, ascertainable that by about 1840 poker was widespread in western America. It seems, too, that this was the time when most of the present rules of draw poker grew up, and they were apparently well established before the Civil War. There is a story according to which the game was introduced in England when the American Minister showed it to Queen Victoria in 1872, but even though the latter event seems authentic, much evidence indicates that poker was played in England as early as 1850. During the nineteenth century the majority of English and American enthusiasts stuck to straight draw; the wilder variations of the game were to be found in mining camps, on the frontier and, according to certain legends, among Negroes in New Orleans, whence poker, like jazz, was supposed to have gone up the Mississippi.

Draw poker was therefore an American or, at the very least, an Anglo-American game. Indeed, it seems that an American innovation gave the game its definite shape as early as a century and a half ago; before that time the Louisiana French had played *poque* with a smaller deck, and with hands of three or four cards each. The introduction of the fifty-two-card deck gave poker a more masculine character, making it what I call a "low-scoring game." In this I tend to see a certain reflection of the characteristics of an Anglo-Saxon and democratic people, since one could win with relatively low cards, without the ubiquitous hierarchical royalty of kings, queens, and knaves. (Thus the face cards became less influential but more rare—as in nineteenth-century England the political influence of royalty lessened but its social influence rose.)

The golden age of poker in the United States seems to have been from 1870 to 1920. It seems, too, that contrary to the general assumption poker was not played mainly on the frontier and was not considered an archetypal gambling game. Poker, in those decades, was often an American drawing-room game, a game played in law offices after hours, a game for men, a game played by small-town friends in thousands of parlors from Maryland to Missouri, a manly and somewhat raffish pastime but one with a solid mahogany core, with a certain late-Victorian tinge. There is no doubt that the wilder variations of the game were already widespread by 1900; but from what I know of its intra-American history, the practice of draw poker began to fade rapidly only after the First World War, and to vanish from large areas during the Second, so that in 1946, by the time I arrived in the United States, it was already something of a rarity.

When certain people tend to act in certain ways, they also tend—note again that I say tend, not will—to play in certain ways. I believe, for example, that the social acceptance of poker-playing women may well have had a bad effect on the game. This began around 1920, after the Constitutional amendment ordering female suffrage and around the time when smoking by women began to be generally accepted. I believe that this wide introduction of the female element diluted the character of poker (just as Prohibition led, however indirectly, to the dilution of table spirits). Women are notoriously bad gamblers; they find it difficult to exclude social considerations from a game that must be organized around a social occasion; whereas in bridge, an intellectual and calculating game, women are equals and often superiors of men, this is not true of poker, with its strongly masculine characteristics.

Another bad influence was the frequency of gambling, under deleterious conditions, among servicemen and officers during the Second World War. These soldiers were playing poker day after day, for exorbitant sums, when they had nothing else to do. To play poker out of boredom will eventually lead to a deterioration of the game: the longer the boredom, the more artificial the excitements demanded by the human spirit. Consequently, during the war years hundreds of thousands of young Americans were introduced to a kind of poker in which "anything went" and wild games abounded, for the earlier mentioned subtle but very important relationship between the players and their normal financial circumstances was missing—in the shadow of possible death and amid the irregular interruptions of Army life, money could not possibly have the same meaning as in times of peace.

Since poker is still probably the most widespread domestic gambling game in America, and since poker playing and the poker player have become accepted and respectable prototypes of American behavior, many young people, from bored interns to the sons of clergymen, craving group acceptance and social sophistication, have chosen to learn and play poker at some time during their early years, even though many of them may have been characteristically or temperamentally better suited to other games of chance. The result of all this, and of many other things besides, is the present degeneration of poker into a game of chance with some of the original vocabulary and framework left to maintain the name of poker —in my opinion, fraudulently so.

In this development I see reflected the erosion of the American national character. The deterioration of poker, I believe, corresponds very closely to a tendency in modern American life that I find most disturbing and dangerous: the inflation (meaning the increasing worthlessness) of words— more menacing, even, than the inflation of money. Seven-card stud poker represents a gross inflation of values. It corresponds to the development of a society where everybody goes to college until the value of the college degree is less than that of a high-school degree forty years ago; where everybody nominally owns a house but with less sense of permanence and of privacy than the owner of a family flat in a Naples tenement; where the Great American Novel of The Generation is published at least twice, and of Our Decade at least five times, a year; and where everybody calls everybody else by his first name. Depending on cards rather than on one's own judgment reflects, too, a deterioration of self-confidence: in this respect the new kind of poker suggests some of the habits of the Organization Man. It also represents a form of immaturity, a strange kind of grown-up disorderliness covering up what is fundamentally an adolescent attitude.

Through seven-card stud and other wild games, poker has been transformed from a low-scoring to a high-scoring game. In this respect it resembles basketball, a sport I abhor, since I cannot find much interest in a game where scores run 158– 142, where even the worst team will make forty or fifty points, and where the gangling six-foot-eight-inch player is the inevitable joker, the wild card in the deck. Seven-card stud and its cousins are also truly Alice-in-Wonderland games of egalitarian democracy, where flushes are as frequent as two pairs in the older draw poker, where everybody wins and therefore nobody wins. In the large-scale limitation on bluffing it is perhaps not going too far to detect a craving for security or perhaps even for the welfare state. Just as those American businessmen who so often cry out against the passing of free enterprise have, through conformity and over-organization, helped to bring about the bureaucratization of business, so the addicts of wild and unruly poker are really conformists at heart. They have grossly exaggerated the element of blind fate; they have weakened the element of self-reliance in what was once a great American game.

A word remains to be said about the crowning absurdity of what has happened to poker: its study in our government-supported research institutes in universities and by our armed services as a science, under the idiotic name of Games Theory. It is difficult for me not to be abusive: for this development is part and parcel of the recent inclination of generals and admirals to listen in awe to the theories of our military intellectuals, usually refugee economists of Central European origin, who more than often cannot tell a shotgun from a rifle. It all began during World War II, this relatively recent American passion—so utterly unlike the Anglo-American past—for intellectualizing everything, from business to military strategy. Thus, while on the one hand the playing of poker becomes perverted, on the other hand poker is given an elaborate theory and becomes an object of scientific study —insufficient seriousness on one end, overseriousness on the other.

The "scientification" of poker has come about in two ways. First, mathematicians and nuclear scholars were for some time compelled to pay increasing attention to theories of probability (because of the collapse of earlier scientific assumptions about absolute mathematical certainty, but that is another story). Consequently some of them tried to examine and to illustrate probability theories through games of chance. The most notable result was a book by two Princeton luminaries, Oskar Morgenstern and the late John von Neumann, called *Theory of Games and Economic Behavior*, which around 1945 stirred the scholarly world to its depths. (It is perhaps symptomatic that during the following decade one of these eminent Central European savants, an erstwhile mathematician, became a hydrogen-bomb chief; the other, an erstwhile economist, a leading war theorist.) In 1948 John McDonald, a writer for *Fortune*, was sufficiently impressed by the book's reputation to consider expanding his excellent article "Poker, An American Game" into a more philosophical volume entitled *Strategy in Poker, Business, and War*. Subsequently, as his acknowledgment reads, McDonald felt compelled to consult not only professors Von Neumann and Morgenstern of Princeton but professors Ernest Nagel of Columbia, J. K. Galbraith of Harvard, John W. Tukey (again of Princeton), E. J. Gumbel of the New School for Social Research, Herbert A. Simon of the Illinois Institute of Technology, Jacob Marschak of the Cowles Commission, University of Chicago; Dr. E. W. Paxson of the Rand Corporation; Dr. Gunnar Boe, former Norwegian representative to the United Nations Economic and Employment Commission; and W. Edward Deming of the U.S. Bureau of the Budget. The result was a book whose chapter on poker, written by its author without the benefit of extensive scholarly consultations, is sensible and witty; and the rest of which is either nonsense or else, as Oscar Wilde would have said, pursues the obvious with the enthusiasm of a shortsighted detective. I cannot, at this point, go into metaphysical and philosophical details about how and why mathematical Games Theory has (or, rather, should have) nothing to do with poker. I have already said that poker is a game which cannot be played against an IBM machine; I must content myself with drawing attention to two principal assumptions of the games theorists. The first assumption—a mathematical *sine qua non*—is, of course, that all players are of the same temperament: an inhuman or nonhuman condition that cannot be found in reality. The second, and perhaps centrally important, assumption of the professorial gamesters represents the crystallization of their arguments. "Like all economic theories," (harrumph!) "the theory of games," McDonald writes, "is based on the assumption that man seeks gain." I have yet to see the man, except for the professional cardsharp, who plays poker because he primarily seeks gain. He plays for fun; and he hopes to make some gain. (Not the reverse. *Homo ludens*; not *homo faber*.)

By 1947 the armed services had given Games Theory a high security classification which, as McDonald put it in 1950, "is a sign that its intent is anything but trifling. A young scientist attached to the Air Force said . . . of its military application, 'We hope it will work, just as we hoped in 1942 that the atomic bomb would work.'" It certainly did. The result is with us, in the seven-hundred- to one-thousand-page volumes of our eminent warrior intellectuals, Professors Kissinger, Kahn, Morgenthau, and Morgenstern, each dealing with missiles, communism, Russia, the moon, hydrogen, war, peace, life, death. It is anything but trifling.

By the end of the fifties the books and articles of the games and military theorists amounted to several hundred, while the editors of American military journals set out on a quest to acquire the brilliant writings of military intellectuals for their professional warrior readership. Finally, as a result, we have reached the logical dead end of this development: a call for banishing the poker mentality from American thinking.

Spurred in part by the great Sputnik Panic of 1957, numerous professors, congressmen, and anti-communist experts have now drawn attention to the important role that chess, together with Marxism, plays in the Russian educational system. An example of this argument appeared in the May, 1962, issue of the *United States Naval Institute Proceedings*, a venerable maritime monthly, originally devoted to problems of naval history and seamanship, but lately more and more concerned with such profound matters as Ideology, Programming, Operational Research. In an article entitled "Contrasting Strategic Styles in the Cold War," which received honorable mention in the annual prize-essay contest of the United States Naval Institute, the author, Professor Charles O. Lerche, announced that "probably the most basic difference in strategic style between the Soviet Union and the United States is dramatically suggested by the Russian preference for chess as an intellectual pastime in contrast to the American predilection for either poker or contract bridge."

"American behavior in the Cold War," according to the author, who teaches international relations at American University, "is rooted—possibly unwittingly—in the bridge-poker school of strategy." This is a grave shortcoming, we are given to understand, since the essence of strategy in chess "is in its integral unity. The entire plan of attack is tied together from the very first move. . . . In chess, victory (checkmate) is won by one move made *at the end of the game*." "The crisis of decision facing the United States at this point in history," Lerche says, repeating an argument that has been made by now not only by our military intellectuals but also by new conservatives and psychological-warfare experts, "is whether the nation can safely go on playing poker with a chess master. . . . Under the conditions of military and political technology in the latter half of the twentieth century, what chance has a strategy of opportunity against a strategy of finality?" The answer, in my opinion, is: Lots.

Poker is a unique game because it approximates life. This is not true of chess, which is circumscribed by a framework of mathematical rules and is therefore irrevocably artificial. Even though the variations of its calculations are almost infinite, the rules are inflexible. That is why there are so many chess players of the rank of genius who are no good at anything else: their extraordinary capacity for mental gymnastics, on the one hand, being offset, on the other, by a generally below-average allowance of common sense (the theme of the late Stefan Zweig's *Royal Game*). Similarly, a thorough knowledge of Marxist epistemology gave precious little help to the Russian generals who faced German Panzer divisions in 1941. I do not remember having read that Stalin was a chess player (but, then, he probably read very little

Marx either). Clausewitz—from whom Lenin learned more than from Marx—is not recorded as having been a chess addict, but he knew an estimable amount of history.

"The chess strategist," writes Lerche, "has a major advantage over the poker player . . . he has a broader strategic outlook and many more analytical criteria." The very opposite is true—fortunately and, also, alas. Alas, because the widespread and fashionable nature of the chess-above-poker argument is, in itself, a symptom of American over-intellectualization, of the fatal departure from earlier American habits and traditions: God save the nation that prepares its young officers for war by making them play chess against business machines. Fortunately, because I believe that the common sense of Americans will in the end assert itself, as befits a nation of erstwhile poker—*draw* poker—players.

I have nothing against chess. I wish the Russians luck with it. It is a game typical of the concentrated and mathematical turn of mind; its character somewhat corresponds to the ironclad (and already greatly superseded) categorical thinking of dogmatic Marxists. Logical, rational, scientific as it then seemed, Marxism represented to certain Russians the very intellectual antithesis to the fatalistic, mystical, irrational inclinations of the Russian character—manifest, for example, in the Russian penchant for mad gambling, described profoundly and inimitably by Dostoevsky in *The Gambler* (his most honest, since most autobiographical, book). For the compulsive gambler the play elements in any game are subordinated to pure chance—as in Russian roulette, which carries to a logical extreme man's challenge to fate—an attitude perhaps not untypical of a people with an Oriental streak in their history and character. It was in resistance to this kind of Byzantine and Oriental fatalism that certain Russian intellectuals turned to the idea that life could be ordered and arranged as a logical and mathematical proposition—with results that are (or, rather, should be) painfully obvious. But life and love and poker and war are not mathematical propositions; indeed, life is stronger than theory—

266

which is just what the nonintellectual genius of the English-speaking peoples has intuitively recognized, and which has been the source of their historical greatness. "The key point," according to Lerche, is that "the conditions under which strategic choices are made are radically different in chess than in the games favored by Americans."

You bet.

NOTES
FROM AN
EMPTY ROOM

JAMES V. McCONNELL

I am writing this because I presume He wants me to. Otherwise He would not have left paper and pencil handy for me to use. And I put the word "He" in capitals because it seems the only thing to do. If I am dead and in hell, then this is only proper. However, if I am merely a captive somewhere, then surely a little flattery won't hurt matters.

As I sit here in this small room and think about it, I am impressed most of all by the suddenness of the whole thing. At one moment I was out walking in the woods near my suburban home. The next thing I knew, here I was in a small, featureless room, naked as a jay bird, with only my powers of rationalization to stand between me and insanity. When the "change" was made (whatever the change was), I was not conscious of so much as a momentary flicker between walking in the woods and being here in this room. Whoever is responsible for all of this is to be complimented—either He has developed an instantaneous anaesthetic or He has solved the problem of instantaneous transportation of matter. I would prefer to think it the former, for the latter leads to too much anxiety.

Yes, there I was walking through the woods, minding my own business, studiously pretending to enjoy the outing so that I wouldn't mind the exercise too much, when the transition took place. As I recall, I was immersed in the problem of how to teach my class in beginning psychology some of the more abstruse points of Learning Theory when the transition came. How far away and distant life at the University seems at the moment! I must be forgiven if now I am much more concerned about where I am and how to get out of here than about how freshmen can be cajoled into understanding Tolman.

Problem number one: Where am I? For an answer, I can only describe this room. It is about twenty feet square, some twelve feet high, with no windows, but with what might be a door in the middle of one wall. Everything is of a uniform gray color, and the walls and ceiling emit a fairly pleasant achromatic light. The walls themselves are of some hard material which might be metal since it feels slightly cool to the touch. The floor is of a softer, rubbery material that yields a little when I walk on it. Also, it has a rather tingly feel to it, suggesting that it may be in constant vibration. It is somewhat warmer than the walls, which is all to the good since it appears I must sleep on the floor.

The only furniture in the room consists of what might be a table and what passes for a chair. They are not quite that, but they can be made to serve this purpose. On the table I found the paper and the pencil. No, let me correct myself. What I am calling paper is a good deal rougher and thicker than I am used to, and what I am calling a pencil is nothing more than a thin round stick of graphite which I have sharpened by rubbing one end of it on the table.

And that is the sum extent of my surroundings. I wish I knew what He has done with my clothes. The suit was an old one, but I am worried about the walking boots. I was very fond of those boots—not because of any sentimental attachment nor because they had done me much good service, but rather because they were quite expensive and I would hate to lose them.

The problem still remains to be answered, however, as to just where in the hell I am—if not in hell itself.

Problem number two is a knottier one: Why am I here? Were I subject to paranoid tendencies, I would doubtless come to the conclusion that my enemies had kidnapped me. Or perhaps that the Russians had taken such an interest in my research that they had spirited me away to some Siberian hideout and would soon appear to demand either co-operation or death. Sadly enough, I am too reality oriented. My research was highly interesting to me, and perhaps to a few other psychologists who like to dabble in esoteric problems of animal learning, but it was scarcely startling enough to warrant such attention as kidnapping. So I am left as baffled as before. Where am I, and why? And who is He?

I have decided to forego all attempts at keeping this diary according to "days" or "hours." Such units of time have no meaning in my present circumstances, for the light remains constant all the time I am awake. The human organism is not possessed of as neat an internal clock as some of the lower species. Far too many studies have shown that a human being who is isolated from all external stimulation soon loses his sense of time. So I will merely indicate breaks in the narrative and hope that He will understand that if He wasn't bright enough to leave me with my wrist watch, He couldn't expect me to keep an accurate record.

Nothing much has happened since I began this narrative, except that I have slept, been fed and watered, and have emptied my bladder and bowels. The food was waiting on the table when I awoke last time. I must say that He has little of the gourmet in Him. Protein balls are not my idea of a feast royal. However, they will serve to keep body and soul together (presuming, of course, that they are together at the moment). But I must object to my course of liquid refreshment. The meal made me very thirsty, and I was in the process of cursing Him and everybody else when I noticed a small nipple which had appeared in the wall while I was asleep. At first I thought that perhaps Freud was right after all, and that my libido had taken over control of my imagery. Experimentation convinced me, however, that the thing was real, and that it is my present source of water. If one sucks on the thing, it delivers a slightly cool and somewhat sweetish flow of liquid. But really, it's a most undignified procedure. It's bad enough to have to sit around all day in my birthday suit. But for a full professor to have to stand on his tiptoes and suck on an artificial nipple in order to obtain water is asking a little too much. I'd complain to the Management if I only knew who the Management was!

Following eating and drinking, the call to nature became a little too strong to ignore. Now, I was adequately toilet trained with indoor plumbing, and the absence of same is most annoying. However, there was nothing much to do but choose a corner of the room and make the best of a none too pleasant situation. (As a side thought, I wonder if the choosing of a corner was in any way instinctive?) However, the upshot of the whole thing was my learning what is probably the purpose of the vibration of the floor. For the excreted material disappeared through the floor not too many minutes later. The process was a gradual one. Now I will be faced with all kinds of uncomfortable thoughts concerning what might possibly happen to me if I sleep too long.

Perhaps this is to be expected, but I find myself becoming a little paranoid after all. In attempting to solve my problem number two, why I am here, I have begun to wonder if perhaps some of my colleagues at the University are not using me as a subject in some kind of experiment. It would be just like McCleary to dream up some fantastic kind of "human-in-isolation" experiment and use me as a pilot observer. You would think that he'd have asked my permission first. However, perhaps it's important that the subject not know what's happening to him. If so, I have one happy thought to console me. If McCleary is responsible for this, he'll have to take over the teaching of my classes for the time being. And how he hates teaching Learning Theory to freshmen!

You know, this place seems dreadfully quiet to me.

Suddenly I have solved two of my problems. I know both where I am and who He is. And I bless the day that I got interested in the perception of motion.

I should say to begin with that the air in this room seems to have more than the usual concentration of dust particles. This didn't seem particularly noteworthy until I noticed that most of them seemed to pile up along the floor against one wall in particular. For a while I was sure that this was due to the ventilation system—perhaps there was an outgoing air duct where this particular wall was joined to the floor. However, when I went over and put my hand to the floor there, I could feel no breeze whatsoever. Yet even as I held my hand along the dividing line between the wall and the floor, dust motes covered my hand with a thin coating. I tried this same experiment everywhere else in the room to no avail. This was the only spot where the phenomenon occurred, and it occurred along the entire length of the wall.

But if ventilation was not responsible for the phenomenon, what was? All at once there popped into my mind some calculations I had made back when the rocket boys had first proposed a manned satellite station. Engineers are notoriously naïve when it comes to the performance of a human being in most situations, and I remembered that the problem of the perception of the satellite's rotation seemingly had been ignored by the slip-stick crowd. They had planned to rotate the doughnut-shaped satellite in order to substitute centrifugal force for the force of gravity. Thus the outer shell of the doughnut would appear to be "down" to anyone inside the thing. Apparently they had not realized that man is at least as sensitive to angular rotation as he is to variations in the pull of gravity. As I figured the problem, if a man aboard the doughnut moved his head as much as three or four feet

272

outward from the center of the doughnut, he would have become fairly dizzy! Rather annoying it would have been, too, to have been hit by a wave of nausea every time one sat down in a chair. Also, as I pondered the problem, it became apparent that dust particles and the like would probably show a tendency to move in a direction opposite to the direction of the rotation, and hence pile up against any wall or such that impeded their flight.

Using the behavior of the dust particles as a clue, I then climbed atop the table and leaped off. Sure enough, my head felt as though a mule had kicked it by the time I landed on the floor. My hypothesis was confirmed.

So I am aboard a spaceship!

The thought is incredible, but in a strange way comforting. At least now I can postpone worrying about heaven and hell —and somehow I find the idea of being in a spaceship much more to the liking of a confirmed agnostic. I suppose I owe McCleary an apology—I should have known he would never have put himself in a position where he would have to teach freshmen all about learning!

And, of course, I now know who "He" is. Or rather, I know who He *isn't*, which is something else again. Surely, though, I can no longer think of Him as being human. Whether I should be consoled at this or not, I have no way of telling.

I still have no notion of *why* I am here, however, nor why this alien chose to pick me of all people to pay a visit to His spaceship. What possible use could I be? Surely if He were interested in making contact with the human race, He would have spirited away a politician. After all, that's what politicians are for! Since there has been no effort made to communicate with me, however, I must reluctantly give up any cherished hopes that His purpose is that of making contact with *genus homo.*

Or perhaps He's a galactic scientist of some kind, a biologist of sorts, out gathering specimens. Now that's a particularly nasty thought. What if He turned out to be a physiologist, interested in cutting me open eventually to see what makes me tick? Will my innards be smeared over a glass slide for scores of youthful Hims to peer at under a microscope? Brrrr! I don't mind giving my life to Science, but I'd rather do it a little at a time.

If you don't mind, I think I'll go do a little repressing for a while.

Good God! I should have known it! Destiny will play her little tricks, and all jokes have their cosmic angles. He is a *psychologist*! Had I given it due consideration, I would have realized that whenever you come across a new species, you worry about behavior first, physiology second. So I have received the ultimate insult—or the ultimate compliment. I don't know which. I have become a specimen for an alien psychologist!

This thought first occurred to me when I awoke after my latest sleep (which was filled, I must admit, with most frightening dreams). It was immediately obvious that something about the room had changed. Almost at once I noticed that one of the walls now had a lever of some kind protruding from it, and to one side of the lever, a small hole in the wall with a container beneath the hole. I wandered over to the lever, inspected it a few moments, then accidentally depressed the thing. At once there came a loud clicking noise, and a protein ball popped out of the hole and fell into the container.

For just a moment a frown crossed my brow. This seemed somehow so strangely familiar. Then, all at once, I burst into wild laughter. The room had been changed into a gigantic Skinner Box! For years I had been studying animal learning by putting white rats in a Skinner Box and following the changes in the rats' behavior. The rats had to learn to press the lever in order to get a pellet of food, which was delivered to them through just such an apparatus as is now affixed to the wall of my cell. And now, after all these years, and after all the learning studies I had done, to find myself trapped like a rat in a Skinner Box! Perhaps this was hell after all,

I told myself, and the Lord High Executioner's admonition to "let the punishment fit the crime" was being followed.

Frankly, this sudden turn of events has left me more than a little shaken.

I seem to be performing according to theory. It didn't take me long to discover that pressing the lever would give me food some of the time, while at other times all I got was the click and no protein ball. It appears that approximately every twelve hours the thing delivers me a random number of protein balls—the number has varied from five to fifteen so far. I never know ahead of time how many pellets—I mean protein balls—the apparatus will deliver, and it spews them out intermittently. Sometimes I have to press the lever a dozen times or so before it will give me anything, while at other times it gives me one ball for each press. Since I don't have a watch on me, I am never quite sure when the twelve hours have passed, so I stomp over to the lever and press it every few minutes when I think it's getting close to time to be fed. Just like my rats always did. And since the pellets are small and I never get enough of them, occasionally I find myself banging away on the lever with all the compulsion of a stupid animal. But I missed the feeding time once and almost starved to death (so it seemed) before the lever delivered food the next time. About the only consolation to my wounded pride is that at this rate of starvation, I'll lose my bay window in short order.

At least He doesn't seem to be fattening me up for the kill. Or maybe he just likes lean meat.

I have been promoted. Apparently He in His infinite alien wisdom has decided that I'm intelligent enough to handle the Skinner-type apparatus, so I've been promoted to solving a maze. Can you picture the irony of the situation? All of the classic Learning Theory methodology is practically being thrown in my face in mockery. If only I could communicate with Him! I don't mind being subjected to tests nearly as

275

much as I mind being underestimated. Why, I can solve puzzles hundreds of times more complex than what He's throwing at me. But how can I tell Him?

As it turns out, the maze is much like our standard T-mazes, and is not too difficult to learn. It's a rather long one, true, with some twenty-three choice points along the way. I spent the better part of half an hour wandering through the thing the first time I found myself in it. Surprisingly enough, I didn't realize the first time out what I was in, so I made no conscious attempt to memorize the correct turns. It wasn't until I reached the final turn and found food waiting for me that I recognized what I was expected to do. The next time through the maze my performance was a good deal better, and I was able to turn in a perfect performance in not too long a time. However, it does not do my ego any good to realize that my own white rats could have learned the maze a little sooner than I did.

My "home cage," so to speak, still has the Skinner apparatus in it, but the lever delivers food only occasionally now. I still give it a whirl now and again, but since I'm getting a fairly good supply of food at the end of the maze each time, I don't pay much attention to the lever.

Now that I am very sure of what is happening to me, quite naturally my thoughts have turned to how I can get out of this situation. Mazes I can solve without too much difficulty, but how to escape apparently is beyond my intellectual capacity. But then, come to think of it, there was precious little chance for my own experimental animals to get out of my clutches. And assuming that I am unable to escape, what then? After He has finished putting me through as many paces as He wishes, where do we go from there? Will He treat me as I treated most of my nonhuman subjects—that is, will I get tossed into a jar containing chloroform? "Following the experiment, the animals were sacrificed," as we so euphemistically report in the scientific literature. This doesn't appeal to me much, as you can imagine. Or maybe if I seem particularly bright to Him, He may use me for breeding purposes, to establish a colony of His own. Now, that might have possibilities. . . .

Oh, damn Freud anyhow!

And damn Him too! I had just gotten the maze well learned when He upped and changed things on me. I stumbled about like a bat in the sunlight for quite some time before I finally got to the goal box. I'm afraid my performance was pretty poor.

Well, it wasn't so bad after all. What He did was just to reverse the whole maze so that it was a mirror image of what it used to be. Took me only two trials to discover the solution. Let Him figure that one out if He's so smart!

My performance on the maze reversal must have pleased Him, because now He's added a new complication. And again I suppose I could have predicted the next step if I had been thinking along the right direction. I woke up a few hours ago to find myself in a totally different room. There was nothing whatsoever in the room, but opposite me were two doors in the wall—one door a pure white, the other jet-black. Between me and the doors was a deep pit, filled with water. I didn't like the looks of the situation, for it occurred to me right away that He had devised a kind of jumping stand for me. I had to choose which of the doors was open and led to food. The other door would be locked. If I jumped at the wrong door, and found it locked, I'd fall into the water. I needed a bath, that was for sure, but I didn't relish getting it in this fashion.

While I stood there watching, I got the shock of my life. I mean it quite literally. The bastard had thought of everything. When I used to run rats on jumping stands, to overcome their reluctance to jump, I used to shock them. He's following exactly the same pattern. The floor in this room is wired but good. I howled and jumped about and showed all the usual anxiety behavior. It took me less than two seconds

277

to come to my senses and make a flying leap at the white door, however.

You know something? That water is ice-cold!

I have now, by my own calculations, solved no fewer than eighty-seven different problems on the jumping stand, and I'm getting sick and tired of it. One time I got angry and just pointed at the correct door—and got shocked for not going ahead and jumping. I shouted bloody murder, cursing Him at the top of my voice, telling Him if He didn't like my performance, He could damn well lump it. All He did, of course, was to increase the shock.

Frankly, I don't know how much longer I can put up with this. It's not that the work is difficult. But rather that it seems so senseless, so useless. If He were giving me half a chance to show my capabilities, I wouldn't mind it. I suppose I've contemplated a thousand different means of escaping, none of them worth mentioning. But if I don't get out of here soon, I shall go stark raving mad!

For almost an hour after it happened, I sat in this room and just wept. I realize that it is not the style in our culture for a grown man to weep, but there are times when cultural taboos must be forgotten. Again, had I thought much about the sort of experiments He must have had in mind, I most probably could have predicted the next step. Even so, I probably would have repressed the knowledge.

One of the standard problems which any learning psychologist is interested in is this one—will an animal learn something if you fail to reward him for his performance? There are many theorists, such as Hull and Spence, who believe that reward (or "reinforcement," as they call it) is absolutely necessary for learning to occur. This is mere stuff and nonsense, as anyone with a grain of sense knows, but nonetheless the "reinforcement" theory has been dominant in the field for years now. We fought a hard battle with Spence and Hull, and actually had them with their backs to the wall at one point, when suddenly they came up with the concept of "secondary reinforcement." That is, anything associated with a reward takes on the ability to act as a reward itself. For example, the mere sight of food would become a reward in and of itself—almost as much of a reward, in fact, as is the eating of the food. The *sight* of food, indeed! But nonetheless, it saved their theories for the moment.

For the past five years now, I have been trying to design an experiment that would show beyond a shadow of a doubt that the *sight* of a reward was not sufficient for learning to take place. And now look at what has happened to me!

I'm sure that He must lean toward Hull and Spence in His theorizing, for earlier today, when I found myself in the jumping-stand room, instead of being rewarded with my usual protein balls when I made the correct jump, I discovered . . .

I'm sorry, but it is difficult to write about even now. For when I made the correct jump and the door opened and I started toward the food, I found it had been replaced with a photograph. A calendar photograph. You know the one. Her name, I think, is Monroe.

I sat on the floor for almost an hour weeping afterward. For five whole years I have been attacking the validity of the secondary reinforcement theory, and now I find myself giving Him evidence that the theory is correct! For I cannot help "learning" which of the doors is the correct one to jump through. I refuse to pick the wrong door all the time and get an icy bath time after time. It just isn't fair! For He will doubtless put it all down to the fact that the mere *sight* of the photograph is functioning as a reward, and that I am learning the problems merely to be able to see Miss What's-her-name in her bare skin!

Oh, I can just see Him now, sitting somewhere else in this spaceship, gathering in all the data I am giving Him, plotting all kinds of learning curves, chortling to Himself because I am confirming all of His pet theories. I just wish . . .

Almost an hour has gone by since I wrote the above section. It seems longer than that, but surely it's been only an hour. And I have spent the time deep in thought. For I have discovered a way out of this place, I think. The question is, dare I do it?

I was in the midst of writing that paragraph about His sitting and chortling and confirming His theories, when it suddenly struck me that theories are born of the equipment one uses. This has probably been true throughout the history of all science, but is perhaps truest of all in psychology. If Skinner had never invented his blasted box, if the maze and the jumping stand had not been developed, we probably would have entirely different theories of learning today than we do. For, if nothing else, the type of equipment that one uses drastically reduces the type of behavior that one's subjects can show, and one's theories have to account only for the type of behavior that appears in the laboratories.

It follows from this also that any two cultures that devise the same sort of experimental procedures will come up with almost identical theories.

Keeping all of this in mind, it's not hard for me to believe that He is an ironclad reinforcement theorist, for He uses all of the various paraphernalia they use, and uses it in exactly the same way.

My means of escape is therefore obvious. He expects from me confirmation of all His pet theories. Well, He won't get it any more! I know all of His theories backward and forward, and this means I know how to give Him results that will tear His theories right smack in half!

I can almost predict the results. What does any learning theorist do with an animal that won't behave properly, that refuses to give the results that are predicted? One gets rid of the beast, quite naturally. For one wishes to use only healthy, normal animals in one's work, and any animal that gives "unusual" results is removed from the study but quickly. After all, if it doesn't perform as expected, it must be sick, abnormal, or aberrant in one way or another. . . .

There is no guarantee, of course, as to what method He will employ to dispose of my now annoying presence. Will He "sacrifice" me? Or will He just return me to the "permanent colony"? I cannot say. I know only that I will be free from what is now an intolerable situation. The chance must be taken.

Just wait until He looks at His results from now on!

FROM: *Experimenter-in-Chief, Interstellar Labship* PSYCH-145

TO: *Director, Bureau of Science*

Thlan, my friend, this will be an informal missive. I will send the official report along later, but I wanted to give you my subjective impressions first.

The work with the newly discovered species is, for the moment, at a standstill. Things went exceedingly well at first. We picked what seemed to be a normal, healthy animal and smattered it into our standard test apparatus. I may have told you that this new species seemed quite identical to our usual laboratory animals, so we included a couple of the "toys" that our home animals seem to be fond of—thin pieces of material made from wood pulp and a tiny stick of graphite. Imagine our surprise, and our pleasure, when this new specimen made exactly the same use of the materials as have all of our home colony specimens. Could it be that there are certain innate behavior patterns to be found throughout the universe in the lower species?

Well, I merely pose the question. The answer is of little importance to a Learning Theorist. Your friend Verpk keeps insisting that the use of these toys may have some deeper meaning to it, and that perhaps we should investigate further. At his insistence, then, I include with this informal missive the materials used by our first subject. In my opinion Verpk is guilty of gross anthropomorphism, and I wish to have nothing further to do with the question. However, this behavior did give us hope that our newly discovered colony

281

would yield subjects whose performances would be exactly in accordance with standard theory.

And, in truth, this is exactly what seemed to be the case. The animal solved the Bfian Box problem in short order, yielding as beautiful data as I have ever seen. We then shifted it to maze, maze-reversal, and jumping-stand problems, and the results could not have confirmed our theories better had we rigged the data. However, when we switched the animal to secondary reinforcement problems, it seemed to undergo a strange sort of change. No longer was its performance up to par. In fact, at times it seemed to go quite berserk. For part of the experiment, it would perform superbly. But then, just as it seemed to be solving whatever problem we set it to, its behavior would subtly change into patterns that obviously could not come from a normal specimen. It got worse and worse, until its behavior departed radically from that which our theories predicted. Naturally, we knew then that something had happened to the animal, for our theories are based upon thousands of experiments with similar subjects, and hence our theories must be right. But our theories hold only for normal subjects, and for normal species, so it soon became apparent to us that we had stumbled upon some abnormal type of animal.

Upon due consideration, we returned the subject to its home colony. However, we also voted almost unanimously to request from you permission to take steps to destroy the complete colony. It is obviously of little scientific use to us, and stands as a potential danger that we must take adequate steps against. Since all colonies are under your protection, we therefore request permission to destroy it in toto.

I must report, by the way, that Verpk's vote was the only one which was cast against this procedure. He has some silly notion that one should study behavior as one finds it. Frankly, I cannot understand why you have seen fit to saddle me with him on this expedition, but perhaps you have your reasons.

Verpk's vote notwithstanding, however, the rest of us are

of the considered opinion that this whole new colony must be destroyed, and quickly. For it is obviously diseased or some such—as reference to our theories has proved. And should it by some chance come in contact with our other colonies, and infect our other animals with whatever disease or aberration it has, we would never be able to predict their behavior again. I need not carry the argument further, I think.

May we have your permission to destroy the colony as soon as possible then, so that we may search out yet other colonies and test our theories against other healthy animals? For it is only in this fashion that science progresses!

Respectfully yours,
Iowyy

VACHEL LINDSAY'S LOST WEEKEND IN URBANA

M. M. MARBERRY

Urbana, Illinois, was no Sauk Centre, and my mother was no Carol Kennicott, but she did have a craving for culture and never missed the Chautauqua —including that memorable Saturday evening in 1922 when Vachel Lindsay came to perform. My father was dubious about spending twenty-five cents a ticket just to see a poet, but he gave in when mother pointed out that Lindsay also delivered temperance lectures. My parents were dry fanatics.

The turnout was surprisingly large, with some six hundred townspeople, faculty members, and college students attending. Everybody came to see a show, and Lindsay did not disappoint them. At first the students were in a challenging and derisive mood, but Lindsay quickly won them over, so much so that they became enthralled and cheered him after each reading just as they cheered when the Illinois football team scored a touchdown. The townspeople and the professors were less responsive. Some stared aghast at the poet, while others cradled their heads in embarrassment; none of them had seen a bona fide poet behave in such an outlandish manner. Lindsay's biographer, Elizabeth Ruggles, wrote that it was a unique experience to see him in the throes of a recital—his arms pumping up and down, his eyes rolling like a man in a fit, his body rocking, and his shoulders weaving. Her description was apt enough, for the auditorium was soon in a turmoil as Lindsay threw back his head, puffed out his chest, and began bellowing out his most spectacular and successful poem, "The Congo":

> *Fat black bucks in a wine-barrel room . . .*
> *Beat an empty barrel with the handle of a broom.*
> > *Hard as they were able,*
> > *Boom, boom,* BOOM,
> *With a silk umbrella and the handle of a broom.*
> *Boomlay, boomlay, boomlay,* BOOM!

Bounding to another part of the stage, Lindsay teetered back and forth on his heels, his hands jabbing the air, and, tipping his head back again, let go—slap, sock, and bang:

THEN I SAW THE CONGO, CREEPING THROUGH THE BLACK, CUTTING THROUGH THE FOREST WITH A GOLDEN TRACK. . . .

> *Then along the riverbank*
> *A thousand miles*
> *Tattooed cannibals danced in files;*
> > *Then I heard the boom of the blood-lust song*
> > *And a thigh-bone beating on a tin-pan gong. . . .*

Lindsay was accompanied throughout this recital by the tom-tom beat of a drum off stage. Suddenly the drum was silent and the poet lowered his voice and delivered the eerie last line in a menacing whisper:

> *Mumbo . . . Jumbo . . . will . . . hoo-doo . . . you.*

After the seven minutes of gymnastics required to complete the poem, Lindsay was hoarse and dripping with sweat, and the audience was almost as exhausted. The windup brought the students to their feet roaring.

"The Congo" was the *pièce de résistance* of Vachel Lindsay's repertoire. He also recited "The Santa Fe Trail," "The Chinese Nightingale," "The Kallyope Yell," "General William Booth Enters into Heaven," "Abraham Lincoln Walks at Midnight," and "The Eagle That Is Forgotten," an elegy about Illinois' liberal governor, John P. Altgeld:

Sleep softly . . . eagle forgotten . . . under the stone.
Time has its way with you there, and the clay has its own.

The audience participated in the rendering of some poems, chanting from the printed program. In his "Daniel" the poet would cry out:

King Darius said to the lion:
"Bite Daniel. Bite Daniel.
"Bite him. Bite him. Bite him!"

and then the audience joined in:

THUS *roared the lion:*
"We want Daniel, Daniel, Daniel,
"We want Daniel, Daniel, Daniel,
"Grrrrrrrrrrrrrrrrrrrrrrrrrrrrr."

It was an unforgettable night. The students felt they had seen the greatest theatrical act of the Urbana season. But the grownups had reservations about such a frenetic performance. They regarded Lindsay as a freak, not as a legitimate artist. To them it was like going to a slightly disreputable side show only faintly redeemed by a façade of culture. My father's reaction was typical of the older generation: the poet had been undignified, prancing and scampering around like an acrobat. This "New Poetry" was pretty obscure stuff. A lot of shouting. Vachel Lindsay was certainly no Longfellow, no Whittier. What was the fellow trying to prove, anyway?

Lindsay could have told him. He thought of himself as an artist originator whose "New Poetry" would, in short order, sweep all conventional forms of verse into the trash heap. As it turned out, he was wrong. Forty years after

Lindsay's death, his influence on modern poets is negligible. They admire his vivid imagery but shy clear of his chanted, syncopated rhythms, deplore his frequent alliteration, and regard him generally as an iambic curiosity.

Yet Lindsay *was* an innovator, though not, as he prophesied, in poetry. He was the first of the traveling troubadours to gain national attention. The Woody Guthries, the Bob Dylans, the Pete Seegers, and other minstrels owe him a debt for being the original voice of protest who performed on platforms before thousands, the man who smoothed the way for the horde of balladeers who today flourish from Berkeley to Princeton. But he is not revered by the current crowd, for they are not aware of his trail blazing, if indeed they know he ever existed.

Lindsay started out reciting protest verse—protest against the liquor traffic, against denial of the ballot to women—to the accompaniment of a stringed instrument, usually the guitar. Today these issues are academic, but platform protesting goes on, with the folk-rock singers using Lindsay's techniques to oppose the draft and the war in Vietnam.

At first Lindsay attracted little attention. Then, in 1913, as his poetic scope widened, he began intoning his verse in ragtime rhythm, in what he called "Higher Vaudeville" presentations. He was convinced that Americans "hate and abhor poetry," and so he sugar-coated the pill in order "to get the public." He developed a bouncy routine, totally unlike the ordinary, tame poetry reading; it was half revivalist and half jazz in style. He explained that his audiences thus were hoodwinked into thinking they were seeing a vaudeville act and were entertained. "And yet," Lindsay insisted, "I try to keep it to a real art." Lindsay's "New Poetry" caught on, his recitals became popular, and he made three successful cross-country tours. To see the poet striding and leaping about on the platform, gesticulating like a Billy Sunday gone mad and at the same time nasally chanting his verse to the tinkle of a guitar or the beat of a drum, was more than startling. Audiences everywhere were stunned, and Urbana was no exception.

Lindsay was scheduled to leave by train the morning after his performance, and was invited by the late Professor Stuart Pratt Sherman to stay overnight in his home. Sherman was well known on the campus as an essayist and a disciple of the Humanists, the literary and philosophical cult headed by Irving Babbitt and Paul Elmer More. I was often in the Sherman home, since I was a friend of the professor's son John. The evening after the recital, I went over to John's house and was surprised to learn that Lindsay had missed the train. Professor Sherman had given him his ticket—transportation to Gilman, then a trip on the Illinois Central spur to Springfield—and yet he was still in bed! John told me that a few selected members of the faculty had been invited to the Sherman house after the reading, and that the poet had entertained them with what amounted to a repeat performance. A raspberry punch—nonalcoholic, of course—had been served, and as the evening wore on, the guest had become more and more exhilarated until finally he collapsed and had to be helped to bed. John and I were mystified. Surely Lindsay could not have been drunk—he was a temperance lecturer.

John said his parents were going out for dinner and asked me to stay around. When the Shermans came downstairs, they found us immersed in our schoolbooks. Mrs. Sherman said Mr. Lindsay was suffering from total exhaustion and was not to be disturbed. The professor looked apprehensive.

As soon as they had left, we threw aside our books, and a few minutes later we heard what we took to be the cries of a man in agony. We rushed up to the guest room and found Vachel Lindsay propped up in bed, wearing his long underwear and downing the contents of a half-pint bottle. Near at hand was a valise neatly stacked with more half-pints. The poet was in no pain. He merely had been reciting his verse.

Lindsay was affable enough, not at all resenting the intrusion on his privacy by a pair of teen-age boys. He motioned for us to sit down, opened another half-pint, and said he would recite to us. John closed the bedroom windows. Neighbors in Urbana had big ears.

Although at the time I regarded anyone over twenty-five as an old man, Vachel Lindsay struck me as being fairly young. No doubt I associated poets with youth, with Chatterton and Keats. I know now that he was forty-three. Anyway, he looked like a poet—and it is difficult to look like a poet when wearing long underwear. I remember to this day how tall and wraithlike he appeared, even though he was in bed. (Recently I came across Lindsay in a group photograph and found him to be, inexplicably, a rather chunky man of medium height.) He was blond, with a long, dangling forelock. His forehead was high, and a protruding lower lip gave him at times a slight pout. His enunciation was precise, his voice resonant—and loud. He would peer at you sharply from the corners of his eyes, without shifting his head. There was decidedly an air of wildness about him. That was the way I thought a poet should look.

We listened to Lindsay deliver his poems for almost two hours. He treated us like grownups, and we were enchanted with him.

John Sherman finally reminded me that his parents would be back shortly. Before we left, I timidly mentioned an ambitious project I had been mulling over in my mind, one that would butter up my public-speaking teacher, who was showing a strong distaste for me. I asked Lindsay if he would read for twenty minutes or so to my eleventh-grade elocution class on the following morning at Urbana High School.

He agreed instantly. He even thanked me for the invitation, and said he was looking forward to the recital. I told him that the class met at eleven thirty and that I would pick him up at eleven. When we left, he saluted us with a gulp that emptied still another half-pint. He disposed of the empty as he had done before, tossing it across the room into an open closet, where it shattered. I have no idea what was in the bottles. Lindsay had mentioned that it was his favorite elixir. "Great as a tonic and bone hardener," he said solemnly.

At school the next day, my elocution teacher was delighted at the prospect of having Vachel Lindsay appear before her class. Then the thing got bigger. The principal heard the news and announced that the entire student body would gather in the school auditorium to hear the famous poet.

Promptly at eleven, I drove up to the Sherman residence in my Model T. I knew instinctively that the raffish Lindsay would enjoy riding to the school in a ramshackle machine that cost twenty dollars secondhand. As I approached the house, I could hear Lindsay singing upstairs. So could the neighbors, I noticed.

When Mrs. Sherman heard my story she was horrified. She said the poet was suffering from severe exhaustion, that he had not left his bed, that she was sending his meals upstairs, and that he could not possibly appear in public. She hustled me out of the house, instructing me, rather mysteriously I thought, to "say nothing about this to anyone."

I was too much of a coward to explain to the principal that Lindsay was not available. I simply stayed home. I learned later that the students, all eight hundred of them, had gathered in the auditorium and were happy about missing a whole class period. When I eventually saw the elocution teacher, I never mentioned the name of Vachel Lindsay, nor did she. But I flunked the course.

Before Lindsay left the Sherman household—a completely disrupted household, I now began to realize—I saw him twice again. I went to John's house Tuesday evening, and he told me that the poet was still staying on. The Shermans were waiting hopefully for their guest to leave; they were too genteel to boot him out. Mrs. Sherman was grim, her husband glum.

The fact of Lindsay's continued presence was kept a secret. He was isolated on the second floor, and the Shermans entertained no one. John told me that two college girls had come tripping up the sidewalk to keep an appointment with Professor Sherman, and that his mother had charged out of the house like a blocking halfback and shooed them off.

Later that evening John and I crept surreptitiously up the backstairs to visit our new friend. He was grumpy, not in the mood for singing or reciting. I noticed that his stock of half-pints had disappeared and that the litter of broken bottles in the closet had been carted away. This visit was not much fun for us. I felt as if I were visiting a man in the death cell.

Evidently Lindsay had forgotten altogether about appearing at the high school, for he did not mention it. In any event, our stay was cut short by Mrs. Sherman, who, when she heard voices in the guest room, bounded up the staircase and dragged us out, one on each hand. "He's still got his nervous trouble," Mrs. Sherman said. John walked half-way home with me and said his mother was upset because Lindsay had spent most of the night making long-distance calls, including a lengthy conversation with someone in Portland, Oregon.

I witnessed the eventual departure. Lindsay had arrived in town on Saturday, and he decided to leave Wednesday. The Shermans were dizzy with relief. As he was saying good-bye, Lindsay turned to me: "Don't forget about that date at the high school. I'm looking forward to it."

Lindsay was carrying his valise, obviously empty of bottles now, but the neck of a small bottle could be seen sticking out of his coat pocket. John told me he had seen Lindsay pouring cooking sherry from a jug he had found in the kitchen into a discarded bay-rum bottle. And later he told me that the poet had absent-mindedly walked off with a dozen of his father's silk socks.

The Shermans were beaming as they said their farewells, and Lindsay at long last walked out of the front door. There he paused. Undoubtedly he had suddenly recalled that Mrs. Sherman had prepared all his meals and served them to him in bed. He wanted to show he appreciated her hospitality. He reached around and patted her gently on the backside. Mrs. Sherman reeled with a horrified gasp. Then Lindsay said:

"The *coffee* was wonderful."

With that, Lindsay departed, and John and I never saw him again. The chances are the Shermans never did either.

Lindsay's farewell remark became a famous saying in Urbana. After a guest had dined particularly well, on a lavish five-course dinner, say, he would compliment the hostess with a casual, "The *coffee* was wonderful."

Vachel Lindsay's popularity as a platform balladeer continued for several years. His poetic powers had waned long before, for his most significant poems were all written before World War I. When the great depression struck, his day was over; people had no use for the frivolities of his "Higher Vaudeville." He was forgotten, just as he is forgotten today. In 1931 he died the hard way, swallowing lye.

BREAKFAST
WITH
OSCAR WILDE

BEVERLEY NICHOLS

O ne might have thought that the last story about Oscar Wilde had been told, that the last *chronique scandaleuse* had been dragged from the remotest volume of memoirs, and that the brains of every ancient Parisian concierge had been picked in the hope that in his guttersnipe days he might have been offered a glass of absinthe by the notorious M. Sebastian Melmoth, as Wilde was then calling himself.

But there is one story that has never been told, and I shall tell it here. And though it could be narrated in a very few words, that is not how I propose to go about it.

Besides, the story needs an introduction.

The scene was the bedroom of a rambling Victorian house in Torquay. I was going on fifteen and I had been rudely awakened from an innocent sleep, in the small hours of the morning, by a burly man with a thick black mustache. My father. He strode over to the window and tore back the curtain with a simple gesture. Then he sat down at my desk and began to write.

I rubbed my eyes and blinked at him with some astonishment. He was evidently in a towering rage—but about what? I knew better than to ask, and waited till he had finished. After a few moments he threw down his pencil, rose to his feet, and glared at me as though I were something unclean.

He pointed to the desk with a trembling finger. "That," he shouted, "is what That Man did." With which he stalked from the room, slamming the door behind him.

I was still scarcely awake, but I slid out of bed and took up the paper on which he had written, in block capitals, this macabre message: ILLUM CRIMEN HORRIBILE QUOD NON NOMINANDUM EST, "that horrible crime which is not to be named."

Then it all came back in a flood of humiliating memory—the violent scene of the night before, my mother's tears, and the flames creeping round my beautiful book, the book bound in white parchment powdered with silver fleurs-de-lis, the book that Reggie had given me, *The Picture of Dorian Gray*.

Reggie was a neighbor of ours, in his early thirties. He was rich, volatile, and extremely popular with the old ladies who formed the majority of Torquay's population. Nowadays, his walk, his clothes, the sinuous gestures of his delicately manicured hands, would have made it screamingly obvious to everybody that he was a homosexual. But Torquay was still sunk deep in the dark ages, as far as *that* sort of thing was concerned. Never for a moment did it occur to anybody that his mannerisms might be more than amiable eccentricities. "Dear Reggie is so artistic," murmured the dowagers, as they sipped their tea in his elegant drawing room. Even when he came to lunch at our house with his cheeks heavily rouged, my mother was merely amused. "Dear Reggie has actually begun to 'touch up,'" she observed to my father. "I wonder whatever he will do next?"

What he did next was to give me *The Picture of Dorian Gray*.

I was a good-looking boy—at this distance of time one may be pardoned for mentioning it—but I was also a strangely innocent one. On the evenings when I went to dine with him, which always ended with music, I sometimes wished that he would not breathe so heavily down the back of my neck when I was playing Chopin, but I suspected nothing sinister. The only thing that disturbed me, ever so faintly, was his apparent anxiety to make me drunk. At the age of fifteen a little Médoc and a glass of vintage port are enough to produce a considerable exhilaration, but at these dinners, when we were served by a young Greek footman who might have posed for Praxiteles, there was always champagne, and Armagnac, and an assortment of liqueurs as colorful as the celebrated passage about the jewels in *Dorian Gray*.

The present of *Dorian Gray*, which arrived on the morning of my fifteenth birthday, was presumably intended to produce another form of intoxication, and in this it certainly succeeded. As I have already mentioned, it was bound in white parchment powdered with silver fleurs-de-lis, but even if it had been a paperback, I should have fallen under its heady spell. From the moment when the curtain rose on the studio scene, with the scent of lilacs drifting through the open window, I was enthralled. True, some of the epigrams were a little over my head, and sometimes I felt faintly cheated because the author was so very mysterious about what Dorian actually *did* that was so unspeakably wicked. (In my innocence I suspected that it must be something to do with naked women.) But these were minor drawbacks to the sheer enchantment of page after page of purple prose, as heavily encrusted with jewels as a Fabergé cigarette case. This, I thought, was one of the great masterpieces of all time. Odd as it may seem, I still think so.

All through that long day of April, I pored over *Dorian Gray*, and in the evening my father found me reading it in the garden by the light of the dying sun. His reaction, as we have seen, was swift and brutal. When he hurled the book into the fire, he shouted that he was sending it back to its accursed author, who was burning in the quenchless fires of Hell. And when I dared to ask "Why? What did he *do?*" he could find no words to answer me in the English language.

"*Illum crimen horribile . . .*"

What has all this to do with our story? Very little, except to date it—and to accentuate the shock it made upon me when at last I heard it.

First the date. That was thirty years later. Incredibly, during those three long decades, the name of Oscar Wilde was never mentioned in our household. Europe might burst into flames—and did; Evil incarnate might stalk abroad—and did; but the author of *The Importance of Being Earnest* represented a sort of Evil beyond Evil. He was the ultimate horror, the Thing.

And then, quite suddenly and casually, my mother mentioned that he had once stayed with her family when she was a girl.

"He stayed with you? Oscar Wilde actually *stayed* with you?"

"I am afraid so."

"Why have you never told me this before?"

The answer was characteristic. "Because if I had known what he was, at the time, I should have run out of the house. I would have rather been in the room with a snake."

But at last she brought herself to speak.

It was in the winter of 1883. Oscar had recently returned from a lecture tour in America where he had been exploited as a sort of brilliant clown. This was the heyday of his aesthetic period, the day of the velvet jacket, the flowing cloak, and the soft felt hat. None of the major works had yet been written; the American dollars were soon spent, and on his return he was obliged to continue lecturing.

His first appearance was booked in that hideous, smoke-blacked center of British industrialism, Leeds.

Now it so happened that on the outskirts of Leeds lived

a formidable old lady called Rebecca Shalders, my grand-mother. Although she was a model of Victorian propriety, she was evidently keenly interested in the arts, and when-ever any celebrities arrived in the city she had a habit of annexing them. As she was rich, hospitable, and not unintel-ligent, the celebrities were only too happy to be annexed. And they usually sang for their supper.

But Oscar did not sing for his supper. He was far too tired. ("Languid" was my mother's adjective.) Besides, he was extremely cold. The lecture hall had been inadequately heated, the audience none too responsive, and afterward there had been a five-mile drive through the snow in my grandmother's carriage—a drive in which she had probably taken more than her fair share of the rug.

So after a large brandy and soda he had excused himself and made his way up the old oak staircase and taken himself to bed. During this brief interlude he had made only one remark which my mother remembered. "One's only real life," he had said, "is the life one never leads."

"Never mind," said my grandmother when he had gone. "At least we will see that the poor man has a good breakfast."

On the following morning my mother came down early to the dining room, to find the old lady hovering round the solid mahogany sideboard. This was laden with a weight of food which, even in Victorian Yorkshire, might have been regarded as almost ostentatious. Here my mother's recollec-tion becomes crystal clear, maybe because she was later to inherit most of the silver plates and dishes in which it was served. Thus, she vividly recalled the chafing dish filled with grandmother's special kedgeree, Georgian platters piled with sliced ham, the Regency sauceboat with the pickled cranberries, the Sheffield plate which accommodated the cold grouse, and the cumbersome Victorian device, mounted over a spirit lamp, for the eggs, the bacon, and the sausages. At various times in my life I too have been served from the same dishes. But not all at once.

Oscar was very late. More butter had to be spread on the

kedgeree, and there was a fear that the spirit lamp might run dry. But at last he made his appearance. He was still wearing his fur coat, and my mother, with a curious flicker of memory (I was a tireless cross-examiner!), recalled that the collar was still damp from the snow of the night before, and that she had thought that the fur must be dyed and not "good." And he looked paler and more languid than ever.

"And now Mr. Wilde," said my grandmother, "what would you like to begin with?"

Slowly he surveyed the sideboard, and a faint but perceptible shudder agitated his body, which even in those days was beginning to run to fat. For a moment he stood there in silence. Then he walked over to the window and looked out onto the cheerless landscape. The standard roses were muffled in straw, and in the distance the lake was a sheet of sullen glass.

He spoke very softly.

"I should like," he said, "some raspberries."

My grandmother felt that she could not have heard aright.

"I beg your pardon, Mr. Wilde?"

He turned and smiled.

He spoke even more softly, as though, in this incongruous atmosphere, at this unpropitious hour, a prose poem were forming in his willful brain.

"Some *pale yellow* raspberries," he said.

And that is the end of the story.

"Story," did I say? How can one make a story from a single word? That is a question I would not venture to answer. For after all, it was not I who said the word, but Oscar. He had a way with words.

DE
MORTUIS

J. H. PLUMB

The British have hilarious fun over the quaint funerary habits of the Americans. The death of Hubert Eaton, the world's greatest entrepreneur of death, and the recent discovery of a funeral home for pets, by a wandering British journalist, released another gale of satirical laughter in the English press. The mockery was hearty and sustained; yet was it deserved? Well, certainly much of Mr. Eaton's Forest Lawn is hard to take—the wet, nursery language for the hard facts of dying ("the loved one" for the corpse, "leave taking" for burying, and "slumber" for death), the cosmetic treatment (the contortions of death waxed away, replaced by rouge and mascara and fashionably set hair)—all of this is good for a gruesome joke. The place names of Forest Lawn appall—Lullabyland, Babyland. The piped guff, the music that flows like oil, and the coy fig-leaved art give one goose flesh.

One turns, almost with relief, to a harsh fifteen-century representation of the dance of death—livid corpses, jangling bones, and skulls that haunt. How wholesome, after Hubert Eaton, seem the savage depictions by Bonfigli of the ravages of plague, or even the nightmares of death painted by Hieronymus Bosch. And how salutary in our own age to turn from Forest Lawn to the screaming, dissolving bodies of a Francis Bacon painting, for surely this is how life ends for most of us, in pain, in agony.

And if Forest Lawn nauseates, what of the Pets Parlor? "Blackie" combed and brushed, stretched out on the hearth rug before a log fire, waits for his sorrowing owners. The budgerigar is wired to its perch. The Ming Room houses the Siamese cats, and if you want to do your kitty proud, you can spend three hundred dollars or so on a stately laying out, a goodly coffin (if you're worried about its fun in the afterlife, you can put an outsize rubber mouse in with it), and naturally a special plot in Bide-A-Wee, the memorial park for pets. President Nixon's dog, Checkers, had the treatment: he lies among the immortals in Bide-A-Wee, like Hubert in Forest Lawn.

However, this will become a mere second-class death if deep-freezing really catches on, as it shows every sign of doing. The Life Extension Society is spreading, and the entrepreneurs have smelled the profit in immortality. As soon as the breath goes, get yourself encapsulated in liquid nitrogen and stored in one of the specially constructed freezers that are springing up all over America from Phoenix to New York. And so wait for the day when they can cure what you died of, or replace what gave way—the heart, the brain, the liver, or the guts—or rejuvenate your cells.

None of this is cheap: the capsule costs four thousand dollars, and then there are the freezing costs and who knows what they may be in fifty years, so it would be imprudent not to make ample provision. Forest Lawn may be death for the rich; this is death for the richer, death for the Big Time. But in America there are a lot of very rich, so maybe soon now, outside all the large cities, there will be refrigerators as huge as pyramids, full of the frozen dead. This surely must be a growth industry.

Perhaps by the year 2000 Hubert Eaton will seem but a modest pioneer of the death industry, for who does not crave to escape oblivion? The rich have always tried to domesticate death, to make death seem like life. The American way of death is not novel: seen in proper historical perspective it reaches back not only down the centuries but down the millenniums, for it is a response to a deep human need.

Some of the earliest graves of men, dating from paleolithic times, contained corpses decked out with bits of personal finery and sprinkled with red ocher, perhaps the symbol of blood and life, done in the hope of a future resurrection. After the neolithic revolution, which created much greater resources and considerable surplus wealth, men went in for death in a very big way. Doubtless the poor were thrown away, burned or exposed or pushed into obscurity, back to the anonymous mind from which they came.

The rich and the powerful, high priests and kings, could not die; they merely passed from one life to another. Because the life hereafter was but a mirror image of life on earth, they took with them everything they needed—jewels, furniture, food, and, of course, servants. In the Royal Graves at Ur, some of the earliest and most sumptuous of tombs ever found, a row of handmaidens had been slaughtered at the burial—death's necessities were life's. No one, of course, carried this elaboration of funerary activity further than the Egyptians. And the tombs of Pharaohs and the high officials of the Egyptian kingdom make Forest Lawn seem like a cheap cemetery for the nation's down-and-outs.

What should we think of vast stone mausoleums outside Washington, stuffed with personal jewelry from Winston's, furniture from Sloane's, glassware by Steuben, food from Le Pavillon, etc., etc., and in the midst of it all the embalmed corpse of a Coolidge or a Dulles? We should roar with laughter. We should regard it as vulgar, ridiculous, absurd. Pushed back three millenniums, such habits acquire not only decorum but also majesty, grandeur, awe.

The Egyptians were as portentous in death as in life, and their grave goods only occassionally give off the breath of life, unlike the Etruscans, who domesticated death more completely and more joyously than any other society. A rich caste of princes built tombs of singular magnificence, filling them with amphorae, jewels, and silver. And they adorned their walls with all the gaiety that they had enjoyed alive. There was nothing solemn about their attitude to death. In their tombs they hunted, played games, performed acrobatics, danced, feasted; their amorous dalliance was both wanton and guiltless. Deliberately they banished death with the recollected gusto of life. No society has brought such eroticism, such open and natural behavior, to the charnel house. But in the annals of death, Etruscans are rare birds.

How different the grandiose tombs of medieval barons, with their splendid alabaster or marble effigies. There they lie, larger than life, grave, portentous, frozen in death, a wife, sometimes two, rigidly posed beside them, and beneath, sorrowing children, kneeling in filial piety, the whole structure made more pompous with heraldic quarterings. Yet these are but another attempt to cheat death, to keep alive in stone what was decaying and crumbling below. And even here a breath of life sometimes creeps in. The Earl and Countess of Arundel lie side by side, dogs beneath the feet, pillows under the head, he in armor, she in her long woolen gown. But, movingly enough, they are holding hands. The sons of Lord Teynham cannot be parted, even in death, with their hawk and hound. Nor were these tombs so cold, so marmoreal, when they were first built. They were painted, the faces as alive with color as the corpses in the parlors of Forest Lawn.

Seen in the context of history, Forest Lawn is neither very vulgar nor very remarkable, and the refrigerators at Phoenix are no more surprising than a pyramid in Palenque or Cairo. If life has been good, we, like the rich Etruscans, want it to go on and on and on, or at the very least to be remembered.

Only a few civilizations have evaded expensive funerary habits for their illustrious rich, and these usually poverty-stricken ones. For all their austerity, the Hindus, burning bodies and throwing the ashes into the Ganges, have maintained distinction in their pyres. Not only were widows coaxed or thrown onto the flames, but rare and perfumed woods were burned to sweeten the spirit of the rich Brahman as it escaped from its corrupt carapace. Cremation à la Chanel!

What is tasteless and vulgar in one age becomes tender and moving in another. What should we say if we decorated our tombs with scenes from baseball games, cocktail bars, and the circus, or boasted on the side of our coffins of our amatory prowess, as erect and as unashamed in death as in life. And yet when the Etruscans do just these things, we are moved to a sense of delight that the force of life could be so strong that men and women reveled in it in their graves.

So the next time you stroll through Forest Lawn, mildly repelled by its silly sentimentality, think of those Etruscans; you will understand far more easily why seven thousand marriages a year take place in this California graveyard. After all, like those Arundels, Eros and Death have gone hand in hand down the ages. The urge to obliterate death is the urge to extend life, and what more natural than that the rich should expect renewal. How right, how proper, that Checkers should be waiting in Slumberland.

THE
ASTROLOGERS

J. H. PLUMB

Are you Taurus or Gemini, Pisces or Capricorn? Does your eye glance furtively at the column headed "The Stars and You," and are you relieved when you read that you could have a "speculative benefit" or worried when you see "changeability in relationships may pose problems"? Or does a slightly sheepish, shamefaced smile flutter across your face as you turn hurriedly to another page of your newspaper? I suspect it strikes few readers that the silly astrological columns are the sad end of an extraordinary human enterprise. The belief that the movements of the stars are related to man's destiny dates back to the very earliest days of the neolithic revolution if not before. And the fact that popular, nonelite newspapers in America, England, France, Germany, Italy, India—indeed in all non-Communist countries—find it worthwhile to publish astrological columns day in and day out, indicates the persistence of that belief.

In addition to the popular astrologers, high priests of the cult still exist. They are masters of intricate calculations who cast horoscopes and predict the fate of individuals with the conviction of scientists, men and women who believe as intensely in the stars as did the astrologer-magicians of ancient China. True, over the last three centuries belief in the stars has steadily weakened, and the market for horoscopes dwindles. With the coming of industrial society and the scientific revolution, which has given us an accurate knowledge of the stars, astrology has become the plaything of the credulous and the ill-educated. But two hundred years ago its power in the West was still strong: both Cagliostro and Casanova cast horoscopes and interpreted the stars in order to bamboozle aristocrats, merchants, and attractive women. And a century before that the stars were playing a truly vital part in human affairs—although historians rarely pay any attention to this aspect of seventeenth-century belief.

The Earl of Shaftesbury, the violent Whig who nearly toppled Charles II from his throne by exploiting the hysteria of the Popish Plot in 1678-79, believed absolutely in astrology. (John Locke, the rationalist philosopher, lived in his household but apparently had no impact on this belief of Shaftesbury's.) A Dutch doctor who dabbled in the occult had cast the earl's horoscope and so, Shaftesbury thought, foretold all that would happen to him. Nor was Shaftesbury an isolated crank. The great Habsburg general Wallenstein, a leader in the Thirty Years' War, took no action, military or political, without consulting the stars, and no one thought him either eccentric or pagan.

In the centuries before the Enlightenment astrology lived quite comfortably with Christianity. Many kings kept astrologers at court and consulted them regularly. Dr. John Dee, the Elizabethan mathematician and astrologer, consulted the spirits in a polished obsidian mirror that he had somehow or other acquired from Aztec Mexico via Spain; and he, too, used the stars to predict the future. He created a sense of fear with his activities, but the most prominent Elizabethans consulted him, and he died comfortably enough in his bed and not at the stake. He might practice magic, but even in that age, terrified as it was by witchcraft, he survived. The stars were beyond the Devil and his work. They belonged to the mechanism of the universe, a piece of God's handiwork—therefore good and open to interpretation. A belief in astrology permeated all heresies and all creeds: Protestant, Catholic, Jewish, Moslem. And in this respect, at least, they were at one with Hindus and Chinese and with the civilizations of the Middle East. The stars influenced the lives of Sumerians, Akkadians, Babylonians, and Egyptians.

The first great historian of China, Ssŭ-ma Chi'en, gloried in the title The Grand Astrologer, possibly because the earliest archives to be kept systematically were those that dealt with astronomical data. Indeed the Chinese not only consulted the stars but devised the most elaborate instruments to determine their precise conjunction at any given moment. One of the most elaborate and complex astronomical clocks of antiquity was built by the Chinese so that the position of the stars would be known, even if the heavens were cloudy, in case the empress should conceive when the emperor paid a visit to her bed. Heaven would naturally be disclosing its hand at such an auspicious moment, either to foretell happiness or doom.

But long before the Chinese had developed their elaborate system of stargazing, the Assyrians and Egyptians had been studying the heavens just as intensely. Of all civilizations the Assyrian was perhaps the most addicted to astrology, and no king of Babylon would act in minor, let alone major, matters without consulting the stars. A great reference library was built up in the king's palaces, so that the predictions and their results could be studied and referred to. By the time Babylon fell the Assyrian astrologers and divinators had reference material dating back nearly a thousand years. The ancient Egyptians studied the stars, too, and believed in their benign or malevolent influence. Nor was belief in astrology derived from a single center. For without any contact with Europe, the Mayas in the Yucatán and Guatemala built huge observatories and watched the stars. From China to Peru, throughout many millenniums, men's lives were star-haunted, and the heavens wrote in cryptic symbols the fate of nations and the destiny of men.

So those foolish columns in the newspapers have a long, long history—a history heaving with portent. The stars have frightened men, made them jubilant, and, above all, strengthened a sense of unalterable fate not only in the hearts of the peasant and craftsman but also in emperors and kings, priests and soldiers. It is easy, of course, to see how relevant initially the position of the stars was to all communities that depended on the soil. Changes in the constellations indicated the coming of spring or winter or foretold rains in the Yucatán or the Nile flood in Egypt, events that, if delayed or inadequate, could mean famine. To the peasant the sky and the seasons were in mysterious harmony, although they were capable of discord. The constellations might appear, and yet the rains might stay away, in spite of sacrifice and religious observance; and then for years the harmony might be re-established. The will of the gods and the stars were interconnected, but not in an obvious way; they needed to be studied with minute care; only then could they be used safely for prediction.

But humanity's need for the stars goes deeper than the need to discern the changing seasons or the coming of rain and water, deeper than the need to foretell the fate of kings. There is a need in man to know and to rationalize his universe through magic and through very precise and detailed knowledge. He derives a sense of security from knowledge, whether it be the very precise and detailed knowledge of territory—of the trees and flowers and animals—such as the most primitive tribes of men acquire, or of the complexities of modern physics and biology. His aim has always been both to control his environment and to banish anxiety. Man has always been, as it were, scientifically oriented, even if his earlier and more primitive sciences did not work very well.

Only gradually did he learn the way to investigate precisely and to control (perhaps one should say exploit) his environment; but he put the same intellectual effort, the same passion to observe and to accumulate knowledge, into his earlier

307

attempts. Magicians and astrologers were but mankind's first scientists. They were men of great intelligence and keen observation, no different in quality from Newton or Rutherford, and essentially dedicated to the same task. Many of their facts were right and beautifully observed; their pursuits led them to invent instruments of great ingenuity. What was wrong was their set of premises. And in the vaporings of a popular newspaper astrologer one sees the pathetic end of a once majestic and comprehensive study of destiny: a science that for thousands of years interpreted men's hopes and fears and that seemed to give them a chance of evading disaster and controlling their fate.

SOME
NON-ENCOUNTERS
WITH MR. ELIOT

FRANCIS RUSSELL

When the St. Louis-born T. S. Eliot returned to the land of his Unitarian ancestors in 1932 to give the Charles Eliot Norton lectures at Harvard, it was his first visit to the United States since 1914. To speed him on his voyage across the Atlantic, one of London's literary magazines published a cartoon captioned "Mr. T. S. Eliot leaves for America Accompanied by the Thames River Maidens," showing him aboard ship with cockney mermaids gamboling in the waves alongside. Now that the new branch he grafted onto our old tree of literature has become so firmly attached to the trunk, it is hard to realize how daring it then seemed to appoint this frosty and formidable modernist, the iconoclast of *The Waste Land*, to Harvard's Victorian-plush Norton Chair. Even more perplexing in that nadir-year of the Depression must have been the knowledge that this very model of a model modern poet came as a self-announced "Catholic in religion, a classicist in literature, and a royalist in politics."

It was on a damp autumn evening that I walked through the Harvard Yard and across the street to the New Lecture Hall to attend his first lecture. The hall's cavernlike interior with its tiers of black wooden seats, each with swinging writing-arm attached, was for me a place of sour memories. How many dull Monday mornings had I sat there as a freshman, through lectures in History I, while Frisky Merriman cavorted about the platform, bald and pink like a depraved cherub, waving an eight-foot pointer and talking leeringly about the Defenestration of Prague!

For Eliot's first lecture the hall was only about two-thirds full. After World War II a lesser figure like Thornton Wilder, occupying the same Chair, could fill the hall, the balcony, and even the window ledges—and not say very much, either. But in the chill and limited mood of Hoover's last year in the White House, the cultural explosion was still a long way off, and poets and Norton lecturers were incidental. I think most of us were there that evening not so much to hear what Eliot had to say as out of curiosity about his person. What was this wild goose like who had winged away in the flood tide of William Howard Taft and returned in the Hoover ebb? And though few of us would have admitted it, one of the things we were all wondering about was what sort of accent he would now have.

Just as the bell in the tower of Memorial Hall was sounding eight o'clock he strode onto the platform—tall, hawk-nosed, offhandedly graceful, a tailor's model in well-cut evening clothes. The former United States citizen, now a British subject, had certainly absorbed his later surroundings. There was nothing American about him. I suppose he was the last Norton lecturer who ever appeared in white tie and tails. His hair was sleekly black, parted just to one side and Brylcreemed to impassivity. Before he began to read his lecture he paused and put on a pair of oval, narrow-rimmed tortoise-shell spectacles. At Harvard tortoise-shells had gone out with the twenties, and everyone from freshmen to emeritus professors wore round steel-rimmed glasses. As for hair, Harvard had proudly originated the crew-cut as a supercilious contrast to the slicked-down midwestern collegiate. Over the sea it was obviously different.

The voice for which we had been waiting was remote and somewhat melancholy. It bore no trace of an American accent, neither did it bear any trace of BBC. I found a certain measured ecclesiastical quality to it, and somehow I thought of Oscar Wilde's remark: "The bishop received him with extreme unction."

That Depression audience consisted mostly of Harvard faculty and graduate students, with a scattering of undergraduates, plus Cambridge's own inimitable breed of lecture-hounds who are to be found taking notes at every university lecture on every conceivable subject. But the two front rows were occupied by a phalanx of white-haired dowagers of the kind one used to see at Friday-afternoon Symphonies, readers of the *Boston Evening Transcript* whom Eliot described in his poem of that name as swaying "in the wind like a field of ripe corn." Most of them were clutching copies of his *Poems, 1909–1925*, containing that very poem, which they intended to have the author autograph at the end of the lecture.

A third of a century later I cannot remember what the lecture was about, or even its title. What has stuck in my mind from that vanished evening is one phrase only. "I don't suppose there is anyone in this room," said Eliot glancing up from his script with his hawklike look, "who has not read Daniel's *Defence of Ryme* and Campion's *Observations in the Art of English Poesie.*" Eliot was paying his audience a Cambridge compliment, but I expect he knew as well as I did that there would probably not be one in fifteen who had read those two essays.

At the end of his lecture the dowagers rose as one and formed up in line to pass by the lecturer, either to speak to him or to hold out a book for autographing. Graciously he bent over the platform, always ready to sign, occasionally shaking hands. Standing out of earshot, I imagined the old ladies with garrulous geniality telling him that they had known his cousins, his sisters, his aunts, his grandfather the Unitarian minister from St. Louis. Yet even when he shook hands, one had—I had, at least—the feeling that there was an invincible barrier between himself and this outside world, that no one could ever get within ten feet of him.

He remained in Cambridge throughout the academic year, having rooms at Eliot House.[*] During that winter I was in Brunswick, Maine, one hundred and thirty miles north of Boston, and the first Norton Lecture was the only one I managed to attend. But whenever I got to Boston for the weekend, I used to see Eliot on Sunday morning in church. That church, St. John the Evangelist, behind the State House on the wrong side of Beacon Hill, happened to be the church I belonged to. It also happened to be the highest of high Episcopal churches, run by an Anglican monastic order, the Society of St. John the Evangelist. The priests were known as the Cowley Fathers from their headquarters near Oxford, and on the street they wore cassocks, capes, and Continental-style shovel hats. St. John the Evangelist, for all its High-Church rigor, was not fashionable like the Church of the Advent at the foot of Beacon Hill, where Mrs. Jack Gardner once scrubbed the front steps for a Lenten penance. Most of our congregation was from the city's lodging-house belt, and notably deficient in both intellectuals and pious old ladies. The atmosphere was just too rare. We had a few communicants like Harvard's Professor Chandler Post, but the rest of us were obscure. I don't suppose there were three people at the eleven o'clock Mass who were even aware of T. S. Eliot. The Father Superior, the shrewd-eyed Spense Burton, of course knew who our distinguished convert was, but he never gave any sign of it as he stood by the door and shook hands with us in turn at the end of the service. As I look back now, I can't think of another church in all Boston where Eliot could conceivably have fitted in. If he had gone to Phillips Brooks's Trinity on Copley Square, the Low-Church rector would have welcomed

[*] Several of Harvard's most distinguished educators were forbears of T. S. Eliot, among them Charles William Eliot, president of the college for forty years in the last decades of the nineteenth century, after whom Eliot House was named; and Charles Eliot Norton, the noted poet, classicist, and art critic, after whom the Norton lectures are named.

him with hearty good fellowship while urging him to speak on "Christianity in Literature" to the young people's group. The old ladies of the Advent would have flung their rosaries at his feet. At Emmanuel, the Buchmanites would have gone all out to sign him up for propaganda purposes. But in the congealed atmosphere of St. John the Evangelist, no one bothered him at all. Each Sunday he occupied the same pew, about two-thirds of the way down the aisle, conspicuously inconspicuous behind a thin pillar. He had a look of pious elegance as he knelt in his beautifully tailored suit—usually of some tightly woven Glen Urquhart check. Beside him were his umbrella, doeskin gloves, and a derby—that he, of course, called a bowler—and his brown handmade shoes were not polished but boned.

Eliot was indeed the most precisely dressed poet since Byron. Not only had he achieved a poetic revolution in his verse: in his person he had achieved a sartorial revolution as well. Virginia Woolf might poke fun at his "four-piece suits," but he had given the death blow to Bunthornism. Yeats as a young man had worn a Windsor tie and an Inverness cape, and even in his hieratic old age still clung to a cut-down version of the tie. The youthful Joyce in his black Latin Quarter hat and thin pointed beard was obviously in the tradition of *Scènes de la vie de bohème*. Even Eugene O'Neill started out with a flowing cravat, as can be seen in old photographs. The aged Ezra Pound has always kept to the romantic tradition in his "poetic" garb. But Eliot changed all that. He made poets look like board chairmen.

The interior of St. John the Evangelist had been designed by Ralph Adams Cram. Like most High Churches it was in chill good taste, tinged with aestheticism. The priests wore Gothic chasubles rather than the square-cut Roman variety, and had even revived such medieval ceremonies as the ritual kiss of peace given by the celebrant to the deacon on the high altar. The music was plain song, then relatively rare, and under J. Everett Titcombe the best in the city. From time to time during the Sunday High Mass, I used to glance at the Eliot profile out of the corner of my eye. From a satirist who, a few years back, had written derisive verses about a hippopotamus being translated into heaven, he had become a scrupulous and exact conformist to the ritual, crossing himself, kneeling at the *Incarnatus*, striking his breast three times at the *Non sum dignus*, making the triple sign of the cross and genuflecting at the proper place in the Last Gospel.

I remember seeing him at the midnight Mass on Christmas Eve, his face highlighted in the semidarkness by the candles, the shadows giving his features an even more aloof and melancholy expression. It was a face that had never been young. I wondered, as I had at times before, whether he held to the Church as an institution or from personal conviction. Some months before, he had said bravely that he was a Christian not because it was aesthetically satisfying but "because it was true." Yet one of his mentors was Charles Maurras, the atheist champion of Catholicism who was like Santayana in thinking the Church a beautiful myth, but who went beyond that in holding it a myth necessary for most men to believe in in order to preserve the fabric of Western culture. The nonbeliever Matthew Arnold had felt that an established church was necessary for cultural continuity. Eliot, with his love of the traditional, who saw literature as a tree with its roots in the past, who must have felt the weight of generations echoing in the noble language of the Book of Common Prayer, who had even come to feel that democracy negated the deeper values of the spirit—was it for such reasons that I saw him decorously kneeling there? Or did he really believe, with what Unamuno called "the coal heaver's faith?"

The following summer, after I came back from Maine, I stayed for a week at the monastery in Cambridge, the North American headquarters of the Society of St. John the Evangelist. It so happened that Eliot, after his year at Harvard, was also staying there. I suppose I could have met him easily enough just by speaking to the Father Superior. But I never did. Somehow, I never could think of anything I wanted to say to him. I remember him most clearly at breakfast sitting at the long refectory table in the basement dining hall, that silent meal broken only by the sound of munched toast. Sometimes, but less often, I would see him at lunch or dinner. Except on feast days all the meals were taken in silence, but at lunch or dinner one of the novices would read aloud from some book—not necessarily religious—that Father Burton considered edifying. The novice always had an approximation of an English accent. It was as if an Anglican east wind were blowing through the monastery. Father Burton, of the Cleveland Burtons, sounded more like a London Burton. And within a few weeks any newly arrived novice, whether from the West or the South, would be modifying his accent to that pattern. Whenever Eliot appeared at lunch or dinner, he always attended the Nones or Complin services afterward in the little makeshift chapel that was also in the basement. That chapel seemed impregnated with incense. It had an uneven but highly waxed brick floor, foam-rubber kneeling pads (fortunately), and a plain altar with a baroque silver crucifix from Spain. Eliot never joined the fathers and their guests in the common room after dinner, though—at least not in the week I was there. All that week Father Burton was complaining rather humorously at the telegrams and cables he was receiving almost hourly from Eliot's wife in England— long, garbled, incoherent, and frantic.

Eliot had been married in 1915 to a ballet dancer, Vivienne Haigh-Wood. Except that it was an unhappy marriage, I know no more of it than that she was mentally afflicted and that after his stay at Harvard he never went back to her. Perhaps his nostalgic and tender poem "La Figlia che Piange"— "The Girl who Weeps"—is about Vivienne. It is said that much of the despair of *The Waste Land* is a reflection of personal disasters. About the time of his writing it, he had a complete breakdown. But always with Eliot there is the qualifying "perhaps," the "it is said." I don't suppose there is any other literary figure of his stature about whose private life so little is known. There has been no full-scale biography of Eliot, and perhaps there never will be. Only in the autumn ripeness of his *Four Quartets* did he at last allow the direct personal note to appear in his poetry. Yet, to my mind, it was always just below the surface.

Living near Boston in the thirties, I was often struck by how descriptive of that city some of his ostensibly London lines were. And though I could in no way prove it, I sensed that the imageries of his earlier poems—beyond the four that obviously refer to the city of Boston—were at core Boston rather than London. As a Harvard undergraduate Eliot certainly must have walked through the honky-tonk of Scollay Square on a Saturday night, traversed the flaring market district, stopped off at some sawdust-strewn oyster bar. The whole atmosphere of the now-demolished Scollay Square area comes back with

> *. . . faint stale smells of beer*
> *From the sawdust-trampled street,*

where anonymous hands

> *. . . are raising dingy shades*
> *In a thousand furnished rooms.*

After Eliot graduated from Harvard, he fled the Boston of his early verses, the city of Cousin Harriet waiting for her *Transcript,* of Cousin Nancy Ellicott who rode to hounds over the barren cow pastures, of Aunt Helen Slingsby in her parrot-and-dog house near Louisburg Square, of dowager Mrs. Phlaccus (Mrs. Jack Gardner) and Professor and Mrs. Channing-Cheetah. That North American Athens of Mrs. Gardner and Major Henry Lee Higginson and Bishop William Appleton Lawrence and Harvard's A. Lawrence Lowell, entrenched within the Beacon Hill–Back Bay redoubt while the Apeneck Sweeneys occupied City Hall, must have been to Eliot like an airtight room in winter with a stove exhausting the oxygen. I could not, and still cannot, imagine him settling down within the triangle of Beacon Hill, Harvard, and the North Shore, where the leading occupation was managing estates, the leading statesman Henry Cabot Lodge, the leading literary gent the novelist Judge Robert Grant, and where the household gods were "Matthew and Waldo, guardians of the faith." Eliot later described proper Boston with lacerating accuracy as "quite uncivilized—but refined beyond the point of civilization." He had to get out. London, the vast and imperial world city, was the only place for him. I think a reading of his four Boston poems shows clearly enough why he left America.

Yet there was another and unsuspected reason, one I learned only by chance some years after the monastery interlude. Just before the Second World War, I ended up in California after some months of wandering across the United States. I went to stay a few days in Pasadena with my college friend Dick, whom I had not seen since my own brief months at Harvard. Dick had never been much of a reader, and the books on twin shelves beside his fireplace looked like what Edith Wharton referred to as a "book dump." Just by chance I happened to notice and take down a small volume of Ezra Pound's *Selected Poems*. Opening it, I found that the selection had been made by Eliot and that the flyleaf was inscribed "T. S. Eliot—To my mother." "Where did you get that?" I asked Dick.

"Oh," he said, "I got it a long time ago, with some other things when Aunt Charlotte died. My cousins and I divided up her books. She was T. S. Eliot's mother, you know."

"Then you must be his cousin."

"Yes, I am. His first cousin. Not that I've read much of his stuff, though, or that book either. I haven't. Aunt Charlotte was a terrible bluestocking. I remember her, all right. She was forty-four when he was born. Not many people know it, but he really left this country to get away from her. He loved her, I guess. He always wrote her and used to send her all his books. But he never really felt safe unless he had the Atlantic between them. He would never come back to America, either, until after she died. She never crossed to England."

After Eliot's return to America in 1932, his visits became fairly frequent. He was at Harvard once more in 1935, lecturing and attending his twenty-fifth class reunion, but I never saw him again until after the war in London. I was living for a time then in Chelsea—where he too lived, although I never knew the address—in one of those renovated cul-de-sacs off King's Road. Chelsea was a London neighborhood with literary and theatrical overtones. Claire Bloom kept decorous house for her mother at one end of our street, Diana Dors camped not so decorously at the other end. Robert Newton, the actor, lived within shouting distance, and we could sometimes hear him. One evening we heard the crash of glass as he broke every window in the front of his house after his wife had locked him out. Sometimes I would see Dame Sybil Thorndike hurrying down King's Road, her string shopping bag full of vegetables. Occasionally I would run into what was left of Augustus John shambling from pub to pub. The biggest stir I remember was the day they took Jacob Epstein's son to a mental hospital and en route an attendant gave him some injection to quiet him, and he died. Ada, our char, swore they killed him on purpose. Such was Chelsea as I used to see it while walking down King's Road toward Sloane Square.

If I took the Number 11 double-decker bus in the morning I would at times find myself riding with T. S. Eliot, bound for his Faber & Faber office at Russell Square. He had not greatly altered in fifteen years, and was still the impeccably dressed city man with derby and rolled umbrella. But he has described himself better than I could:

How unpleasant to meet Mr. Eliot!
With his features of clerical cut,
And his brow so grim
And his mouth so prim
And his conversation, so nicely
Restricted to What Precisely
And If and Perhaps and But. . . .

He always sat upstairs in the front row and spent the time

between Sloane and Russell squares doing the *Times* cross-word puzzle. I usually stayed downstairs, in the profane hope that Joyce Redman might get aboard and fill the bus with her enchanting presence.

Eliot, the upper-deck crossword puzzler, had become a fixture of the Establishment, a dictator of literature second only to Dryden. He had refurbished the metaphysical poets, he could turn Milton off or on like a water tap, and in a few select words he could make the impossible Kipling possible again. An informal dinner guest of George VI's at Buckingham Palace (though it is a question whether that conga-loving king had ever read a line of anybody's verse), a vestryman of St. Stephen's, Kensington, and a holder of the Order of Merit, he still kept his high seat among the moderns.

Yet, seeing him at bus-stop distance and having no reason to come closer, I nevertheless felt a sympathy for his withdrawn presence that I had not felt in the earlier years, based mostly, I think, on a feeling of gratitude for his autumnal achievement in the *Four Quartets*. These poems came out individually in pamphlets just before and during the war, and I first read them in the Victorian rigor of the Corunna mess in Aldershot as a Canadian infantry reinforcement in those dragging months before D-Day. In the last section of his second quartet, "East Coker," I found the moving apologia for his creative self:

> *So here I am, in the middle way, having had twenty years—*
> *Twenty years largely wasted, the years of l'entre deux*
>   guerres—
> *Trying to learn to use words, and every attempt*
> *Is a wholly new start, and a different kind of failure*
> *Because one has only learnt to get the better of words*
> *For the thing one no longer has to say, or the way in which*
> *One is no longer disposed to say it. And so each venture*
> *Is a new beginning, a raid on the inarticulate*
> *With shabby equipment always deteriorating*
> *In the general mess of imprecision of feeling,*

Undisciplined squads of emotion.

Within the aspects of this extended poem, Eliot attempted to come to grips with the deepest problems that human beings have to grapple with: his own and human destiny, life and death, life *or* death, the mystery of time passing and time to come, the ultimate meaning of his religious beliefs. The *Four Quartets* are not easy reading. But where they are difficult, they are so in a very different way from the symbolist-derived difficulties of *The Waste Land.* And, as one always finds in Eliot though rarely in his imitators, there are lines touched by the music of incantation, the indefinable quality of true poetry:

> *The brief sun flames the ice, on pond and ditches,*
> *In windless cold that is the heart's heat,*
> *Reflecting in a watery mirror*
> *A glare that is blindness in the early afternoon.*

In his culminating poetic phase Eliot could turn back to his American past that he had once rejected, to his early memories of the tawny vastness of the Mississippi and the violence of the New World seasons. "My poetry is American. Purely American," he told V. S. Pritchett on his seventieth birthday. Sometime during the middle thirties he read *Huckleberry Finn,* and perhaps through the experience of that river idyll he was able to recapture the river of his childhood, as he did in the opening of "The Dry Salvages"—that quartet otherwise so haunted by the fog and sea echo of the New England coast.

> *I do not know much about gods; but I think that the river*
> *Is a strong brown god—sullen, untamed and intractable,*
> *Patient to some degree, at first recognized as a frontier;*
> *Useful, untrustworthy, as a conveyor of commerce;*
> *Then only a problem confronting the builder of bridges;*
> *The problem once solved, the brown god is almost forgotten*
> *By the dwellers in the cities—ever, however, implacable,*
> *Keeping his seasons and rages, destroyer, reminder*

Of what men choose to forget. Unhonoured, unpropitiated.
By worshippers of the machine, but waiting, watching and
*   waiting.*
His rhythm was present in the nursery bedroom,
In the rank ailanthus of the April dooryard,
In the smell of grapes on the autumn table,
And the evening circle in the winter gaslight.

"In my beginning is my end," he commenced the quartet "East Coker," reversing the phrase that Mary Queen of Scots had embroidered on her Chair of State. East Coker was the Somerset village where the Eliots lived before they emigrated to America in the seventeenth century. That deep-laned, obscure village was the beginning for all the Eliots—Puritans, divines, scholars—who had made their name noted in the New World. The living descendant of so many generations, reverting to the older beliefs that they had repudiated, had ended by coming back to the very spot as the last Tory émigré of the American Revolution

With the *Four Quartets* Eliot completed his cycle. His three last verse plays, written afterward, achieved some popularity through his reputation, but they are failures. Eliot wanted to revive the verse play. Christopher Fry proved that it could be done, but Eliot's attempts are tedious and insignificant for all his good intentions. If they had been written by an unknown Thomas Stearns, they would neither have been printed nor performed.

In 1957, ten years after his first wife's death, Eliot married his secretary, Valerie Fletcher, a young woman thirty-nine years his junior. The remaining seven years of his life were his most contented and serene. Then in his last year the acute and probing transplanted intellect dimmed. *"Omnia fert ætas; animum quoque"*—"Age bears away all things, even the mind." So wrote his prophetic mentor Virgil in the "Ninth Eclogue."

He was buried in the place he had chosen for himself, the churchyard in East Coker. Of time, he wrote in "Burnt

Norton":

> *Time present and time past*
> *Are both perhaps present in time future,*
> *And time future contained in time past.*

It might serve for his epitaph.

WHERE
ART THOU,
MUSE?

MAURICE SAGOFF

With all the science fiction produced in the past two hundred years, why hasn't there been at least a smattering of science verse?

"The subject, Sir, cannot be made poetical," was Dr. Johnson's damping comment about a contemporary who tried in a poem, "The Fleece," to describe scientific sheep farming. Some years later, Erasmus Darwin in "The Loves of the Plants" and "The Economy of Vegetation" tried to cross-pollinate botany with poetry. These went over like lead balloons. Another epic failure was "The Newtonian System," versified by a Fellow of the Royal Society; and if you look long enough in old bookstores, you may find a copy of Sarah Hoare's "Poems of Conchology." A pretty thin showing, the lot.

Yet there is no question that science poetry will be the next great breakthrough on the literary frontier.

Indeed, a little group of writers and scientists living in and around Cambridge, Massachusetts, has already organized to do the job. We have named our project *Scientific Poetry: Lyr-*

icism Applied To Technology, or SPLATT; and we welcome all
who seriously wish to advance the new art form. Our team is
presently made up of four writers and two scientists. We know
we aren't going to set the Charles on fire, but after only five
meetings we have already produced our first fruit, a Shakespearean sonnet on the Second Law of Thermodynamics.

It hasn't been easy. Our first meeting was marred by bicker-
ing and jockeying for status, like an acting out of C. P. Snow's
Two Cultures and the Scientific Revolution, but we are moving forward. Here are excerpts from the minutes of the initial
SPLATT meetings.

May 8. Opening session at the home of Dr. B., attended by
sixteen writers and twelve scientists. Dearth of science verse
discussed. Ancient poets cited as scientists of their day—Lu-
cretius's *De Rerum Natura* (forerunner of atomic theory),
Virgil's *Georgics* on the subject of scientific manuring, etc. Re-
freshments were served. All present were asked to bring ideas
to next meeting.

May 15. Many members absent, but a nucleus of ten proceeded with the meeting. Miss C. told of Shelley's devotion to
science, quoting Alfred North Whitehead: "What the hills
were to the youth of Wordsworth, a chemical laboratory was
to Shelley. . . . Physical experiments guide his imagery. For
example, the Earth's exclamation [in *Prometheus Unbound*]
'The vaporous exultation not to be confined!' is the poetic
transcript of 'the expansive force of gases,' as it is termed in
books on science. . . ." Prof. G. said this shows there need not
be any hard dichotomy between poet and scientist, and the
whimsical bit that goes

> Poet: *"O Cuckoo, shall I call thee bird*
>   *or but a wandering voice?"*
> Scientist: *"Mark X against the one preferred;*
>   *Give reasons for your choice"*

is grossly misleading.

Members were asked to select a theme for the first SPLATT
verse. The following were offered and eliminated for one rea-

son or another: Botulism in Food Fishes, Functional Calculus of First-Order Identities, Cybernetics, Stress-Strain in Precast Concrete. The theme finally agreed upon is the Second Law of Thermodynamics. The sonnet form has been selected as having the highest reliability factor. Next meeting will program the input.

May 29. Five members present. The Second Law of Thermodynamics defined as dealing with dissipation of energy; i.e., *it is impossible to construct an engine operating in cycle whose only effect is to transfer heat from one body to another at a higher temperature.* Simply stated, heat will not pass automatically from a cooler body to a hotter body. We will attempt to translate this into human values and insights—as great poetry must do with any theme—while at the same time satisfying the scientific mind. (Mr. G. offered a mathematical formula explaining the Second Law. It did not scan.) The committee on materials analysis suggested that since most sonnets are about Love, our subject with its warm and cooler bodies had possibilities for a kind of contrast structurization; e.g., the power of love to stoke up and incandesce a cooler element by heat transfer versus the impossibility of this happening in thermodynamics. Our Shakespearean expert, Mr. W. H., took up the idea, and we evolved the following opening lines:

> *Two hearts, one cool, one ardent, when they meet*
> *May work an alchemy of wondrous force . . .*

We have a feeling of elation. We are off the ground at last!

From these few excerpts you can see the work involved, the problems in creativity that had to be overcome by really inspired teamwork. Here is our completed sonnet:

> *Two hearts, one cool, one ardent, when they meet*
> *May work an alchemy of wondrous force:*
> *The warmer, pulsing with augmented heat*
> *Returns the flow to warm its cooler source.*
> *No man-made instrument can thus perform!*
> *Ingenious though it be, and free of flaw,*

The mightiest engine must obey the norm
  Of Thermodynamism's Second Law:
Heat cannot be reversed. By slow degrees
  It wanes each time the action is replayed,
The villain Friction drains its energies
And by its own device the plot's betrayed;
  The Law emerges evermore the hero

So long as $\int \frac{T-T_0}{T} \, dQ = 0.$

TO THE VALLEY OF THE ASSASSINS

TIMOTHY SEVERIN

The mountain trail was narrow, far too narrow for an inexperienced motorcyclist and his justifiably terrified pillion passenger. To make matters worse, a drenching mist had reduced visibility to a few yards and turned the rocky surface of the track into a treacherous slime. On our left the edge of the trail dropped away sharply, and an occasional stone, dislodged by the tires, would clatter and bounce for several seconds before it smashed on the rocks below. Once, through a gap in the mist, we peered down into the abyss and saw the burned-out wreck of a jeep that must have skidded on one of the hairpin turns and tumbled off the trail. Seventy-five miles behind us was Teheran, capital of Iran, and ahead through the mist lay the reason for our venture—the Valley of the Assassins.

My companion—Michael de Larrabeiti—and I had undertaken a journey to trace Marco Polo's route across Asia, and because the great Venetian traveler had written at length about the legendary valley, Mike and I were determined to visit the place. But the valley was accessible, or so we had been told in Teheran, only by mule train. It had seemed logical that where a mule could go, a motorcycle could go too. Struggling up the mountainside five hours later, we were not so sure.

The valley is a great gash, some twenty-five miles long and from three to ten miles wide, locked in the heart of the Elburz Mountains, which rim the southern end of the Caspian Sea. The spine of the valley is the Alamut river, rising at one end of the gash and cutting its way out at the opposite end of the valley via a spectacular sandstone gorge. This gorge and a half-dozen mule paths are the only routes into the valley and could be defended by a handful of men. For this reason the Alamut valley became in 1090 the headquarters of Hasan ibn-al-Sabbah, better known as the Old Man of the Mountain and First Grand Master of the Assassins.

In the preface to his translation of Omar Khayyám's *Rubáiyát* Edward FitzGerald offers a popular version of Hasan ibn-al-Sabbah's rise to fame. According to this story, Hasan was a fellow student of Omar Khayyám and a certain Nizam-al-Mulk. The three young men made a pact that whoever made his fortune first would share it with the other two. In due course it came about that Nizam-al-Mulk rose to be vizier to the sultan Alp Arslan and became second in power to the sultan. Then Omar Khayyám visited his former schoolmate and reminded him of their agreement. But Khayyám did not ask for riches or political advancement, only that he be allowed to live in the shadow of the vizier's fortune so that he could devote his life to the study of science and the arts. This boon was granted. But when Hasan ibn-al-Sabbah in his turn came to see the vizier, he demanded nothing less than a post in the cabinet. When this was given to him, Hasan used his position to undermine the authority of his benefactor. The final clash came when Hasan, eager to prove his superior ability, promised the sultan that he would prepare the royal budget more quickly and efficiently than Nizam-al-Mulk. Indeed, Hasan would have succeeded had not the vizier at the last moment jumbled together the sheets of Hasan's final ledger. Thus, when he read out his accounts to the sultan, Hasan lost his place, was thrown into confusion, and disgraced.

This story, like most contemporary tales about the Assassins, suffers from the fact that it was the theme of Hasan's enemies. On the other hand the official Assassin version of Hasan's life raises the First Grand Master to semi-divine status. Whatever the case may be, Hasan's early career was certainly more prosaic than the storytellers would have us believe, though it is not easy to unravel the twists and turns in his climb to power.

The first important step was taken when Hasan, who is thought to have come from a middle-class background, became a convert to the religious sect known as the Ismailians. A branch of the Shiite Moslems, the Ismailians claimed that Ismail, son of the Imam Jafar, was wrongfully deprived of his inheritance and was therefore the true Seventh Imam, tracing his descent back to the Prophet himself. The religious tenets of the Ismailians were extremely strict, and their spiritual leaders had absolute authority. Hasan rose swiftly in the Ismailian hierarchy, and in 1078 he went to Cairo, where the ruling Fatimid caliphs were themselves Ismailian supporters. At this point the Fatimid caliphate, once the foremost power of Islam, was in decline, weakened by the ineptitude of its leaders and torn by a dispute for succession. Cairo was seething with plots and counterplots, and Hasan took advantage of the turmoil to build up a personal following of dissidents who were attracted to the astute and ambitious visitor. Two years later he suddenly reappeared in Persia, this time at the head of a band of retainers who followed their master on a strange and erratic tour of the country.

Hasan visited isolated Ismailian communities and, significantly, inspected several mountain fortresses. Then, in 1090, he seems to have found what he was looking for in the Alamut valley; there, perched on the side of the valley, was a

Seljuk castle that would be impregnable if garrisoned with loyal troops and strengthened with additional fortifications. By now Hasan's odd wanderings had aroused the suspicions of the vizier, the same Nizam-al-Mulk of FitzGerald's tale. An order for Hasan's arrest was sent out, but it came too late. The garrison of the Alamut had defected, and Hasan ibn-al-Sabbah was safely ensconced inside the stronghold. The reign of the Assassins in the Alamut had begun. During the next thirty-four years, it is said, Hasan emerged only twice from his lair.

Two years later the Seljuk sultan Malik Shah (Alp Arslan's son) died, and his vast empire disintegrated into quarreling pieces. From his refuge in the Alamut, Hasan preached adherence to the strict beliefs of Ismailianism and encouraged local Ismailian cells to rise up against their rulers. When the other Ismailian leaders disapproved, he broke away from them and proclaimed that he represented the true belief. To give his independent movement a sense of legitimacy Hasan took up the cause of Prince Nizar, one of the claimants to the Fatimid caliphate. When Prince Nizar was defeated and killed, Hasan promptly announced that the prince's infant son had been smuggled to the Alamut, whence he would one day come forth to lead his people to victory. In the meantime Hasan himself was to be the Grand Master, guardian and spirtual leader of the rebels.

The extraordinary aura of myth, rumor, and religious fanaticism that surrounded Hasan ibn-al-Sabbah in his own lifetime distinguishes him from the run-of-the-mill mountain brigand. With real political skill and an uncanny sense of psychological legerdemain Hasan developed the Nizari Ismailians from an obscure religious minority group into a widely respected brotherhood of believers, responsible only to the Grand Master. He radiated personal magnetism, and he was shrewd enough to discern how he could twist the religious nature of Ismailianism to suit his own purposes. It is quite possible that Hasan himself was a sincere believer in his own creed, but his success lay in the fact that he diverted the Nizaris' intense religious loyalty into absolute obedience to himself. With this cult of personality Hasan ibn-al-Sabbah was the genius of the Assassins, and without him the word "assassin" would never have entered the languages of the West.

The root form of "assassin" is the Arabic word *hashshāshīn*, meaning "those addicted to hashish." By association with Hasan's fanatical followers it came to mean "a person who murders, particularly one who kills an important public figure from fanaticism or for money or other reward," because political murders soon became the hallmark of the Nizari Ismailians. There are several theories about how this association came about: the medieval Crusaders thought that the men whom Hasan sent out to kill his enemies committed their murders under the influence of hashish; contemporary Arab sources give the impression that the Nizari killers were called *hashshāshīn* not because they actually used the drug but because their religious mania resembled nothing so much as the effects of smoking hashish.

Marco Polo's version (see below), which received wide currency in the Christian West, describes how the Old Man of the Mountain would have young men drugged and carried into a lush garden filled with dancing girls and flowing with wine, milk, and honey. When the youths awoke they would think themselves in Paradise and thereafter, though returned to their native villages, would obey the Old Man's every command, hoping to return to the garden.

Marco Polo's tale cannot be dismissed as a complete fabrication, since the idea of a secret paradise flowing with milk and honey has obvious affinities with the existence of the green and fertile Alamut valley hidden in the midst of the barren mountains. But though the Alamut valley provided the grain of truth around which the legend was built, the skill of the tale was its appeal to the universal fascination for the concept of an earthly paradise where all sensuous pleasures abound. The wine, milk, and honey, the voluptuous damsels, and, in some versions, the nightingales specially imported to fill the valley with the sweetness of their singing—these were magical ingredients to the medieval imagination, whether Moslem or Christian. As Marco Polo said: "Mohamet assured the Saracens that those who go to Paradise will have beautiful women to their hearts' content to do their bidding and will find there rivers of wine and milk and honey and water."

In Christian Europe, too, there was the long-standing tradition of an Oriental paradise, a luscious garden filled with every delight, from which the angel had driven Adam and Eve. The story of Hasan's secret garden thrilled medieval society. The tale had just the right mixture of horror, fantasy, and exquisite enjoyment, and there was dreadful pleasure in contemplating the idea that the wicked Old Man of the Mountain had warped Paradise to his own evil purposes. Furthermore, the legend provided an explanation for the amazing devotion the Grand Master was able to instill in his followers.

Impressive examples of this devotion were common knowledge during the Middle Ages. Henry, Count of Champagne, was believed to have been invited to visit an Assassin fortress in Syria (the Nizaris spread there during the last years of the eleventh century), and as his host led him around the ramparts, the two leaders discussed the importance of personal devotion from their retainers. To illustrate that he could command instant and absolute obedience, the Assassin sheik turned toward a group of his *fida'i*, or fanatical followers, who were standing on a nearby tower, and with a wave of his arm directed that they should leap from the walls. Without a moment's hesitation the entire group of men jumped straight to their deaths.

This tale may or may not be true, but it was certainly believed by many people, and this was precisely the aim of Assassin policy: to build up a horrendous reputation for themselves. Hasan ibn-al-Sabbah and the Grand Masters who followed him relied not only on the devotion of their *fida'i* but also on a war of nerves, a medieval application of psychological warfare. To compensate for their own numerical inferiority the Assassins seldom allowed themselves to be drawn into open battle. Instead they withdraw into their mountain strongholds until any besieging armies lost heart and went home. This was the defensive side of their strategy. To conduct an offensive the Grand Master would send out hand-picked bands of Nizaris, disguised and carrying concealed weapons, to penetrate the court of a hostile ruler and murder him. The most important aspect of the assassinations was that they were conducted *in public,* as when the Prince of Homs and the Prince of Mosul were both struck down in full view of their subjects in their own mosques. In Nizari policy, assassination, like justice, had not only to be done but had to be seen to be done. Thus other rulers would learn their lesson and not interfere with the plans of the Grand Master.

Among the early victims of Assassin daggers was the man reputed to have been Hasan's schoolmate, the vizier Nizam-al-Mulk. His death was a typical Nizari murder. The vizier was killed at a public audience after an unidentified assailant had approached him as if to present a petition. When the vizier leaned forward to receive the petition, the killer snatched out a dagger and mortally wounded him. In later years Assassins were blamed for the deaths of at least two caliphs, the governors of Aleppo, Baghdad, and Khurasan, the son of Nizam-al-Mulk, and sundry emirs, sheiks, muftis, and rich merchants. Their near misses were also impressive. On June 16, 1272, Prince Edward of England, while on Crusade at Acre, was badly wounded with a poisoned dagger; and among the Saracens (who, as more orthodox Moslems, were repugnant to the Nizari Ismailians) the famous Saladin was rescued by his bodyguards from a suicide squad of Assassins who had penetrated to within a few yards of his tent. Louis IX of France, the Holy Roman Emperor Frederick II—the list of near victims goes on and on; and almost every sudden death, whether by illness, knife, poison, or garrote, seems to have been attributed to the malicious intervention of the Assassins. Such accusations are undoubtedly exaggerated, for the turbulent situation of the Middle East encouraged bitter enmities among squabbling princes as well as the wider conflict between Cross and Crescent. Individual rulers, even when officially allied with one another, were not at all averse to sending out their own men to murder their rivals and, when the job was done, blaming the Assassins for the killing. There was seldom any way of tracing the identity of the murderers because few of

---

MARCO POLO'S REPORT
OF THE GARDEN OF DELIGHTS

He (the Old Man of the Mountains) caused to be made in a valley between two mountains the biggest and most beautiful garden that was ever seen, ornamented with gold and with likenesses of all that is beautiful on earth, and also four conduits, one flowing with wine, one with milk, one with honey, and one with water. Fair ladies were there and damsels, the loveliest in the world, unsurpassed at playing every sort of instrument and at singing and dancing. And he gave his men to understand that this garden was Paradise. That is why he made it after this pattern, because Mahomet assured the Saracens that those who go to Paradise will have beautiful women to their hearts' content to do their bidding and will find there rivers of wine and milk and honey and water. So he ordered this garden made like the Paradise that Mahomet promised to the Saracens, and the Saracens of this country believed that it really was Paradise. No one ever entered this garden except those whom he wished to make Assassins. At the entrance stood a castle so strong that it need not fear any man in the world, and there was no way in except through this castle. The Sheik kept with him at his court all the youths of the country from twelve years old to twenty, all, that is, who shaped well as men at arms. These youths knew well by hearsay that Mahomet their prophet had declared Paradise to be made in such a fashion as I have described, and so they accepted it as truth. Now mark what follows. He used to put some of these youths in this Paradise, four at a time, or ten, or twenty, according as he wished. And this is how he did it. He would give them draughts that sent them to sleep immediately. Then he had them taken and put into the garden, where they were wakened. When they awoke and found themselves in there and saw all the things I told you of, they believed that they really were in Paradise. And the ladies and the damsels stayed with them all the time, singing and making music for their delight and ministering to all their desires. So these youths had all that they wished for and asked nothing better than to remain there.

Now the Sheik held his court with great splendor and magnificence and bore himself most nobly and convinced the simple mountain folk

them ever escaped with their lives. Angry mobs or palace guards cut them down before any questions could be asked.

Toward the end of their reign of terror, which lasted more than one hundred and fifty years, the Nizari Ismailians were accused of selling their services to the highest bidder. Originally, under Hasan ibn-al-Sabbah, the Assassins murdered only to further Nizari policies, but from there it was only a short step to committing murders on behalf of their allies. Naturally, once murder for hire became possible, assassina-

---

that were around him that he was a prophet; and they believed it to be the truth. And when he wanted emissaries to send on some mission of murder, he would administer the drug to as many as he pleased; and while they slept he had them carried into his palace. When these youths awoke and found themselves within the castle, they were amazed and were by no means glad, for the Paradise from which they had come was not a place that they would ever willingly have left. They went forthwith to the Sheik and humbled themselves before him, as men who believed that he was a great prophet. When he asked them whence they came, they would answer that they had come from Paradise, and that this was in truth the Paradise of which Mahomet had told their ancestors; and they would tell their listeners all that they had found there. And others who heard this and had not been there were filled with a great longing to go to this Paradise; they longed for death so that they might go there . . .

When the Sheik desired the death of some great Lord, he would first try an experiment to find out which of his Assassins was the best. He would send some of them off on a mission in the neighborhood at no great distance with orders to kill such and such a man. They went without demur and did the bidding of their Lord. Then, when they had killed the man, they returned to court—those of them that escaped, for some were caught and put to death. When they had returned to their Lord and had told him that they had faithfully performed their task, the Sheik would make a great feast in their honor. And he knew very well which of them had displayed the greatest zeal, because after each he had sent other of his men as spies to report which was the most daring and the best hand at murdering. Then, in order to bring about the death of the Lord or other man which he desired, he would take some of these Assassins of his and send them wherever he might wish, telling them that he was minded to dispatch them to Paradise; they would go accordingly and kill such and such a man; if they died on their mission, they would go there all the sooner. Those who received such a command obeyed it with a right good will, more readily than anything else they might have been called on to do. . . . Thus it happened that no one ever escaped when the Sheik of the Mountain desired his death.

tion became a less effective political weapon. There is the story of the potentate who offered the men who came to kill him twice their blood money if they would murder the man who sent them. This was far removed from the ideas of Hasan ibn-al-Sabbah, who believed that the death of a hostile ruler was a neater way of protecting the Nizari Ismailians than sending an army into the field for a bloody clash in which many men would die. Often, in fact, the actual assassination was not necessary; a threat—the dagger found plunged into the ground beside a sleeping prince, or the ostentatious gift of a winding sheet and a pair of knives—would be enough to make the opposition see reason. Hasan was aware that a co-operative ruler was more useful than a dead one.

When Marco Polo wrote about the sinister Old Man of the Mountain, the power of the Nizari Ismailians had been crushed forty years earlier. Marco Polo was particularly interested in the Assassins because his route to China took him close to the Alamut. The narrow mule track that Mike and I were finding so difficult to negotiate turned off the medieval caravan road and threaded its way up into the mountains, which stretched away in rank upon rank to the north. We expected to find the Alamut valley on the far side of every ridge, but it was not until the afternoon that our path at last began to descend. Then, quite suddenly, we emerged from the mist into brilliant sunshine. There, dropping away beneath our feet, lay a deep valley cleft and the silver thread of a river wriggling between the feet of the mountains. On the other side of the river rose the almost vertical wall of a great razor-topped ridge. This final barrier stood like a gigantic castle battlement, a huge reef of rock running directly across our path, and over the ridge we looked down onto a sea of white clouds pooled between the mountains' crests. The clouds hung like a canopy over what we knew must be another valley, the secret valley of the Assassins. By some trick of the light the flank of the final barrier ridge was glowing with reds, greens, grays, and browns of every shade where the different rock-bands had weathered into a random mixture of colors.

Cautiously we rode down the trail until it reached the riverbank and turned downstream. Our road petered out when the river disappeared between tall cliffs, and there, at the end of the track, we found a tumble-down caravansary and a party of Iranians having a picnic in the shade of a large tree. They invited us to join them and, after a meal of unleavened bread and creamy yoghurt, told us how to find our way into the Valley of the Assassins. First we had to leave our motorcycle behind and wade across the river to a tributary gorge on the far side. After passing through this gorge we would find ourselves on the floor of the Alamut valley. Then, about ten miles up the valley on the left-hand side, they said we would find the "Eagle's Nest," Hasan ibn-al-Sabbah's castle.

It was not too difficult to ford the river, because a line of submerged boulders marked the crossing. But on the other side our difficulties really began. There, sure enough, was the entrance to a narrow, winding gorge that opened like a slender knife thrust in the side of the ridge of many colors. The Alamut river had carved out that gorge—a thousand feet deep and about a quarter of a mile long—and now the river was pouring through like a mill-race. Mike and I had no choice but to plunge into the swirling water and thrash our way upstream, holding our cameras above our heads. Once I watched Mike being picked up by the current and tossed about in a graceful pirouette before being deposited with a bump into the shoals. Once we stopped to take some photographs, and Mike suggested that I pose in midstream. The photograph was not a success, for the shutter clicked just as I stepped into a large pothole and disappeared from view.

On the other side of the gorge Mike and I emerged onto a flat, fertile valley floor that gurgled and trickled with rivulets and irrigation channels. It was indeed a green paradise when compared with the harsh mountain slopes, though the lush vegetation made miserable terrain for walking. We blundered about for a couple of hours, falling into muddy ditches and squelching across paddy fields before we chanced to come across a rather surly muleteer who agreed to take us up the valley on his animals.

We spent that night at a small village some five or six miles from the gorge. It was not an experience that I would care to repeat; all night we tossed and turned under the searing fire of bites. Whoever concocted the story about the specially imported nightingales forgot to mention the ravenous insect population of the valley. Our blankets had just been taken from the mules and they crawled with vermin. For reinforcements every crack in the mud floor yielded up its scuttling column of bugs.

The next morning our muleteer suddenly and quite irrationally asked to be paid off, demanding far more money than we had brought with us. He stormed and ranted, and there was little use in haggling or offering to send him the extra cash when we got back to Teheran. The mule driver was determined to make trouble and refused to believe us, even trying to search us for hidden coins. Finally he grabbed Mike's camera and tried to make off with it. This was a mistake. Without a word, Mike and I sprang at him in calculated, flea-bitten fury. The ensuing brawl was very brief, for our opponent had obviously not expected that two Europeans would indulge in what Mike lovingly described as a "punch-up." A few wild blows and the whole affair was over. The muleteer lay on the ground and Mike had his camera back.

The court of enquiry that the village headman convened to investigate the fracas was a solemn affair. The council of elders sat in judgment, and while the sun rose higher the long arguments flew back and forth. Mike and I kept silent, since anything else seemed a waste of effort, and besides, our Persian vocabulary did not measure up to the occasion. Nevertheless, by midday we appeared to be winning our case, for the unfortunate mule driver had several counts against him: he was from a rival village; he had a reputation as a troublemaker; and, to clinch the argument, he had already been going up the valley with his mules when he met us. Under these circumstances it was deemed an act of charity to pay him anything at all for his miserable beasts. With profuse apologies for the muleteer's behavior the headman told us that we owed nothing and then sent his own nephew to guide us to the castle of Hasan ibn-al-Sabbah.

The Eagle's Nest is built on the flat crown of the Rock of Alamut, a vast sandstone boulder that juts out from the side of the deep valley. To reach the top of the rock one climbs a narrow footpath that curls around into the gap between the rock and the mountain behind it. There, in the shadows, one has a few moments of tricky footwork on the loose, crumbling surface of the trail before stepping out onto the crown of the rock to take in the view that the Grand Master must once have enjoyed. The only horizon is the long gray line of mountain peaks, half shrouded in clouds and appearing to hang in space. Far below, the cloud shadows chase each other across paddy fields divided by the glint of sunlight on streamlets, and from one end of the valley to the other there are the little groves of trees that surround the toy-like Assassin villages.

Today there is very little left of Hasan's fortress on top of the rock—only a few rather disappointing stumps of stone walls and a couple of caverns in which, it is said, the Assassins stored honey and grain that never spoiled during the one hundred and sixty-six years of their rule of the Alamut. Seven Grand Masters followed Hasan ibn-al-Sabbah, but they failed to match the founder's genius. Gradually the power of the Assassins ebbed away.

The end came in 1256; yet, in a sense, the *fida'i* were not disgraced since they were defeated by one of the most ruthless military machines of all time—the Mongol army under Hulagu Khan. The Assassins were forewarned that the Mongols had decided to crush them, and they appealed to the Christian princes to come to their aid against a common foe. But Europe was only too pleased that the Assassins had at last met their match and, in the words of the Bishop of

Winchester, sent back the cold reply "Let Dog eat Dog."

So Hulagu came with his squadrons of mounted archers, his Iranian auxiliaries, and his Chinese engineers skilled in siege warfare and equipped with mangonels and giant cross-bows capable of hurling a javelin more than twenty-five hundred paces. The Alamut could, perhaps, have held out; there were tanks of food and ample supplies of weapons, and water was piped to the Eagle's Nest through channels hewn into the solid rock. But the heart had gone out of the Nizaris. Their last Grand Master, Kwur Shah, vacillated. His councilors advised him to sue for peace, and so Kwur Shah left the Alamut to surrender himself to Hulagu. For three days the inhabitants of the rock were allowed to carry away their possessions, and then Mongol troops moved in to pull down the walls and demolish all standing fortifications. Several of the other Assassin castles put up a fight, but without the Alamut and their Grand Master it was hopeless. Kwur Shah was eventually executed by the Mongols and thousands upon thousands of Nizaris were systematically rounded up and put to death. The power of the Assassins was snuffed out; in the words of the Arab historian Juvaini: "Of him [the last Grand Master] and his stock no trace was left, and he and his kindred became but a tale on men's lips and a tradition in the world."

But history was to prove Juvaini wrong. At the end of the fifteenth century there was a Nizari revival, and a new imam came forward. Much later, in the nineteenth century, the reigning imam fled from Iran to India for political reasons, and the large overseas community of Nizari Ismailians accepted him as their leader. His heir, of the same name, and spiritual descendant of the Lords of Alamut, is the present Aga Khan.

ALWAYS
BE THANKFUL
WHEN YOU
CATCH WHALES

STAN STEINER

North of the Arctic Circle, on the icy fingers of land that border on the Chukchi Sea, there is the tiny Eskimo village of Point Hope. By the most recent nose count the Eskimos of this Alaskan settlement, some three hundred and twenty-four inhabitants, own twenty-five "magic machines"—their name for the Japanese tape recorders that have captivated the igloo market.

One tape recorder for every thirteen Eskimos!

Hunters of the polar bear celebrate a kill. But before the banquet of bear meat they tell the tale of their heroism, how they stalked the Goliath and how they killed him, to the spinning magnetic tapes. . . . It is a new moon and the "Song of Allingnuk," the Giver of Whales, is sung by the wives of the whaling-boat captains. Go bring out the tape recorders. . . . Young lovers are to be joined in Eskimo marriage. Record the wedding ceremony. . . . Sealing time has come and the little seals, the *nachik,* are stripped of their skins and cleaned and dried. Record the work songs. . . . Caribou has been hunted and the aromatic "ice cream" of the Arctic, the *akoo-tuk*, is to be boiled from the suet of the animal. Then seal oil must be added, and the frothy, snow-white soufflé frozen; it is much the same as frozen custard. Record the recipe. . . . *Oogruk*, the huge bearded seals, have been sighted near the village. Umiaks, the open whaleboats, set sail in the narrow ice channels, in pursuit. The old men sing to the success of the hunt. Record these songs too. . . .

On the icebound coast and in the inland settlements that burrow under a labyrinth of snow, the recorders wind and unwind the long hours of the Arctic night. Eskimos gather in sod igloo and log hut, not merely for social contact, but to record their vanishing culture before the jukeboxes of the youngsters drown it out with the wail of the Twist, "that animal dance," as the elders call it.

All this is a kind of reverse of the usual situation, where the professors and researchers descend with their equipment on some remote culture—which usually doesn't care whether it is recorded for history or not. But the Eskimos are creating a do-it-yourself anthropology, and the johnny-come-lately researchers of the future may find themselves quite useless. From Kwigillingok to Koyuk, Klukwan to Kwethluk, Kotzebue to Kalskag, Eek to Goodnews Bay—there are few villages not adept at modulating the treble or lowering the bass. And it would appear that there are few family circles that do not own their own "magic machines," for their personal pleasure and for the edification of visiting anthropologists.

Because of their geographical isolation, the Eskimos have been one of the most reticent of all the native people on the continent. Turn-of-the-century traders and explorers found them remarkably hard to tempt with the lures of a mechanized civilization. Even today, such developments as the supermarket and the automobile have a negligible influence on the frugal lives of the Eskimos, who still cling to subsistence hunting as a way of life. The reluctant acceptance by them of "non-native" culture, where it has occurred, has been largely due to practical necessity: an outboard motor for a whaling boat, a store-bought steel knife, a cooking stove for blubber.

Weather no doubt has played a major part in helping the Eskimos to avoid the usual fate of so many indigenous peoples of the Americas. Temperatures of 60 below zero have undoubtedly cooled the enthusiasm of many entrepreneurs, but the native character is obdurate, too. Until the tumultuous arrival of the present teen-age generation, the Eskimos have kept their traditions deep-frozen and almost untouched.

The Tundra Times, a newspaper of the Eskimos, Aleuts, and Indians of Alaska, has commented on this ironically: "In the case of the Arctic people, it is a well-known fact that they do not feel that civilization is adverse altogether. They have accepted many of the fine things civilization has to offer. On the other hand, the Eskimos especially, are resisting those things that seek to undermine their culture."

How, then, have the tape recorders charmed the reluctant Eskimos?

Although Eskimos have a written language, it is not generally known to Alaskan Eskimos and hence, until these handy devices arrived, there was no recorded literature. English, their language of literacy, is the speech of the children, learned in government schools. The old people, the traditional leaders of community life, use English mainly out of politeness to strangers—and when they have to talk to the tax collector. In their daily lives the Eskimo tongue prevails.

Legends of the past, ceremonials, and the songs of celebration and religion have had to be memorized. Much of this ancient lore has been lost in the endless retelling, from generation to generation. But magnetic tape has made it possible to halt this atrophy of a culture and thus preserve the best legends as passed on by the best "teller" in the village.

The "Song of Allingnuk," transcribed in this fashion, tells of Nikuwanna, the young wife of a whaling captain who on the spring night of a new moon, dons a beautiful squirrel-skin parka, climbs out of the *pallisuk,* the sky hole of her igloo, and lifts a stone vessel in prayer to the "Dweller of the

Moon." She sings:

> *O, Allingnuk, Dweller of the Moon,*
> *Allingnuk, great and generous Giver of Whales,*
> *I, Nikuwanna, whose wife I am of Killigvuk,*
> *A young and hopeful new whaler of Tigara,*
> *Implore thee for thy life-giving gift.*

One of the venerable Eskimo singers, Jimmy Killigvuk, who at seventy-one professes to remember the coming of the first white man to Point Hope (the Tigara of the song), has recorded a number of the old songs. Here is his mocking version of the "Eskimo Woman's Love Song," with its understated envoy:

> *Here I am sitting*
> *And I am sitting still.*
> *And I see two kayaks coming.*
> *Here I am sitting*
> *And I am sitting still.*
> *And two men are coming*
> *To court me.*
> *And here I am a ne'er-do-well*
> *And not very good-looking.*

Killigvuk has also recorded a hunting song which came down from his great-great-great-grandfather Karairnok:

> *Who am I?*
> *Watch me! I am the mouth of the river!*
> *I have killed the caribou and the oogruk!*
> *I have also killed the whale!*
> *Who am I?*
> *Watch me! I am the mouth of the river!*
> *I sing a song to Sunikpeak.*
> *Sunikpeak did not get a caribou.*
> *He did not get an oogruk.*
> *He did not get a whale.*
> *The reason Sunikpeak did not get these animals:*
> *Because he has a long, long beard.*

Songs of this sort, enlivened by the mock-heroic boast and the rejoinder so typical of the Eskimo's sardonic humor, have a buoyancy that probably would be dulled by the techniques of scholarly field workers. In doing their own tape recording the Eskimos seem to feel free to be themselves. In similarly intimate surroundings they record their dances, while an announcer identifies the persons who are dancing and describes their gestures.

"Letters" preserved on tape recorders journey from village to village. These have become the spoken newspapers of the North. Once the teller of a letter has recorded his message on his magic machine, he sends it, by umiak or dog sled, to his relatives far down the coast, or to a lonely inland settlement where it is welcomed much as a nomad troubadour of old. It has the advantage that nothing has been lost in translation.

These Eskimo letters are often orchestrated by a whole community, which gives them a choral effect. In the neighboring villages a communal communication of this sort is eagerly awaited. Local government matters and meetings of officials are recorded in a similar way. When the Inupiat Paitot ("People's Heritage") Conference was convened in Kotzebue last year, the speeches and discussions were taped and sent home with the delegates to their constituents. And it was suggested that such a procedure might have a salutary effect if it were instituted elsewhere. When officials of the Atomic Energy Commission came to Point Hope to hear the objections of the Eskimo leaders to the proposed "Project Chariot"—the explosion of a nuclear device in the area of Cape Thompson to create a polar harbor (a plan since shelved)— the proceedings were recorded by *two* tape recorders, kept "going full blast."

The most unusual and perhaps most important use of the magic machines by the Eskimos has been in the preservation of their folk-ways. It has helped to unify the scattered people of the tundra and create a sense of community in a society that had become diffuse.

So much, after all, is "on the brink of being lost," in the words of Mrs. Lorraine Koranda, a former teacher at the University of Alaska who has been recording Eskimo songs and customs since 1950. One of her recordings is of Chief John Oolanda of King Island in the Bering Strait, who, in a message to his relatives at Point Barrow on the mainland, intones a eulogy for himself and his way of life. His faltering words hint at a resilience of traditional values which may help to explain why the tape-recording fad has captured the Eskimo's imagination. Chief Oolanda's message is brief:

"I am sending greetings to the families of Kunaluk, Kokokruk, Kunungowruk, and Koonookyak. I have traced my ancestry and yours and found that I am related to all you men I mentioned.

"I am old now, and I do not believe I will see you again in this life. Someday we will meet somewhere else—out of the reality of this land—in a place that is not here on earth.

"I believe in God and with thoughts of Him I pray to you. I pray that you will have great success in your whaling. I pray that you will live the ways God wants you to. Then He will bless you with whales.

"Everyone who was born on the island is well. The aged ones are gone now. I had known them since they were children. I am eighty-one years of age now. My body is lessening in strength as I grow old. My friends, every day God comes nearer to me and I trust He will be here soon. Do not forget God.

"Always be thankful when you catch whales."

Seldom has a society had the good fortune of enjoying its own anthropology; even while it lives it.

INSIDE
XENOBIA

WILLIAM K. ZINSSER

It always surprises me that so few tourists have discovered Xenobia. In twenty years of roaming the world for my syndicated column, "Mister Footloose," I have never found a country so blessed with all the features that your average traveler is looking for. Truly it can be said of Xenobia, "It has everything."

Typical is the "all-purpose cathedral" that dominates the pretty capital city of Djrug. Begun in 1018, it has a Romanesque facade, a Gothic north side with flying buttresses, a south side in the Italian Renaissance style with an adjoining campanile, and a Byzantine dome. One of the spires is Baroque, as is the ambitious new transept begun in 1670 but never finished because of the plague. The plague was arrested in Xenobia, most authorities agree, though an occasional runny nose is still to be seen in the outlying areas.

The cathedral's interior likewise represents all forms of ecclesiastical architecture, from the pendentives which support the mosaic-studded dome (the figure of St. John the

Least is particularly striking in the late afternoon light) to the Saxon rood screen which separates the piscina from the tomb of King Retrograde II. Of special fascination—at least to me—are the frescoes in the nave. Every two years they are peeled off to reveal another layer of frescoes beneath. Since Professor Zinshausen of the Academy began this scholarly task in 1926, nineteen different sets of frescoes have been exposed—none, regrettably, as good as the one that preceded it.

Most notable of all, however, is the unfinished masterpiece by Xenobia's greatest artist, Ugo da Fat Lippi, which may be found in the apse. From this huge boulder of Carrara marble, Ugo lived long enough to carve only the superb foot on the southeast side. But in this foot any student of his work will discern the power and beauty of the total statue conceived by "the little chiseler," as Ugo is affectionately known.

Like the cathedral, Xenobia as a whole has something for everybody. I personally can recall no other climate where it is winter and summer at the same time. The lovely Struwwelpeter Mountains are draped all year in snow ideal for skiing and sliding downhill on an aluminum tray (it will be recalled that Xenobia won this event at the 1964 Olympics), yet the slopes end at the sun-kissed beaches of the Côte Jaune, where the summer-long film festival is held.

Surely, of all film festivals, none is as picturesque as this one. It begins every night at eight o'clock and is raided by the police before eight twenty. Strollers gather in the square outside the ornate Palais du Cinéma to watch the film makers being hustled out the front door and into the police wagon. Frequently they wager on the exact moment when this will occur.

Xenobian law allows every film maker two and one half minutes to tell the crowd that his film is not obscene but merely avant-garde and that his artistic freedom has been violated. *Aficionados* love to hear these impassioned speeches, much as your bullfight fan enjoys a well-executed veronica, and in reply they josh the film makers with genial cries of

"Dirty old man!" etc. Last year's entries were so avant-garde that none were shown beyond the opening titles, and the crowd saw many spectacular exits between 8:06 and 8:08.

Members of the international film colony stay at the unspoiled coastal village of Porto Veduta, where they may be seen "at play" every weekday afternoon from three to five and on Sundays from one to six. Inevitably the village becomes more and more spoiled as film folk keep arriving, and by autumn its sleepy charm is marred by souvenir stands, fast motorcars, and jazz music from the transistor radios that the screen personalities carry in their quaint sisal baskets.

But every year on October 6, known as "Landslide Day," the natives unspoil the village again and restore its rustic simplicity. Actors, producers, and agents who fail to reach their yachts in time are dug out and buried in the unpretentious little "Celebrities' Cemetery." This has become a popular shrine, along with the adjacent museum which houses the artifacts that they left behind. In row after row of glass cases one can study the myriad objects of Filmland, from sun lamps and toupees to screen treatments of Genesis.

This museum is but one of many that Xenobia boasts, Djrug alone has thirty-two, of which my own favorite happens to be "Galoshes from All Nations." Also popular is the Gallery of Art in Unusual Materials, noted for its Laocoön carved in fat and for the Monet *Water Lilies* in punched leather. And for fanciers of fine blown glass it is still rewarding to visit Glassblower House on Fünfjahreszeitenstrasse. Naturally one keeps wishing that the curator had not forgotten to close the door during the hurricane of 1958. But nothing has been swept up, and many exquisite fragments may still be seen here and there on the floor. Thick-soled shoes are advised.

Music is another art that is woven into the very soul of Xenobia. Thousands flock every May to pay homage to the revered ninety-three-year-old master of the ocarina, Ferenc Kolodnyí, at the festival held at the spa of Bad Bimstein. Nor can one overlook the open-air concerts presented twice weekly by the Klog Family on their chromatic goat bells. It speaks for the musical genius of the country that Baroness von Klog was able to train her eleven children, six nieces, four nephews, two uncles, three aunts, five cousins, and mother-in-law, as well as a stranger who stopped one day for lunch, to play the goat bells with such precision and feeling.

Space does not permit listing the one hundred and fifty-six annual folk pageants and outdoor events (three a week) that give Xenobia its Old World charm, nor would it be fair to suggest that one is more colorful than another. Sportsmen claim that the semiannual Rock Throw, though lacking some of the traditional graces, affords a thrilling spectacle of strength. Others prefer the Running of the Roosters, down the narrow Via Pamplona, which launches the long-awaited rooster-fighting season.

I myself, if pressed to name a favorite, would vote for the unique "Mayor Catch." Every July 12 the good townspeople of Djrug grease the mayor and send him dodging through the main square. The person who catches him becomes burgomaster for the next twelve months. Apart from the pure excitement of the event, which has its origins in a very old and unusual legend, it is a sterling example of democracy at work, reassuring the citizen that there is a system of "checks and balances" within the constitutional monarchy that has ruled Xenobia for centuries. Incidentally, the handsome cenotaph at Tarmac International Airport marks the spot where King Ribald VI absconded with the national treasury in 1928.

That the nation could rebound from this financial setback to the position that it occupies today—Xenobia is unquestioned leader of the "Outer Eleven" countries—is proof of its amazing financial health. The economy is geared to the fact that Xenobia can produce every item that tourists want, including simulated antiquities from each era dating back to prehistory.

Its current "best seller," of course, is the Pugotti VII, advertised as "the smallest car in Europe." This remarkable car folds up and can be carried in an ordinary suitcase. I never leave the country without taking one along in my valise, and as soon as I unpack it, I want nothing so much as to drive right back and "do" Xenobia all over again. Truly it can be said that there is still power in the old superstition about throwing one shoe in the fountain at Djrug. You will not be at peace with yourself until you return.

THINGS ARE IN THE SADDLE

WE CANNOT TAKE THEM WITH US, BUT IT SEEMS THEY CAN TAKE US WITH THEM

RUSSELL LYNES

A French sociologist named Georges Perec has written a novel called *Les Choses* that has recently been published in this country under the title *Les Choses,* which goes to show how international things are becoming. The novel, essentially an elaborately embroidered household inventory, sold 100,000 copies in France and won one of their innumerable literary prizes, the Prix Renaudot. It is about a young couple called Jérôme and Sylvie, who must be one of the most boring couples in French, or any other, literature. These young people are impressed by things, all sorts and manner of things, so long as they bespeak the good life, which to them is the life of the upper classes (though they also seem to settle for what we might call Upper Bohemian); and they are voyeurs, because they are too lazy to earn enough money to buy the things they letch after. I am devoted to things myself, up to a point, but I left Jérôme and Sylvie staring into a shop window along about page fifty, and I hope never to meet them again.

One thing that 100,000 Frenchmen are not wrong about is that this is an age uncommonly concerned with things, with their manufacture, their distribution, their acquisition. Things are endowed with mystical powers beyond the dreams of those who make them, with social influence, political significance, international prestige. The world has become, if you will excuse the expression, a *thingdom;* and the importance of its several provinces is more and more determined by how many things they can make, consume, waste, and have left over to sell (or, even better, to give) to other provinces. In general, things (more viable today than ideas) are divided into two principal categories—consumer goods and military hardware—and it is a tossup which has more international status. The great debate in most provinces of thingdom is which category shall be allocated the greater part of the wealth.

It is infra dig for a "great nation" today not to have the most destructive thing of all, and scientific progress (or "who's ahead") is measured by how many things a nation can put in orbit and how big they are. Less great nations settle for dams to create power to make things, and emerging nations momentarily settle for a jet transport (which is called an airline) or a railroad: things that will transport other things when there are any to transport. Total progress is measured by improved "standard of living," which, of course, is measured primarily by things—refrigerators, clothes, automobiles, houses, furniture—not by education, say, or health. We even take nonthings like food and by processing them, freezing them, packaging them, make them into things. A thing is easier to cope with than a fact of nature in the raw. You can store it, break it, put it on the mantelpiece, forget it. If you can't think of anything else to do with it you can use it, or if you're a great nation you can negotiate about not using it.

There is a story of a little boy who was given a couple of chocolate rabbits at Easter that, I think, must have a profound meaning for our thing-ridden society. By the end of the day the rabbits had disappeared, and the boy's mother asked him what had become of them. "They got too dirty to play with," he said, "so I ate them."

If more of us could establish as logical and direct a relationship with things as this, think what a different world we would live in. There are some people who give the appearance of staying a pace or two ahead of things, men for example whose desks are always neat and uncluttered, tidy altars ornamented with the ritual accoutrements of business —the onyx-based pen stand with gold swivels, the monogrammed silver frame with pictures of wife and children, the tooled leather portfolio, the empty "in" and the full "out" baskets, symbols of decisiveness, of mastery over things. I am suspicious of such desks and darkly believe that beneath their pristine surfaces the drawers groan with indecisions— undigested memorandums, knots of rubber bands, dried-up erasers, pennies, unused date books with one's name stamped on them in gold letters by insurance brokers: things, in other words, that are in *my* desk and seem impossible to throw away and, no matter how dirty, are impossible to eat.

We are creatures of clutter in an age of clutter. Clutter is what happens to things when they become useless but friendly. The Victorians made it into an ideal of decoration, a nice try at turning man's natural instinct for indecision into a domestic virtue of sorts. Emerson, who lived through the height of that Age of Clutter said, "Things are in the saddle, and ride mankind." The history of civilization is the history of things—things made of stone, of bronze, of iron, of clay and glass and precious metals, things for survival and for vanity. The history of mankind is one big desk drawer.

I sometimes think that the world would be a better (certainly a more orderly) place if man could "take it with him" to the grave—especially his indecisions. Consider, for example, the problem of the wire clothes hangers. Do you save them or throw them away? Or do you save the ones with the cardboard still on them and throw the others away? It is a little thing, but it is symptomatic. There is something of the pack rat in all of us.

We are forced, however, to make decisions about things lest we be defeated by them, lest, as consumers, we become consumed, buried, overwhelmed. Every so often one has to turn over a new leaf, start fresh, face the facts, and perform (or try to) other such clichés of salvation. This very day I am going to start ruthlessly throwing away things, and as a symbol of my emancipation, the first thing I am going to throw away is *Les Choses*.

THE
GRAND
ACQUISITOR

FRANKLIN RUSSELL

The nervous, black-eyed pack rat is a nut gatherer, thief, and collector in the most active sense of the word. If he can carry it or drag it, he collects it, he stores it, he hoards it. He is supremely a creature of things, of utterly useless things, of things that trip him as he scuttles for his daily bread.

His brown fur sleek, his stomach white, his long tail bushy, he looks more like a chipmunk or a squirrel than a rat, and it seems a pity that science calls him a wood rat.

He belongs to a phenomenally successful order of mammals, *Rodentia*, two thousand species of which, like one other mammal, teem everywhere on earth except at the poles and on distant desert islands. Rodents all do their separate things; while the pack rat is collecting, others are burrowing with similar zeal, or jumping or swimming with equal energy, and a few have even learned to fly. The pack rat is a member of the *Cricetidae* family, the genus *Neotoma*, and has, in twenty-two species, fitted himself into a variety of habitats from

Guatemala to British Columbia, from the deserts of Arizona to the Alleghenies.

As successful as he is, he appears a bit schizophrenic to the human observer. He is ostensibly a vegetarian; however, he has no trouble switching to meals of lizards or warblers or young rabbits when the opportunity arises. He is beaverlike in his propensity for girdling small trees, lopping down shrub branches to drag off to his nest. But in times of danger he becomes a rabbit and hammers his feet on the ground in warning. With a coyote, a fox, or dog, or owl, or mammalogist at his nest he may skin up a tree faster than a squirrel. He has the eye of a crow for shiny things, including alarm clocks, dishpans, watches, money; but unlike the crow his fascination for manufactured objects is not discriminating, and he collects shotgun shells with the same zeal as hair curlers. He has even been known to drag away the traps that are set to catch *him*.

He is, in short, endearing in his affinity for man's works, but infuriating in his ingenuity in converting them to his purposes. He has a mythology, attributed to him by trappers, miners, and campers. He has, they say, a sense of morality in that when he steals one item, he leaves another in its place. These people call him a trade rat, but they do not quite understand that his commerce is unwitting, made so by an agony of choice that makes him drop one stolen item when he sees another, more larcenable piece. He is the totally indiscriminating thief, a tiny Willie Sutton who cannot spend the loot he has stolen.

One pack rat, working a girls' dormitory lodge in the Cascade mountains of Washington, gives us a profile of the schizophrenic pack-thief. He stole an onion peel, a piece of bacon rind, some figs, lemons, beans, potatoes, and peanuts; and we may understand all this, even the lemons, as evidence of a catholic appetite. But what did he want with handkerchiefs, stockings, and string, when his nest was already made up nicely with a shredded comforter? We might go along with his acquisition of cantaloupe rind, bread crusts, puffballs, and biscuits, but remain baffled at his interest in a newspaper clipping on forest fires.

He went on a ten-bar chocolate binge, and we can identify with this. He went into the dried apricot business, but surely he must have gagged on half a dozen bars of soap after the apricots. He went after candles with a really ratlike hunger for tallow; but no self-respecting rat would have followed this with a sugar chaser—fifteen lumps packed into his capacious cheek pouches. This dormitory *Neotoma* wound up his thieving with a shining coffee-can cover, perhaps to examine the reflection of such a smart fellow.

To be missing a sense of enough is the lot of the pack rat (and one other important mammal), and his nest—up to twenty feet off the ground, a tangle of twigs, thorns, and grass—may bulge with hundreds of trivial items scattered through its maze of corridors, bedrooms, pantries, and toilet areas. Ten generations of pack rat may use the nest, extending it many times—a new rat (but only one) moving in on the demise of the previous owner until the debris in it may become an unnatural history of the area, a Collyer house in miniature.

The pack rat must outbreed his manifold enemies, and he keeps his numbers up, in favorable habitats, to about four animals to the acre. This can mean a fairly urgent sex life, up to three families raised every year. Young pack rats, fastened by notched teeth to their mother's teats, are not fazed or dislodged by copulation or bumpy sprints up trees as mama flees her enemies. A pack rat's split personality makes him neither careful nor quiet in his wanderings in a woods cabin —a favorite haunt—and he bumps around like an amiable Dr. Jekyll until everybody is awake. Then, at the first creak of a bedspring, he hammers his feet and scuttles like Mr. Hyde.

Is he, then, a rat fink, or just lovable? To find out, we corner him in our cabin. Trembling, he stands up abruptly, and now we know he is a squirrel. But no! Suddenly he has become a tiny kangaroo with his forepaws raised in a Jim Jeffries stance of resistance. He is going to punch the hell out of our ankles. But no; he backs up, still standing, still squaring off, whiskers blurred with movement. So cute! But schizophrenic to the end. We reach down and he either lets us catch him or, faster than the eye can follow, sinks his teeth into our hand and disappears.

But, we know one thing clearly. In two minutes or less he will be back, like an old friend, or enemy, for our transistor radio, our calendar watch, our gold signet ring, our electric toothbrush, our silver-trimmed comb, our miniature reading light, our wrist compass, our three-color ball-point pen . . .

But what were *we* doing with those things in the first place?

DOES
YOUR ROOM
LOOK LIKE
THE COLLYER
BROTHERS'?

ROBERT COWLEY

As I begin, I think of my cardboard boxes. There they are, crammed with the debris of a decade at least: childrens' drawings, aged desk calendars, a 1948 copy of *Life* with the stories of Truman's victory and the Donora smog, a guarantee for a long-defunct vacuum cleaner, letters and bank statements, an old Army Air Corps surplus map of Borneo, and—why?—a photo engraver's wood block with a picture of a gorilla. In my case, a move is rarely as good as a fire; the boxes not only travel with me but they multiply. Don't be disdainful. You, too, have your piled attic, your "hell corner," your Fibber McGee closet ready to trip its booby-trap freight of old Muriel cigar boxes and baseball mitts with the Snuffy Sternweiss autograph imprint. We keep them, perhaps, because they are the closest representations that we have of our selves: these are the things that have formed the shape of *our* time, and it would take a revolution to get rid of them. And yet, there must be moments in our nightmares when the boxes or the stubborn roomful of junk seems to swell and we see ourselves engulfed by our own useless accumulations—our thing Triffids, our paper-and-metal Venus Flytraps.

How often do nightmares become real? There is the old story about the difference between a neurotic and a psychotic. The neurotic builds dream castles; the psychotic builds dream castles and lives in them—and the psychiatrist collects rent from both. In the home of Homer and Langley Collyer we find such a dream house, except that it is a Castle of Otranto in the middle of Harlem and its two inhabitants are uncomfortably real. For three weeks twenty-two years ago, we all took inventory of its contents, truckload after truckload; by the time the last of the Collyers' effects had been carted away and their house had fallen under the wrecker's ball, the obsession of two old men had permanently entered our language. For years my mother put it to me this way: "Aren't you ashamed? Your room looks like the Collyer brothers'."

The story broke on March 21, 1947. It was a typical first day of spring in New York City: a greymetal overcast, rain, and a temperature that felt much colder than the 45 degrees on the thermometer. At about ten that morning, a call came in to police headquarters. The voice of a man who identified himself as "Charles Smith"—and no one ever satisfactorily established who he was—announced, "There is a man dead in the premises at 2078 Fifth Avenue." Here, for almost forty years, had lived two legendary and mysterious recluses, Homer and Langley Collyer. Homer, paralyzed and, as *The New York Times* said, "blind as the poet he was named for," had been seen only twice since 1934; Langley, his younger brother (they were respectively sixty-five and sixty-one), prowled the city at night, as furtive as one of the alley cats that made their home in his basement. About the only people who had ever been inside the house—and just once past the entrance hallway—were process servers: the brothers did not believe in paying taxes. Occasionally Langley would give an interview to the press; for all his anchoritic ways, he seemed to delight in teasing the public with the details of his life with Homer.

A newspaper picture of Langley taken in 1938 shows a man in an oversized cloth cap peering down from a window. He has a long nose with great nostrils, deep-set, dark-ringed eyes, and a scraggly moustache that looks like a clump of grass growing from a crack in the pavement. A man named Gruber had made an offer for some land the brothers owned in Queens, and for the purpose of the legend the picture caption is worth quoting. It alleged that Langley "never leaves the house until dark" (true); that "he owns 17 grand pianos, one for every room of the house" (he owned fourteen, some less than grand); that "he has a Model T Ford in his basement" (he did, more or less in pieces); that "he doesn't believe in banks" (he did, to the extent that thirty-four bankbooks were later found, eleven of them canceled); that "there are 25,000 books in his library" (it was closer to five thousand); and that "he owns half of New York's waterfront" (the one statement that was completely untrue).

When the enigmatic call came on that morning in March, a patrolman was dispatched to the Collyer house. He found himself pounding at the front door of a weathered three-story brownstone on the northwest corner of Fifth Avenue and 128th Street. Getting no response, he summoned the emergency squad. With axes and crowbars they broke down the door and were confronted, the *Herald Tribune* reported, "with a wall of newspapers, folding chairs, broken boxes, part of a wine press, half a sewing machine, folding beds, parts of a rocking chair, and innumerable other pieces of junk." They tried the front basement door and again found their way barred by junk. It was the same at the back: the areaway was piled to the ceiling with, among other things, an old stove, umbrellas, wrapped packages of newspapers, a broken scooter, and a gas mask canister.

A policeman climbed up on a fire ladder to one of the second-floor windows. He could not even get a foot inside. By this time a crowd of some six hundred people had gathered below, and they gaped at the things that came hurtling out of the window: a rake . . . a baby carriage frame . . . the New York *Evening Telegram* for November 24, 1918 (REDS KILL 500 WHILE RUSSIANS FIGHT FOR FOOD). At last the patrolman disappeared from view, only to return to the window a few moments later.

"There's a D.O.A. here," he called down.

Behind a stinking mountain of junk the beam of his flashlight had fallen on the body of a tiny old man sitting on the floor. His matted hair reached down to his shoulders, and he wore only a ragged bathrobe. Next to the corpse were a half-eaten Washington State apple, a leaking container of rancid milk, and a copy of the Philadelphia *Jewish Morning Journal* of Sunday, February 22, 1920. Homer Collyer, it first appeared, had been dead at least ten hours, though that estimate was later revised upward to from four days to a week; he had apparently succumbed to heart disease aggravated by starvation.

But what had become of Langley?

"That the collecting mania," writes A. A. Brill in *Fundamental Conceptions of Psychoanalysis*, "is a reaction to an unconscious need, to an inner feeling of voidness concerning some particular craving is best seen in the collections made by the insane." In the case of Langley and Homer Collyer we know of the void only through inferences. They were born in New York in the 1880's and grew up in the city. Their father, Dr. Herman L. Collyer, was a prominent and wealthy gynecologist. This circumstance seems noteworthy, since neither of his sons ever married or had, as far as is known, any contact with women. At any rate, father and sons did not get along: their allegiances belonged all to their mother, a doting and possessive woman who was fond of reading the classics aloud to them in Greek. Homer went to the City College of New York, studied admiralty law, and practiced for a time. Langley majored in engineering at Columbia but never held a job. He aspired to become a concert pianist: "My last concert was in Carnegie Hall, a week before Paderewski's first. He got more notices than I, so I gave up. What was the use?" Whether the story was apocryphal or not is unimportant; it is the visible part of the iceberg —along with the pianos, the five violins, the several pipe organs, the cello with the phony "Stradivarius, 1727" imprint, the two cornets, the bugle, the trombone, and the musical clock weighing two hundred pounds.

When the family moved into the 128th Street house, Harlem was a neighborhood favored by the white middle class. But in the early 1900's Manhattan suffered one of its periodic real-estate collapses; Negroes began to migrate to Harlem, and a white exodus followed. Dr. Collyer himself moved to West 77th Street, but his sons could never bring themselves to leave the Harlem house. It was as if their own fear kept them there, these two frail, genteel men with their fine old New York accents, barricading themselves against a world that was in every sense getting blacker and blacker. Police turned up four revolvers and a hundred rounds of ammunition, a shotgun, two rifles, a cavalry saber, and a twenty-four-inch French bayonet.

Dr. Collyer died in 1923. He must have been a little odd himself. When his house was sold in the 1930's, the new owner found, to her consternation, a Model T Ford in the basement. How had it got there? Finding neither window nor door wide enough for it to pass through, she paid a man $150 to take it apart and leave it out on the pavement. Somehow Langley heard. He carted the car uptown, piece by disassembled piece, chassis, engine, and all, and put it in his basement. But that is going ahead of the story. In 1929, when the brothers were in their late forties, their mother died. By this time their eccentricity had already become marked. They cut off their utilities, used a kerosene stove for heat and cooking, carried water in demijohns from a nearby park, and tried to generate their own electricity.

Homer started to go blind and in 1934 decided that he would never go outside again. But Homer was seen outdoors one more time. Early on New Year's morning, 1940, a policeman caught sight of the brothers carrying the branch of a fallen elm tree across the street to the basement of their house.

Not long afterward Homer lost the use of his limbs as well as his sight. He refused to see a doctor—or was it that Langley would not let him? "You must remember we are sons of a doctor," Langley said. "Homer eats 100 oranges a week— and is improving." Langley would appear after dark, a wraith in a greasy cloth cap, pulling a cardboard box on the end of a long rope. Sometimes he would walk as far as the Williamsburg section of Brooklyn for whole-wheat bread. As for the tons of newspapers in the house, he explained that he was saving them for the day when Homer regained his sight: "He can catch up on the news."

That was the only reason Langley ever gave for their collecting. "A passion for collecting is frequently a direct surrogate for a sexual desire," wrote the psychiatrist Karl Abraham. But there is something monstrous about the Collyers that defies psychological explanation. One thinks of the police officer who, on a day in 1942, decided to check on a rumor that Homer was dead. After considerable hesitation, Langley let him in at the basement door and then led him up a pitch-black stairway through precarious canyons of newsprint, under alarm systems that would spew garbage and tin cans on the heads of the unwary and the uninvited— delicately poised booby traps that would bring down a suffocating edifice of junk. Did the policeman trip on the jawbone of the horse? Did he collide with the chassis of the Model T or brush against the skeletons used by the late Dr. Collyer? It took him half an hour to reach the second-floor room, a small cleared section of which Homer inhabited.

"I switched on my flashlight," the policeman related, "and there was Homer sitting up like a mummy . . . 'I am Homer L. Collyer, lawyer,' the old man says, in a deep voice. 'I want your name and shield number. I am not dead. I am blind and paralyzed.'"

Five years later Homer was buried in the family plot in Queens. The funeral was delayed in hope that Langley would miraculously show up, but he did not. An eleven-state alarm was sent out. He was variously reported in Atlantic City, in Asbury Park, New Jersey, where policemen rummaged through boarded-up summer cottages, on a subway in Brooklyn, and floating in a creek in the East Bronx. One old man was observed carrying a hand-lettered sign: "I am *not* Langley Collyer." Even Andrei Gromyko, the Russian delegate to the Security Council, looked up from his newspaper to comment, "Who knows, we might find out today where Langley Collyer is." As the headlines subsided and the story moved to the back pages, the *Daily News* wondered out loud: "We find ourselves wishing the New York policemen would just sweep Langley's place up a little more, and then quietly steal away, maybe leaving a little bowl of milk for him on his doorstep."

Meanwhile the clearing out of the house continued, day after day. In room after room junk was stacked to the ceiling, and Langley's alimentary burrows were the only way through. Nineteen tons were brought out one day . . . eighteen another . . . twelve tons, including five from a single six-foot area. By the time police and sanitation men were finished, 140 tons—280,000 thing-pounds—had been carted away. The search was becoming a "nightmare," the police said, and a hazardous one at that. Two detectives were almost buried by a booby trap on the stairs: "Close behind them," reported the *Herald Tribune*, "came two seventy-five pound chunks of concrete, two feet square, cardboard boxes containing tin cans, crowbars, and other inconceivable kinds of inutile material . . ."

Then, on April 8, nineteen days after the search had begun, a detective rooting not ten feet from where Homer had died looked down and saw a hand. Langley Collyer had been crushed by one of his own booby traps as he carried food to his brother through a tunnel lined with a chest of drawers and an old bedspring. On the body there rested bundles of newspapers, a suitcase filled with metal, a sewing machine, and three breadboxes.

INDIAN GIVING

FREDERIC V. GRUNFELD

The problem, as every member of the acquisitive society will have noticed by now, is not in amassing things but in getting rid of them. Look into your closets, O Western World, and you will see a rising flood of things threatening to engulf you—a surfeit of all the fair and flagrant things that human and mechanical ingenuity can devise. One acquires them as desiderata; afterward, many of them turn out to be things that the department of sanitation cannot be prevailed upon to haul away. Sometimes, by happy chance, one can manage to lose things, and three moves are as good as a fire, as my New England grandmother used to say. But a far more stylish way of disposing of a lot of things in a hurry is the time-honored northwest-coast Indian potlatch. In the midst of our great crisis of the Malthusian supermarket a study of the ways of the potlatchers can teach us something.

The Indians of the Pacific coast used to be very good at making things, and they produced vast quantities of them, for they lived in a region where the salmon and halibut were so thick they did everything but catch themselves. That left the human population with time on their hands for making spruceroot rain hats, mountain-sheep horn spoons, cedarwood boxes inlaid with haliotis shell and snail opercula, argillite grease-dishes, maplewood soapberry-beating paddles, blankets of mountain-goat hair and cedar bark, whale's-tooth amulets, and such.

Since arts and crafts (and, to a lesser extent, sex) were the Indians' main preoccupation before the white man introduced liquor, money, and bookkeeping, their longhouses would periodically fill to overflowing with the results of everybody's incessant basket weaving, wood carving, and stone chiseling. But to keep these from becoming a burden on the tribal psyche, their chief would hold a potlatch and give everything away in one great orgy of generosity. Potlatches were given to celebrate the accession of a new chief, the raising of a totem pole, the assumption of a crest or title, and so on; the word derives from the Nootka *patshatl*, "to give." If the potlatching chief impoverished himself and his clan in the process, so much the better, for by his very lavishness he acquired an unpurchasable esteem in the community. Besides, custom dictated that the recipients of his gifts must go him one better at their next potlatch.

A proper potlatch involved prodigious displays of eating, since it was a point of honor with the host to provide much more food than his guests could consume. The eating would last for days, interspersed with singing, belching, speechmaking, dramatic performances and the ceremonial conferring of honorific names. But the vital part of the occasion was the bestowing of gifts—bowls, boxes, baskets, blankets, canoes, ornaments, sculptures—that the chief had collected among his people, from each according to his ability, and now distributed among his guests, to each according to his rank.

Potlatching replaced warfare and violence as a way of settling tribal disputes after the Canadian and United States governments began asserting their authority along the coast.

"When I was young I saw a stream of blood shed in war," said an old Kwakiutl in a speech in 1895. "But since that time the white men came and stopped up that stream of blood with wealth. Now we fight with our wealth."

The Hudson's Bay Company's factory-made blankets replaced deerskin and mountain-goat robes just at the time when potlatching reached new heights of conspicuous consumption, having been accelerated by the tribal chiefs' need to assert their prerogatives in a rapidly changing world. A chief grown wealthy in the fur trade would demonstrate his contempt for property by giving away and destroying whole households—burning canoes, clubbing slaves to death, and breaking his most valuable "coppers" in the process. The coppers—shaped like shields and embossed with totemic figures—were, in effect, bills of high denomination that enabled a chief to get rid of a great deal of wealth at one go. Often they were worth more than their weight in gold, for they had the disconcerting habit of doubling their value every time they changed hands; and it was not uncommon for a copper to be worth ten or fifteen thousand trade blankets.

To be able to break so powerful a copper before an audience of one's invited rivals was a tremendous honor. But the game was usually rigged, since the broken pieces could be picked up and either resold at a profit or used to embarrass a neighbor. "A chief may break his copper and give the broken parts to his rival," explains the pioneer anthropologist Franz Boas, who watched a lot of potlatching before the turn of the century. "If the latter wants to keep his prestige, he must break a copper of equal or higher value, then return both his own broken copper and the fragments which he received . . ."

Later, when coppers went out of circulation, the potlatch people shifted to trade goods and introduced a whole department-store repertory to take their place. The Kwakiutl chief Daniel Cranmer drew up a partial inventory for the anthropologist Helen Codere when he described a memorable potlatch he held at Village Island, British Columbia, in

1921: "I gave him [the chief of nearby Cape Mudge village] a gas boat and $50 cash. Altogether that was worth $500 . . . The same day I gave Hudson's Bay blankets. I started giving out the property. First the canoes. Two pool tables were given to two chiefs. It hurt them. They said it was the same as breaking a copper. The pool tables were worth $350 apiece. Then bracelets, gas lights, violins, guitars were given to the more important people. Then 24 canoes, some of them big ones, and four gas boats." Later he handed out jewelry, shawls, sweaters, and shirts for women and young people; button blankets, shawls, and four hundred trade blankets; washtubs, teapots, cups, and about a thousand washbasins. Handfuls of small change were flung to the children. "The fourth day I gave away furniture: boxes, trunks, sewing machines, gramophones, bedsteads and bureaus. The fifth day I gave away cash. The sixth day I gave away about 1,000 sacks of flour worth $3 a sack. I also gave sugar." When it was over, he was unchallengeably one up on every other chief in the region. "All the chiefs say now in a gathering, 'You cannot expect that we can ever get up to you. You are a great mountain.'"

Potlatches of a sort are still given occasionally in the northwest-coast Indian country, but nowadays the institution retains only a faint glimmer of its former magnificence. Since they no longer have art objects to give away, they simply throw parties at which everybody receives . . . money. The end is clearly in sight. The white man has never shown much understanding for the potlatch; it was outlawed by the Canadian government, and even the most sympathetic anthropologists have described it as an "atrocious" and "paranoid" pursuit of social prestige. Most of them have missed the point; namely, that potlatching was essentially a primitive, preliterate form of investment banking.

From an economist's standpoint the wealthy Indian chief accomplished the same results by ostensibly giving things away as does the modern millionaire by supposedly holding on to them. In our paper economy the millionaire doesn't keep his wealth around the house, either—except for a Modigliani or two. What he doesn't need for his personal consumption he gives to a bank, in the form of pieces of power-paper inscribed with totems. The bank, in turn, ladles it out to the economy as a whole in the form of loans. The main thing is that people (beginning with the bank manager) must know that the money, though invisible, is actually there. It is this knowledge that determines a man's status as a millionaire; otherwise he's just a Collyer brother.

A Kwakiutl chief, depositing his wealth with his rivals, also depended on that public knowledge for his power, though he never had to worry about bankruptcies or a drop in the price of coppers. At the highest level, the cycle of acquisition and distribution is virtually identical in both cases. If our millionaire is very, very rich, social pressure and the tax structure will induce him, sooner or later, to do some heavy potlatching of the modern sort: the name of the game is Rockefeller Foundation.

GARBAGE,
OR,
CAN WE EVER
GET AWAY
FROM IT ALL?

ROGER STARR

O n a narrow strip of Jersey marsh, garbage men are building a land bank; it grows day by day, stretching always a little farther from the black, polluted waters of Newark Bay toward its final limit: the edge of a six-lane interstate highway. At any hour, one can watch at least thirty sanitation trucks making their way across the top of the new bank. The covered trucks follow rutted roadways built from loads of broken brick and concrete that have been set aside from the flimsier trash, garbage, and household refuse. The trucks rock slowly up and down over the ruts, like heavy work-boats pitching in an oily sea, as they head for the open face of the bank, the slope on which loads are currently dumped. In fifteen years, more than a thousand acres have been covered with a waste twelve feet deep from the cities of northern New Jersey. The speed of covering continually increases, both because the population of north Jersey is growing and because every American discards more waste each year.

New Jersey is one of the few states with strict regulations governing the operation of sanitary landfills. The proprietors of this marshland site must cover the dumped material with clean soil six inches deep, leaving only one day's working surface open and uncovered, to a limit of 15,000 square feet. Following the trucks out to the working face, one meets the smell of refuse only when one approaches that uncovered space, where five Caterpillars rumble back and forth over recent dumping, compacting the fill and spreading the dirt that lies in piles on the already completed surface. When the smell comes, it is not the heart-stopping stench of sewage and animal decay but the stale, dusty odor of trash and chemicals, sweetened by only an intermittent whiff of the sickly scent of wet garbage. Papers that have been blown loose from the heavier material before the dirt can be pushed over it dart fitfully across the landscape. They provide the only sign of life: the papers and the birds. Small bands of starlings, stubby creatures, peck at scraps of food caught in the soil cover; they are ignored by the great crowd of sea gulls. A few of the gulls work their way up into the sky on heavy wingbeats, to glide there, high above the emptying trucks; thousands squat near the trucks on a layer of fill already discovered, waiting for news of sudden riches from the air-borne birds above.

Across the highway from the fill a great international airport spreads one runway parallel to the road. One herring gull, beating upward across the nose of a climbing airliner, can be sucked into one of the plane's mammoth jet pods where, dying, it may snuff out a hundred lives in a thunderous catastrophe. The public authority that owns the airport has shown its uneasiness over the proximity of gulls to jet planes, but no government has clear, final power to determine how great the danger is or what should be done about it. The question hovers over the landfill rather like the gulls themselves.

The strange possibility that buried refuse can reach up from the ground, as it were, to snatch an airliner from the sky, symbolically suggests the complex scope of industrial man's unprecedented need to shed the substances he has used but no longer wants. When men were farmers the problem was simpler; they threw away what they could not eat, and patched, mended, spliced, and sewed their other possessions forever. Industrial society discards a flood of objects so torrential that it may well drown us. Each year, in the United States, the trash contains a smaller and smaller portion of organic residues, which gradually change into humus, and a bigger and bigger portion of change-resistant, man-made artifacts and potions: old machines and their parts, bits of cities knocked down or dug up to be discarded, plastic containers in which men deliver their goods to one another, useless when emptied, tubs of chemicals that have served their purpose and represent the now-worthless distillate of vast quantities of raw materials extracted from the earth.

For an added irony, consider that the attempt to salvage useful flotsam from the flood founders on the very productivity that originally created it. A system capable of producing eight million automobiles a year must run smoothly; it cannot be slowed down to adjust to the slight irregularity in its operation that re-used components might cause. A labor force that is paid enough to buy back its produce cannot be put to work digging for valuable sherds in the wrack of last year's mechanical marvels, or yesterday's.

A calm marble statue with missing head and arms may well be the supreme symbol of the Greek desire to achieve order and moderation in a turbulent world. The descriptive modern artifact may well be the automobile hulk with shattered windows and missing wheels, the object of supreme romantic love reduced to a cause for mere embarrassment in only ten years.

Everyone remembers the glowing pride that suffused the family lined up along its driveway as Dad arrived from the dealer's in his new car; we reeled at the fresh scent of the synthetic leather, a perfume that vanished almost as quickly as the glow of a martini. The new car's glory is so brief that the first fender dent affects us like the clap of doom. How evanescent our life is! In the movie *Goldfinger* violent death for hundreds of male and female agents evoked not a quiver from the audiences, but the premature pressing of a mint-new Lincoln Continental into a block of scrap metal brought gasps of horror. By the time Dad turns into his driveway for the first time, his car has lost perhaps one-third of its value. Within a year it is no longer even thought of as new; within ten years it has become completely valueless. Some of its components—the wheels and tires, for example—may bring a few pennies from a scrap dealer, but not enough to pay anyone to remove them. The body is virtually worthless at the moment of its obsequies, even though it still holds several electric motors, intricately machined pistons and gears, laminated safety glass, to mention only a few bits of junk that could not have been purchased for an emperor's treasure only a hundred years ago. They will be buried now under twelve feet of other trash, there to remain until some day when, the relative values of labor and natural resources having changed, they will be dug up to provide raw materials for no-one-knows-what new artifacts to please no-one-knows-how-many hundreds of millions of men and women, who will then be discarding no-one-knows-what miraculous products not yet invented, until the globe—unless already terminated for some other reason—will consist only of a mass of discarded material in which all the elements needed to sustain organic life will be locked in a permanent but sterile chemical embrace. But automobiles—Americans throw away more than four million of them a year—are only a small part of America's garbage heaps. No figures are readily available to indicate the number of refrigerators and other major mechanical appliances discarded each year, but these, too, constitute a tremendous total of technical complexity, weight and bulk.

A visit to a landfill operation, or a drive through the streets of an American city during "Clean-up Week"—an annual period in some cities when residents are permitted to discard without penalty *any* object, however large, for disposal by the sanitation department or sanitary contractors—will quickly indicate that Americans also throw away sofas, mattresses, lamps, bent gutters and leaders from their houses, jarfuls of flammable paint thinners and cleaning fluids, and broken clocks, radios, television sets. During clean-up week these objects are piled on the curbs, a melancholy fringe along the trimmed edges of suburbia.

And then there is the simple daily disgorging of soda-pop bottles, soup cans, cardboard and plastic containers, orange peels. Statisticians estimate that the average American home produces four and a half pounds of solid waste per person per day, more by far than any other nation.

This rough tally of identifiable municipal wastes has skipped the anonymous commercial and industrial waste products that constitute the largest single segment of the disposable tonnage: vast quantities of fly ash, the residue of pulverized coal that has been burned under electric generating-station boilers; debris from construction and demolition sites; by-product chemicals perhaps too degraded for any commercial re-use, but flammable nonetheless and hence a nuisance in a sanitary landfill; restaurant garbage; rock and dirt dug up from excavation sites within the city.

Modern man can no longer avoid the consequences of his own productivity: all these things must be put *somewhere*. Almost every city in the nation is embroiled in some sort of controversy over the final disposition of its own waste, but the vigor of the arguments cannot stretch the possibilities for disposal. There remain only four possibilities on this planet, if one dismisses the likelihood of shooting the earthly waste out into space. Of the four the most sanguine hope is that waste can be reclaimed for future use. Hardly a month passes without a happy announcement that someone has developed a method for turning garbage into topsoil, or mining it for small quantities of rich metals like gold and silver. So far no reclaiming system has proved economically attractive to

American mayors, under the local ground rules that govern this subject. This comes as bad news to those who remember that when they pulled K.P. in the army they were expected to divide wastes carefully into separate cans, presumably to facilitate the re-use of fats for explosives, paper products for new paper manufacture, and bones for chemicals and soap. The army system depended upon the availability of low-paid and underemployed laborers with a plethora of sergeants aching to keep their charges busy.

When reclamation is not feasible, some solid wastes can be disposed of in the air. They need only to be combined with oxygen; that is to say, burned. Large-scale municipal incinerators can, in theory, be designed to operate with great efficiency at very high temperatures. Such incinerators would not at all resemble the messy steel wigwams, now in use in many dumps, that merely create a slightly improved draft in a smelly bonfire. Since paper and paper products constitute almost half of present solid waste, a large, efficient furnace could be designed to burn this material at a temperature of 3,000 degrees Fahrenheit. Such a furnace would require no other fuel than the combustibles contained in the waste. It could actually generate enough heat to serve some useful purpose, perhaps making steam to warm nearby apartments. An efficient incinerator produces neither smoke nor odor, but it is costly to build and requires expert supervision and maintenance.

Even the most efficient and smoke-free incinerator, however, creates an invisible residue in the form of carbon-dioxide gas, the result of combustion. If all the solid wastes in the world were burned daily, a considerable quantity of carbon dioxide would be added to the volumes already produced today by the combustion of fossil fuels like coal and oil. Does this matter to anyone? The question is less easily answered than framed. But as the rate of combustion increases and, coincidentally, as the stands of forest and other plant life throughout the world decrease, the measurable carbon dioxide content of the atmosphere is increasing.

Clearly the maintenance of the oxygen–carbon-dioxide balance is vital to all forms of life on this planet. Would large-scale, efficient incineration of waste affect this balance? Nobody quite knows.

If depositing wastes in the air, even under the best possible circumstances, raises questions that no one can answer, what about stowing wastes on the land? This possibility raises a different question: which land shall be used? Traditionally, municipal sanitation commissioners and private landfill operators have chosen swamps or marshes for their landfill operations. No one particularly wanted the wetlands. The very word swamp suggests uselessness. It is easy enough to convince the governing body of a city that the fill will simply be making a beautiful golf course out of a mosquito incubator. Landfill operations designed only to hide waste have not been the only consumers of wetlands, which have also disappeared to create land for housing developments, highways, and harbors. But garbage disposal is a relentless need that cannot be long deferred. Only recently has anyone begun to notice how much coastline has been changed to make room for garbage. Connecticut, for example, watched more than half its wetlands disappear before the state passed a law that lends them a measure of protection against bulkheading and fill.

Marine and ornithological biologists have been able to establish that wetlands breed far more than mosquitoes; in fact the tidal marshlands produce more usable protein per acre than the richest farm land in the world. The protein, however, is not consumed directly by men and women, an unfortunate accident, for the small aquatic animals that do consume it are not represented in the state legislatures or Congress. These small creatures are in turn eaten by shellfish or the fry of important fish, including menhaden, winter flounder, and striped bass. Decline in the productivity of offshore fisheries can be traced to the obliteration of coastal marshes, not only because the nutrients for young fish disappear, but also due to the disappearance of the small coastal watercourses in which pelagic fish spawn and are hatched. Unfortunately, fishermen who depend on the fish population for their livelihood have only recently gained the sophistication to add their voice to those of the conservationists.

Fresh-water wetlands, also popular for landfill, are not the nuisances they have generally been taken for. They are natural sumps, gathering rainfall that penetrates the substrata of the land and keeps the water table constant. It is ironic that in some areas, Long Island for one, where natural fresh-water wetlands have been filled in for housing sites, artificial sumps have had to be dug to replace the hydrologic function. There are in many parts of the country far more suitable barren areas, productive of little wildlife, that could be used effectively for depositing solid waste if the filling operation were intelligently handled and carefully controlled. There are many big holes in America—the holes of vast mining operations—that could be filled successfully with solid wastes to everyone's benefit, but few municipalities are ready to spend the money to transport their wastes to the places where they would be welcome. Solid wastes, moving to these mines, may someday be the most dependable bulk cargo of the railroads. Used properly, these wastes can even create attractive surroundings. In the vicinity of Chicago a combination of waste and excavated material has been used to build up a hill that is now used as a ski slope. Its stability indicates that compacted fill, placed intelligently, can modify flat land and turn it into interesting landscape with unexpected recreational uses.

If the uses of land are limited, the only remaining depository is the water. But here the courts have raised a cautious hand. The Supreme Court has held that wastes cannot be simply dumped into the ocean, for no government in the United States has the right to inflict a nuisance on the beaches of its neighbors. Too much of the solid waste load floats. The key to the constructive use of water as a final disposal site for solid waste lies in the compaction of the waste to increase its specific gravity. The Japanese have developed a press capable of compacting solid waste so tightly that it will not disintegrate. The compaction raises the specific gravity so high that the material sinks like a rock. These bundles, dumped at sea, would simply settle on the bottom, where they would not harm anything and might form artificial reefs that would be of help to the fish population. Land for unwelcome uses—monster jetports, for example—might be constructed from bundles of supercompacted waste, which would save precious wetlands and the ears and nerves of those living nearby.

Ultimately it becomes clear that our planet is limited, like any house, and that the time will come when its attic will overflow with the accumulated debris of years of habitation. There is the difference, however, that when the attic of a house fills up, one may clean it out and pay someone to take the debris away. But things cannot be carted away from the earth; our planet, as the economist Kenneth Boulding has told us, is a spaceship to which nothing can be added and from which nothing can be taken away. The ultimate problem of solid waste is not that the waste itself takes up valuable room on the spaceship but that the stock of elements is limited, and if the elements are locked into waste irretrievably, they are lost to human life. As the character of man's waste has changed—from organic compounds capable of decomposition and regeneration through the metabolic process of life, to compounds such as plastics, which resist decomposition—so the ability of the earth to sustain life may have been impaired. It is quite possible that at some time or other so much of the needed life matter will be locked into waste that the earth will not be able to sustain the population living on it. One assumes that the earth will reach this tipping point slowly, after a long period during which raw materials will become scarcer and more expensive, the standard of living will decline, and the quality of the natural environment deteriorate. And one assumes that given warning, mankind will do something to stave off disaster.

But even with ample warning there is little to suggest that

men will be able to change direction. At stake here is man's ability, nay willingness, to control his own productivity, to measure the seriousness of the waste that will result from each extension of his productivity, each new artifact, each new human life. The control over inventiveness, love, and hunger that would be required in order to utilize natural resources wisely and avoid crossing the balance point might well destroy so many of the human values that man would be incapable of asserting this control. Will men prefer to drown in the waste of their pleasures? Or will they prefer to control them in the hope of prolonging life? This, nothing less, is the question that lies burning at the bottom of the dump.

THE
MANY FACES OF
KARL MARX

JOHN W. BURROW

One can imagine few greater shocks to our sense of the fitness of things than a revelation that Karl Marx without his beard had the face of a romantic poet, another Byron or Shelley. We are used to seeing him in the guise of an angry prophet, beard bristling with outrage at the iniquities of his opponents; or nobly marmoreal in profile, with a similar profile of Engels or Lenin apparently adhering to one of his ears, as one sees them on innumerable communist posters. The beards of the saints of European communism seem a part of their roles: Marx's leonine and denunciatory; Engels's brisk and worldly; Lenin's a jutting icebreaker, forging forward toward the happy land over the always-receding horizon.

Yet the suggestion that the young Marx might have had a face of dreamy, romantic sensitivity—though literally speaking highly improbable, to judge from the clues among the bristles—is not altogether symbolically inappropriate. Marx was an idealistic young man, born into a romantic environment, whose early ardors bear unmistakably the marks of a youth of the generation of Hector Berlioz and Victor Hugo, a generation to which Byron and Napoleon, Prometheus and Faust, were the symbols of their own thwarted aspirations, pent up by the stuffy reaction that gripped Europe in the years after Waterloo. To many of that generation "revolution" was a holy word, and the spirit of freedom appeared, as in Delacroix's famous painting, as a beautiful barebreasted woman leading the workers at the barricades. The years of Marx's youth and early manhood were the years before the European revolutions of 1848, when it seemed that with one final titanic effort humanity might throw off all its oppressors at one blow and create from the ashes of the old social order a new world of justice and freedom. Paris was revered by young men as the holy city of revolution. As the Russian socialist Aleksandr Herzen put it, "I entered the city with reverence, as men used to enter Jerusalem or Rome."

The fate of captive countries like Italy and Poland, ruled by oppressor nations whose domination had been reaffirmed at the Congress of Vienna, touched liberal consciences as Spain was to do in the 1930's and Hungary in the 1950's. Not only proletarians but artists and intellectuals of all kinds felt, during these years, the revolutionary itch; when revolution came to Europe's capitals in 1848–49, they went with the workers to the barricades.

It was to this generation that Karl Marx, born in 1818, belonged. There is no cause for surprise that he became a revolutionary; it would almost have been surprising if he had not. What distinguished him from most of his contemporaries was that in Marx youthful fervor soon became transmuted into scientific rigor, without abating its revolutionary character. Marx's revolutionary zeal thus acquired a staying power, while that of most of his contemporaries—vaguer, more hazily idealistic—faded with age and disillusionment. Nevertheless, Marx's "scientific" socialism never altogether lost a visionary, apocalyptic aureole that occasionally gives a lurid glow to the gray pages of *Capital* and recalls the ardent years before the false dawn of 1848. In his personal tastes, too, Marx remained a man of his generation; he shared that passionate love of Shakespeare that struck the intellectual youth of France and Germany in the early nineteenth century with the force of a revelation; for him, too, Prometheus, the archetypal rebel, the Titan who had defied Zeus, was a potent symbol, as he was for Shelley, Goethe, and Beethoven. Marx's taste in novels, again, was not chiefly for realistic novels of industrial England or Flaubert's brutal dissection of the French bourgeoisie, but for Sir Walter Scott and Alexandre Dumas the elder. Karl Marx, economist and visionary, German scholar and international revolutionary, contemptuous as he was of revolutionary phrasemakers and conspiratorial play-acting, was yet himself a powerful rhetorician and prophet of doom and regeneration, a romantic realist, a man of many faces.

The paradoxes begin with his birth. He was born of comfortably-off middle-class parents, not in one of the great centers of population and industry whose portentousness for the future he was so vehemently to proclaim, but in the ancient city of Trier. Marx was to experience poverty, but after, not before, he became a revolutionary. He never gained the firsthand experience of factory conditions possessed by his partner Friedrich Engels, the son of a Bremen manufacturer. Trier is a city of ancient monuments, set among the castle-dotted, vine-clustered terraces of the Moselle valley, only a few miles from the Luxembourg border and the forest of Ardennes. In one respect only was it an apt birthplace for Karl Marx. Trier, or Treves, which at the time of Marx's birth formed an outlying part of the dominions of the king of Prussia, had once been the gateway between the Latin and the Teutonic worlds; the great gate that marked the limits of the power of imperial Rome still stands, like a grandiose, abandoned Checkpoint Charlie, in the midst of Trier's traffic, a suitable reminder of a German who was also a cosmopolitan, to whom Paris and London were not only homes but the focus of his thoughts as the breeding grounds of revolution, a man who looked always to the West and has been honored in the East.

Marx's dreams were imperial in scale, ecumenical in scope, and grounded on a panoramic view of world history. Such cosmopolitanism, too, is characteristic of his generation. The French Revolution, the great beacon, extinguished yet still smoldering in the minds of men, especially of those too young to remember it, had been an ecumenical event; the fall of the Bastille, of little importance in itself, became a universal symbol, welcomed as eagerly in Britain and in Germany as in France itself. The nineteenth century is the classic age of the émigré intellectual, the cosmopolitan revolutionary, and the ideological *condottiere* fighting in a foreign land because liberty is every man's cause or because the proletariat has no fatherland. Besides the prototype, Byron, there were Mickiewicz, Polish poet and professor at the Collège de France, who raised a Polish legion in 1848 to fight for Italian independence against the Austrians; the Russian anarchist-nobleman Bakunin, later to be Marx's archenemy in the First Workers' International, organizing revolt among the artisans of the Jura and leading the Saxon workers at the Dresden barricades; and the aged Garibaldi, leading an irregular and somewhat undisciplined column of volunteers against the Prussians in 1870 on behalf of the newly reborn French Republic. When Friedrich Engels and a handful of fellow communists stood by the graveside of Karl Marx in Highgate cemetery, London, in 1883, they were honoring one of the last, as well as one of the most intransigent and least fraternal, of that unofficial fraternity of revolt, dating from the days when romanticism and revolution were almost synonymous terms. The earliest, Byron, had died at Missolonghi nearly sixty years before. Engels at Marx's graveside acclaimed him as the man who had made socialism "scientific," but to the young Marx as a scholar in Germany forty years earlier, politics had come first in a different guise, through the medium of philosophy and the romantic rhetoric of the emancipation of the human spirit.

In his secure niche in the placid, comely, preindustrial world of Trier and the German university towns, it was not personal oppression or the sight of proletarian misery and industrial squalor that first turned Marx into a revolutionary, but the enthusiasms of his generation and the theories of his elders, the intellectual diet he encountered as a student, on which young Germany was eagerly feeding. Marx the philosopher and the romantic humanist preceded Marx the politician and Marx the anatomist of industrial society. The philosophy Marx imbibed at the universities of Bonn and Berlin taught that man is truly himself, truly human, only when his activities are willed by himself, when he is not manipulated by others, by blind forces, or brute *things* as a mere object, only when he chooses, rationally, to act as his own human essence dictates. The young Marx, applying this philosophy with his own uncompromising rigor, came to the conclusion that however free men might be in the abstract, legally speaking, as workers the majority were not free at all. Labor was, or should be, the highest expression of humanity, the activity by which men freely shaped and changed the world, subjecting *things* to the creative power of man. But labor, the essence of man's humanity, his godlike creative power, had itself been degraded into a thing and was bought and sold as a commodity. Instead of productive labor being used by humanity, human beings were used to produce products. The workers, the proletariat, were not free in practice, whatever the law said. The State was not their state, nor was it impartial, because it upheld the domination of the property owners. Man could only be free if labor was an assertion of men's own wills and creative power, rather than a commodity that they were forced to barter for wages, and this could only happen by the proletariat overthrowing the existing property relations and creating a state of real, as distinct from merely abstract, legal, freedom. As Marx wrote at this time: "Philosophy finds in the proletariat its material weapons." Marx the philosopher had become Marx the revolutionary politician.

He had also become a radical journalist, and it was this that led to his first self-enforced exile, to Paris and Brussels. In Paris Marx, now a committed socialist, saw for the first time the visible reality of the urban proletariat—which he had invoked as the savior of society—on a far larger scale than anything Germany could yet show. There, too, he found groups of other socialists. He learned from them, particularly from their critiques of capitalist economics; but chiefly it was in his intellectual struggles with them, his attempts to define his own position as a way of repudiating what he saw as the mistakes and eccentricities of theirs, that the "Marxism" of the *Communist Manifesto,* published in 1848, was born. The historian and social scientist was taking over from the idealistic philosopher of freedom.

The *Communist Manifesto* differs from most political pamphlets precisely in the breadth and grandeur of its historical perspective. The message is that history both promises victory and imposes conditions. From the ringing opening ("The history of all hitherto-existing society is the history of class struggles") to the final celebrated call to action ("The proletarians have nothing to lose but their chains. They have a world to win. Working men of all countries, unite!"), the idea is hammered home that capitalism is not the permanent state of mankind but simply the latest phase of historical development. The bourgeoisie is not respectable and law-abiding; it is dynamic and rapacious; it has won its way to power by smashing the ancient privileged regime of feudalism. Seldom has a political movement received such a gift as the *Manifesto:* at once an indictment, an analysis, and a promise of victory. Marx and his collaborator Engels, in the *Communist Manifesto,* join Jean Jacques Rousseau and Abraham Lincoln among the rare few who have given to a political attitude a classic rhetorical form. Like Magna Carta and the Declaration of Independence, the *Manifesto,* especially in its concluding sentences, has the resonance and power of myth; like *The Social Contract* and the Gettysburg

Address, it gives definitive form to a hunger of the human spirit.

In the short run the prophecy was false, nor has the ensuing century done much to make it valid. The specter of communism, which Marx and Engels had declared to be haunting Europe, proved in 1848, not for the last time, to be a wraith. The masses in France, enfranchised by the new Republican government, voted overwhelmingly for property and order; the resistance of the Parisian workers was trampled into the gutters of the capital by the government's cavalry, and Marx, doubly exiled now that he had made France too hot for himself, arrived penniless in London, the grimy citadel of capitalism itself, where he was to spend the rest of his life. For Marx the would-be man of action the best years of his life were already behind him; the years of patient research had begun. Here in London he was to work, mole-like, dogged by poverty, exasperated by the political moderation of the English working class, laboriously documenting his thesis of the inevitable downfall of capitalism, adding to the philosophy of human emancipation and to the incandescent rhetoric of the *Communist Manifesto* the technical apparatus of economic analysis, the patiently accumulated facts of a massive indictment of a whole social system, and detailed analyses of the failure of the recent revolutions on the Continent.

It is the last that, together with the economic sections of *Capital*, establishes Marx as a great historian—probably, in terms of sheer intellectual power and penetration, the greatest historian of the nineteenth century, an author to whom modern historians, no matter how hard they try, can scarcely avoid being indebted. His most masterly work of detailed history, a study of the rise to power of the new French emperor, Napoleon III, by a *coup d'état* over the ruins of the short-lived Republic established in 1848, is only an extended essay, yet it contains a revolution in the writing of history. Using the concept of a socioeconomic class not merely as part of a political indictment but as a tool of

388

historical explanation, Marx provides what is still the most penetrating and stimulating analysis of the character and the success of Napoleon III and also gives the classic account of the situation of the fascist dictator who claims to be "above" class and politics and to represent symbolically the unity of the nation.

Marx's essay is outstanding for the subtlety and minuteness with which he lays bare the ironies of history and the intricacies, the agitated twists and turns, of the various sections of French society, particularly the French bourgeoisie; parodying its cult of "order," Marx represents it as capitulating to Napoleon III by its bleating: "Only theft can still save property; only perjury, religion; bastardy [Louis Napoleon's legitimacy was doubtful], the family; disorder, order!" Marx's contempt is tellingly balanced by the glimpses he gives of the perspectives of world history; they are, in a sense, his justification for treating Napoleon's regime as a comic masquerade. The spectacle of the great Napoleon's nephew stepping into his uncle's boots offered opportunities that Marx was not the man to miss. The note is struck in the first sentence: "Hegel remarks somewhere that all facts and personages of great importance in world history occur, as it were, twice. He forgot to add: the first time as tragedy, the second as farce." This tone, sometimes of polished irony, sometimes sheer vaudeville, is maintained throughout. As an example of the first, take Marx's dismissal of French liberals' excuses for Napoleon III's success: "It is not enough to say, as the French do, that their nation was taken unawares. A nation and a woman are not forgiven the unguarded hour in which the first adventurer that came along could violate them."

The essay on Louis Napoleon is not only the work of a profound and original historical and sociological intelligence; it also has the verve and impact of first-class journalism. It was a talent Marx was to need in his exile, not merely as a political weapon but as a means of staying alive. One of the many ironies in Marx's career is that he quarried his indictment of capitalism from the British government's reports in the scholarly security of the British Museum Reading Room, but another is that in the 1850's he saved himself and his family from destitution partly by becoming the respected London correspondent of the New York *Tribune*. The managing editor, Charles Anderson Dana, had met Marx in Germany when the latter was winning notoriety as the crusading editor of the *Neue Rheinische Zeitung*. After Marx fled to London, Dana asked him for regular articles, at five dollars apiece. At first Engels wrote them for him, but when Marx's English improved he took heart from Engels's declaration that the *Tribune*'s own English was appalling and began to write them himself. Fortunately Marx's attitude toward British imperialism and the British governing class was pretty much the same as that of his American employers, and the relationship was a moderately harmonious one.

The meager pay of the New York *Tribune* and the subsidies of Engels enabled Marx and his family to survive the first bitter years of exile in London. Turned out of their first lodgings into the street because of a mix-up over the rent, the family settled in two small rooms at 28 Dean Street, Soho Square, in a poor exiles' quarter, where the house is now surrounded by restaurants and strip-clubs. There they endured the hardships of genteel poverty. Marx wrote to Engels in 1852: "For a week past I have been in the pleasant position of being unable either to go out for want of my overcoats, which are at the pawnshop, or to eat meat because the butcher has stopped credit. The only good news we have here comes from my sister-in-law, the minister's wife, who announces that my wife's uncle is ill at last." In these circumstances, most witnesses agreed the Marx family created something very like a domestic idyll. Of the many faces of Karl Marx not the least surprising or remarkable is Marx the family man, a devoted husband, a jovial and indulgent father.

In 1843 Marx had married Jenny von Westphalen, the beautiful daughter of a neighbor in Trier, a Prussian government official. When they came to London, there were already three children, Jenny, Laura, and Edgar. Shortly after their arrival Guido was born and inevitably was nicknamed Fawkes, after the would-be dynamiter of the British Houses of Parliament; Marx's own nicknames were "the Moor"—a reference to his dark hair—and "Old Nick." Two more daughters, Franziska and Eleanor, were born later. The household was completed by "Lenchen," the Westphalens' family servant, who was said to be the only person who could subdue Marx. There may have been a reason for this. There were rumors at the time that Marx or Engels was the father of Lenchen's illegitimate son Frederick, and subsequent evidence points to Marx. Whether this was the result of an isolated lapse from fidelity to Jenny or a protracted liaison, we do not know.

Details of the Marx's family life are preserved by another exile and a disciple, Wilhelm Liebknecht, in a series of descriptive scenes that have the slightly comic naïveté of the sentimental paintings of domestic scenes of the period so beloved by the nineteenth-century bourgeoisie: pictures of a benign Marx patting urchins' heads like a Mr. Pickwick and giving them pennies and apples, or of the family picnics on Hampstead Heath. Liebknecht, who was obviously often hungry, recalled with particular tenderness a "substantial joint of roast veal . . . consecrated by tradition for the Sunday outings to Hampstead Heath. A basket of a size quite unusual in London, brought by Lenchen from Trier, was the tabernacle in which the holy of holies was borne. . . . Bread and cheese could be bought on the heath, where crockery, hot water and milk were also to be had, just as in a Berlin *Kaffeegarten*." After lunch the adults would sleep on the grass, read the Sunday papers, or give piggyback rides to the children, Marx being, according to his daughter Eleanor, a splendid horse. On the walk home they would sing German folk songs, or Marx would recite Shakespeare or Dante from memory.

Three of the children died, Guido and Franziska before

391

reaching their first birthdays, so that Marx was especially agonized by the death of Edgar at the age of nine. To his daughters he was an indulgent and fascinating companion, joining in their horseplay and telling fantastic stories in the manner of E. T. A. Hoffmann. To his daughter Eleanor he was "the cheeriest, gayest soul that ever breathed . . . a man brimming over with humor and good humor, whose hearty laugh was infectious and irresistible . . . the kindliest, gentlest, most sympathetic of companions. . . . His kindness and patience were really sublime."

Marx's political opponents would have been intensely surprised to hear it. They knew Marx in another of his incarnations, as a practical politician, a man of domineering temper, brutal speech, and implacable rancor. His opponents were, of course, not only the bourgeoisie, which was virtually unaware of his existence, but his fellow socialists. Many of Marx's key works are polemics against the errors of some erstwhile comrade. A long succession of socialist theorists and leaders felt the edge of Marx's scorn and the crushing weight of his erudition as he fought them for control of the socialist parties and movements to which he at various times belonged. Marx was a formidable political opponent, but he had no conception of consensus politics; again and again he showed himself ready to abandon or wreck a promising movement rather than allow it to fall into the hands of those he regarded as doctrinally in error. His deliberate destruction of the First Workers' International to save it from the Russian anarchist Bakunin and his followers was only the most notable of these fatal self-administered purges.

Marx's irritability was no doubt exasperated by persistent ill health. When writing *Capital* he was severely troubled with hemorrhoids. As he wrote plaintively to Engels, "to finish I must at least be able to *sit down*," adding grimly, "I hope the bourgeoisie will remember my carbuncles." Utterly dedicated to the idea of revolution, Marx spent his life as an exile, despite his attempts to organize the German exiles and to collaborate with English working-class leaders, essentially

as a scholar. He would have nothing to do with merely conspiratorial politics; there was no substitute for the travail of
history and the political education of the workers by the
class struggle. Marx's rejection of conspiracy was not due to
moral objections or to natural coolness of temperament, but
to a massive intellectual self-restraint, a contempt for im-
practical revolutionary dreaming and frothy oratory. He was
in fact a man in whose nature aggression and revolt ran deep.
In a questionnaire composed by his daughter Laura he once
gave the answers: "Your idea of happiness. *To fight;* The vice
you detest most. *Servility;* Favorite hero. *Spartacus, Kepler.*"

The official name of Marx's circle was the German Workers' Educational Society, and the educational aspect was
taken seriously even when it had nothing to do with politics.
Marx in this context wears the face of the German *Gelehrter,*
with all the strengths and weaknesses of the type. There was
nothing narrow about his intellectual interests. He could
read all the main European languages and taught himself
Russian when he was in his fifties. He read Greek and regularly reread Aeschylus. He was interested in the natural
sciences and, of course, technology; he acclaimed Darwin
and became highly excited when he saw a model of an electric train engine in a shop window. For relaxation he would
do mathematics; during his wife's last illness he could find
solace only in working on calculus. In his dealings with his
young followers one sees not only Marx the political doctri-
naire but also, more surprisingly, Marx the pedagogue. On
the whole the latter sounds a good deal more intimidating:
"How he scolded me one day," Liebknecht lamented, "because I did not know—Spanish! . . . Every day I was questioned and had to translate a passage from *Don Quixote.*
. . ." Educational bullying was obviously part of Marx's nature, even apart from politics, and one can see in these reminiscences the professor he at one time seemed destined to
become.

But ultimately, of course, the politician and social scientist
were uppermost. Marx had already, before he came to Lon-

393

don, developed his characteristic theory of history: that a society's legal and political institutions are an expression of its economic substructure. But it was in England, in the British Museum, that Marx did his fundamental research as an economist and social scientist and prepared his most celebrated work, *Capital*. Marx's book is a strange amalgam: it is a highly abstract theoretical economic analysis designed to show that the capitalist annexed all the surplus value produced by the worker, leaving the latter nothing but his bare subsistence, and himself contributing nothing; there is a good deal of detailed economic history, of which Marx was a pioneer, analyzing the earlier stages of capital accumulation, the dispossession of the European peasantry, and the development of European industrial and mercantile civilization. And there is the statistical demonstration of the human cost of early industrialism, compiled chiefly from the evidence of the British government's own commissions and the reports of its factory inspectors. Marx here joins Dickens, Disraeli, Carlyle, and other Victorians appalled by the conditions of industrial and urban life. These pages of *Capital* are, for all Marx's attempts to refrain from mere denunciation, the work of an angry moralist who could see in the cold figures "the motley crowd of workers of all ages, and sexes, that press on us more insistently than did the souls of the slain on Ulysses."

Finally there is prophecy, deduced from a model of capitalist competition and production—intended to show the inevitability of increasingly frequent and disastrous economic crises and the ultimate revolt of the masses. In the *Communist Manifesto* Marx had called for this revolt and predicted its success. Now in *Capital* he thought he had demonstrated its inevitability, the result of the self-destructive character of capitalism, doomed to perish by its own inherent contradictions: "The centralization of the means of production and the socialization of labor reach a point where they prove incompatible with their capitalist husk. This bursts asunder. The knell of capitalist private property sounds, the expropriators are expropriated."

Marx thought that his conclusion was the verdict of social and economic science. More evident to us is the face and voice of the angry Hebrew prophet, denouncing the worship of the golden calf and the human sacrifices to a mechanical Moloch and trumpeting the wrath to come in the careless ears of the unrighteous. Capital is a "fetish," a false god. Marx's intellectual career comes full circle; the face of the economic theorist melts into that of the young idealist philosopher, to whom the ultimate evil is the subjection of mind and spirit to the domination of brute *things*.